ALSO BY NADINE COHODAS

Queen: The Life and Music of Dinah Washington

Spinning Blues into Gold:
The Chess Brothers and the Legendary Chess Records

The Band Played Dixie:
Race and the Liberal Conscience at Ole Miss

Strom Thurmond and the Politics of Southern Change

Happy Birthday Leah,

Love ——— U.Charles,
A. Mary,
Zack & Eli
(+ Josh)

Princess Noire

Princess Noire

The Tumultuous Reign of NINA SIMONE

Nadine Cohodas

The University of North Carolina Press
Chapel Hill

Originally published in 2010 by Pantheon Books. Paperback edition published in 2012
by the University of North Carolina Press, by arrangement with Pantheon, an imprint of
The Knopf Doubleday Publishing Group, a division of Random House, Inc.

Manufactured in the United States of America

The paper in this book meets the guidelines for permanence and durability of the
Committee on Production Guidelines for Book Longevity of the Council on Library
Resources.

The University of North Carolina Press has been a member of
the Green Press Initiative since 2003.

Grateful acknowledgment is made to the following for permission to
reprint previously published and unpublished material:

Alfred Publishing Co., Inc.: Excerpt from "Four Women," words and music by Nina
Simone, copyright © 1966 (renewed) by EMI Grove Park Music, Inc. and Rolls Royce
Music Co. All rights controlled and administered by EMI Grove Park Music, Inc.; and
an excerpt from "Mississippi Goddam," words and music by Nina Simone, copyright
© 1964 (renewed) by WB Music Corp. All rights reserved. Reprinted by permission
of Alfred Publishing Co., Inc.

Pantheon Books: Excerpts from *I Put a Spell on You* by Nina Simone with
Stephen Cleary, copyright © 1991 by Nina Simone and Stephen Cleary.
Reprinted by permission of Pantheon Books, a division of Random House, Inc.

Carrol Waymon: Excerpt from "The Tryon-Town Public Library" by
Carrol Waymon. Reprinted by permission of Carrol Waymon.

The Library of Congress has cataloged the original edition of this book as follows:
Cohodas, Nadine.
Princess Noire : the tumultuous reign of Nina Simone / Nadine Cohodas
p. cm.
Includes discography, bibliographical references, and index.
1. Simone, Nina, 1933–2003. 2. Singers—Biography. I. Title.
ML420.S5635C65 2010
782.42164092—dc 22
[B]
2009022252

ISBN 978-0-8078-7243-7 (pbk.)

Frontispiece: Nina at London's Dorchester Hotel, December 1998
(Steve Double, www.double-whammy.com)

16 15 14 13 12   5 4 3 2 1

Contents

Princess Noire

Prologue

I understood fully for the first time the importance of black song, black music, black arts. I was handed my spiritual assignment that night.

OSSIE DAVIS, after seeing Marian Anderson
at the Lincoln Memorial, Easter Sunday, 1939

It was more a path emerging than a promise fulfilled that put Nina Simone on a makeshift stage in Montgomery, Alabama, on a sodden March night in 1965. She wanted to sing for the bedraggled men and women who had trekked three days from Selma to present their case for black voting rights to a recalcitrant Governor George Wallace. Nina was following the lead of James Baldwin, her good friend, mentor, and sparring partner at dinner-table debates, a role he shared with Langston Hughes and Lorraine Hansberry. They were her circle of inspiration, writers who found their voice in the crackling word on the page—the deft phrase and the trenchant insight that described a world black Americans so often experienced as unforgiving.

Nina linked her voice to theirs, understanding from the time she was Eunice Waymon, a precocious little girl in Tryon, North Carolina, what it was to be young, gifted, and black, even if she couldn't find the words to express it. On that stage in Montgomery, long since transformed into Nina Simone, she sang "Mississippi Goddam," her litany of racial injustice and a signal that she, too, had found her spiritual assignment: to use her talent for the singular cause of freeing her people and not incidentally herself. She never suggested the task was easy, and anyone willing to listen, willing to heed her exhortations, could engage in the struggle at her side.

"I didn't get interested in music," Nina explained. "It was a gift from God." But when private demons besieged her, a rage of breathtaking dimension obscured that gift, blinding her to everyday realities even as the anger informed her creations and at the same time served to attract, provoke, and on occasion repel an audience. Yet through it all came the unmistakable pride of accomplishment. "When I'm on that stage, I assume honor. I assume compensation," she declared, "and I should."

In the best of times Nina could embrace the mysteries of her art, finding comfort in the ineffable. "Did you know that the human voice is the only pure instrument?" she wrote one of her brothers. "That it has notes no other instrument has? It's like being between the keys of a piano. The notes are there, you can sing them, but they can't be found on any instrument. That's like me. I live in between this. I live in both worlds, the black and white world. I am Nina Simone, the star, and I am not here. I'm a woman. My secret self is between these worlds."

1. Called For and Delivered

~ June 1898–February 1933 ~

The gifts that would turn Eunice Waymon into Nina Simone were apparent by the time she was three, though the passions, the mood swings, and the ferocious intensity that marked her adult life were buried for years under her talent. She was born on February 21, 1933, the sixth of eight children, in Tryon, North Carolina, a town perched at the border between North and South Carolina, on the southern slope of the Blue Ridge Mountains. The beautiful surroundings, the pleasant climate, and the good railroad service established by the turn of the century helped Tryon grow from a rural outpost to a haven for white artists and their friends, many of them from the North. Visitors stayed and put down roots, those with keen business instincts making investments that gave the town its municipal backbone.

Eunice's birth certificate listed her father, John Davan Waymon, as a barber and her mother, Kate Waymon, as a housekeeper. But these descriptions, necessitated by the limited space on the state's official form, failed to capture the creative, entrepreneurial path John had woven through a world both circumscribed and defined by race. Likewise, "housekeeper" did not do justice to the pursuits of his equally determined wife to stretch the boundaries of their lives and give the family its spiritual core.

They were respected members of black Tryon and were treated with the patronizing courtesy whites traditionally reserved for those black residents deemed "a cut above." The Waymons set an example of hard work for their children, underscored by a deep faith that from Kate's perspective could ease disappointment and loss. Eunice had her doubts, and in her troubled moments as an adult, she would take little solace from her mother's lessons. Her father's buoyant spirit and pragmatic outlook, on the other hand, drew her in. "He was a clever man," she recalled. "Although he wasn't educated, he had a genius for getting on."

John Davan Waymon and Kate Waymon came from South Carolina, each the descendant of slaves. John, born June 24, 1898, in Pendleton, a small town near Clemson University, was the youngest of several children. A gifted musician, he played the harmonica, banjo, guitar, and Jew's harp. "He could take a tub and make music out of it," one of his children would say later with evident admiration, noting, too, that his father had the unique ability to whistle two notes at once. "We could hear that many blocks away—Daddy whistling in the night." Tall, with a high forehead and prominent cheekbones, he looked the part of the song-and-dance man he became in his teens, dressed in a sharp white suit, spats over his shoes, cane in hand when he entertained the locals.

Kate was born November 20, 1901, and christened Mary Kate Irvin (though some family members spelled it Ervin), the baby among fourteen children—seven girls and seven boys. She was never sure what town her parents lived in when she arrived, only that it was in South Carolina, probably Spartanburg County. Her father was a Methodist minister, and while her mother was not officially trained, she had absorbed enough religion to carry on the ministry if Reverend Irvin was called away. Kate's heritage on her mother's side was an unusual mix. She took after her maternal grandfather, who was a full-blooded Indian, tall "and of the yellow kind," as she recalled, and her maternal grandmother, who was short and dark with luxuriant black hair, which Kate inherited. She often wore it in a braid wrapped around her head.

One of Kate's sisters, Eliza, was married to a pastor who led the congregation in Pendleton where John Davan worshipped. Sometime in 1918 he introduced John, then twenty-one, to Kate, only seventeen. Kate remembered that they sang "Day Is Dying in the West" together at church. John was smitten, and he promptly wrote Kate asking to visit her in Inman, where she now lived with her widowed mother. On that first visit they went for a buggy ride, and soon John was coming by every Saturday and staying through Sunday evening. Their routine on these visits usually included a ride in the countryside, the couple entertaining themselves with duets. Kate's alto blended easily with John's tenor on their favorites, "Whispering Hope" and "Sail On." At the Irvins' they sang around the little organ Mrs. Irvin had bought for her daughter. She paid for a few lessons, and then Kate taught herself the rest.

Few of their friends were surprised when John and Kate married in 1920. They moved to Pendleton to live briefly with John's mother, and then they settled back in Inman. Their first child, John Irvin, was born in March 1922. The year after that Lucille arrived, and then came the twins, Carrol and Harold. When he was just six weeks old, Harold contracted spinal meningitis. He wasn't expected to live, but he survived, with a permanent paralysis on one side.

Though he still loved music, John gave up entertainment to take a job in a dry cleaning plant. He learned the business so quickly and with such thoroughness that he decided to open his own shop. He was also a part-time barber, and to earn extra money he took on work as a trucker. Just as important, he moved comfortably between the worlds of black and white, reaping rewards on both sides of the color line. He prospered enough in Inman so that Kate could stay home to take care of the four children. She even found time to take piano lessons to burnish her natural talent.

On one of his truck-driving jobs, John took a load of goods into Tryon, and right away he saw business opportunities for someone with ingenuity and energy. Years later the children remembered the prospect of opening a barbershop as the family's reason for moving, but more likely it was the chance to run a dry cleaner's that would serve the burgeoning tourist trade. John, Kate, and the children moved to Tryon early in 1929, taking a small house just off the main street. John opened his shop as planned, proudly announcing in a small ad in the *Tryon Daily Bulletin* "Dry Cleaning and Pressing—Called for and Delivered." He even had a phone and listed himself by his nickname, "J.D." Waymon. On March 7, not long after settling in, Kate gave birth to Dorothy, her fifth child in barely seven years.

THE FOUR GAS STATIONS—Gulf, Sinclair, Texaco, and Standard—on Trade Street, Tryon's half-mile-long main street, testified to the town's prosperity, as did the two livery stables that served the hunt-and-riding set who rode the bridle paths through the town's hilly outskirts. The two large hotels built years earlier were still thriving, and their success meant steady work for Tryon's black commu-

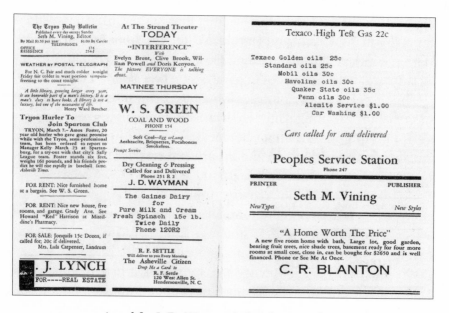

An ad for J. D. Waymon's dry cleaning shop
(name misspelled) in Tryon, North Carolina, March 1929
(Tryon Daily Bulletin)

nity as waiters, housekeepers, and gardeners. Though the geography differed, the atmosphere evoked "that familiar hospitality of the Old South," as one travel writer noted in *The Charlotte Observer*, North Carolina's largest newspaper. "You envision snow-white linen, gleaming silver service and sparkling crystal, a smiling colored waiter, and you imagine you can smell the tantalizing odors of a delectable plantation dinner. . . ."

The heart of Tryon's cultural life was the Lanier Library, founded in 1889 by five women to foster the civic and educational welfare of the small community. They started with a few donated books and gradually raised money to buy more and a bookcase to hold them. Within six years, the white community put up a building named for the poet Sidney Lanier, who spent his last months in Tryon. By 1930 the Lanier Library had turned into a community center where white patrons came not only to read books but to attend lectures and classical music recitals.

Though the railroad tracks ran through the center of Tryon, blacks and whites did not live exclusively on either side. Rather the two races lived near each other in checkerboard clusters, an arrangement that fostered, depending on one's viewpoint, an inchoate integration or an imperfect segregation. Families exchanged pleasantries and the bounty from one another's gardens; the men worked alongside one another on construction jobs. But these lives mixed only up to a point. Black laborers, including the teenage John Irvin, helped build the bowling alley and movie theater, but the alley was whites-only, and when the theater first opened, blacks had to wait for special showings so late in the evening that the children fell asleep before the feature was over. Eventually blacks could go whenever they wanted, but they had to purchase their tickets from a separate window, buy their popcorn and soda from a separate makeshift stand, and sit in the balcony. The man in the booth would sell a ticket to a white customer at the front and then pivot to the left to sell one to his black customer. White families occasionally treated their black help to movie tickets, gently instructing them where to go as employer and employee went their separate ways before the movie started. Blacks appreciated such gestures, and took them as a sign of working for good folks who looked after them. Black and white children went to separate schools. If they played together as youngsters, that ended by the time they were teenagers. The color line could nonetheless be a rude awakening, perhaps because it existed in such a seemingly benign atmosphere. Nine-year-old Carrol couldn't understand at first why he wasn't allowed to take out a book from the library. He turned the rebuff into a poem.

> *They said the library was for everybody,*
> *I thought that meant me, too—I was a body—*
> *It was the Tryon town Public Library—*
> *I lived in Tryon town, too—I was a public.—*
> *They said they wanted all the kids to come.*
> *I thought that meant me, too—I was a kid—*
> *'Cause I didn't know what they meant when*
> *they told me what they said . . .*

Though no one talked much about it, J.D. and Kate and their friends remembered the lesson Scotland Harris, a teacher, learned about the town's racial norms. He had come to Tryon at the behest of the Episcopal diocese to open the Tryon Industrial Colored School. His first few years went smoothly, but when his classes grew more adventuresome, the city's white elders spoke up. They chastised him for teaching his young black charges to aspire to lives and careers beyond Southern custom and tradition, and they told him to stop. "Of course he continued," recalled his granddaughter, Beryl Hannon Dade.

The white elders also looked askance at the large house Harris built at the crest of a hill on Markham Road, which wound its way from the north end of Tryon through the east side of town. Harris's students had helped with construction as part of a real-world exercise in their shop class, and the house was among the grandest in Tryon, even including the white areas.

The final straw for Harris came when he accepted a white friend's invitation to attend the man's church, Holy Cross Episcopal, on the fashionable Melrose Avenue. On the appointed Sunday, Reverend Harris and his entire family entered the sanctuary with other congregants and sat down in one of the Holy Cross pews. "Well, of course you don't do that," Beryl Dade said. "It was a social barrier that was crossed." A short time later the head of the diocese, a white bishop, asked Harris to leave Tryon. He leveled no threats, but Harris got the message. He chose not make a fuss and agreed to take another post. His departure highlighted the precariousness of black life in Tryon, its residents ever mindful that in more hostile communities such a moment could easily explode into violence.

The *Tryon Daily Bulletin*, the town paper, documented social life along with the news, recording the comings and goings of the celebrities who vacationed there as well as showing through its copious ads the latest at Ballenger's department store, the specials at the A&P, and the host of items that could be found at the two drugstores nearly adjacent to each other on Trade Street, Owen's and Missildine's. Both served as gathering places for the town's business folk, like-minded white men adopting one or the other as their haunt, though the Missildine's lunch counter was considered the elite spot and Owen's "the subsidiary." "You only went to Owen's if you got mad at somebody at Missildine's," recalled Holland Brady Jr., who watched some of these tête-à-têtes with the enthusiasm of a teenager learning the ways of the world.

The *Bulletin* devoted most of its stories to Tryon's white community, though the paper included short articles about black Tryon under the heading "Colored News." Black residents also used the *Bulletin*, listing notices for PTA meetings or special programs at the Tryon Colored School or announcements of events at their churches. Specific requests for assistance, each carefully worded, conveyed not only what was needed but gratitude that such a request could even be made and then granted. "Donations or will buy a used typewriter to be used at colored school," said one. "We have a project outlined to make our school more progressive. We are asking our white friends to continue to support us as you have done in the past. We always appreciate the interest you manifest in us." Famous gospel groups such as the Dixie Hummingbirds advertised their local performances, and on occasion they agreed to match voices with the area's top groups. "White friends invited," the ads concluded.

The *Bulletin* didn't have a regular classified section, but residents were free to write their own ads seeking help or offering their services. Racial preference was explicit in both categories: "WANTED: White girl to stay on place. Must be able to cook." "WANTED: Colored Farm Hand to do general work. Unfurnished house. free milk; garden space of his own." "Experienced colored butler (old school) wants job. Excellent references."

J.D.'S DRY CLEANING STORE sat right on Trade Street snug up against the railroad tracks, not far from the depot and catty-corner from the A&P and the Sinclair station. His prized possession—and he was sure it was the first in Tryon—was a Hoffman finishing press fired by a boiler and controlled with a foot pedal. The other cleaners (as far as he knew) still had to contend with the cumbersome routine of a hand-held iron. Because J.D. sewed, he offered customers repairs and alterations. When the jobs were done, he delivered the clothing as promised, and almost always took John Irvin with him. Eager to get the most out of his space, J.D. also started a barber business, tucking his barber's chair in a little room next to the dry cleaning apparatus. Word spread through town that "Mr. Waymon can do white hair"—even the popular "Washington Square," a cut named for the squared-off look at the back just above the collar. J.D. got so busy that he hired a Mr. Broomfield to help him.

J.D.'s smooth transition into Tryon was shattered one day in the most unusual way. He and John Irvin arrived early, as was J.D.'s custom. Before making a fire in the boiler he always cleaned out the flue. Then he took old newspaper and rolled it into tight cylinders to use as kindling. On this morning when he lit a match to start the fire, nothing happened. He tried again with the same result. After the third time, he went outside and up on the roof to see what the problem might be. That's when he noticed an inner tube full of gasoline that someone had stuffed at the top of the chimney. Had the rolled-up newspaper started to burn, the shop would have been destroyed and J.D. and John Irvin injured or even killed.

J.D. didn't know whether this was a prank or a more sinister act to put him out of business. Years later a couple of the children claimed it was the Ku Klux Klan that tried to intimidate their father. But John

Irvin doubted it. "I didn't know nothin' about the Klan" in Tryon, he said, and while the town itself had never been a hotbed of Klan activity, the organization did have a foothold in more rural—and racially tense—parts of Polk County. J.D. credited a "higher power" with preventing a tragedy.

Her husband's spiritual explanation made sense to Kate; it matched her growing interest in religion, specifically activities at St. Luke CME, one of Tryon's black churches. "She went Christian," as John Irvin put it, and he felt the change. Music still filled the Waymon house, but now it was the sacred instead of the secular when Kate sang and accompanied herself on a little pump organ, just the way she had as a child in Inman.

The family's life was actually disrupted not long after the incident at the shop, when their rented house caught fire in the middle of the night. John Irvin never forgot how his father tumbled out of bed, grabbed a shotgun with one hand and his pants with the other, and ran outside to shoot off the gun, a signal for help. One of the pant legs had turned inside out, and though John Irvin knew it was a serious moment, he couldn't help laughing at the sight of his father tipping back and forth to get to the door. "But he shot that shotgun," John Irvin said. Help came, and no one was injured.

It was probably in 1931 or 1932, after the fire, that the family moved to a house on a curving, hilly road, later named East Livingston Street when Tryon authorities finally established more precise municipal boundaries. Though not large for a family of seven, the house had a number of advantages, best of all a yard big enough so the family could have a garden and keep some chickens. A fence in the back separated the house from a pasture where the neighbors kept their cow.

The large main room had one of the two stoves, and the children usually slept there. The other stove was in the kitchen. When bath time came in the evening, either J.D., Kate, or one of the older children heated a tub of water on top of the living-room stove, and the children took turns cleaning up. John Irvin got so close to the stove one chilly night that he burned himself, the scar a permanent reminder of the bathing ritual. Kate and her good friend Alama

King, who lived down the road with her husband Miller and daughter Ruth, used the front steps and the little porch as their visiting spot. Ruth was the same age as the twins, Harold and Carrol, but best friends with their older sister Lucille. Dorothy considered those steps her private domain. She pretended the front of the house was her classroom, and she would carefully set her dolls on the steps facing the road and then stand out in the yard to give them "instruction."

As far as the children were concerned, the best part of their new home was the tennis court and little store right across the dirt road to the west. They belonged to Fred and Blanche Lyles, who lived in a house next to the court with their four children. Lyles had been a dining-car waiter, but with an entrepreneurial spirit and a savvy wife to tend the shop while he was away, he had used his savings to open a neighborhood store. Even though their children went to boarding school, the community-minded couple set up a playground in the big yard next to their house for the all the neighborhood kids.

The original store was a small wood-frame building. When it prospered, Fred built a larger brick structure that faced Markham Road. Decades later the Waymon children couldn't remember why their father had closed his Trade Street dry cleaning shop, but by this time, roughly 1932, J.D. rented the small building that had been the Lyleses' store and opened a dry cleaning business in it, reinstalling the Hoffman press in the new place. He renamed the operation the "Waymon Pressing Club," as noted in the *Bulletin*. The Waymons' house was barely a five-minute walk down the hill to St. Luke CME Church, where East Livingston Street joined Markham Road. Garrison Chapel Baptist Church was right behind St. Luke, making this east Tryon's holiest corner. Kate was about to be ordained as a minister, so having the church close by was convenient. J.D. found his niche as deacon and then superintendent of the Sunday school. He also joined the Simpson Quartet, named for leader Bossy Simpson. It was one of several quartets that formed in and around Polk County, and they all competed against one another at church-sponsored events. The Waymon household erupted in delight when the Simpson Quartet won a contest over the Spindale Quartet, one from Tryon High School, and the Littlejohn Quartet of Thousand Pines. The prize, according to the *Bulletin*, "was a big watermelon."

·

THOUGH THE DEPRESSION had affected Tryon's bustling tourist industry, J.D. and Kate managed to stay afloat. "We was doing pretty good," John Irvin recalled, noting that his father took in $100 a week, if you counted the bartering that went on, one family to another—dry cleaning or haircuts in exchange for chickens, meat, vegetables, or maybe milk. Food provided by the federal government through its various national recovery programs also helped. Tryon had been designated one of the distribution sites for western North Carolina, and the government needed local drivers. J.D. already had trucking experience, and he got a job distributing goods throughout the area. Not only that, he could also take home extra flour, sugar, apple butter, and the powdered eggs that made such an impression on the children, who only knew the real eggs that came from chickens.

J.D. figured out a way to get free coal, too, following the freight train as it came through town, made a turn west, went up the mountain to unload, and then came back. Heaps dropped along the tracks, and J.D., with John Irvin and Carrol in tow, joined other townspeople to gather up what the railroad had left behind.

By 1932 the Waymons enjoyed the friendship of neighbors, the fellowship of church, and the more tangible assets of living next door to the Lyleses. John Irvin was ten and a frequent tennis partner for Blanche, Georgia, and Lulu Lyles when they were home. Lucille was nearly nine, the twins seven, and Dorothy three. Kate became pregnant again in the summer. Sometime in the evening of February 20, 1933, she went into labor. Midwife Lucinda Suber was called to the house, and at six a.m. on the twenty-first Eunice Kathleen Waymon entered the world. "I knew she was a special child," Kate said, "because her name was given to me before she was born."

2. We Knew She Was a Genius

~ March 1933–August 1941 ~

John Irvin sang in a St. Luke quartet and played guitar with his father; Lucille, Carrol, Harold, and Dorothy sang in the church choir, but even before their baby sister could walk, they realized she had more musical talent than all of them. "When she was eight months old, my daughter hummed 'Down by the Riverside' and 'Jesus Loves Me,' " Kate said. "I had a quilt that I had on the floor for her, and she wanted to look at magazines. Every time she saw a musical note, she tried to sing."

Parishioners at St. Luke commented, when they saw little Eunice at church, that she clapped in time to the hymns. She must be blessed, they told her parents. By the time she was two and a half, Eunice could hoist herself onto the stool in front of the organ, sit at the keyboard, and make sounds come out, and not just any sounds. One time she played her mother's favorite hymn, "God Be with You Till We Meet Again," without a mistake.

"We knew she was a genius by the time she was three," her brother Carrol declared, and it is a tribute to her parents that Eunice's brothers and sisters did not begrudge the attention and opportunities that came her way. "She was preserved," Dorothy remembered, exempted from the typical chores, washing dishes and the like. "Her fingers were protected. She was always special in that way. Nobody was jealous," Dorothy added. "We adored her."

Eunice took this special status in stride because her parents insisted on it. She didn't dare get a swelled head. Yes, she had talent, her parents told her, but the talent was God-given, and she should be grateful. Eunice didn't know what a "prodigy" was when people called her that, and no one at home explained it to her either. All she knew was that she absorbed the music she heard, especially the religious songs her mother sang around the house, "I'll Fly Away" and "If You Pray Right (Heaven Belongs to You)." Kate sang when she cleaned and when she baked, and Eunice loved it when her mother, rarely missing a beat, sat her on the countertop, gave her an empty jam jar, and let her cut out shapes from the biscuit dough about to go in the oven.

As a full-fledged minister now, Kate traveled through the surrounding counties preaching and leading services. When Eunice turned four, Kate took her out on the road to open her events. Most of the time Eunice could barely reach the pedals on the church piano, which made the sight of this little girl dressed in her Sunday best even more arresting. The audience was primed to be impressed before she struck the first note, and Eunice didn't disappoint. Though it might have seemed inappropriate, even cruel, to put a toddler to work, even the Lord's work, Eunice liked the adventure of seeing new places and visiting new churches. If she was tired at the end of these services, she slept in the back seat of the car on the way back to Tryon, undisturbed by the occasional jostling on the bumpy rural roads.

J.D.'S JOB in the federal recovery program ended just as Kate's preaching duties began to consume more of her time. At some point in this period, probably 1935 or 1936, he also closed the dry cleaning shop and took a new job cooking at a Boy Scout camp on Lake Lanier, the large man-made lake just south of town. Created in 1924 by damming one of the creeks, the lake now served the dual purposes of recreation for well-heeled white residents and a reservoir for the surrounding area. An ad to induce the sale of lots promised "They Rise Together—Land Values—Water Values," with a barometer for illustration. The fringe benefits of J.D.'s new job included the extra food he brought home from camp and the chance to take his oldest son with him.

No matter how busy the week had been in the Waymon household, Kate insisted that Sunday be devoted to church, so every Saturday night the children had to shine their shoes, which they'd learned to do with a professional's touch from their father, who had started a little shoeshine business, too. "We'd leave there [the house] on Sunday morning, and didn't get back till Monday morning," John Irvin explained. "We'd have the children's service, then go right in the main service, and then stand up and sing." The family might walk back to the house for a sandwich, and then it was back to church for the late afternoon and evening services. If one of the children had the temerity to ask, "Mama, why can't we go home?" the answer was always the same: "Be quiet."

When the family finally returned home, often at midnight, "Mama would walk out of the kitchen to get a chicken, wring its neck, and while that chicken was dyin' out there, kickin' and goin' on, she would put water on the stove, make a fire, clean that chicken," John Irvin explained. "We'd have chicken and gravy at one in the morning. Mama would say, 'All right, wake up if you want to eat. Now come on.' We used to do that all the time."

SOMETIME EARLY IN 1937 things changed dramatically in the Waymon household. The children noticed that J.D. was not working anymore. Instead he stayed at home because he hadn't been feeling well. Most days he just tended the garden. One night he took ill and was rushed to the hospital. Doctors diagnosed an intestinal blockage. John Irvin and Carrol remembered that their father had some kind of complicated operation, though they were unaware of the details. In her memoir, Eunice described it as "one of the first type in the world." As she understood it, his stomach was washed and the wound left open to heal in the sun-drenched fresh air.

Kate spent weeks going back and forth to the hospital, and John Irvin and Lucille had to care for their siblings until J.D. was strong enough to come home. His illness also meant that Kate had to find work beyond her preaching. Options for black women were limited, even in Tryon, which considered itself progressive about race. A few women taught at the black school, but most did domestic work, either in the hotels or in the homes of their more affluent white neighbors. One of Kate's first jobs was washing windows at a building on Trade Street. She took Carrol to help, and it proved to be a rude awakening for a boy who had been sheltered in the relative comfort of east Tryon and as the child of respected parents—"My daddy and mama's name was all around Tryon," John Irvin proudly recalled. Carrying a wash bucket and a mop behind his mother and then seeing her struggle at this manual labor made Carrol aware of the discrepancy between black and white. "It was the first time I felt humiliated and ashamed of the fact that we were poor," he said. He was certain the family had suddenly tumbled down from its exalted perch to some lowly station, and it made him cry.

If Eunice was too young to appreciate all that was going on around her, she was delighted that her father had finally returned from the hospital. Though she was barely five, it fell to her to become J.D.'s nurse. Kate had to work; Lucille, Carrol, Harold, and Dorothy were in school; and John Irvin had a part-time job at a lumberyard, too. But this new arrangement suited father and daughter just fine. "She was the apple of his eye," Carrol remembered.

Eunice went about her nursing duties with the utmost seriousness. Every day, weather permitting, she helped J.D. settle on a cot out in the yard just across from the Lyleses' tennis court, so he could take in the sunshine as the doctors ordered. Strolling down Livingston to her family's house, Ruth King would often see Eunice sitting attentively by J.D.'s side.

"The wound from his operation was a big ugly thing with a tube coming out of it, which drained fluid from his stomach," Eunice wrote years later in near-cinematic detail. "I kept washing him, more than ten times a day, trying to keep that wound clean." J.D. couldn't eat solid food, so he made up a lunch of liquid ingredients every day, his favorite a combination of "raw eggs beaten with a little sugar and vanilla, mixed with Carnation milk," Eunice recalled. She liked the taste of it, too, but she took only a sip now and then "because I knew we had to make him better."

At first J.D. could only lie down. As he got stronger, he took walks around the yard and then in the neighborhood, one of the children at his side. "Hey, J.D.," a friend might holler, and ask how he was doing. And J.D., with one hand on his child's shoulder for support, raised his cane with the other in salute.

Eager to do some kind of work again, J.D. rigged up a little barber-shop at the back of the house and taught John Irvin, who was now fifteen, how to give a proper shave. All the children marveled at their father's ingenuity—he repaired worn-out shoes with a little leather and fine wire, he was a mechanic, and of course he made his own shaving soap from a special recipe. When his strength permitted, J.D., oldest son in tow, went to his customers' homes to cut their hair and give them a shave. Though he couldn't reestablish a full-fledged dry cleaning operation, J.D. occasionally took in sewing and laundry, mostly menswear. It was a cumbersome operation at home that nonetheless fascinated Eunice and her siblings as they watched this new ritual. First J.D. washed the clothes in a big tub in the kitchen, with special care given to the men's pants. He would turn each pair inside out and hang them up so the water would drain. He explained that it kept them from "drawing up" or shrinking. He heated the iron, which was the extra-long heavy industrial model, on the stove to press the pants. But first he grabbed a few pine needles from a tree in the yard and ran the iron over them so it wouldn't stick. Finally he put a damp cloth over the clothes and started the pressing. Because he was the oldest, John was allowed to participate as long as he followed directions and ironed the pants in proper sequence: first the apron and then each leg, carefully handled to avoid wrinkling and to keep the seams crisp.

DESPITE J.D. AND KATE'S best efforts to stay afloat, they couldn't maintain the house on Livingston Street, and sometime after J.D. was strong enough, the family moved to a smaller house about a half mile north. They were barely there a year when a fire broke out in the middle of the night. Eunice remembered that the treasured pump organ was the first piece of furniture to be rescued. It was understandable that the Waymons might feel hexed. This was the second fire that had taken their home in six years, but they refused to lose faith, reminding themselves that no one had been hurt either time.

After this latest fire the Waymons settled on the second floor of the Episcopal Center, a building that was part of the Good Shepherd Church, which, along with its small school, served the black community. But the cramped, noisy lodgings hampered J.D.'s recovery. He and Kate realized they had to move, and the only place they could afford was a small house in Lynn, a hamlet roughly three miles north of Tryon on the road to Columbus, the Polk County seat.

Lynn was so primitive some families didn't have outhouses, but when one turned away from the shacks and toward the woods the beauty was unsurpassed. Eunice loved the family's new garden, and she delighted in following J.D. up and down the rows, pulling the weeds that he pointed out. "When we got tired, we'd sit down and play patty cake or just talk," she wrote later.

J.D. had always had some kind of car, and now that the family was in the country, they needed his Model-A Ford. The children loved the way their father could maneuver up and down the hills, knowing precisely when to shut off the engine and let the car coast to save gas. They thought it was natural to peer through the floorboards and see the ground below, and they giggled when J.D., concerned for his wife's safety, would instruct her to sit in the front seat and then take a piece of rope to tie her in because the passenger door was so flimsy.

On winter nights J.D. backed the Model A up the hill near the house and stopped it at just the right angle so he could drain the radiator. The next morning he took the water he had collected, heated it for a few minutes on the stove to get the chill off, and then put the water back in the radiator, got in, and started the car. "We didn't know nothin' about antifreeze," John Irvin chuckled years later, reminded of his father's creativity.

A bus was supposed to pick up the black children in Lynn and take them into town for school. On the days it didn't come, the kids had to walk. Sometimes it felt like thirty miles instead of three, and when it was cold, parents came up with clever ways to keep their children warm. Ruth Hannon, who was between Eunice and Dorothy in age, recalled her father heating stones on the fireplace hearth at night. The next morning, he would wrap up a few and put them in the pockets of her jacket and her twin sister Rachel's before they headed into town.

SHORTLY AFTER THE FAMILY settled in Lynn, John, now seventeen, went to work at the Civilian Conservation Corps camp in Spindale about forty miles east of Tryon. Everyone called it the "Three C," and as one of the federal programs created to get the country out of the Depression, the camp offered men a way to make money by doing work on public land. John was a truck driver who ferried other "Three C'ers" through the countryside to lay sod on the side of highways, fix fences, and occasionally fight fires. His camp mates called him "Pee Wee" because he was smaller than most of them, but he proudly held his own. He was paid $30 a month and sent $22 home as required by program regulations. He insisted that his parents use one of the payments to buy the family's first piano, an upright that their neighbor Martha Brown wanted to sell.

Mrs. Brown, who worked for one of the white doctors in town, and Kate shared the same belief about music. They disdained anything that wasn't religious—blues, jazz, Tin Pan Alley. Kate referred to this as "real music," and she never forgot the time her own mother chastised her for singing "Everybody's Doing It," which Kate had heard at a minstrel show. But J.D. still had a taste for "real" music, and when he sat down at the keyboard and played "real" songs for Eunice, she picked them up by ear, and the two had a grand time. Periodically J.D. went to the window to watch for Kate, and if he saw her, he signaled Eunice with a whistle to make a fast segue into one of her mother's favorite hymns.

When John returned from the Three-C camp, he liked a turn at the piano, too. "I'd be playing 'Coonshine' or 'Love Oh Careless Love,'" he said, and then he'd hear Kate's voice.

"Hey boy!"

"What's a matter, Mama?"

"That don't sound right." And John Irvin knew he'd been caught.

Every now and then John teased his baby sister by hogging the piano—at least that's how Eunice saw it. He would sit down on the bench and prop his feet on the keyboard so she couldn't play.

"Mama," she wailed, "John Irvin is on the piano. He won't let me have it." After a stern warning from Kate and a few tears from Eunice, John relented, and Eunice had the piano all to herself.

SOMETIME IN 1940 the Waymons moved back to Tryon. Carrol and Dorothy remembered that first year as a blur of two temporary stops before the family resettled on the east side. This last house was less than a mile from the Livingston Street place, but it felt much farther because the streets wound back and forth up the hills. By this time, Lucille had moved out—she had married Isaac Waddell, one of the family's neighbors. Not long after, John left, too, prompted by an argument with his father that made him realize that at nineteen he was old enough to be on his own. In 1941 Kate and J.D. had their fourth daughter, Frances, and three years later Samuel—instantly known as Sam—was born, the last of the Waymon children.

Always on the lookout for the next opportunity, J.D. put a small extension on the house and bought an assortment of provisions to outfit the room as a store. He sold candy and food and then realized he could earn extra money making sandwiches in the morning and taking them later to construction sites to sell to the men along with drinks. You could even order ahead if you wanted. "John imagined up his own career," according to Holland Brady, who would go from the observant teenager at Missildine's to one of Tryon's respected white architects. "I always say he invented the ten a.m. coffee break."

Eunice was so accomplished at the keyboard now that the congregation at St. Luke designated her the regular Sunday pianist even though she had just turned ten. It was often an all-day affair that began with a morning service, continued through Sunday school, and finished with the six o'clock evening prayers. She also played Wednesday nights at a prayer meeting and Friday nights at choir practice. Her perfect pitch allowed her to identify any note, and she could play something back after a single hearing.

Eunice had almost no formal training to supplement her natural talent, which was influenced by what she heard and felt intuitively. And though these early years were also shaped by her mother's insistence that she stay away from popular music, it didn't take much listening to realize that the rhythm, the beat, and the melody that she loved in that forbidden music could be found in church music, too. She'd heard it herself, at the evangelical Holiness Church tucked away on one of the streets south of St. Luke. "Their prayer meetings were one great commotion," Eunice remembered, "with people testifying and shouting all night." The music sounded as though it came straight out of Africa, or at least how Eunice imagined Africa would sound. She loved hearing the revival drums beating while the congregation rose up in song. Dorothy, who sometimes went, too, was fascinated by the woman who beat the drums, tapping out one rhythm with her hands while her stomping feet were doing something entirely different.

Revival time at St. Luke, when parishioners rededicated themselves to God, ran a close second to the Holiness Church. Out-of-town preachers came in for the two-week stints of nightly prayer meetings. Congregants who felt the spirit stood up to testify, shouting and speaking in tongues with such intensity that it spread to other worshippers who started their own testimony. Pretty soon people ran up and down the aisles under the practiced watch of the Saints, the church women in their crisp white dresses, white stockings, and white shoes who stepped in to administer the necessary aid if one of the testifiers was overcome. Occasionally, a testifier had to be taken to the hospital.

Eunice's job was to keep playing regardless of the commotion. She realized that if she repeated the distinctive gospel chords she knew so well, she could get the congregation back on track. But with all the frenzy around her, it was hard to pay attention, and it took all of her concentration not to leap up from the keyboard and run down the aisle, too.

Most evenings Eunice was tired when the prayer meeting ended, but she woke up excited the next morning, knowing she would do it all over again. She might not be able to explain or describe what was happening, but she understood already that the keyboard gave her power. With soft, slow chords she calmed the congregation. When the chords crescendoed faster and faster, she lifted them up, and in those moments she could think of no more thrilling place to be.

LIKE THE OTHER black children in town, Eunice attended Tryon Colored School. It was a wooden building whose few rooms served all the classes, which encompassed elementary, secondary, and high school through the eleventh grade. It had no central heat or running water. To keep down the dust, boys from the upper grades were recruited to spread creosote, a mixture of chemicals used as a preservative, over the floors every day after school. The enrollment was usually about two hundred, and longtime principal LeRoy Wells supervised a staff of five who divided up the grades among themselves.

As was the custom in the South, the black schools received hand-me-down materials from the white schools. Textbooks were often in tatters, their back covers a roll call of the white youngsters who had thumbed their pages when the books were new. Biology and chemistry experiments were difficult if not impossible because the school had so little equipment. But the dedicated teachers insisted that substandard materials would not interfere with their mission to give Tryon's black children the best education possible. The teachers routinely supplemented the textbooks with other books or pamphlets, usually from their own collections and at their own expense. Parents, too, made sure their children understood the importance of education. "I always had aimed to learn," Kate told hers. "I even stayed in at recess because I wanted to make a hundred if I had to stay in school all day." She brought home old copies of *Reader's Digest* and *Look* magazine from her housecleaning jobs so her children could keep their reading skills sharp and keep up on current events.

Of all the teachers, Orine B. Wiggins was considered the strictest. Stern and demanding, she nonetheless earned her students' grudging respect. If she complimented you, you knew you deserved it. If she chastised you, you knew you deserved that, too. "Give me your hand," she would say to someone who had misbehaved. And when the guilty party complied, she rapped the child's knuckles with a ruler to make her point. "She wouldn't pass you if you didn't deserve it," recalled Artie Hamilton. "If you got through, you were high school equivalent. She taught you more than what was in the text. She taught the ways of life."

For all the intellectual effort inside its walls, Tryon Colored School made a mockery of "separate but equal," the standard of the Jim Crow South. Principal Wells had been lobbying for a new building for some time to no avail, and at the end of the school year in the spring of 1940, his patience gave out. Sometime during the first week of June, Wells contacted a local man, Arthur Suber, and gave him $25 to burn down the school. Suber recruited two other people, Cleveland Rice and Hattie White, and told them they could make "easy money" on a "small job."

On June 9, the three of them went to the school, pried open a door, and doused the floors with kerosene. They lit a match, and the place went up in flames, fueled by all the creosote that had built up during the school year. The fire department came, but the firemen didn't have enough water to douse the blaze. No part of the building could be saved. Five days later the police arrested Suber, Rice, and White, and on June 19, ten days after the fire, Wells was arrested as well. Suber told authorities that Wells had furnished the money for the arson "so that they could have a nice brick building like other schools."

(The four were convicted on arson charges in August and sentenced to prison. Wells appealed his conviction, won a new trial, was convicted again, and eventually served a prison sentence that began in 1942.)

The school burning tore a hole in the town's fabric, reminding black and white alike of the inequalities that lay beneath Tryon's amiable surface. In more personal terms, Wells's action—dramatic, intemperate, foolish, however one described it—proved that anyone could succumb to the pressures of the moment. The entire episode hit close to home for J. D. Waymon. He knew Wells as more than the principal at his children's school. They were friends and cooks

Eight-year-old Eunice Waymon in Tryon,
North Carolina
(Courtesy of Frances Fox)

together during the summer at the Boy Scout camp at Lake Lanier,
and he could only guess at what finally drove Wells to strike out.

With Tryon Colored in ashes, the black students moved to the
school building at Good Shepherd, the Episcopal church that had
once employed Reverend Scotland Harris. The church had closed
its school operation in 1936, but fortunately the building was still
there to accommodate the public school students until Tryon Colored could be rebuilt. (The new school opened in December 1942,
and Polk County officials applauded its "modern" plan.)

Eunice was only seven when Tryon Colored went up in flames
and too young to understand. She was simply happy to go to school,
and she took to her studies the way she took to the piano. On those
occasions that the *Tryon Daily Bulletin* published the honor roll

from the colored school, at least two or three Waymons made the list, including Eunice. A photo of Eunice a year later shows a serious girl whose bright eyes cast a knowing look at the camera. Her immaculate appearance suggests the great care that was taken before she left the house.

Eunice's chum Fred Counts considered himself her competition; they vied to see who could be the star of the class. "We were one and two in the class," he said. "Of course she was number one."

3. Miss Mazzy

~ September 1941–August 1947 ~

It was Eunice's good fortune that Kate Waymon regularly cleaned house for Katherine Miller, a widow who lived in Gillette Woods, the affluent Tryon neighborhood that meandered from the far west side of town right up to the South Carolina border. The development traced its origins to 1893, when William Gillette, an actor famous for his characterization of Sherlock Holmes, was en route to Florida by train and was delayed in Tryon for several hours. To pass the time, he walked around the countryside and was so impressed with its natural beauty that he returned and purchased the seven hundred acres that became known as Gillette Woods. After building homes for himself and family members, Gillette sold the property in 1925 to a group of businessmen with the proviso that it be mapped for further development. The new owners trumpeted their holdings as Tryon's most "exclusive residential section."

Mrs. Miller and her husband George arrived in 1933 from Rochester, New York, and bought two adjacent homes on Glengarnock Road. A retired printer, George Miller was eccentric even by Tryon standards. He devoted one of the houses to his model railroad and installed a railroad signal out front instead of a doorbell. If it showed red, the visitor didn't dare open the door because it meant that the train was about to cross the doorway on the other side. "Nobody ever saw Mr. Miller," Holland Brady remembered, "except if you were interested in trains." He died suddenly in 1938, and afterward, Mrs. Miller immersed herself in the typical activities of Tryon's society women, the Lanier Library Association and the garden club.

Eunice often accompanied her mother to the Millers' house on Saturdays, and Mrs. Miller was the first white person she had ever known to speak to. Eunice liked her because she seemed kind. Not only that, the Waymon children noticed that Mrs. Miller always referred to Kate as "Mrs. Waymon" rather than by her first name as most overly familiar whites did, even those much younger than their mother.

Mrs. Miller had become the guardian for David Johnson, a five-year-old who was the child of a previous housekeeper with two other children. His mother and Mrs. Miller had worked out the arrangement after Mrs. Johnson realized she couldn't properly care for her youngest child. Eunice often played with David at the Miller house until Kate finished her work. Though Mrs. Miller often sent a taxi to pick up Kate on the days she cleaned and called a taxi to take her home, occasionally she drove her back herself, David in tow, so he could play with whoever was at the Waymons'. David loved it best when Kate let him eat her homemade biscuits. "I'd sit till I'd bust if she let me," he admitted. The children were as curious as David when he asked Kate a question they'd wondered about, too: why was her skin so much darker than his? Realizing the answer required diplomacy, Kate came up with a genial story that had only the slightest barb to hint at much more complicated realities. In the beginning, she said, everyone was dark. Then there came a big vat of liquid that would turn skin white. The greedy folks jumped in and took most of that liquid. "What's left," she explained, "was just for the soles of our feet and the palms of our hands." The explanation satisfied David, and he didn't bring up the subject again.

Kate periodically talked to Mrs. Miller about Eunice's talent, and one day Mrs. Miller went to hear Eunice, probably at the Tryon theater, where she accompanied her sisters Lucille and Dorothy during a concert. They billed themselves as the Waymon Sisters—Lucille, the soprano, Dorothy the contralto, and Eunice, if a song called for her to sing, alto. After the performance, Mrs. Miller said she was amazed that Eunice had never had any lessons. She told Kate it would be "sinful" if Eunice didn't have proper study to nourish her talent. Kate responded honestly: the family couldn't afford it. So Mrs. Miller made Kate an offer: she would pay for a year's worth of lessons, and if Eunice showed promise, then she would find a way for the lessons to continue. Mrs. Miller even had a teacher in mind, her neighbor across the street on Glengarnock, Muriel Mazzanovich, a native of Britain who had moved to Tryon in 1927 (as Muriel Harrington) and then two years later married Lawrence Mazzanovich, a painter of some reknown and another Northern transplant. Eunice would walk to her piano lesson every Saturday morning and then go across Glengarnock to the Millers' to wait for her mother to return home. Mrs. Mazzanovich received seventy-five cents per lesson.

ON THE TWO-MILE WALK that started at the Waymon house on Jackson Street, Eunice planned a route that took her through the gravel streets of east Tryon up to Trade Street. She might pass a little café behind the A&P and wave to "Jewbaby," a fixture downtown beyond his unusual name because he was such a good shoeshine man and kept the café spotless. Jewbaby was a stocky, light-skinned black man with yellowish curly hair. Nobody claimed to know his real name, and folks could only guess at the origins of his nickname. Passing Newman's livery stable, Eunice imagined the magic show her brother John told her about when she was a toddler. It sounded unbelievable, but he swore it was true: this white man would lie down on the ground and put a couple of crates on his stomach, and then a truck would drive over him.

Eunice occasionally stopped at Owen's pharmacy to pick up a cheese sandwich, which she ate outside, rain or shine, because blacks couldn't eat inside with the white patrons. The children didn't talk much about such things among themselves; they accepted it as the required custom. But if the subject did come up, it was usually on summer days, when they bought their lemonade—at full price—but had to drink it in the hot sun. More than once they cast an envious, even angry look at the white kids sitting at the counter cooled by the breeze from the ceiling fans that twirled overhead. Eunice and her friends would later realize that whatever prosperity they achieved never erased the memory of their second-class status.

Crossing the street from Owen's, Eunice might wave hello to the policeman who was stationed at a kiosk at one of the intersections with Trade Street. Some of the kids called him "Crip" because he had a bad leg and walked with a limp. Nobody knew what he did except walk back and forth along Trade to keep an eye on things.

When she reached the other side of the railroad tracks, Eunice walked past the Lanier Library and Oak Hall, the town's main hotel, with its inviting wraparound porch. It was the place where elegantly dressed white people ate, drank, and danced at their parties, though the people Eunice knew who had actually been inside were the waiters and housekeepers who tended to these patrons and felt lucky to have their jobs. She knew this not just because the men and women said so. She could see it in the way they went about their work, pride on their faces and no less elegant in their carriage than the individuals they served.

After a few more blocks, Eunice made the turn onto Glengarnock and headed up the hill to the Mazzanovich house, nestled amid tall trees on the right-hand side of the road. The house had stucco walls; the sloping roof accommodated a cathedral ceiling inside. A gable hung over the front stoop, and except for a small opening next to the front door, the side that faced Glengarnock had no windows.

The house didn't look like much from the outside. But inside three or four easels, each of them holding a Mazzanovich work in progress, were arrayed at one end of the large room that comprised the ground floor. A north-facing skylight took up much of the ceiling. A Weber concert grand piano stood against the street-side wall, and right behind it stood an upright, also against that wall. Windows filled the entire opposite wall, which provided a glorious view of the woods. A fireplace right inside the entry faced a sitting area where

The home of Muriel and Lawrence Mazzanovich,
where Eunice took her first piano lessons
(Joan Nash)

the Mazzanoviches had set up a round table and chairs. From the table or a window seat nearby, one could look out into the open room.

Beside the back of the fireplace, a stairway led down to the basement, where the kitchen was, and up to the bedroom, which was in a balcony that ran the width of the house. It could accommodate another easel if Mr. Mazzanovich wanted to paint in the light of this upper room.

Eunice hardly knew where to look first and wondered for a moment if she might faint right there on the spot. But she caught her breath, determined to absorb all the details and catalog them forever, not just what she saw but what she smelled, which was not like anything she was used to—her mother's biscuits coming out of the oven, the fried chicken cooking after church, or the livestock that roamed near their house. This scent was sweeter and more delicate, a mixture of the fresh flowers that adorned the big room and the swatches of paint that sat on Mr. Mazzanovich's easels.

When the door closed behind her, Eunice felt so far away from Tryon that she could have been on another planet.

Muriel Mazzanovich
(Courtesy of the Upstate Newspapers)

Muriel Mazzanovich was waiting for her at the grand piano, and she instantly reminded Eunice of a little bird. She was petite and about fifty-five or sixty years old, though Eunice couldn't be sure. Her silvery hair was pulled back in a bun, but because of her delicate features the hairstyle didn't make her seem severe. When Miss Mazzy, as Eunice called her, spoke, the accent of her native England was obvious, something Eunice had never heard before. They shook hands, and then Miss Mazzy introduced her husband, who was working at one of his easels. He nodded and smiled hello. Miss Mazzy motioned Eunice to the Weber grand to begin. It looked like the typical moment played out in countless cities and towns across the country, the student coming to the teacher for a lesson. And Eunice and Miss Mazzy treated it this way, too, neither openly acknowledging that *this* lesson was unusual. In how many other Southern towns could a black child take lessons at a white teacher's home with no fear of retribution for either one?

Before letting Eunice play a single note, Miss Mazzy instructed Eunice to hold her hands at the keyboard just so, with the fingers spread for maximum advantage. Eunice felt lucky she had good hands—long, slender fingers that tapered slightly at the tips. Next, Miss Mazzy said, it was important to play from the shoulder rather than the wrist. These preliminaries out of the way, they were ready to begin. Though Miss Mazzy started her younger students with selections from *Teaching Little Fingers to Play*, a virtual standard since it was published, and supplemented the book with exercises from *Hanon*, another staple of music education, she knew that Eunice didn't need them. She wanted to dive into the classical canon, especially Bach. Eunice was excited but intimidated, because Bach was so much more intricate than anything she could have imagined. When she wanted to stop, Miss Mazzy wouldn't allow it. "You must do it this way, Eunice. Bach would like it this way. Do it again."

This first lesson was over in two hours, and Eunice floated home, already dreaming about all the lessons to come. She realized that although she hadn't left Tryon's city limits, now she inhabited a larger world.

SERIOUS WORK TOOK UP the first hour of each lesson in Eunice's new routine, with a focus on Bach. He had captured her interest once she understood that all the notes had a purpose, like a mathematical equation, only one that kept growing in force and intensity as the notes added up. Miss Mazzy helped her appreciate that every note had to be executed properly or the entire effect would be lost.

Miss Mazzy didn't only teach Eunice the music. She talked to her about Bach and other classical composers, and she was so engaging that Eunice was sure the men were right there in the room with her. Teacher and student usually took a break for a piece of candy from a big basket Miss Mazzy kept filled to the brim. Then, instead of going back to the Weber for more classical pieces, they sat down at the upright for duets of lighter fare, which Eunice took as a welcome relief. In the warmer weather, Miss Mazzy prepared lemonade, and they took their breaks outside in the garden looking at the beautiful vistas from the top of Glengarnock. On colder days, a fire burned in the fireplace, but never warmly enough for Miss Mazzy, even when she wore her thick hose. "Uninhabitable, Eunice," she complained.

"Simply uninhabitable." But Eunice knew Miss Mazzy really didn't mind because the memories of a chilly winter evaporated on the first beautiful spring day.

Miss Mazzy had no children of her own (Mr. Mazzanovich had a son from his previous marriage), and Eunice had no way of knowing if she was as kind to other students as she was to her. What Eunice did know is that after only a few lessons, she blossomed under Miss Mazzy's affectionate attention. At home, Eunice had to share her mother with the rest of the family and, as Kate gained prominence as a minister, with the Methodist Church. She may not have uttered the words out loud, but in Eunice's mind, Miss Mazzy became "my white mama."

THE FIRST YEAR of piano lessons flew by, and Eunice wanted to continue. J.D. and Kate Waymon couldn't afford the lessons out of their own pockets, however, so they needed to find a sponsor. To a child already receiving so much attention, it must have seemed that the entire community rallied behind her, and years later Eunice wrote about the creation of the "Eunice Waymon Fund" of Tryon to further her studies. But the "fund" appears to have been confined to the generosity of two white women, Mrs. Miller and Esther Moore, another Northern transplant who was, like Mrs. Miller, a pillar of Tryon society and appreciative of Eunice's talent.

Mrs. Moore's son Tom remembered hearing his mother talking on the phone about Eunice and her potential. "My mother was telling Miss Mazzy to give her whatever she needed and she [Esther] would cover it." Esther Moore's generosity might have stemmed from her fondness for J.D. and Kate. As a jack-of-all-trades, J.D. helped Mrs. Moore around the house. "He did all kinds of nice thoughtful things. He was a cut above," Tom Moore said. And Kate helped Esther Moore when she entertained. "She wasn't just a maid," Tom Moore said, but more like a caterer.

Miss Mazzy's lessons now covered stage comportment for the recitals she wanted Eunice to give: how to walk gracefully to the piano, sit up straight at the keyboard, look elegant and composed even before striking a single note. All of this was especially important if Eunice was going to become the classical concert pianist they had envisioned. Eunice's friend James Payne remembered one recital at a church in Forest City when either Miss Mazzy or Eunice had forgotten some of the music. "Eunice went right on and improvised," James recalled. "No one knew it."

When Kate wasn't around to complain about "real" music, and she wanted a break from Bach, Eunice played for her friends at school. They gathered in the auditorium during a free period, and "she played for just about anyone who thought they had a little talent," Ulysses Counts recalled, each of her chums vying for her attention. Eunice's fast friend Patricia Carson might be the first to start, the girls urging each other on with tunes they heard on the radio. It felt like a guilty pleasure when Patricia broke into an impromptu "Soothe me baby, soothe me, make me feel good" or tried "Straighten Up and Fly Right."

Sometime in 1944, after Eunice had turned eleven, Miss Mazzy arranged for her to give a recital, probably in the main room of the Lanier Library. It was going to be the kind of afternoon that would make an impression for a lifetime, savored (and maybe even embellished) with each retelling. Though this event was for white Tryon, Eunice insisted that her parents attend. As she remembered it, J.D. and Kate, dressed in their churchgoing best, came into the library and sat in the front row. The host introduced Eunice, and she walked to the piano with practiced elegance, just as Miss Mazzy instructed. But when she looked out, she saw that her parents were being asked to move from their front row seats so that a white couple whom Eunice had never seen before could sit there instead.

J.D. and Kate didn't object and were in the process of moving, when surely by instinct—because she had never been encouraged to be a rabble-rouser or to cause trouble, had never heard her parents complain or even talk about race—Eunice spoke up. If anyone expected her to play, she told the audience, they better let her parents sit right where she could see them. The host, perhaps startled by such a direct outburst, obliged. Eunice went ahead and performed. She remembered her parents seemed embarrassed by the momentary ruckus, and in subsequent retellings, she asserted that some of the white patrons snickered.

Around the time of the recital Polk County's black community moved to establish its own chapter of the NAACP, the acronym for the venerable National Association for the Advancement of Colored People. The timing was probably a coincidence, but it nonetheless reinforced the fact that race mattered, even in Tryon. An NAACP representative came to town in July to host an organizational meeting at St. Luke—"white friends welcome," the *Bulletin* notice stated. The Polk County branch of the NAACP received its official charter in November during a ceremony at the church led by an NAACP representative from nearby Asheville. J.D. was appointed chairman of the membership committee, a post he held for three years, apparently with some success. In the first year, the new chapter recruited ten members. By 1946 there were sixty-one.

4. We Have Launched,
Where Shall We Anchor?
~ September 1947–May 1950 ~

Eunice idolized her older sister Lucille, who seemed more like her mother than Kate did. Kate was working twelve- and fourteen-hour days cleaning houses on top of her church duties, so it fell to Lucille to teach Eunice how to dress and wear her hair. She walked her to school and talked to her about boys; one or two of them always were around seeking Lucille's company—and Dorothy's, too. Four years older than Eunice, Dorothy was pretty and spirited in her own way. Temporarily defiant when her mother and teachers vetoed her plan to wear a strapless gown to a school function, Dorothy consented to wear a borrowed dress whose poofy sleeves were tasteful yet still met her sense of style.

A photo of Eunice taken when she was twelve, perhaps for school or for another recital Miss Mazzy had organized, shows a casual pose but a serious mien. She is leaning over the back of a chair, her left hand placed over her right. She is wearing a simple dark blouse. Her hair is short and slightly curled in the front. The haircut accentuates her high forehead, round cheeks, and full lips, which hint at a smile. In the upper-left-hand corner, she wrote an inscription that suggests an uncommon seriousness of purpose for someone not yet a teenager.

"All music is what awakes within us when we are reminded by the instruments; It is not the violins or the clarinets—It is not the beating of the drums—Nor the score of the baritone singing his sweet romanza; nor that of the men's chorus, Nor that of the women's chorus. It is nearer and farther than they."

Though Eunice was as interested in boys as her girlfriends were, she was too shy to act on her feelings. But when a new family moved into the neighborhood, Mr. and Mrs. Whiteside and their son Edney, Eunice was smitten. The family had actually lived in Tryon for a few years, and Mrs. Whiteside had helped Kate right after Frances was born. But Eunice was sure she didn't know Edney, who was four years older, and she was even more sure she had never seen such a handsome boy. His Cherokee Indian heritage gave him tawny skin, shiny black hair, brown eyes, and an oval-shaped face. "I just looked at him and got torn up," she recalled.

Eunice didn't speak to Edney at first, and he was busy anyway, helping his parents around the house. But because the Whitesides belonged to St. Luke and Edney was in one of the choirs, Eunice could steal a glance or two every Sunday. Her heart leapt the day she saw him glancing back. After church Edney asked if he could walk her home. Of course, she said, thinking to herself, "He could have rolled me home in a barrel if he wanted."

It wasn't long before the teenagers met every Sunday after church to ride bicycles and stop at the Lyleses' store for ice cream. Edney would buy a pint, "and she would eat it all," he said. Kate had eased up on her Sunday routine, so the family wasn't in church all day anymore. When Eunice and Edney came to the house, which J.D. and Kate enjoyed because they liked Edney, Kate still kept a watchful eye and ear on activities. If the kids were at the piano and the spirit took them into "real" music, Kate came in the room in a flash to steer them back to spirituals and hymns.

After Edney bought a green 1939 Chevrolet, their Sunday afternoons became more adventurous. As soon as church was over, they might drive an hour or so north to Hendersonville or perhaps over to see Edney's grandmother in the little town of Edneyville, which was right in the middle of apple country. "We had a good bit in common," Edney explained, "because I was kind of a loner, and I think she liked being alone."

Eunice loved their quiet times together. She leaned her head on his shoulder, sometimes running her fingers through his hair and stifling the urge to kiss him, she later wrote, "for fear of starting something I wouldn't have the will to stop." Mostly Eunice and Edney enjoyed talking to each other, and Eunice felt she had found a confidant. She told him how much she loved music, but she also admitted her private worries about living up to other people's expectations. She hadn't sought the spotlight that came along with her talent, and some days, the pressure was overwhelming, especially when she wanted to go outside and play but had to stay at the piano and practice. "Sometimes I thought I'd go crazy locked up with that piano," she later recalled, "but I just kept playing and getting better." Eunice wondered if the goal she had set—to be the first black American concert pianist—was her own dream or her mother's. But if she had frankly discussed this with Miss Mazzy, surely she would have learned that there were already other accomplished black women classical pianists, among them Hazel Harrison, Natalie Hinderas, and Philippa Schuyler. This needn't have diminished Eunice's aspirations, but it might have made the task seem less daunting. Edney didn't have to say anything when Eunice talked about this grand ambition. It helped just that he listened.

EUNICE REMAINED THE STAR of her class at Tryon Colored, impressing even the formidable Orine Wiggins. She recommended that Eunice be allowed to skip the ninth grade. Fred Counts wasn't surprised. Any time Miss Wiggins asked a question directed to older children, he remembered, Eunice's hand went up to give the answer. "She didn't need ninth grade."

Miss Mazzy was likely the person who suggested that Eunice leave Tryon and continue her studies at the Allen School in Asheville, one of only three private accredited secondary schools for black girls in North Carolina. It was founded in 1887 by the Women's Home Missionary Society of the Methodist Episcopal Church, and to anyone familiar with the corrosive aftermath of Reconstruction, it came as no surprise that a Northern Church led efforts to improve the education of Southern blacks. Dr. and Mrs. L. M. Pease, white Methodist missionaries, settled in Asheville after working with the poor in New York. A few months into their new life in western North Carolina, they realized what limited schooling was available for black children and resolved to do something about it. They purchased property in the eastern corner of the city and converted an old livery stable that sat on the land into their private school for blacks.

In 1892 the institution was renamed the Allen School in honor of an English Quaker, Mrs. Marriage Allen, who was so impressed with the school after seeing it during a trip to Asheville that she offered the Missionary Society $1,000 for improvements. The organization used the money to build a dormitory for girls, determining that the students could learn to be better homemakers and citizens if they lived at the school. Boys initially studied at Allen, but they were phased out by 1941. Roughly 150 young girls enrolled each year now, with most of the students living on campus. The rest were day students from the Asheville area. At least half of the teachers were white, several of them from the North. All in all, the experience would give Eunice a more sophisticated education than Tryon Colored, the bountiful efforts of Orine Wiggins and her colleagues notwithstanding.

Katherine Miller and Esther Moore likely covered Eunice's tuition to Allen, and Kate and J.D. gave their consent. Eunice and Edney resolved to write every day, and he promised to visit every Sunday. Right before she left for school, Eunice played a special recital at St. Luke, accompanying the choir and earning a mention in the *Tryon Daily Bulletin* as a "noted pianist."

EUNICE'S ROOM was in Allen's main dormitory—she had two roommates, and they shared the community bathroom that was on their floor. She settled into a routine, getting up no later than five-thirty in the morning to practice the piano in the school's auditorium before breakfast at seven. Her classmates grew used to waking up to the sound of Bach or perhaps scales in every key wafting up the hallways. After breakfast came "duty work," when the girls divided up chores around the school: cleaning classrooms or the bathrooms, or sweeping the halls. After morning classes and lunch there was another duty period, followed by afternoon classes.

Though Eunice made friends, none of her classmates felt they knew her well. "She was so focused on her music," recalled Christine Ivey, a day student who was a year behind Eunice. "She didn't spend a lot of time joking around." But Christine loved it when Eunice stopped her classical exercises and played popular tunes—with no Kate to shush her. While she still loved Bach, she had found a new, contemporary idol, Hazel Scott, the glamorous singer-pianist who could play Liszt's Hungarian Rhapsody as Liszt intended and then turn on a dime to give it a modern-jazz interpretation. Eunice had covered one wall of her room with photographs of Scott.

When the Allen staff realized Eunice was already beyond what the school's music staff could teach her, she was allowed to take private lessons off campus with a tutor Miss Mazzy had arranged, most likely Grace Carroll, a well-known pianist who had won a scholarship as a young woman to study in Europe. She also apparently studied with another area pianist, Clemens Sandresky.

The Allen girls didn't have to wear uniforms, but they did have to dress properly—skirts well below the knees, blouses and sweaters and simple jewelry if they wished, such as a tasteful necklace or string of pearls. Shorts or pants were allowed only for physical education or when Maud Worral, the beloved science teacher, took the girls for hikes in the hills outside of Asheville to study the plant life or maybe catch tadpoles to bring back for class.

Proper behavior was a must. The girls could chew gum only in the privacy of their rooms, never in public. They had to go in groups to the movies or shopping, and they had to sign out before they left. Gloves and a hat were required for church. The girls received fifty points each semester, and if they broke any of the rules, points were deducted—chewing gum in public, one point for the first time, second time four points, third time six points. If you lost all fifty points, you were sent home. A model student, Eunice never came close to losing the points that her Tryon friend Patricia Carson did for saying "damn" within earshot of a teacher.

At first Eunice could hardly believe her surroundings. Instead of studying from books cast off by white students and crowding into a single room, she now was learning from brand-new texts and in small classes—the student-teacher ratio was something like twelve to one or maybe even ten to one. And she found the same standards that Orine Wiggins had sought to impart. "They were helping nurture us as we grew into young women," said Cordelia Pedew, another Allen contemporary.

Eunice was the same good student at Allen that she had been at Tryon Colored, and by her junior year, she had thrown herself into the school's activities so completely that she was president of the eleventh grade. A photo of the class, the officers sitting in the front row, shows her in the middle wearing a tan jumper with a white blouse, white socks neatly folded down above her dark shoes. Like her classmates, she sits with her legs delicately crossed at the ankles—the kind of ladylike posture expected of an Allen girl. The class chose as its motto: "We have launched, where shall we anchor?" Eunice was also president of the dramatics class, which met three times each week to rehearse one-act plays that were performed during the year, and she joined the student council, helping to raise money from candy sales after school to buy records for the music department and clocks for three classrooms.

She also accompanied the glee club, which not only performed at the school but at various churches in the area and at the nearby Veterans Hospital. A caption under one photo of the glee club (some thirty-two strong) praised Eunice for doing a "splendid job." She joined the Allen chapter of the NAACP, formed the semester before she arrived, and by her junior year she was the club's treasurer, helping organize a presentation by the poet Langston Hughes for students from the area's black schools. He spoke in Allen's auditorium, and the older students, who were allowed to gather on the floor around him, sat mesmerized as he read his poetry.

In the first year Eunice was away, she and Edney wrote each other all the time, and he drove to Allen to see her almost every Sunday.

Eunice at the Allen School
in Asheville, c. 1949–50
(*Courtesy of Dr. Patricia C. Caple*)

"Neither one of us liked being away from each other all that time," he said. Their visits were hardly private, however. A teacher sat right in the middle of the dormitory parlor—the only place boys were allowed—and surveyed the entire scene. But Eunice and Edney didn't mind. They still talked and planned for the future, and even discussed getting married when she finished her studies.

WHEN EUNICE CAME HOME on a school break in late March of 1948, Miss Mazzy hosted a recital for her at the house on Glengarnock. She picked Sunday afternoon, March 28, at four p.m., when the sun—assuming good weather—was going down but still shimmered through the skylight. Eunice and Miss Mazzy had selected an ambitious program. She started with her favorite composer, Bach— the French Suite in E-flat, which was made up of seven pieces. Next came Beethoven's Sonata in F Minor. After an intermission she played three pieces by Chopin, Etude in A-flat Major, Nocturne in E Major, and Etude in C Minor, followed by Debussy's Doll's Serenade. She finished on a light note, with his Golliwogg's Cakewalk.

One of Miss Mazzy's other occasional students, Garland Goodwin, a white teenager, carefully hand-lettered enough programs for all those invited, taking care with his budding engineer's talent to center each line and make sure each word was precisely printed. Eunice's beautiful tone from the Weber impressed him. He knew it didn't sound like that when he played. During an encore Miss Mazzy had Eunice improvise short pieces from musical notes suggested from the audience. After that she told Eunice to turn her back to the piano while she struck a note and then had Eunice identify it. Garland knew Miss Mazzy only wanted to demonstrate Eunice's singular gift, though he was certain she "felt like a circus act or a freak show. But she was very gracious. Her mama raised her to be polite no matter what."

EUNICE GRADUATED FROM ALLEN on May 30, 1950. She shared top academic honors with classmate Olivette Jackson. But problems in her relationship with Edney marred this otherwise joyful moment. A long-distance romance was difficult under any circumstances, and this one was made more so by Edney's moving to Cleveland for almost two years to live with relatives. He returned to Tryon during Eunice's senior year, and while they kept up a correspondence and he visited, it wasn't the same. Edney had also begun seeing another young woman in town, Annie Mae Burns.

When Edney had told her he was building a little apartment in Tryon, Eunice assumed he was building it for them. But it turned out to be for him and Annie Mae. The news devastated Eunice. She went back to Allen and studied with a vengeance in her last months to make sure she received those top academic honors. She practiced the piano in every spare minute, hoping that Bach and the other classical composers could somehow take Edney's place, though she knew it wasn't so. He had made her feel special and anchored her in the real world, and in her mind their talk about marriage was no fantasy. But even if Eunice couldn't see it, Edney understood that her talent had set her on a separate path, and Miss Mazzy and Kate were determined that she make the most of her gifts. Miss Mazzy had secured a scholarship for Eunice to study at the famed Juilliard School of Music in New York City for the summer session in 1950. The idea was to use this study as preparation for the scholarship examination to the Curtis Institute of Music in Philadelphia.

Eunice was torn. She didn't want to believe that she and Edney were through, though he told her, not unkindly, that if she went to Juilliard, he knew she wouldn't come back. When she added up all her hard work with Miss Mazzy, the hours and hours of practice, the expectations of her family, and weighed them against what was just the hope of a life with Edney, she knew the only choice was Juilliard.

"We were very close. We had a lot of good times together," Edney said years later, recalling those days in Tryon with a gentleness that spoke to the innocence of a much simpler time.

5. Prelude to a Fugue

~ June 1950–May 1954 ~

Eunice's first trip to New York City, when she was twelve, had scarcely prepared her for life as a Juilliard student. It was an eight-week summer vacation organized around family, with everyone—Kate, Eunice, Dorothy, and the babies, Frances and Sam—staying on 129th Street where Lucille, Eunice's oldest sister, lived. Her husband was in the service, so she was glad to have the company even if things were crowded.

Kate had used that summer of 1945 to earn some extra money at a factory job, but work took second place to her love of the church. The side benefits were visits to other boroughs as she preached her way around the area's black church circuit, her three daughters in tow reunited as the singing Waymon sisters.

Now Eunice was on her own in New York and on the next phase of her mission to become a concert pianist. She was determined to throw herself into her studies with all the energy she could muster. She had to forget about Edney, too, or at least try to. He was going to marry Annie Mae, and that was that.

Through church connections, Kate had secured a room for

Eunice in a house in Harlem, at 355 West 145th Street, right at St. Nicholas Avenue. It was on the edge of Sugar Hill, Harlem's high-society neighborhood, where some of the most affluent and influential blacks lived, among them the activist intellectual W. E. B. DuBois, NAACP lawyer Thurgood Marshall, and Langston Hughes, whom Eunice had heard at the Allen School. The location meant that Eunice could walk to Juilliard, which was on West 122nd Street near the north end of Columbia University, or ride the bus. The walk was shorter than the regular ones she had taken from her house in east Tryon to Miss Mazzy's in Gillette Woods, and it couldn't have been more different: no trees and more traffic in the first five minutes than Eunice might see in two days in Tryon.

Juilliard's concrete building, decorated with only a few parallel lines etched into the first-floor facade and brass-framed lamps on either side of the door, spoke to the school's serious purpose. The imposing Riverside Church, a Gothic structure modeled on a thirteenth-century French cathedral, was across the street and only emphasized the grandeur of this unfolding moment. The church was easily twenty times the size of St. Luke CME and like nothing Eunice had ever seen before.

But for all that was different, something was familiar, too. Once again Eunice lived in two worlds, among white students and teachers at Juilliard during the day (though a handful of other blacks were also in the summer program) and among other blacks in Harlem in the evenings and on weekends. Yet if the challenge of negotiating the turf in each world remained the same, Eunice was older now and more practiced in moving through this complicated terrain.

REGISTRATION FOR THE SUMMER SESSION began on June 29. Eunice signed up for three classes. Piano 250 was her private instruction for a half hour each week. Fundamentals of Piano Practice met weekly for three hours and was designed to emphasize "thoughtful practice as the key to achievement," according to the Juilliard handbook. The class included exercises in the "interrelation of touch and technique, essentials of pedalling and cues for memorizing." Eunice's other class was in Repertoire, where attendance was required but no credit was given.

Luisa Stojowski, the widow of the Polish composer Sigismond Stojowski and a pianist of note who had trained in her native Peru, taught the fundamentals course. She looked about the same age as Miss Mazzy but had a much more exotic presence: dark, deep-set eyes, arched eyebrows, and silvery hair that was braided and wrapped three times around her head like a crown. Though she could seem forbidding on first impression, her ready smile eased any tensions the students might have felt.

Eunice's principal teacher was Carl Friedberg, an elfin older man who had retired from full-time teaching in 1946 but was still part of the summer school faculty. As a young man in Europe, he had studied with Clara Schumann, who with her husband Robert made up one of classical music's celebrated couples. Friedberg made his debut in 1892 with the Vienna Philharmonic, and after considerable success in Europe, he came to the United States in 1914. He was much in demand as a performer with the top American orchestras, but always interested in teaching, he had joined Juilliard in 1923. Friedberg was so beloved by colleagues and students that in 1949 some of his former pupils created the Carl Friedberg Association to provide scholarship money for gifted young pianists.

Eunice was Friedberg's only black student, but it didn't bother her and didn't seem to bother Friedberg either. From their first meeting she understood why his students were so devoted to him. Though he was formal—he almost always wore a suit—he exhibited an obvious and genuine concern for his students' well-being. Did Eunice have a comfortable place to stay? Did she have enough to eat? Was she able to find a practice room when she needed it?

Eunice felt the same way with Friedberg that she had with Miss Mazzy—full of anticipation for each lesson, excited to think about what she might learn next. The sessions were similar to Miss Mazzy's, too. Eunice played a piece she had prepared and then Friedberg offered his comments. His observations were so subtle she doubted at first they could make much difference. But when she tried to emulate what Friedberg suggested, the piece was transformed, glistening "like polished silver." She found it exciting, too, when she realized she was studying with someone who had a direct connection to one of the masters, given Friedberg's early work with Clara Schumann. It was as close as she could get to having met Schumann herself. Like Miss Mazzy, Friedberg worked on Eunice's technique, giving her exercises for finger, knuckle, wrist, and back movements. Sometimes he demonstrated at the piano, playing each exercise with the precision and grace of a recital piece.

Eunice felt at home at Juilliard, immersed in music and surrounded by classmates, 336 in all, full of the same passion she had, whether they played the clarinet, played the violin, or sang. Adjusting to life in Harlem, on the other hand, was more difficult. Though the other young women at the house on 145th Street were friendly enough, everything was different from Tryon and Asheville, not simply the hustle and bustle but that ineffable sense of excitement and even danger that existed right beside the ordinary and the mundane. The *Tryon Daily Bulletin* never published headlines that blared "Schoolboy, 8, Hangs Self on Fire Escape," as the July 1 *New York Amsterdam News* did. Even grocery shopping was an adventure with so many little stores piled high with goods Eunice had never seen before, many of them reflecting the mix of cultures that made up Harlem. She wasn't use to seeing women sashaying down the street in midday dressed in expensive silks and high-heeled shoes either, and though she had an inkling of how some of them earned a living, she refrained from passing judgment, church training notwithstanding. From her vantage point it looked like a fine life.

Eunice mostly kept to herself at 145th Street, content to sit on the porch swing and listen to the other young women talk about their plans for the evening and what handsome man they might find at one of the clubs. They seemed so sophisticated, and they certainly had more clothes than she did. Eunice wore her one fancy dress whenever she ventured out into the neighborhood, and with the necessary repeated washings, it looked threadbare in no time at all.

By coincidence Eunice found a welcome face at Columbia. Ruth Walther, the math teacher from the Allen School, was taking summer classes to earn an advanced degree, and she invited Eunice to have dinner with her at the International House, where she was living. "I think she was hungry," Walther recalled. Though Eunice's tuition and basic necessities had been taken care of by her sponsors in Tryon, "it wasn't quite adequate for New York, for her to live and so forth."

The Juilliard summer session ended August 11. Friedberg gave her a B+ for her piano studies, and she earned a B– in the Fundamentals of Piano Practice course from Stojowski. She faithfully went to the no-credit Repertoire class and received the appropriate mark for her attendance. A B+ and B– were not the norm for someone who had stood out in every class up to then, but Eunice had at least proved she could hold her own among other Juilliard students, and she decided to stay in New York to study with Friedberg on a private basis. Her new goal was to prepare for the entrance examination to the Curtis Institute in Philadelphia as Miss Mazzy had planned. It was at least as prestigious as Juilliard, and with its enrollment of no more than 136, much smaller. Founder Mary Louis Curtis Bok wanted to make sure that those selected were provided significant one-on-one study, and the best way to accomplish that, in her view, was to limit the enrollment. Curtis was different in another respect. Since its founding in 1924, the school had provided full scholarships to all students who were accepted, regardless of need. Given its size, the competition for admission was intense, even more so because the school granted auditions in the various disciplines only when there were openings in a particular department. One piano slot had existed for the 1949–50 year, and for the 1950–51 class, seventy-two applicants now competed for three spots.

In addition to studying with Friedberg, Eunice worked briefly back in North Carolina with Miss Mazzy and Grace Carroll, the tutor in Asheville. She wanted to make sure she was ready when Curtis assigned her audition slot in the spring of 1951. The school had very specific requirements: each applicant had to play from memory some Bach, either a prelude and a fugue from the Well-Tempered Clavichord or a three-part invention; a complete Beethoven sonata; and one slow and one "brilliant" composition from the works of Chopin. While it is impossible to know which particular piece Eunice chose, she must have been thrilled that the audition included Bach. "He is technically perfect," she announced to anyone who asked her opinion.

When she arrived in Philadelphia on the appointed day in April 1951, Eunice felt certain that she was well prepared, if slightly in awe of the elegant surroundings: Curtis was made up of four stately mansions on Rittenhouse Square, one of Philadelphia's toniest addresses. She was given a practice room in one of the mansions and had thirty minutes to warm up beforehand. She had to be mindful of the time because if she was late, the judges could refuse to let her audition. There was no guarantee either that Eunice or any other applicant could play all the pieces he or she had prepared. The judges had the leeway to dismiss a student after one selection.

When it was over, Eunice felt she had played well. Now she simply had to wait for the school's decision, which probably would come by the end of spring.

BEYOND CURTIS, Philadelphia had taken on added importance because Kate, with Eunice's younger siblings, Frances and Sam, had moved there in the fall of 1950. J.D. made his way up from Tryon when he could. One of his older brothers, Walter, a contractor, had lived in the city for years and was well established. It was part of the reason Carrol settled there in 1946 when he got out of the army.

When Kate and the children first arrived, they lived temporarily in south Philadelphia, not far from Walter. Most important to Kate, this temporary home was only a ten-minute walk from Tindley Temple United Methodist Church, one of the influential black churches in the city, with a claimed membership of ten thousand and a sanctuary that could seat more than three thousand. The church was named in honor of pastor Charles A. Tindley, widely considered to be the father of American gospel music. His "I'll Overcome Some Day" later became the basis for the civil rights anthem "We Shall Overcome." Most church hymnals featured other Tindley songs, including "We'll Understand It Better By and By" and "Stand by Me." The importance of music in the church was underscored by its distinctive organ, which had more than six thousand pipes, and by the creation of a special position in the church hierarchy, minister of music.

Eunice had already moved to Philadelphia to join her family

when she received unimaginable news. Curtis had rejected her. She was convinced her dream of being a classical pianist lay in ruins, her plan not deferred but unequivocally derailed. Over the ensuing half-century that moment of despair would resurface, sometimes unexpectedly, with all the anguish of a fresh betrayal, and it would shape forever more how she viewed her past.

"I just couldn't believe it had happened," she wrote later, "and all I could think about was what I had given up over the years to get to where I was the day I heard that Curtis didn't want me, which was nowhere. . . ."

Kate's reaction only intensified Eunice's sorrow: this was "God's will" and it had to be accepted. Kate had suffered her own disappointments, she reminded her daughter, and survived. Snap out of it, she seemed to say. Get some kind of job and keep working at the music.

"How in the name of God was I going to be the first black concert pianist in my spare time?" Eunice retorted, convinced no one would "pay money to a failure." Hard as it was to believe, Eunice still carried around the burden of her misguided dream: that she could break the color barrier in classical music. She was still unaware that several accomplished black men and women were already on the concert stage, including Natalie Hinderas, who had studied at Juilliard when Eunice did.

Most troubling, Eunice couldn't shake the notion that she simply wasn't good enough, and she found no solace in compelling statistics that showed every applicant, white or black, faced long odds. Sixty-nine other piano applicants didn't win acceptance either. In fact, overall 165 young people had auditioned across the disciplines, and only thirty-five were chosen—barely one for every five who applied. The total enrollment had dropped, too, to 123 from 136.

EUNICE CAME UP WITH a new strategy when her melancholy lifted: to work twice as hard, if that was possible, and audition for Curtis the next year. The plan made sense until her brother Carrol repeated what he had learned from their uncle Walter, well connected in certain black and white circles: Eunice had been rejected from Curtis because she was black. Not that Curtis had never had black students before. One of them, George Walker, a piano and composition student, would go on to win a Pulitzer Prize.

But Eunice was convinced that an unknown black girl from a small Southern town never had a chance. It was actually a comforting thought, because putting the pieces together this way meant it wasn't a question of talent. Her rejection was based on the immutable factor of skin color, something she had no control over. One could rue the imperfections in a society that operated by unspoken bias, but it certainly wasn't her fault. And there was a larger truth. If racism indeed was at play, it had shaped Eunice's chances long before she sat down to audition in one of Curtis's elegant mansions. Her competition had better and more training simply because they were white.

Convinced she had no future in music, Eunice declared herself "a stranger to the piano." She took a routine job in a photographer's darkroom, grateful for the monotony. All she had to do was lift film out of a solution every time a bell rang, she recalled. "It left me free to think about anything that came into my head." She did, though, honor a request from the Town and Country Club, a black civic group, to play for the organization's annual summer fashion show. It earned her two mentions in the *Philadelphia Tribune* society pages.

BY 1953 THE WAYMONS had moved to predominantly black northwest Philadelphia. Carrol had found a two-story brick row house at 4221 Wyalusing, which was typical of the other houses on the block: a good-sized kitchen and living room, a bedroom and a bathroom on the first floor, and three smaller bedrooms upstairs— large enough so the family would be comfortable.

Though Eunice hadn't officially assigned him the role, Carrol took it upon himself to be his sister's adviser-cum-protector. He could see that in spite of her declaration to be "a stranger to the piano," ignoring music made her miserable. She finally admitted it, too, and Carrol told her she had to get back to serious study. He promised they would find a way to pay for the lessons, and Eunice took it from there. She found Vladimir Sokoloff, a supplementary piano instructor at Curtis for students majoring in another instrument, and he agreed to take her on as a private student to prepare her for an audition the following year. His immediate encouragement and praise softened the blow of her rejection and restored her confidence. "Once the terrible insecurity of wondering if I had overestimated my talent was gone, my bitterness went too," she explained later. But not the anger. Only now it was the kind of anger that motivated her. The goal of being a classical concert pianist was back on track.

Sokoloff held firm on one point, however. He dismissed the notion that Eunice had been turned down because she was black and of modest means. "Oh no, it had nothing to do with her color or her background," he told French television reporters for a 1992 documentary. "She wasn't accepted because there were others who were better, and that was the whole posture of the Curtis Institute." She wasn't a "genius," Sokoloff went on, "but she had talent. She had a great talent. I accepted her on the basis of her talent and with the understanding that I would prepare her for an audition at Curtis."

AFTER SHE STARTED her private lessons, Eunice gave up the photography job. But she still needed to earn money, and when she heard about a job as an accompanist for Arline Smith, who ran a vocal studio on South Eighteenth Street, near Rittenhouse Square, she took it. Coincidentally, the studio was barely two blocks from Curtis. The music might be a world apart from classical study, but at least she would be playing. Plus, Eunice admired the way Smith, a white woman, did business. Her prime clientele, as far as Eunice could tell, were barely talented teenagers supported by their optimistic parents, who were charged $10 per lesson. Smith only paid her accompanists $1 an hour, though she provided them hot meals every day prepared by her housekeeper. The easy math showed that Smith made a nice profit.

Another accompanist named Ingrid was already working when Eunice started. She wasn't as serious about music and she wasn't very attentive either. More than once Ingrid chewed gum right through her lessons, blowing bubbles in a kind of contemptuous counterpoint to her students' vocal efforts. Whatever Eunice thought of the teenagers, her manners kept her from being so rude.

Though hardly a perfect fit, the job provided one benefit—the chance to learn new music, mostly the current hits the students liked, along with older standards their parents favored. Eunice had to admit that she liked the variety, playing either from the sheet music Smith scrounged up or, thanks to her good ear and perfect pitch, devising her own accompaniment after hearing a song only once.

Eunice also enjoyed the challenge of trying to make even bad singers sound good. Classical training tethered her to the written page, but she could transpose a song to any key instantaneously so her students never had to stretch beyond their range. They might not say a formal thank-you, but she caught the looks of relief in their eyes and appreciation on the faces of their parents when they came by to listen, thrilled at how good their children sounded. She realized, too, that she actually knew something about singing, from her time as one of the Waymon Sisters and from listening to the glorious music that was part of all the church services she had either played for or attended.

She had no formal vocal training, but Eunice knew that the kids who came to the studio were too restrained. She tried her best to explain that singing meant more than learning the melody and the lyrics. They needed feeling, too. If she couldn't get through to them any other way, she sang the songs herself to demonstrate. She didn't mean to be conceited, but when the students tried to copy her, they sounded better. Until now, Eunice had never given much thought to her voice. But one day she had a revelation: she was earning money singing.

Smith usually supervised the first sessions with a new accompanist, but having quickly proved herself, Eunice was on her own almost from the start. Not only that, the studio was busy enough that she worked steadily, though she found four or five hours a day to practice. She was earning $50 a week, paying $25 to Sokoloff for each lesson, giving a few dollars to Kate to help with household expenses, and keeping the rest.

Eunice had a stage all to herself for an afternoon of Chopin when she played at a seventh-grade assembly at the end of February 1953 at the Mayer Sulzberger Junior High School. The event dovetailed with her realization that she needed to make more money and could do so through music. To make it work, though, she had to open her own studio. In short order she rented a small storefront at 5705 West Master, about two miles west of the family house on Wyalusing, and set up shop with the essentials: a piano, a few pieces of furniture, a phonograph and some cherished records, and a new dog she named Sheba. She charged $2.50 an hour, which turned out to be cheaper than a lesson at the Smith studio. Eight students followed her, and though Smith was initially irked, she didn't hold a grudge. Before long, she was giving Eunice part-time work.

Eunice taught during the day, and in the evening the studio turned into her apartment, her time at the piano devoted to preparing for her next lesson with Sokoloff. But she also had opportunities to perform. She put on an afternoon program with Carrol's girlfriend, Doris Riley, for an organization that helped place black children for adoption. She had an even bigger audience February 19, 1954, when the Philadelphia Branch of the National Association of Negro Musicians, with help from the Young People's Music Club, presented her in a recital at the New Century Auditorium. Her program is lost to history, but it must have been gratifying to present the music she loved to an audience eager to hear it, and unlike those at the Tryon recitals, one that was almost entirely black.

A few months later, Eunice was invited again to play for a fashion show, this one to raise money for the *Philadelphia Tribune* charities. It was one of black Philadelphia's biggest social events, and the sponsors billed Eunice as the "well-known pianist on the east coast." The *Tribune* reported afterward that she received "a tremendous ovation" for playing "Yankee Doodle Fantasy."

Despite this strong response to her music, Eunice was still lonely. "I didn't seem to fit in with any of the people I met," she recalled in her autobiography, though she apparently had some social life. *The Philadelphia Tribune* listed her among the young women attending a formal gala in May 1954 hosted by Phi Beta Sigma, a historically black fraternity founded at Howard University in 1914. "Eunice Waymon was stunning in aqua blue chiffon with drape of pink enhanced with roses," the paper noted. But this was perhaps an anomaly. Eunice became distraught enough that she spent some of her money to see a psychiatrist once a week, on Thursdays. After a year, though, she decided the sessions weren't doing her much good. Eunice made another friend through neighborhood coincidence, a woman who introduced herself as Faith Jackson. She was tall and elegant, her honey-colored skin three shades lighter than Eunice's, and she was a prostitute. Her street name was "Kevin Matthias." Eunice remembered the provocative women she had seen strolling the streets of Harlem, but Kevin was the first she'd actually met in this line of work. Kevin took a liking to her; Eunice couldn't figure out why, but she didn't dwell on it. She resolved to enjoy getting to know this exotic woman who was beautiful, seemed so free, and "could get men all the time. They gave her money and clothes, and what they didn't give her she bought. . . ." She didn't belong to any pimp "because she never needed one; she was totally independent."

When Eunice took Kevin to Wyalusing to meet her family, she didn't worry about their reaction. "We weren't into judgments," her brother Carrol said. "Everyone knew she had her 'clients,' her weekend company," as Carrol put it, but all that mattered was that his sister and Kevin were good friends.

Kevin occasionally invited Eunice to parties or had her over for dinner. A memorable one took place on Christmas, probably in 1953. Eunice graciously asked if she could bring a dish or help with the preparation. Thanks, but not necessary, Kevin told her. At the appointed time on Christmas day, Eunice was welcomed into a spotless apartment, Kevin already stretched out on the sofa looking elegant. The aroma of roast turkey filled the place. A man appeared and took Eunice's coat as he offered her a drink. When the man went back in the kitchen, Kevin explained that he was a customer "who paid her to let him cook and serve Christmas dinner. All she had to do was go in every half hour or so and beat him with a whip," Eunice said. "I swear this is true," she might add when retelling the story. "I almost died."

6. The Arrival of Nina Simone

~ June 1954–June 1956 ~

It was through her students that Eunice got to Atlantic City, New Jersey, the beachfront resort town about an hour's drive from Philadelphia that was famous for three things: the annual Miss America pageant, which had been held at the convention hall since 1940; the Boardwalk; and the topflight performers who entertained the white tourists flocking to the grand hotels. As segregated as any Southern town, Atlantic City had its own black section, here a few blocks north of the Boardwalk, with nightspots that drew the best black talent. Blacks were also found on the Boardwalk, but as the mainstays of the housekeeping and custodial staffs at the hotels. Carrol had been a bellhop at the Claridge for a couple of summers after he got out of the service.

Eunice got curious about the place when she learned that a few of her college-age students took summer jobs at the hotels. One of them said he played the piano in a bar, and Eunice's surprise must have shown on her face—she didn't think he was very good. "Yeah, I know"—he shrugged—"but they're going to pay me $90 a week." And that didn't include tips. It was nearly twice as much as Eunice made on her own. She was intrigued enough to follow up, and through the student, she found an agent who in turn booked her into the Midtown Bar on Pacific Avenue. It was one block away from the Boardwalk and in the heart of the white entertainment district. Carrol remembered that her first booking was on the weekends. They would go together, and she could commute back and forth from Philadelphia.

Early in June 1954, Eunice made her way to 1719 Pacific Avenue, a nondescript one-story building with a sign out front that said "Midtown." She didn't know what to expect, having never been in a bar before, but standing outside, she took a deep breath, opened the door, and went in. She stopped abruptly, overwhelmed by the smell of the place and barely able to see. The smoky air made her eyes water, but she collected herself, walked to the bar, and asked to see Harry Stewart, the owner.

What did she want? the bartender asked. Eunice told him she was the new piano player. The man said she'd have to wait a few minutes because Stewart was busy, but would she like a drink in the meantime? That would be nice, Eunice replied, and asked for a glass of milk. The request brought good-natured laughter from a few of the regulars sitting at the bar. Eunice blushed, and looked around to get her bearings while she waited.

The Midtown was a long, narrow room with a bar that stretched about two thirds of the way down one wall. A few tables and chairs were laid out in the remaining space, and a piano stood on a tiny raised stage at the back. Eunice noticed sawdust on the floor. Locals thought of the place as "just a plain bar—almost a neighborhood type bar," as one put it, for working people. A kitchen was in the back, "Open All Night" under the direction of "Chef Alberto," a newspaper ad announced. Stewart advertised himself as "your host."

"He was a little Jewish guy and had a fat cigar in his mouth as a permanent fixture," Eunice remembered, though she didn't recall how she knew he was Jewish. Perhaps it was just a guess, given the standard view that men who ran nightclubs were usually Jewish. Stewart took Eunice over to the piano, which was no worse than many she'd seen, but it distressed her to see water dripping down from a leaky air conditioner exactly where she would sit. Stewart noticed the same thing, excused himself for a moment, and returned with an umbrella. He opened it and jammed it up into the ceiling near the air conditioner so that now the water was rerouted into a bucket in front of one of the tables.

How did Eunice want to be billed? Stewart asked. The question brought her up short. In the excitement over the new job, she had forgotten about what her family, particularly her mother, would think about her playing in a bar. She might as well tell Kate she was consorting with the devil. But even if Kate never found out, Eunice also realized she could lose students if their parents knew she was slumming in Atlantic City.

"Nina," Eunice replied on the spot.

"She'd always liked 'Nina,' " Carrol explained, noting that Niña was Spanish for little girl.

Fine, Stewart said. But what about the last name? "Simone," she said without hesitation.

"It was not contemplated," according to Carrol. "It was a natural. It seemed to go with it."

The two names together suggested a certain panache. And when pronounced with a Latin flavor, they sounded vaguely foreign: "Nee-na . . . See-mone." "I chose the name Nina because I had always been called Nina—meaning little one—as a child," she told the Philadelphia *Sunday Bulletin* in 1960, though neither Carrol nor her older siblings had any recollection of the nickname. In a different interview the same year with the magazine *Rogue* she said "Nina" was adapted from a boyfriend who called her Niña. "I don't know where the hell I got Simone from." When she published her memoir in 1991, Nina said that "Simone" came from her appreciation of the French film star Simone Signoret. Variations on the theme, "Nina Simone" felt right as soon as Eunice put the two names together.

Stewart told her to come back in an hour and start to work. When she returned, the regulars at the bar stared in bemusement. Apparently they had never seen a black woman entertainer in the Midtown dressed like Nina. She had changed into a chiffon gown, applied makeup, and fixed her hair as though she was performing at one of her classical recitals. She didn't mind the customers, but she was anxious in this new setting because she didn't know what was expected of her. She calmed herself by ticking off all the pluses: she had talent, she was well trained, and whatever these snickering men at the bar thought of the way she looked, she was the finest pianist they had ever heard. She didn't know anything about this Count Smith, who got top billing in Stewart's ad, but he couldn't be any better than she was even if Stewart advertised him as "royalty at the piano." Nina might be playing at a bar for a bunch of men who were drinking too much, but if she closed her eyes and thought only of the music, she could be onstage at Carnegie Hall.

Once she sat down Nina drew on more than a decade of experience, though she was only twenty-one: gospel from church, Bach and the others from her work with Miss Mazzy, Carl Friedberg, and Vladimir Sokoloff, plus all of the popular tunes she had learned playing for Arline Smith's students and her own. She could mix and match and meld, improvising as she went along. She wouldn't be tied down to three- or four-minute songs like most piano players, and that first night what she played weren't really "songs" at all but extended poems made up of musical notes instead of words, none of it on paper, all of it in her head. Some of them went on for thirty minutes.

Shortly after four a.m., when the last of the diehards had shuffled out of the bar, Nina asked Stewart for his opinion. The piano playing was very nice and interesting, he said, but why wasn't she singing?

"I'm only a pianist," Nina replied.

Not according to Stewart. Tomorrow night, he told her, "you're either a singer or you're out of a job."

On the ride back to Philadelphia with her brother, Nina realized she had only one alternative: turn herself into a singer. She had used her voice before only as sidelight, when she sang as one of the Waymon Sisters or when she gave occasional pointers to her students. Her limited range allowed her to do only so much with her voice, so the solution was to make singing just one element of her performance rather than the centerpiece. Her voice, she decided, would become "the third layer complementing the other two layers, my right and left hands." To put theory into practice, at her next performance she picked an easy popular song, sang a lyric, and then played around with it, repeating a line once or twice and then moving on. In another song, she repeated an entire verse and then started to improvise the lyrics as she went along. She reminded herself of the congregants at some of those revivals she had played in Tryon, when folks got up to testify, shouting out their revelations over and over. When the night was over, Nina had her own revelation: she was having fun. But more important, Harry Stewart enjoyed it, too.

Nina got more comfortable with each performance, and it dawned on her that she was creating something uniquely hers, even if what came out was Eunice Waymon of Tryon, North Carolina, filtered through Johann Sebastian Bach of Eisenach, Germany. But however unusual, she welcomed the synthesis. For the past year Nina had kept the different parts of her musical life separate. One part was her storefront business, the work to make money. The other part was her real life spent with Bach, Liszt, and the other great composers. She practiced every minute on her own time and then polished the various pieces once a week with Vladimir Sokoloff. She could tolerate the work at the Midtown by making her sets as close to classical music as possible, even though she had to play popular tunes and sing. "The strange thing," she recalled later, "was that when I started to do it, to bring the two halves together, I found a pleasure in it almost as deep as the pleasure I got from classical music." What's more, Nina had to admit that after so many years of feeling pressure to achieve at the keyboard, "the Midtown had made me looser."

WORD SPREAD QUICKLY that something special happened at the club. After midnight new people were coming in, whites, but younger whites than the regulars and much more attentive. They were the hotel waiters and bellhops looking for entertainment before heading home. Happily for Nina, they were more attuned to her style and expectations than the usual barhoppers.

Remembering Miss Mazzy's instruction, Nina treated the Midtown like a concert hall, and she was dumbfounded the first time one or two patrons who'd had too much to drink were so boisterous they could be heard above her playing. It broke her concentration, and she resolved right then not to tolerate it. She simply stopped and waited until they quieted down and then returned to the music. Apparently no one had ever done that before at the Midtown, and the regulars were surprised. But these new customers appreciated it, and almost immediately they became her unofficial bouncers, shushing the noisy patrons and, when necessary, escorting them out of the club.

Nina didn't care what Harry Stewart thought about the new rules of decorum. In fact, he didn't seem to mind, and with good reason. Nina was good for business—she was told the place was busier than it had been in years. It was in midsummer, as Carrol remembered it, that Stewart extended her playing time and gave her a schedule of nine p.m. to four a.m., with fifteen minutes off every hour and all the milk she wanted. By this time, Nina had found a place at a rooming house on New York Avenue, which was close to the black clubs but not too far from the Midtown. Now when she finished her last set, she didn't face a long drive home. Instead, just before sunrise she walked the few blocks to her room and collapsed into bed for six or seven hours. When she got up, she might listen to some music and visit with a friend, but most of the time she was by herself.

Despite Nina's obvious popularity, Stewart had hedged his bets. He didn't include her in the Midtown's regular weekly ads in the *Atlantic City Press*, which continued to promote Count Smith. The ad promised "continuous entertainment," which presumably was Nina.

Some of the regulars, many of them Nina's age, introduced themselves over the summer, but she didn't consider them friends. Nina could be anything but welcoming, sitting at the piano overdressed for the surroundings, playing for hours with her eyes closed, almost imperious in her brief acknowledgment of the audience. She didn't mean to be uninterested or remote, and she was tickled when they stopped at the piano to compliment her, even if she didn't make a big show of her appreciation. That's just the way she was, a bit shy, and perhaps, even without thinking about it, she kept her distance because these folks were white. One night Nina overheard someone explain that she played with her eyes closed because she was a drug

The first ad for "Nina Simone" at
the Midtown bar, June 3, 1955
(Atlantic City Press)

addict and was always high. She drank only milk because she got sick
from drinking liquor. This was so far from the truth it should have
been comical. Instead, the comments hurt Nina to the point of tears.

But she knew that only Harry Stewart's opinion counted, and he
wanted her back the next summer. This got Nina thinking as she
returned to Philadelphia in September to resume her old routine as
Eunice Waymon, piano teacher and piano student. She had never
enjoyed accompanying the aspiring singers, and by early 1955, she
resolved to find more work performing because it paid better. Her
goal, however, was still the same: to earn enough money to study
full-time at a music conservatory. She continued to find her instruction with Vladimir Sokoloff rewarding, and during one lesson or
another she must have shown him what she had been playing at the
Midtown. He was impressed.

"Why don't you pursue this as your profession?" he asked her. He
remembered the passion in her reply: "Oh no. My first love is classical music, and I want to be a pianist."

NINA WAS NOT QUITE A STAR when she returned to Atlantic
City in June 1955, but she had a following, and Harry Stewart and the

regulars at the Midtown were waiting for her. Stewart spent money now to get the word out. The Midtown's regular ad in the *Atlantic City Press* announced her first performance, Wednesday, June 1, with her name in all capital letters, and proclaimed her the "new sensation at the piano." She had displaced Stan (The Man) Facey, who had gotten top billing in May. Now he was relegated, in smaller type, to the "plus" category.

Opening night was gratifying: the place was full and Nina was relaxed. She eased up with the customers, too, and as the days went on, she made friends with the regulars. One of them, Ted Axelrod, initially had kept a respectful distance, but finally he approached her to say how much he enjoyed her music. Could he share some of what was in his collection with her? Sure, Nina replied. "He'd play me songs I never heard before, and every so often he'd suggest I include them in my live set," she recalled. One evening he came in with a Billie Holiday record and said he'd like to hear her sing "I Love You, Porgy," from George Gershwin's *Porgy and Bess*. As a favor to Axelrod, Nina said she would work up the tune.

Holiday's version was a delicate rendering that featured an understated piano and a barely perceptible bass. She also smoothed away some of the nonstandard English in the lyrics—Gershwin's title was "I Loves You, Porgy." Nina followed her lead and adapted the song to her strength, her piano playing. She tapped into her classical music training for the opening bars, evoking Debussy with arpeggios and Bach with a few trills. Her voice was duskier than Holiday's, but she gave the lyrics a similarly poignant reading. After the first chorus, she repeated the melody on the piano before picking up the next verse. Holiday's version, which was recorded for the Decca label in December 1948, went on for just over two minutes. Nina's piano and vocal embellishments made hers twice as long, but the overall subdued sensibility was the same.

The Midtown regulars made "I Love You, Porgy" their private hit, so Nina sang it every night. Kenny Hill, a twenty-one-year-old Atlantic City native who had just gotten out of the navy, was one of those regulars. He had found temporary work as a bellhop at the Haddon Hall hotel on the Boardwalk and often passed by the Midtown after work. He stopped in one night shortly after Nina started and became an instant fan, astonished that a down-home place offered such sophisticated entertainment. "Once you heard her— she had a way of getting you," he explained. "You knew that she had to go places."

Hill was the friendly sort, rarely if ever intimidated. He introduced himself to Nina, and this summer, more at ease than the last, she was friendly in return. She had given up the formal concert-hall dress and now showed up for her sets in casual clothes. Hill called it "Bohemian. She dressed like a New Yorker." Most evenings he stayed through Nina's last set, sat around to chat with her, and often escorted her back to the rooming house on New York Avenue. "I was in love with her talent," Hill admitted. It wasn't a romance, just a nice summer friendship.

NINA'S SETS HAD EVOLVED into a merry-go-round of styles and genres that was rarely the same on any given night: folk songs, show tunes, hits, and some that should have been hits, along with her own creations, which sometimes were the extended piano compositions she played that first week at the Midtown. As the summer drew to a close, the thought of going back to teach untalented kids was unbearable, and through her agent she found a job in Philadelphia at the Poquessing Club on South Nineteenth Street. It had opened about eighteen months earlier and was a step up in decor, pay, and clientele from the Midtown. Because the first audiences didn't know her at all, she could play her Midtown sets in the opening weeks, and they turned out to be as well received in Philadelphia as they had been in Atlantic City. In a repeat of that experience, word quickly spread. In December, Frank Brookhouser, who wrote the Evening Bulletin's "Man About Town" column, included Nina in his installment on the eighth. "Kept hearing about a girl who plays the piano and sings at the Poquessing Club. Finally heard her last night. Will hear her again many times. She's sensational, the finest new talent we've heard in this town in many years."

Brookhouser thought Nina's looks were similar to Marian Anderson, one of her idols, "but she's very very different, weaving a singular spell all her own at the keyboard with her husky, emotionally charged voice and a completely individual piano style which reflects her classical training." With an uncanny prescience, Brookhouser also picked up a tinge of the melancholy, finding in her music "an atmosphere of blue lights and sad memories."

NINA'S FAME HAD BROUGHT another pressing problem: she needed to tell her mother about her club work. She decided to take the direct approach and frankly admitted that she played in nightspots as Nina Simone but that she was doing it—and this was absolutely true—so that she could pay for continued classical lessons. She had not, she wanted Kate to know, given up her dream of being a classical concert pianist. What's more, she never drank liquor in the clubs, and the music she played was not the bump-and-grind, gutbucket blues Kate had so disdained. In fact, Nina explained, she mixed in classical music whenever she could and gave a classical twist to tunes usually played with a pop arrangement.

As Nina remembered it, Kate was unmoved, wanting nothing to do with her daughter's new, if temporary, career and that hurt. But Nina wasn't surprised. She knew Kate could never accept certain things—"although that didn't include the money I gave her every month earned 'out in the world' "—Kate's derisive term for any place that wasn't the church.

Nina forged ahead anyway. Her growing reputation led her to another agent, who booked her into more upscale supper clubs. She was no less committed to proper decorum in these new places than she had been at the Midtown, only now she had a new tactic. Instead of stopping the music altogether, she simply stared at the offending parties. The unblinking eyes and the stern look on her face left no doubt about her feelings. Besides, the hard stare was more polite than calling out the loud patrons.

Nina continued her studies with Sokoloff even though both of them knew she had passed a line of demarcation. The cutoff point for Curtis applicants was twenty-one. Nina was already twenty-two. Sokoloff agreed to keep working with her, but now her pursuit of a classical career would have to be without a degree from Curtis.

In the meantime Nina readied for her return to the Midtown in the summer of 1956. She started at the end of June, and Harry Stewart welcomed her with a new ad that anointed her "the incomparable Nina Simone." Ted Axelrod had also returned with a new group of friends eager to hear her, and while she enjoyed his company, Nina wanted something more than friendship with a fan. One evening she struck up a conversation with a young good-looking white man who had a nice smile. He was sweet but not in a cloying way, and his sense of humor made Nina laugh. His name was Don Ross, and he came back the next evening, waiting for her at the bar with a glass of milk in his hand. She was charmed.

7. Little Girl Blue

~ July 1956–December 1958 ~

Nina's relationship with Edney had been, for all its intensity, a meeting of the heart and mind, stopping short of the physical intimacy she longed for. In the months after she left Tryon, Nina found little social life of any sort, although there was one brief episode with a young man from home that was, in a way, connected to Edney because they knew each other. The day Nina ran into him on a Harlem street she was particularly lonesome, and, as it happened, so was he. New York City was "too much to deal with," she said. He reminded her of Edney and took his place that night. "It wasn't what I expected, not at all. It hurt like hell and put me off the whole idea of men for a good while."

Sometime later in Philadelphia a young man named Ed, who sang in the Tindley Temple choir, prompted Nina to examine her thinking. He was handsome, shared her love of music, and was also the child of a minister. That his name reminded Nina of Edney might have made him that much more attractive. One Sunday Ed offered to walk Nina home after church, and their afternoon together turned into the evening and then into a romance that lasted a few months. "He taught me a lot," Nina said. "He even talked about marriage, which was when I finished with him."

By the time Don Ross sidled up to Nina at the Midtown with that glass of milk in his hand, she was ready to reciprocate. She let him walk her back to the rooming house on New York Avenue after her last set, and pretty soon he came by in the daytime to visit or take her out to meet his Atlantic City friends. She got so used to seeing him every evening at the Midtown that if he wasn't in the room, "the place felt empty and I got lonely again."

Don was a "pitchman," a salesman-for-rent for whatever product needed selling. He worked fairs up and down the East Coast and wasn't particular about what goods he was pushing. He would earn enough money to get by, and when a certain amount accumulated, he stopped in a place where he had friends until he had to go out and earn more money. A self-styled hipster, he claimed to be a drummer or painter, depending on his mood.

Don moved in with Nina that summer. They "slid into bed together" was how she put it, no big declarations of love, no emotional fireworks. But having Don around took the edge off a lingering isolation that Nina couldn't shake, even with the accolades that accompanied her growing popularity. She liked waking up in his arms rather than by herself, and she got used to it. Before she knew it, she recalled, "the idea of being without him was unthinkable. He loved me, and I needed to be loved."

When Nina brought Kevin, the call girl, home, the family hadn't flinched. They didn't flinch when they met Don either. "We didn't care whether he was black, blue, green or yellow," Carrol said. He fit in easily and "could hang out with anybody. He was just part of the group . . . And he loved Mother's cooking." Sam Waymon, Nina's youngest sibling, was only twelve, and Don intrigued him. He'd never seen a man who wore a beret. "He was a cool cat, a bohemian," Sam remembered. Though Nina and Don clearly cared for each other, Carrol doubted the relationship would last. His sister was a professional, "up and coming." Don was not.

•

DON'S PRESENCE HELPED MAKE the summer at the Midtown go by quickly. Harry Stewart, happy to have his star for another three months, declared her "back by popular demand" in the bar's weekly ads. But Nina knew that when her contract with Stewart was up at the end of August, she was finished. Offers were coming in now from clubs outside Atlantic City and Philadelphia, and Don thought she should take them. She was of two minds. She liked the income, and most of the time she enjoyed the work, but this was still a means to an end: earning enough money to return to classical study full-time. Besides, when she allowed herself even to think about a life in popular music, Nina realized she didn't know anything about the business and had no way of sorting out which offers were real and which were empty promises. If she was going to continue with nightclub work, even temporarily, she needed someone to manage these affairs.

One evening her concerns dovetailed with Harry Stewart's connections. Stewart introduced Nina to a man from New York named Jerry Field. He was a friend who happened to be an agent, Stewart told her. He had heard about her and had come to Atlantic City especially to see a show. Later Nina learned that only part of this was true. Field had already been in town and had just met Stewart when he happened to stop in the Midtown the previous night. But it was true that he was an agent and that he came back to the bar a second time because he liked Nina's music. Field told her she was an unusual talent and that he wanted to represent her. She liked that he was confident but not a braggart. "You can do better," he declared, alluding to the Midtown. Nina could see that he was more professional than the small-time bookers she knew. He didn't work out of his house but had a real office in New York on Broadway, near Central Park, and he tried to develop his clients by putting them in the venues best suited to their talents.

Field promised Nina he would find her better-paying jobs, and he thought he could get her a recording contract. He was ready to seal the agreement with a handshake until a proper contract could be drawn up and signed. Nina wanted to think about it.

"I'm offering you more money so what's to think about?" he asked.

"I thought about that for a few seconds," Nina recalled, "and then stretched out my hand across the table." The deal was done. She might not have admitted it at the time, but if she pointed to a moment when a choice had to be made, one path taken over another, this was it. Saying yes to Jerry Field ultimately meant saying no to Bach and Beethoven.

NINA RETURNED TO PHILADELPHIA to play a few dates that were already in place. Then in late fall she headed north to start the jobs Jerry had arranged at East Side supper clubs in New York City and a few others upstate. Jerry seemed to know what he was doing, and when Nina had introduced him to Carrol, her brother liked him, too. "He was genuine. He also knew there were crooks out there that would take her for a ride, and Jerry wasn't going to let that happen."

Back in Philadephia in the spring of 1957, Nina played a new venue, the Queen Mary Room in the Rittenhouse Hotel, a small establishment at Twenty-second and Walnut whose uncertain past lent a bit of excitement to its present reputation as "a swinging place on the midtown after dark scene," according to one local writer. A few months before Nina's opening, police arrested several patrons for public drunkenness and charged bartenders with serving minors. Entrepreneur Jack Dubin had heard Nina at the Poquessing Club and wanted to hire her for the hotel. But he didn't want to disturb the setup he'd created in the Hi-Fi Room, whose walls were lined with high-fidelity speakers to play stereo records all night. So Dubin worked out a deal to put Nina in the Queen Mary at $100 a week, counting on her singular stylings to bring in the customers. "When Nina is on," bartender Teddy Weintraub joked, "I feel like I'm tending bar at the Academy of Music," a reference to Philadelphia's premier spot for classical music.

Nina had become a more confident singer, too. On some tunes, "Black Is the Color of My True Love's Hair" and "Since My Love Has Gone," for example, she let her vocals carry the moment. The intricate accompaniment, spiced with allusions to all her favorite composers, was just that, a supporting element. Though her sets could be somber, she usually included the up-tempo "Lovin'

Woman," a welcome respite when her fingers flew over the keyboard in a rollicking Caribbean style.

In no time at all Dubin boosted Nina's salary to $175 a week. On top of that, she caught the attention of Philadelphia's social elite and was invited to perform at a charity event in the affluent suburb of Merion. Nina agreed to do so even though she was not paid, understanding the benefits that were likely to flow from the people who would hear her.

In late summer Nina took a booking at the Playhouse Inn in New Hope, a small town in Bucks County about forty miles north of Philadelphia and a popular tourist destination. The inn was right next to the Bucks County Playhouse, whose high-quality theatrical productions featured stars from Broadway and Hollywood. The theater had done well since its founding twenty-two years earlier, but the inn had languished until 1955, when Odette Myrtil, a French-born entertainer, took over. An actress and musician with a flair for food and fashion, she elicited testimonials from satisfied guests and published them every month in the *Bucks County Traveler*. She promised hunters that her chef "will prepare and cook free of charge, any game you've bagged, short of an elephant!" And she brought in entertainment, mostly piano trios, for dancing in the main dining room and in the "Bistro," a room intended to evoke "a bit of fabled Paris" on the banks of the Delaware River. In the September 1957 *Traveler* Odette gushed about Nina's imminent arrival. "Come hear my newest exciting discovery—Ninia [*sic*] Simone and her boys, making heavenly music in the Bistro." The ad suggests that at least for this engagement, Nina had picked up a couple of sidemen, though there is no mention of who they were, and in subsequent years, Nina never spoke of them.

The Playhouse Inn was among a dozen or so nightspots in the New Hope area, most of them, like the inn, featuring jazz trios for entertainment. Al Schackman, a guitarist, had been playing on and off in New Hope for at least a year, and while Nina was at the Bistro, one of either his friends or hers suggested that Al sit in. She was dubious. She knew jazz musicians liked to jam, "but I wasn't a jazz musician, and I didn't see why I should be expected to play with a man I had never met before." Reluctantly, Nina agreed to let Al join her, and the next night she barely acknowledged the tall, slender man who walked into the Bistro carrying a guitar in one hand and an amp in the other.

Nina sat down at the piano and waited for Al to set up. She looked at him but didn't say a word before starting the first song, "Little Girl Blue," which she had worked up at the Midtown a couple of summers earlier. Only she didn't begin with the song itself. Instead she improvised on the Christmas carol "Good King Wenceslas," turning it into a fugue in the style of her beloved Bach.

Al didn't know what song Nina was playing, but he could feel what she was doing. Because he, too, had perfect pitch, he had no trouble finding her key, and he wanted to harmonize. He started playing his guitar a third above her. When she moved into something akin to a two-part invention, he played a counterpoint to that. Nina looked up, startled, but kept going. The two of them reached a crescendo and then in an instant, Nina got quiet. "Sit there and count your fingers," she sang, the opening lines of "Little Girl Blue."

Al was floored that Nina could make a ballad work in the midst of all that intensity. Nina was floored that someone she'd never met before and had never played with understood her so intuitively. "It was as if we were one instrument split in two—I, the piano, Al, the guitar," she said. "It was like telepathy—we couldn't lose each other . . . We played Bach-type fugues and inventions for hours. . . ."

Nina wanted to make more music with Al, and the feeling was mutual. "By the time we got to the downbeat, BAM. It was a lifelong thing," he said. Their respective schedules, however, wouldn't allow a collaboration in the near term. They promised each other they would reunite as soon as possible.

BETHLEHEM RECORDS, a small independent label devoted to jazz, employed Lee Kraft as an occasional talent scout. He brought musical prospects to Gus Wildi, Bethlehem's founder, and then Wildi and his associates decided if they wanted to make a record. Kraft had heard Nina at a club in Philadelphia and thought Bethlehem should record her. But Vivian Bailey, a Philadelphia businessman who first heard Nina at the Rittenhouse, said he had arranged for her to make a demo that included instrumentals and vocals, with the idea of getting a recording contract. He took the tape to New York and played it for Wildi. "Her beautiful and unique vocal quality caused us to sign her immediately to a recording contract," Wildi recalled. They met at the label's office, and Wildi told her he intended to treat her like other Bethlehem artists. She could record whatever she wanted.

The precise date of Nina's session is not known, but it was probably in the late fall of 1957. Bethlehem secured space at Beltone, one of several independent studios in New York. Nina asked Jimmy Bond, whom she knew from Philadelphia, to play bass—he had done a couple of nightclub jobs with her, and the fit was good. "They told me to find a drummer," Bond recalled, and he recruited his friend, Albert "Tootie" Heath, the younger brother of well-known bassist Percy Heath. When they got to the studio, Nina told Beltone engineer Irv Greenbaum that she would accompany herself on the piano. She asked him to turn the lights down and put a small lamp on the piano. Then, Greenbaum said, "it just went."

Nina had selected fourteen tunes that she regularly performed in the clubs, and while some were well known—"I Love You, Porgy," "He's Got the Whole World in His Hands," which Nina had sung with her sisters, Rodgers and Hammerstein's "You'll Never Walk Alone"—Nina gave each of them a makeover, just as she had done with "Little Girl Blue." She reimagined "You'll Never Walk Alone" as an instrumental, starting dirgelike on the piano and echoing the first movement of Beethoven's Moonlight Sonata until she shifted into another gear. The increasingly ornamental piano work was punctuated by a few well-placed cymbal strokes from Heath. "Central Park Blues," another instrumental, was an original tune Nina and Jimmy Bond put together a day or so before the recording session.

"Nina could be a handful," Bond said. "She's just difficult. But she was so talented it didn't bother you." During some moments in the studio, he felt as if he was flying by the seat of his pants trying to follow her.

Greenbaum was mesmerized. "Nothing like Nina's artistry had ever happened in the studio before," he said. Heath and Bond were plenty talented, but he would have been satisfied with only Nina: "Her voice and the keyboard playing were so rich and interesting that they could have stood alone." Greenbaum remembered that Nina came to the session with a white man about her age, probably Don Ross. He sat at a little table away from the musicians, and in between each take, Nina went over to sit with him, and they huddled together discussing the music until everyone was ready for the next tune. Vivian Bailey said he was also at the session, having made all the arrangements to get Nina and the sidemen to the studio. Bailey had also signed a management agreement with Nina and was determined to watch over his new client, though he would later terminate their association on less than amicable terms.

Though Nina had picked the music and recorded with the musicians she wanted, she took little pleasure from the session. She still considered herself on a musical detour dictated by financial necessity. She went back to Philadelphia, she wrote later, and immersed herself in Beethoven for three days straight.

BETHLEHEM HELD OFF RELEASING the disc in part because of problems within the company. Wildi found himself in a cash crunch, and in the middle of 1958 he sold a half interest in Bethlehem to Syd Nathan, who ran King Records out of Cincinnati. This changeover, coupled with professional differences between Wildi and Nathan, must have delayed the release even more. So even though Nina had made an official studio recording, there was still nothing tangible to show for it.

As Nina remembered it in her memoir, Jerry Field suggested she move to New York to advance her career, and she agreed to do so, even though it wouldn't do anything to further her classical ambitions. She also had mixed feelings about returning to Manhattan, remembering her time there, apart from Juilliard classes, as a lonely period. It had been difficult to make friends in Philadelphia, too, and she worried about going into a new situation by herself. "I knew I had to move—I decided I must—but only if I was sure I wouldn't ever be left on my own, that Don would be with me." He had wanted to get married for some time, and Nina had resisted. Finally she relented, and toward the end of 1958 they went to the county clerk's office in Philadelphia and were married in a brief civil ceremony. No family was present; the only witness was a county employee who happened by. The couple left immediately for New York. Nina was filled with as much trepidation as excitement.

8. A Fast Rising Star

~ 1959 ~

After staying with friends temporarily in Greenwich Village, Nina and Don found their own place on Central Park West at 101st Street, about a mile south of Harlem. The apartment was on the top floor of a fifteen-story building typical of the neighborhood: marble floors and accents in the lobby, plenty of windows to capture the view of Central Park across the street. The apartment was big enough for her piano, Don's drum kit, and his painting paraphernalia. It seemed like an ideal setting as well as a testament to Nina's growing success and the money that came with it. But Don's bohemian qualities, so endearing when they met, now felt like the trappings of an upper-class bum. Most of the time, Nina complained, he just wanted to drink, smoke, "and talk poetry, jazz and all the usual beat bullshit." She felt more like the hired help than a wife, and she resented it, especially because she was the one working. To make matters worse, "he spent my money when he had none of his own."

Don wasn't an alcoholic, but he liked to have liquor around. Nina wasn't used to that, but she found herself taking a drink more often now when she was irritated about one thing or another. She didn't handle it well, and she knew it. "Don drank when he was relaxed, and I drank in order to try and relax—there was a difference." Nina started to have a glass of champagne after a show, and when she wasn't looking, one or another of her fans would give her a refill. Before she knew it, she was drunk, "frightened and rushing to make it home before I got sick." When she got there, Don was often out or "sitting on the floor smoking a reefer, stoned again."

In the midst of this bumpy transition from single to married, from Philadelphia to New York, Bethlehem finally released Nina's album the first week of February 1959, about sixteen months after it was recorded. An advance mention in the January 17 *Cash Box*, a major music trade journal, listed the release as *Nina Simone*. But three weeks later Bethlehem executives changed their minds. The album was released as *Little Girl Blue*. Given that it had been his project, Gus Wildi probably selected the eleven tracks from the 1957 session that made up the album, opening with "Mood Indigo" and finishing with "Central Park Blues." And the label hired Chuck Stewart, who was Dinah Washington's personal photographer, to shoot a cover photo. He picked Central Park for the setting of what would be the general public's first look at Nina. She curled up on a bench, her head resting on her right hand. She wore a red-checked poncho over black slacks and stared straight ahead. Though she half-smiled, her eyes were serious. Stewart had captured an arched stone bridge in the background that provided the perfect balance to Nina perched in the foreground.

Joseph Muranyi, a writer who had worked on several Bethlehem projects, composed the jacket copy. Complimentary without being effusive, his notes contained the kind of thoughtful praise intended to stamp Nina as a serious, distinctive musician. Her arresting voice, Muranyi wrote, was "a vibrant and husky contralto that tonally sounds like a blend of an unlikely combination of Marian Anderson and Ma Rainey," that is, the great opera singer and the seminal blueswoman. The sympathetic comparison placed Nina between two well-known extremes, even if the reference diminished his point that she was an authentic original.

(Muranyi's essay included one false note, his reference to Nina's singing with her sisters, "the Simone girls," failing to tell readers Nina's real family name. And another paragraph appears to be the first time that Nina's six-week summer stay at Juilliard in 1950 expanded into "two years of serious piano studies" at the school, an embellishment that would be carried forward for decades without correction by Nina herself.)

It was always a gamble when an album was released, even by a big label with a major star. Success was never guaranteed. When the reverse was true, expectations for attention and sales were generally low. *Little Girl Blue* did nothing to change the conventional wisdom for a small label and an unknown. The music trades—*Cash Box, Billboard, Variety, Down Beat, Metronome*—ignored it, though the *Philadelphia Bulletin* ran a short item noting that a hometown favorite had an album out. But if the release of *Little Girl Blue* did little to change Nina's day-to-day professional life, it was nonetheless an important marker, another irreversible step toward a pop career.

In March Nina joined a five-act bill for a few dates in the mid-Atlantic states. Clyde McPhatter, who was riding a new hit, "A Lover's Question," headlined. The group's short swing through Baltimore and Washington filled time before an eleven-act package started a month-long tour March 28. But Nina was excluded from that lineup, probably because the booking was not a good fit for artist or promoter.

The ad for the show in the *Baltimore Afro-American* turned out to be a barometer of Nina's standing in pop music circles. It listed "glamour and songs at the keyboard—Lena Simone," a typesetter perhaps confusing her with Lena Horne. By the time the group got to Washington to play a week at the Howard Theatre, the ad had been corrected, the buzz reduced to "Glamour on the Keys—Nina Simone."

Though Nina left the McPhatter tour, she did go on to a date back in Atlantic City at the Club Harlem, just a few blocks from the Midtown. The most noteworthy element was the *Philadelphia Tribune* ad for the show, which told readers with some hyperbole that in addition to being the "Nation's newest sensation," she also had an album out: "Jazz As Played in an Exclusive East Side Street Club"—which had apparently been one of the proposed titles for *Little Girl Blue* and was featured as a subtitle in some versions.

UNBEKNOWNST TO NINA, discussions about her career were going forward on two fronts. Bethlehem's option to renew her contract was coming due, and Gus Wildi wanted to extend it in spite of the tepid response to *Little Girl Blue*. Syd Nathan did not. "We don't need the broad," he told Wildi. The two fought, but Wildi lost. "He was the lord and master of his operation," Wildi explained, wincing four decades later at the memory of their verbal altercation.

At the same time Joyce Selznick, the East Coast talent scout for Columbia Pictures—and a niece of the producer David O. Selznick—thought Nina should come to Colpix, the studio's record division. She arranged an audition, and the label wanted to sign Nina immediately. As Nina remembered it, this time she used a lawyer, Max Cohen, whom Jerry Field had recommended. Cohen represented other entertainers, and Nina liked the fact that he appreciated her classical training. He encouraged her to keep studying even though he was helping turn her career in a different direction.

With the Colpix deal signed, Nina was in the studio by July for a session completely different from the Bethlehem record, which was an intimate production in every sense of the word—a small studio, three musicians, an engineer, Nina in control of everything. At Colpix she was part of a larger mosaic assembled by others, from song selection to arrangement. Hecky Krasnow, the man behind "Rudolph, the Red-Nosed Reindeer" and now a freelance producer, put together the sessions, with Bob Mersey, a staff arranger and composer for Columbia and CBS television, in charge of assembling the orchestra—though Nina wouldn't be playing the concerto she might have envisioned at Juilliard. Krasnow had picked an eclectic mix of songs that ranged from "Stompin' at the Savoy" and "You've Been Gone Too Long" to "Willow Weep for Me" and "Blue Prelude," the latter recorded by no less than Mildred Bailey, Lena Horne, and Paul Robeson. Mersey surrounded Nina with violins, muted trumpets, and flutes, a prescription Colpix hoped would bring crossover sales in the pop market.

Among the fourteen songs recorded, Nina's piano was evident only on five. Perhaps most striking was her arrangement of "Children Go Where I Send You," which began with a blast of chords that receded as Nina began to sing. An insistent snare drum complemented her all the way through, suggesting a brisk march.

Nina had fit the studio sessions around her debut appearance July 14 at the Village Vanguard, a nightclub in the heart of Greenwich Village popular with left-leaning hipsters. Guitarist Kenny Burrell's trio, which included drummer Ben Riley and bassist Major Holley, headlined and backed up Nina, who had recently picked up a percussionist, Buck Clarke, to accompany her during her thirty-minute set.

Billboard and *Variety* covered her show, and she impressed both reviewers. Nina "scored brightly," said *Billboard*'s Bob Rolontz, who called her "a real talent who can go far." *Variety* found "a song stylist with something to say and she says it differently and interestingly." But each reviewer had quibbles. Rolontz was put off by some of the lengthy arrangements, and *Variety* said a few songs were stretched "to their limits," criticisms suggesting that originality pushed too far could be tedious. If neither review was a complete rave, together they served as the perfect spotlight for a single Bethlehem had just released, "I Love You, Porgy" backed with a fast-paced "Love Me or Leave Me."

Nina was so pleased with Riley's drumming that she asked him to join her on her upcoming dates. "I understood immediately when I heard her playing what she needed and how I would try to give it to her," Riley recalled. He agreed to go out on the road with Nina but with the caveat that he would stay only until she could find some full-time musicians. He wanted to play straight-ahead jazz and not be confined to accompanying a singer, even one as interesting as Nina.

SID MARK, a young disc jockey in Philadelphia, was just starting his career when Nina played at the Rittenhouse. "I used to hang out there," he said, and periodically he and Nina chatted. Not long after *Little Girl Blue* was released, Nina happened to be in Philadelphia and brought a copy of the album to Mark at WHAT, where he was working. "I fell in love with 'I Love You, Porgy,'" Mark said. He started to play it "every day, three or four times a shift." Listeners caught on and requests poured in. Mark was sure Nina had a hit in the making. He called the record company to let them know, and as he remembered it, they just said, " 'Forget it, kid. It's a local rumble.' And they hung up."

Gus Wildi, who by now had relocated to the Cincinnati headquarters of Syd Nathan's business, was certain he never got such a call. If he had, he would have listened because he was doing his own "Porgy" promotion. "I went around with records under my arm, traveled around the New England area, Massachusetts and Connecticut," he said. Whatever the case, by late summer Mark's enthusiastic response and Wildi's travels seemed to be paying off. On August 1, just as Nina was getting ready to perform at the Playboy Jazz Festival in Chicago, "I Love You, Porgy" registered on the Cash Box pop singles chart at number ninety-two. It would eventually hit number fifteen. Two days later the record was on the Billboard chart at number eighteen. The entire Little Girl Blue album was also selling well, according to a Cash Box tally, which showed the album—albeit listed as Nina Simone—at number thirty-four out of forty on its top Monaural album chart. Evidence that "Porgy" was catching on came in the Chicago Defender, which featured a prominent photograph of Nina to publicize her appearance at the Playboy Jazz Festival, even though other performers were far better known.

"Porgy" stayed on the charts for fifteen weeks, but Nina insisted in her memoir that she hardly noticed. She wasn't interested in a pop career. She was still headed for the classical stage. All the nightclub work, even the new deal with Colpix, was only to make money so she could resume her studies. Nina had been keeping Miss Mazzy abreast of her career and apparently made sure she got a copy of Little Girl Blue. "Eunice Waymon now Nina Simone is doing night club work," Miss Mazzy wrote to Garland Goodwin, the young man who had so carefully hand-lettered the programs for the recital at Miss Mazzy's home eleven years earlier. But her reaction was hardly what Nina would have wanted. "I have one of the records. The piano is OK but I don't like what she does!"

·

THE AUGUST 29 ISSUE of the *New York Amsterdam News* ran a long piece about the concert series "Jazz at Town Hall," devoting much of the story to Nina. Headlined "You Know What We Mean— Jazz Man!" the article extolled Nina as "a rare commodity . . . She plays the piano, vocalizes, and composes." The story was a prelude to her biggest outing yet. The promoters for Town Hall, the venerable auditorium just off Times Square, had booked her as the headliner September 12 on a bill with the Horace Silver and J. J. Johnson quintets. "For this affair," one of the promoters told the *News*, "we chose Nina because her singing, in our opinion, is one of a fast rising star in jazz."

Nina was nervous the day of the performance. She didn't worry about the music. It was the venue that made her uneasy, even though playing in a concert hall had been her dream and now, finally, her elegant white satin ball gown, sleeveless with a drape over the left shoulder, would be appropriate to the surroundings. When she played in nightclubs, there was no "backstage" to speak of. Here all sorts of people she didn't know wandered around, and though things were hardly perfect with Don, his familiar face kept her calm.

Just how different Town Hall would be struck Nina right before she went onstage, when she saw the audience sitting in orderly rows—no drinks being served, no cigarette girls selling their packs. In the middle of the stage sat a beautiful grand piano, lid off, two microphones carefully placed to capture the instrument and her voice. When the MC called Nina's name, she reached back for everything Miss Mazzy had taught her in their Saturday afternoons together. She made her entrance, she recalled, "like an Egyptian queen, slow, calm and serious." This was going to be her night.

For the next forty minutes Nina crafted a distinctive set of ballads, show tunes, movie theme songs, and original material. On a few numbers she played a long piano solo before she sang. It was her way of finding the right mood. When she was ready, she nodded to her sidemen, most likely Riley on drums and Wilbur Ware on bass, the signal for them to join her. Nina barely said a word for the first twenty minutes except "thank you" between songs. But when she jumped into "Under the Lowest," she perked up. "Yeah," she exclaimed during a revved-up exchange with Ware and Riley. She punctuated the final three notes with a buoyant "ba-ba-BA." Nina told the audience she wanted to try "a little Afro-Cuban" music, adding, "We're all out in the jungle right now. We're going to see what happens when we're out there." In the ensuing five-minute instrumental, "Return Home," her piano played off the drums with escalating intensity, and she hummed every few bars in counterpoint to the heavy beat. "That's it!" she exclaimed at the final bar.

Nina closed her set with "Fine and Mellow," a nod to Billie Holiday, whose "Porgy" had inspired her and put her on the pop music map. Holiday's "Fine and Mellow" was subdued, if suggestive. Nina's high-energy treatment delivered vocal swoops and bursts of chords. At the end, she couldn't resist another "Yeah! All right," shouted above the applause and whistles, which confirmed that the night had indeed been hers.

Writing in *The New York Times* two days later, John S. Wilson, the paper's influential music critic, appreciated Nina's allure even if he found her set wanting. Noting that she was "new to the local concert stage," Wilson wrote that she used jazz "only peripherally in her performance but by bolstering some minor talents with an assured and perceptive sense of showmanship she easily held her own with Mr. Johnson and Mr. Silver," who were described by Wilson as "two of the more stirring of today's jazz musicians." Though other performers might sing and play the piano better, he added, her "consummate assurance, skillful pacing and attractive good nature" made her "an extremely winning performer." Wilson had picked up something Nina would not yet admit: she loved creating her own music.

NINA TOOK HER FIRST TRIP to California in early October to play a jazz festival held at the Hollywood Bowl. At the same time Colpix released her first single from the July sessions, "Children Go Where I Send You" backed with "Willow Weep for Me." Whether she intended it or not, the music press identified Nina as a jazz artist; it hardly seemed to matter that, as Wilson noted, she was not in the traditional mode. The Hollywood date was the third jazz booking in a row since her appearance in Chicago, and the October 3 bill put

Nina among heavyweights Count Basie, Coleman Hawkins, George Shearing, and Joe Williams. She regarded her current status with some bemusement, because in her mind a Nina Simone set was a distinct recipe: "popular songs in a classic style with a classical piano technique influenced by cocktail jazz."

By the time she got to Washington, D.C., on October 20 for a week at the Casino Royale, *The Washington Post* had listed *Little Girl Blue* as number three on the local "pop poll of the week" that tracked albums. As it happened, the soundtrack from the recently released movie *Porgy and Bess* was at number two.

NINA AND AL SCHACKMAN had hardly played together since their first meeting in New Hope two years earlier. The first week in December he joined her and Ben Riley for a week in downtown Chicago at the Blue Note. The *Defender* noted that the club was "jam packed" on opening night and was full the rest of the week. Frank Holzfeind, who ran the Blue Note, admitted that he booked Nina solely on the basis of "Porgy." "That's the first time I've ever done anything like that," he added. Even more important, while she was in the city, *Playboy* impresario Hugh Hefner invited Nina to perform on his weekly *Playboy's Penthouse* television program, a lounge version of Ed Sullivan's Sunday night variety show from New York that was broadcast from Hefner's Chicago mansion. (On this evening Nina was joined by comedians Professor Irwin Corey and Gary Morton, among others.)

Host Hefner was the epitome of *Playboy* cool, dressed in a tuxedo, as were all the male guests. The women dressed accordingly: cocktail gowns that were revealing but still tasteful enough for television. Sitting at the piano, Riley on one side, Al on the other, Nina half-smiled as Hefner introduced her as a star "who came out of nowhere last year." She was *Playboy*-ready, too, in her spaghetti-strap white gown. Her short dark hair framed her face, and a pair of unusual knoblike earrings dangled gently as she moved her head. She opened with an understated version of "The Other Woman," the rueful song about that other woman who has to "cry herself to sleep." Some unusual camera work, shots from behind Riley's shoulder, framed Nina between his metal brushes, the visual matching the aural given Riley's deft touch.

When the applause died down, Nina did a fast run of sixteenth notes. "Let's do 'Children Go,'" she said with a determined nod. Then she barreled into those distinctive opening chords. As the camera panned the audience several of the men slapped their knees in time with the music.

"Do you want to hear 'Porgy'?" Nina asked when she finished, knowing full well the answer. Though she had sung this song so many times, each version was slightly different. Here she tossed in a "sweetie" before one line, and repeated another phrase twice for emphasis. She played chords and trills as the spirit moved.

Syd Nathan had put "Porgy" in the news a week before Nina's *Penthouse* performance, but it had nothing to do with her arrangement and everything to do with a growing scandal in the music business. Nathan complained publicly that a Cincinnati disc jockey wouldn't play the tune because of a "dirty line" about Porgy's "hot hands." Nathan alleged that the deejay would relax the ban if Nathan paid him. "He made no bones about it," Nathan told newspaper reporters. He refused to make the payment, though he acknowledged that his company had paid jockeys for air play and never tried to hide it. "We have always paid by check, not cash," he said, though he considered the practice "blackmail." Nathan had made his remarks in response to a wide-ranging investigation about the practice of "payola" to disc jockeys, and documents from King Records had been subpoenaed by New York authorities.

Though Nathan had refused to renew Nina's contract, he tried to cash in now that she had a hit. Bethlehem released another single from the 1957 session early in November, the title track, "Little Girl Blue," with "He Needs Me" on the flip side. Undaunted by sluggish sales—and the Colpix single hadn't made much noise either— Nathan released a third single from the 1957 session a few weeks before Christmas, "Don't Smoke in Bed"/"African Mailman." Nina claimed she was never consulted on any of the releases, and it only confirmed her initial distaste for the record business and for Nathan in particular. Her later description of the Bethlehem years might have distorted the facts, but it left no doubt that she detested the man. Nina's career, though, was thriving in spite of her mixed feelings. It had come to her, not the other way around.

Nina hadn't given any specific thought to her audience either. They found her. She didn't seek them. But like her life since that first lesson with Miss Mazzy, when she straddled the worlds of black and white in Tryon, Nina's fans crossed racial lines, too. The first were the young white men and women who crowded into the Midtown in Atlantic City after finishing their jobs at the oceanfront hotels. Then came the mostly white audiences at the clubs in and around Philadelphia. But now there were black fans, too, evident when *Ebony*, the popular black monthly that was modeled down to its white-on-red logo on *Life*, featured Nina in a four-page spread in the December issue.

Most of the *Ebony* feature was photographs, and Nina was quoted only in snippets, but she must have talked enough to give the writer a sense of her mercurial personality. Where the *Times*'s John Wilson found "attractive good nature" and an "extremely winning performer," *Ebony* found a "wiry, moody girl." But the magazine was hardly finding fault. "The puzzlement she has stirred up in the music world is a product of her odd style: a strange grafting of a thick, abrasive almost masculine sound onto a sophisticated classical music training." Whether or not Nina would have chosen those words to describe her playing, she had to be pleased that the magazine considered her an original.

The accompanying photos showed Nina backstage with Faye Anderson, a white woman who had become an assistant-cum-traveling companion, onstage in performance, and with Don in two cozy shots, which belied the turbulence that reared up so often when they were together. Ben Riley didn't think much of him. "He would bring parties of people in [a club] and they would be talking while we were playing. He wasn't a very nice person." Riley thought Don took advantage of Nina, and he tried to keep his distance. "But I had to threaten him once," he recalled. "He wasn't going to let her go to work. I said, 'You're messin' with my money now. Let this woman go to work.' "

9. Simone-ized

~ 1960 ~

In the middle of January, Colpix put out another single from the July 1959 sessions, "The Other Woman" backed with "It Might as Well Be Spring," a sign the label intended to make Nina one of its stars. The record was a teaser for the anticipated release of two full-scale albums, *The Amazing Nina Simone*, made up of a dozen tracks from those sessions, including the songs on the single, and the Town Hall concert, marketed simply as *Nina Simone at Town Hall*. But before Colpix could get the LPs in circulation, Syd Nathan issued another album called *Nina Simone and Her Friends*, even though only four tracks were from Nina and only two of those, "He's Got the Whole World in His Hands" and "For All We Know," had not been previously released. Songs by Carmen McRae and Chris Connor made up the rest of the album.

Nina was livid. "I had no idea that Bethlehem had any intention to do such a thing until I saw it on display in a record store window in Greenwich Village," she fumed. In one way, though, Nathan's move brought Nina extra exposure. As *Cash Box* noted, she was given featured billing over Connor and McRae, who seemed like afterthoughts. Nina also received the headliner slot on a three-act jazz show in Chicago February 12.

So much had happened since Nina last played the Queen Mary Room at the Rittenhouse Hotel that she might have forgotten her free performance at a 1957 benefit for disabled children. But the officers at the Mildred Malschick Fuhrman Charities hadn't. They were sponsoring the first annual jazz festival at Philadelphia's Academy of Music March 13, and they wanted Nina. This time she would be paid $2,000 for two performances as the headliner, even though the Dizzy Gillespie quintet, the Four Freshmen, and Art Blakey and the Jazz Messengers were also on the bill. A few days before the event, Nina sat down with Frank Brookhouser of the *Bulletin*, who was still writing his "Man About Town" column, and together they traced her trajectory from child star in the church to acclaimed jazz singer. "I formed a group called the Waymon Sisters with two of my sisters," she told Brookhouser, a description of its origins that would have bemused Lucille and Dorothy. Even while she was playing church music, Nina went on, "I found it hard to resist sneaking in an extra beat in the arrangements now and then, although mother didn't approve." In her more recent creations, she said, "I wanted to get into my music more of the feeling I had once put into those spirituals."

If she hadn't completely given up her dream of a classical music career, Nina was now rewriting her narrative as though this state of affairs had been in the cards all along, improvising with words the same way she wove Bach into her blues.

NINA SPENT THE REST of March in New York at the Village Vanguard, this time with her own trio. The otherwise routine engagement was broken up by two events that reflected Nina's growing profile. On March 24 she made her first national television appearance on the NBC *Today* show. She played it safe with two mainstream selections, each coincidentally cowritten by Jule Styne, "Just in Time" and "Time after Time." Two days later she headlined another jazz event at Town Hall on a bill that included drummer

Nina Simone, c. 1959–60
(*Author's photo*)

Max Roach, saxophonist Sonny Stitt, and pianist Thelonious Monk's quartet. But for all its potential, this night would have none of the charm of the previous September evening. A faulty microphone prevented host Mort Fega, a jazz disc jockey, from being heard when he introduced the acts, and a glitch in the lineup delayed Nina's appearance. When she finally came on, she told the audience that some of the music was "created right here on the stage." The *Times*'s Wilson, who was intrigued enough to see Nina again, found her anything but creative. He said her set was based "on the valid theory that if one note is repeated often enough, a jazz audience will eventually applaud."

BEN RILEY AND AL played regularly now with Nina, but the bass chair remained unsettled. Ben's friend Ron Carter, who would go on to a distinguished career with Miles Davis and countless other musicians, filled in when Nina spent a week at Storyville, the Boston jazz club opened by impresario George Wein. But although the fit was good, Carter wanted to work with an instrumental group and chose not to stay on for Nina's upcoming dates. Riley scouted around for another bass player who could meet the group in Milwaukee April 22 for a week at Henri's Show Lounge, one of the better-known downtown clubs. He settled on Chris White, a young bassist from Brooklyn who had studied at the Manhattan School of Music. Ben had seen Chris at some of the regular jam sessions at small clubs around 125th Street and thought he could do the job—exactly why Chris had joined as many of those jams as he could.

The timing couldn't have been better. Ben called just as Chris was prepared to give up on music and take a job at the post office. So instead of donning a uniform and sorting mail, he received a plane ticket to Milwaukee and instructions to meet Nina at 730 North Fifth Street, where Henri's was located. The music would be waiting for him.

This was Nina's first time at Henri's, and the minute she walked in, she sought out the manager. "Could you please wipe down the piano?" she asked in a tone that suggested only one right answer. "I'm not going to touch that instrument." The moment told Chris everything he needed to know about this new job: Nina had standards, and he had to toe the line, musically and otherwise.

Before more out-of-town dates in Atlanta, Miami, and Detroit, Nina called a rehearsal at the apartment on Central Park West. When Chris got off the elevator and entered the foyer of 15D, he noticed a big umbrella on the floor bent at an unusual angle just as a white man walked out, head down, a bloody gash visible on his forehead. The white man, he came to realize, was Nina's husband Don, and he surmised that the two had had a fight. Nina said nothing about it, and they went right into rehearsal. "It was sort of awkward at the beginning," Chris admitted.

Faye Anderson had made the Milwaukee trip to help with suitcases, scheduling, and the like, but Don had not. It was symptomatic of their marital troubles, which now provided fodder for gossip columns. Dorothy Kilgallen led her April 4 installment with the news that Nina and Don "have separated for the fifth time they say." Eight days later *The Philadelphia Tribune* reported that Nina's "friends and relatives are working 'overtime' in efforts to patch up her differences with her white husband. But other talk is that Nina and Don have already agreed to disagree in Reno fashion."

"I had originally married Don so I'd never be alone," Nina wrote in her memoir. But more often than not, she would return from a job "hoping he wouldn't be there. Some stupid arrangement," she conceded. She had mused that they reconciled those four other times because "we can't keep away from each other." But now the separation was for good.

The rupture in Nina's personal life coincided with another change in her musical life. Ben told her he was leaving in the middle of June to take the drum chair with the Eddie "Lockjaw" Davis–Johnny Griffin quintet. "It was me playing with the hard core and how I wanted to play," he said. "Nina was more of a quiet accompaniment. She was a tremendous musician. She had a good feel—that's what made me stay as long as I did."

Chris White recommended Bobby Hamilton, whom he'd known since they played together as teenagers in the "Stablemate Quintet," their high school band in Brooklyn. Bobby studied at the Hartnett School of Music and had also taken lessons with one of the percussionists from the Boston Symphony. Nina told Chris to have Bobby make the next rehearsal at her apartment. He arrived on time to find the other band members but no Nina. The men sat around for what seemed like hours, and when Nina finally came in she offered no explanations and barely acknowledged Bobby. "Let's get this rehearsal going 'cause I got to get to Pep's in Philadelphia," she told them, referring to the popular jazz club. After the group ran through some numbers, Nina reminded Bobby to make the Pep's date, which was her way of saying he had the job.

·

THE JUNE 1960 *METRONOME*, a national magazine for jazz enthusiasts, devoted a full page to Nina. "Tense, taut, sensitive, religious, intelligent. Rare," the piece began. "A singer of rich versatility." After providing the usual background on her life, the article let Nina speak in her own words to answer radio host Ralph Berton of New York's WNCN.

"Frankly, I don't like what you do," Berton had said in an on-air interview. "It's stagecraft, commercial."

Instead of taking offense, Nina delivered a variation on the theme of survival, words once again embroidering her story and once again evoking the "blue lights and sad memories" Frank Brookhouser had picked up in her earliest club dates. "I don't know how this will go down with listeners," she said. "Perhaps, if it's understood, it won't hurt. You are right to a certain extent. For years I worked only on my music. I very nearly starved to death," she added. "It had a profound effect on me. I don't want that to happen again. Sure there's staging and commercialism now."

The same sober themes had emerged a couple of months earlier, when Nina talked to a reporter from *Rogue* magazine and alluded to childhood deprivations much more stark than any her siblings recalled. "I'm scared, scared of many things, but mostly scared of poverty. All of my life I've felt the terrible pressure of having to survive," she said. "Now I've got to get rich . . . very very rich so I can buy my freedom from fear and know I'll always have enough to make it."

The "staging and commercialism" would disappear, she told *Metronome*, when "I don't have to worry about food, about money and rent, then people will hear the real Nina Simone. I can promise you that." She gave no clue about who the "real" Nina Simone was, though evidence was mounting, even if she didn't acknowledge it, that Nina was finding her niche in the world of jazz.

NINA HAD HIRED a new agent, Bertha Case, whose primary work was representing writers. She first heard Nina in New Hope in 1957 and wanted to represent her right then. But Nina said no. They reconnected in New York nearly two years later when the most unusual coincidence brought them together. A young writer had submitted a television play to Case and had included in the package special music and lyrics made in a home recording. As Case listened, she recognized Nina's voice. She renewed her offer immediately, and this time didn't take no for an answer. Case got to work right away on Nina's behalf, and NBC paperwork suggests that it was she who booked Nina's second appearance on the *Today* show, to air June 9. Nina actually taped the show the day before, and perhaps because this was a return visit, she seemed relaxed in the studio, chatting amiably with host Dave Garroway as she waited to perform her numbers. Before she went on the set, she sought out Fred Light, who was the only black associate director employed at NBC-TV.

Garroway introduced Nina as she might have described herself: "fairly new and very different . . . and she's got a way with songs that combines the musicianship of Juilliard with the liveliness of a schoolyard . . . at recess time that is." Nina sang her signature "I Love You, Porgy," then switched to traditional blues, "Nobody Knows You When You're Down and Out." It was a more daring choice than the show tunes of her previous appearance, and Garroway seemed to appreciate it. "Who wants to be reminded of the harsh fact that nobody wants you when you're down and out? You will . . . when you hear Nina Simone sing it. . . ."

On June 30 Nina and the trio played the opening night at the fifth annual Newport Jazz Festival, an event that was for many—performers and audience alike—a highlight of the summer. Al had played all around the United States, and Europe, too, so he barely raised an eyebrow at the heady milieu. But Chris and Bobby were wide-eyed with excitement. Everywhere they looked was someone important—Cannonball Adderley, Dave Brubeck, Dizzy Gillespie, Maynard Ferguson.

"We had a case of the jitters," Chris admitted. But Nina took charge.

"Just walk out there," she told them. "And focus on me." Chris and Bobby nodded and waited along with Nina and Al for MC Willis Conover to introduce her. She couldn't have asked for anything more. Nina, Conover said, "is in the tradition of pianists who also sing and of singers who also play piano, such people of course as Nat King Cole, Jeri Southern, Carmen McRae, Erroll Garner." But perhaps the best part was the way he pronounced Nina's name. He hit each vowel with a continental flare, exactly as she had imagined it six years earlier at the Midtown: "Miss Nee-na See-mone."

Nina opened with a piano solo, thick major chords that were more gospel than blues, to set up "Trouble in Mind." Bobby came in with a simple repeating pattern, a steady thump of the bass drum and one beat of the cymbals in each bar. Nina played the intro another five times, but she was still finding her groove. "One more!" she shouted. On the seventh pass she signaled that she was ready: "Go boys!" she said as the song took off: "Trouble in mind, I'm blue." By the end Nina's arrangement had evoked a revival meeting as much as a smoky club, but it underscored the optimism suggested in the last line, "The sun's gonna shine in my back door someday."

Nina was in good spirits after finishing "You'd Be So Nice to Come Home To." "Hi everybody," she said. "We're sorry we can't see you, but we want to say hi anyway." The crowd gave her an appreciative chuckle. "Can you hear me?"

"Yes," the audience shouted.

"It feels kind of strange to be up here," Nina went on. "I've heard about this place for five years. This is the first time we've ever been here, and we're happy to be here. I want you to know that." Nina had gotten up from the piano and sat down at a stool in front of one of the microphones. She asked for a tambourine.

"This is a folk tune—you must have heard it all your life. I did. It's called 'Little Liza Jane.' We'll get some rhythm started here and see what happens." Al and Bobby responded with a brisk pace, but Nina wanted more. "Come on!" she exhorted.

They picked it up and got louder.

"That's better!"

Now she turned to the audience. "I can't hear you," she hollered. "I think they're shy." But by the time she shouted "Let's go now!" hitting the tambourine for emphasis, the crowd caught her mood, and together they turned the Newport festival into a foot-stomping hoedown. Nina closed her set with a rollicking "In the Evening by the Moonlight" that would have been equally at home at St. Luke

CME. She built to the final crescendo, punctuated with that familiar "ba-ba-BA," and as the audience responded enthusiastically, she declared, "Yeah! All right!"

As happy as Nina looked onstage, John Hammond, a producer, writer, and all-around musical entrepreneur, remembered that later she was in a bad mood backstage. Nobody knew why. Jane Pickens, a former member of the singing Pickens sisters, found Nina's set thrilling and wanted to congratulate her. Hammond took her to see Nina but was waved off by a man outside her dressing room. "Stay away," he told them. "She's in a rage."

Pickens would have none of it. As Hammond recalled, she barged right in and gave Nina a big hug. "Honey," Pickens said, "you're the most wonderful singer in the world. This was the greatest experience of my life."

Nina just melted, Hammond said. "She loved it."

COLPIX HAD RELEASED two more singles from the 1959 sessions, though since "Porgy" Nina had yet to return to the charts. The label was also trying to broaden her reach, having made an arrangement with an Italian company to release an Extended Play 45 made up of four Colpix tunes. *Musica Jazz,* an Italian magazine, published a story about the record along with a photograph of Nina offering a new professional look, that of sophisticated chanteuse. She wore a braided hairpiece on the top of her head, which made her look a little like Luisa Stojowski, one of her Juilliard teachers, and she had on an off-the-shoulder black evening dress.

On the recommendation of his friend Max Cohen, who was still Nina's lawyer, Art D'Lugoff booked her for most of July at the Village Gate, his club on the corner of Bleecker and Thompson not far from the Vanguard. Art had opened the Gate in 1958 and immediately earned a reputation as an adventurous programmer. One of his first shows packaged the American premiere of Edgard Varèse's "Poème électronique," which called for a darkened room and music made entirely by electronic equipment, with contemporary classical music performed by a quintet and an octet. With a seating capacity of 450, the Gate was one of the larger club venues, and when he took it over, the acoustics impressed him. Friends in the record business said that if he didn't like running a club, he could turn the place into a recording studio. Art realized that he could do both, and because he had enough room to separate the equipment from the stage, live recordings would sound better at the Gate than at other nightspots.

Art took to Nina's music immediately, though he could see that she "had an attitude." But given his penchant for innovative shows, he appreciated more than most Nina's improvisations, even when they didn't work. In his mind that's what made them "true improvisation." He had a feeling that this first booking could be the start of a long relationship. If Nina failed to reciprocate immediately, she had to admit she was enjoying the job. The music, the venue, and the city combined to make her feel like "Queen of the Village." She'd found the same audience that had kept her going at the Midtown—the kids, as she called them, "the hip New York jazz crowd, and the people who hung out in the Village coffee bars and clubs," the beats like Don, "and they all hit on my music." A writer from the *Citizen Call*, another of New York's black newspapers, had taken in one of Nina's shows midrun and later dubbed her music "chamber jazz."

Her growing success brought more attention from the press, and during a mid-August week in Detroit, where she was booked at the Flame Show Bar and a local jazz festival, the *Michigan Chronicle*, the city's black newspaper, sent a reporter to the Statler Hilton to talk to her. Like her comments to *Metronome* and *Rogue*, Nina's reflections on this afternoon were another pained reverie on the past. Tryon became a place not only of poverty but of put-down, too, the lessons with Miss Mazzy and the encouragement of family exiled from memory. "The kids made me sing bass . . . or so low you couldn't hear me," she told the *Chronicle*'s Paul Adams. "Darling, I was poor, poor, poor, too." A split second later she picked up the phone in her room to illustrate how much things had changed. "Waiter," she instructed with prima donna flair, "bring me up a nice lobster and a champagne cocktail."

Her jocular mood disappeared as soon as she hung up the phone. "Darling, I was poor, poor, poor and they made me sing bass," she repeated. "After that there was high school—I felt trapped and scorned in a hostile world. But there was a piano," she continued, and then Juilliard. "Then there was 'I Love You, Porgy,' " the very mention of the song lifting her spirits. "And darling, today, they don't make me sing bass anymore." Nina threw back her head "and laughed and laughed," Adams reported. She disclosed she was seeing a psychiatrist, only hinting at the reasons why in a seeming stream of consciousness. "Fear—Yes, I am afraid, so afraid. Maybe I'm afraid because I don't want to sing bass anymore. Maybe I'm afraid of this cold, hostile world, of life, of love, of poverty . . . and of people. People can be very vicious. Believe me, I know. Can't they, Faye?" Nina was looking at her friend Faye Anderson, who had come on this trip, too, and she nodded in agreement.

Such complicated emotions inevitably found their way into the music, and when Nina plumbed the depths, she turned a song from the routine into an intoxicating drama. Collins George of the *Detroit Free Press*, who had attended the jazz festival, marveled later at how she held the audience in thrall, building one number to what sounded like its climactic end only then to "let out her voice. It weaved in and out of the instruments in a low moaning wail that only served to intensify the fever heat of the performance. It was utterly breathtaking."

By the time Nina and the trio returned to New York for their September engagements, her second single had reached the *Billboard* Top 100. "Nobody Knows You," which she had performed on the *Today* show, registered at number ninety-three September 5. But it only stayed another week before dropping below the cutoff. Nina barely noticed. She was preparing for her most important booking the following week, Sunday evening, September 11, on *The Ed Sullivan Show*, which in typical fashion would include a comedian, a dancer, an "illusionist" from Europe, a juggler, and the self-described sex kitten Eartha Kitt.

Nina came on in the last segment. "The winner of all the polls this season for the most promising young recording star is a girl from North Carolina via Philadephia," Sullivan said as he introduced her. "Let's have a big hand for Nina Simone." Nina was sitting at the piano when the camera showed her. She was wearing a long print cocktail dress with the same kind of drape as the white satin ball gown she had worn at Town Hall. Her elaborate makeup—eyeliner to accentuate her dark eyes and pencil applied to thicken her already heavy brows—only served to emphasize her facial expressions.

Sullivan had announced that Nina would play "Love Me or Leave Me." Her arrangement began with a few heavy chords before she shifted into single notes struck briskly and with purpose. Then she launched into an up-tempo version of the song. After the first chorus, a guitar could be heard—probably Al—accompanying her on a variation of Bach's Fugue in C. Their point-counterpoint went on for nearly a minute, and television viewers could see Nina's hands racing over the keyboard. She resumed the vocals and ended the song with a triumphant flourish of chords.

By the time the applause subsided, Sullivan had come over to the piano. "Congratulations, young lady," he said before introducing her other number, "I Love You, Porgy." Halfway through the song, Nina took her hands off the keyboard and rested them in her lap. "Someday I know, I know, someday he's coming," she sang soft and slow, turning to the audience in that moment. Then without looking, she put her hands back on the keyboard in exactly the right place to play an unusual trio of chords as the bridge to the final two choruses. Nina got up from the piano and walked over to Sullivan.

"Wonderful," he told her as they shook hands.

From the first night she sang at the Midtown in Atlantic City, Nina thought of her voice as "a third layer" of music to complement her right and left hands on the keyboard. Though she wanted to disguise her limited range, a dusky timbre made her voice a distinctive one, and this night's performance confirmed that her plan was a good one. The audience, and Sullivan, too, let Nina know that she had drawn them into her world in the short time they were together.

RIGHT AFTER THE SULLIVAN SHOW Nina and the trio headed to Chicago for a week at the Lake Meadows Restaurant, known to aficionados as "Stelzer's," even though its original owner had long since departed. Current manager Dick Benjamin got all the mileage he could out of Nina's Sullivan appearance, promoting her in *Defender* ads as "direct from Ed Sullivan's Toast of the Town." Though the restaurant had been created to serve the surrounding

Lake Meadows development at Thirty-fifth Street and South Park on Chicago's South Side, it also drew students from the nearby Illinois Institute of Technology, making it the kind of place for the same audiences Nina had found in Atlantic City and New York.

Brigitta Peterhans, a white foreign student who had come to love jazz, and her local classmates John Vinci, who was white, and David Sharpe, who was black, were typical of the IIT students who came over to Lake Meadows as often as they could. Catching one of Nina's shows, they loved the music but were unprepared for the edgy personality on display. If anything, Nina had become even more insistent on proper decorum when she played. She might be firmly in the world of nightclubs, but she refused to drop the sensibility of a concert pianist. Unhappy that some of the men at the bar were talking loud enough to be heard over the music, Nina stopped. "I'm the one getting paid here," she snapped. "If you guys sit over there talking, I might as well quit."

Such confrontations notwithstanding, Nina was a good draw in her first week. So good that she was asked to stay on for a second. But Charles Walton, a music teacher who practically made Lake Meadows a second home, remembered Nina as "moody" and reluctant to sing for much of the second week. "She just had her evil moments," Walton said, finding no other explanation. "She just played the piano. It killed her crowd."

HAVING ALREADY BEEN FEATURED in *Ebony*, Nina was profiled in the October issue of *Sepia*, an *Ebony* look-alike. This story, too, which included a full page of photos, highlighted Nina's melancholy side, starting with the headline "Little Girl Blue" and a subhead asserting that "the bluesy gal who whispered 'I Love You, Porgy' is still sighing sadly." Perhaps because the article was prepared so far in advance Nina and Don were depicted as a couple. Several of the photos showed them together, some of them in the apartment on Central Park West. Nina did allude to their troubles when she explained that "Porgy" was so successful "because I am singing about myself, and I think my audience realizes this, too. This song is for real, and I am singing about my husband," she said, noting how many times they had broken up. Don told *Sepia* the couple was planning to go to Europe, probably France, where he could paint and Nina could compose. "Let's face it," she interjected in a now-familiar refrain. "I'm doing what I do now for money, and I hope the money I make can help me achieve the things I really want," though she did not specify.

A trip to France with Don was scarcely in the cards, so Nina stayed busy with present commitments. On October 21, Art D'Lugoff, who had been a concert promoter before he opened the Village Gate, sponsored Nina and the trio for a full evening at Hunter College. It was a solo bill, so she didn't have to confine herself to a half-dozen tunes that would fit into a thirty-minute set. She could stretch out her piano interludes as long as she wanted. During the evening she introduced a song she called "one of our favorites—we've been doing it all of four days and we're scared to death of it." It was her first public performance of "Zungo," an African chain gang song arranged by one of her new friends, Michael Babatunde Olatunji, a Nigerian conga drummer who was currently playing with the Herbie Mann Afro Jazztet. Though Nina had been incorporating African motifs into her music almost from the beginning, this was the first time she gave them such full expression.

The concert was also a chance to showcase the trio, together four months now and clicking. Nina remained enamored of Al's guitar work, and she gave him a solo instrumental in the second half. Chris and Bobby were increasingly comfortable even when Nina went off on a tangent in the middle of a song. They were confident she wouldn't call them out onstage even if they failed to follow her. "Her thing with me was always more intonation," Chris explained. "If you're going to play B flat, give me a B flat. Don't give me something between B flat and B." She also chided Chris for relying too much on the written charts. "When are you going to learn, when are you going to memorize that?" she would ask. "If you're going to be my bass player, I want you to be off the book."

The *Times*'s John Wilson was at this concert, too. He coined a new term, "Simone-ized," to describe the way Nina poked experimentally into "unexpected crannies" of a song. His main criticism of her work were the many "thunderous Brubeckian endings . . . There are, as she must know, some things that end not with a bang."

IN THE MIDDLE OF NOVEMBER, Nina stepped forward purposefully—and at this moment uncharacteristically—as an agent of social change. She was a lead plaintiff in a lawsuit challenging New York City's cabaret card regulations, which, since 1941, had required all cabaret employees, including performers, to get police identity cards. All applicants had to be fingerprinted and photographed in addition to paying a $2 fee. Anyone with a criminal record was ineligible for a card under rules issued by the State Liquor Authority. Most famously, Billie Holiday was unable to perform in New York City clubs—though she could play Carnegie Hall—because of a narcotics violation and subsequent prison sentence. And Frank Sinatra refused to play the city's cabarets because he considered the card requirement to be "demeaning." The lawsuit, also joined by orchestra conductors and music technicians, challenged the right of the police commissioner to require the identification cards. It was prompted by the case of humorist Richard Buckley, known as "Lord Buckley." His card had been confiscated by the police, who claimed he had lied about his prior drug arrests. Buckley was struggling to regain his card so he could work in the city when he died of a sudden stroke.

Nina took another decisive step a week after the lawsuit was filed. She signed a carefully worded letter to Art D'Lugoff, quickly made public, explaining that "I do not recognize the authority of the Police Department with regard to my employment contracts unless there is something inherently criminal or illegal in these contracts. There are no such elements in my contracts with you or with anyone else. I, therefore, decline to make available to you any information as to whether or not I possess a Cabaret Employee's Identification Card." Max Cohen, still Nina's lawyer, drafted the letter, having done most of the legal work on the lawsuit. His concluding rhetorical flourish was the verbal equivalent of one of Nina's "thunderous Brubeckian endings": "I have not abdicated my status as a citizen of the United States by becoming a performer and therefore refuse to have my Constitutional rights and privileges unlawfully assaulted by the Police Comissioner of the City of New York."

Nina's embrace of the cause—completely voluntary, Art said—actually brought her more publicity than her recent performances. *Variety*, which had ignored them, made much of her new stand. A story in the December 14 issue put Nina in the headline about the conflict: "Songstress Won't Tell if She Has Card in New Test of N.Y. Police Authority."

The "test" would turn into a six-year effort that finally resulted in the end of the cabaret card system in 1967, though Nina was not a part of the case on a continuing basis.

WHEN SHE WAS STILL Eunice Waymon, Nina couldn't know that her brief encounter with Langston Hughes at the Allen School presaged one of her most cherished friendships. He made the first overture in his newspaper column, "Week by Week," with a fan letter that was more imaginative tone poem than journalistic prose: "She is strange. So are the plays of Brendan Behan, Jean Genet, and Bertolt Brecht. She is far out, and at the same time common. So are raw eggs in Worcestershire and THE CONNECTION. She is different. So was Billie Holiday, St. Francis, and John Donne. So is Mort Sahl, so is Ernie Banks. She is a club member, a colored girl, an Afro-American, a homey from Down Home. She has hit the Big Town, and the big towns, the LP discs and the TV shows—and she is still from down home. She did it mostly all herself. Her name is Nina Simone.

"She has flair," he went on, "but no air. She has class, but does not wear it on her shoulders. She is unique. You either like her or you don't. If you don't, you won't. If you do—wheee-ouuueu! You do!"

Hughes's column first ran November 12 in the *Chicago Defender* and was picked up later by other newspapers. It made for an intriguing confluence of events, to have one of black America's most prominent literary figures champion Nina at the moment that she was beginning to see her art as something larger than herself, connected to the world around her in a way that remained to be fully defined.

10. You Can't Let Them Humiliate You

~ January 1961–December 13, 1961 ~

Nina's weeklong booking at the Apollo Theater in February was her second at the storied venue. She had appeared there in the spring of 1959 but at the bottom of a jazz bill, playing solo piano for $350. This time Nina, with her trio, was the headliner, and she was earning exactly ten times more. "Friends said I might have trouble with the crowd because the Apollo was well known for giving artists a rough time," she recalled. But Nina hardly flinched from the challenge. She had already shown she could dish out "a rough time," too. "So the two of us getting together was kind of a championship boxing match with the Apollo as the champ and me the contender."

Opening night, February 10, Nina prepared a comfortably polished set but with enough room for the spontaneous moment. In the past few months, she had discovered the music of Oscar Brown Jr., and spent time with him when she and the trio were in Chicago in September. She had already performed his "Brown Baby" as an encore at the Hunter College concert earlier in the year. Now Nina made "Work Song" (music by Nat Adderley, lyrics by Brown) an integral part of her set. It was about the travails of men on a chain gang, and Nina felt compelled to tell the audience her brother had been on a chain gang, too, perhaps referring to her brother John's voluntary stint with the Civilian Conservation Corps when he was a teenager.

Some of the audience giggled—or at least Nina thought they did. She dropped all pretense of politeness. "For the very first time in your lives, act like ladies and gentlemen at the Apollo," she snapped. An uneasy quiet spread over the crowd, and Nina performed her song.

More trouble ensued as the trio prepared to play "Falling in Love with Love." Bobby couldn't get a special sound effects device attached to his drums to work properly. *New York Citizen Call* writers Ted Handy and Ralph Matthews Jr. were sitting close enough to see Nina glowering while Bobby tried feverishly to fix the problem. Matthews had come to see Horace Silver and Sonny Stitt, but Nina made the most vivid impression with what he could only describe as her "pure and powerful hostility" toward the audience and her musicians. Ted Handy thought she was needling Bobby when she sarcastically ordered the Apollo technician to change the lighting: "a white spot on my drummer, and a small baby blue one for me."

"Falling in Love" was finally performed, and Nina closed her set with "I Love You, Porgy." The sustained applause suggested the audience didn't hold a grudge. But on the way out a few patrons complained to Handy, who groused that "this was one of the most nerve-wracking and unnecessary moments in the history of show business."

Nina didn't care what anyone else thought. "If you can get an audience to like you, that's fine," she said later. "If you can't, then you must get them to respect you. You cannot let them humiliate you."

Matthews was so taken aback by Nina's behavior that he devoted an entire installment of his "Mainstream" column to the evening. "The audience, while exuberant, was by no stretch of the imagination disrespectful of her talent," he wrote. "I would say after the fact that the audience was overly generous . . . and for Miss Simone to suggest that we were less than polite to her suggests to me that the behavior problem is hers, not that of the audience she faced . . . [She] seems to be a very angry young woman."

AS SOON AS THEY FINISHED at the Apollo, Nina and the trio along with Art D'Lugoff, now acting as her manager, went to Chapel Hill, North Carolina, to play an afternoon event February 18 at the University of North Carolina. Although Chapel Hill, with its leafy campus, elegant brick buildings, and well-tended stores, was much bigger than Tryon, it, too, prided itself on being a bastion of liberal thought, a place where modernity thrived amid history. But the same racial stratifications of Tryon existed here, too. Chapel Hill's blacks mostly found work in the service of the white community, the surface calm masking the tension underneath. Two days before the concert some of it boiled over, though in a way that confirmed to Chapel Hill's most liberal precincts that the town's progressive reputation was deserved. Three hundred fifty UNC faculty and staff took out an ad in the *The Daily Tar Heel*, the college newspaper, supporting a group of blacks who had been picketing the local theater after being denied admission. The UNC personnel called on the theater owners "to admit all persons, without regard to race, on an equal basis."

The picketers were only a few blocks from Memorial Hall, where the concert took place, but they didn't disrupt the afternoon. Nina played a well-received set, and the next day's *Tar Heel* highlighted her in a two-column photo. Frank Craighill, the president of the social club that had sponsored the concert, was thrilled. He was a big fan and could hardly believe that he had been able to book her. After the concert, he arranged for Nina and the trio and Art to have dinner at one of the area's newest steak houses, the Angus Barn. Craighill had picked the restaurant with care, particularly in light of the movie theater protest, and when Nina and the trio walked in as guests of the university, a big round table was already set and waiting for them. It was easily one of the most elegant meals any of them had eaten on the road. Bobby loved the way the steak was prepared, with a pickled apple in the middle, and Chris used the occasion to have his first-ever glass of merlot.

An encounter later at the train station in Raleigh left no doubt they were in the South. As the group waited for the train to New York, a white woman claimed she had lost her purse. The station manager was called, and he found the purse in the men's restroom. One of the waiting passengers asserted that Bobby had been the last person to use it, and in a flash, police surrounded the group, three blacks and two whites whose status as outsiders was only accentuated by Art's yarmulke. The authorities zeroed in on Bobby, all but accusing him of theft. But Nina leapt to his defense. She was not going to let her drummer be intimidated simply because he was a black man, and certainly not in her home state. "She just went crazy," Chris remembered. "She read them the riot act . . . She was just as black as she could be with these guys, and they left us alone."

THE FIRST WEEK OF MARCH Nina started a two-week job at the Roundtable, a club on Manhattan's East Side. Miles from the Apollo in distance and atmosphere, it nonetheless sparked a replay of Nina's impatience with an inattentive audience, this time a white one. On opening night, she sensed the crowd was not ready for her usual fare. The tables crowded the bandstand, drinks flowed, and men puffed on cigars while they chatted. Bobby joked that it was the kind of club "where the boss takes his secretary but not his wife." So instead of setting the mood with a couple of vocals, Nina opened with an instrumental. When the audience still didn't quiet down, she continued in that vein except for a harsh version of "I Love You, Porgy" with impromptu lyrics to chide the patrons.

The second night was more of the same. On the third night, Nina had enough. She came out after a break and stood at the piano for what seemed like an eternity. She sat down and played the piano very softly for perhaps a minute or two. Then she stopped. "Pack up," Nina told the trio. The men looked confused. She repeated her instruction. "Don't worry. I'll pay you for the week." When the Roundtable manager saw the musicians leaving the stage, he raced up to talk to Nina. A few minutes later she came to the dressing room and told her musicians to go home. In an interview with the *New York Post* that was supposed to publicize the engagement, a defiant and defensive Nina harked back to Tryon, the town still a convenient symbol for her conflicting emotions apparently brought close to the surface by those noisy club patrons. "When I was a child, no one was ever proud of me, and my people were never proud of themselves— or anything they had ever done," she declared. "Well, that's different now. *I'm* proud of myself, and I'm proud of my music . . . The dirt and squalor and the *hate* there," she continued. "But it's beautiful, too. And I don't just mean the countryside. The people are beautiful. *All* of them. I hope to go back some day when I'm a little more confident of myself, when I can face it."

Nina's behavior at the Roundtable caught *Variety*'s attention, which put news of the flap on the front page of the March 15 issue. The paper sensed a trend because Johnny Mathis had walked out of a job at the same time in Puerto Rico, upset with the noisy audience. *Variety* also reported that Nina, General Artists Corporation, her booking agent, and the Roundtable mutually agreed to cancel her engagement. But she disputed that notion. In April she filed a complaint with the musicians' union asking for a full week's salary, $2,500, claiming that she had been booked for at least two weeks and had agreed to a one-week payout and not the mere three days' pay she received. There was no further reporting on the eventual settlement.

BY THE TIME NINA RETURNED to the Village Gate at the end of March, Art had already done a number of live recordings at the club. Now he and Colpix wanted to record Nina, and Cal Lampley, a freelance producer with a classical background like Nina's and extensive recording experience with Miles Davis, Dave Brubeck, and Leonard Bernstein, among others, was hired for the job. Chris mentioned to some of his friends that a live recording was in the works, and one of them, Judy Goldstein, came by with a package of homemade cornbread. "Sweets for the sweet. Make a beautiful record," her card said.

Surrounded by fans, Nina was at her improvisational best, fueled by their applause and appreciative hoots. Once again she mixed genres, a six-minute version of "Just in Time" from *Bells Are Ringing*, a mellow and introspective "House of the Rising Sun" with none of the bluesy muscle that would inform the Animals' hit three years later, and a virtuoso instrumental of the standard "Bye Bye Blackbird" that clocked in at just under nine minutes.

Although the recording went smoothly, Colpix held off releasing *Nina Simone at the Village Gate* for more than a year. The decision was surprising given that an album released a few weeks earlier, *Nina Simone at Newport*, stayed on the *Billboard* album chart for more than a month, rising to number twenty-three. And Colpix had also just made a deal with Pye Records in England, which brought out *Nina Simone at Town Hall* to good notices.

NINA'S FIRST APPEARANCE at Carnegie Hall came on May 21, an event both a milestone and resonant with personal history. The concert was a benefit for the Presbyterian Church of the Master in Harlem, and it didn't matter that Nina was raised a Methodist. She knew her mother would be pleased. Nina shared the bill with Miriam Makeba, a Xhosa tribeswoman from South Africa who ventured beyond her country's folk music with its distinctive clicks to sing Zulu, calypso, English, and even Yiddish. She had burst on the scene a year and a half earlier, one critic describing her as "a piquant combination of the exotic, the primitive and the sophisticated." He could have been talking about Nina, too. Yet the Carnegie afternoon was not a competition but rather the opportunity to witness eclectic musicality, one part complementing the other. Nina offered an inventive "When I Was a Young Girl," singing with long attenuated phrases and giving her sidemen free rein with their improvisations. Bobby used Arabic finger cymbals and Al added Middle Eastern flavoring with his guitar work. Robert Shelton in *The New York Times* wasn't sure what to call Nina's music, so he offered alternative hybrids. It was either "the extreme of 'folk jazz' or 'jazzed up folk' . . . It all had little to do with the traditional song she was working on," he wrote, "but it is useless to measure the unpredictable and whimsical Miss Simone by any narrow standards."

By the time of the concert, Nina and Don had formally divorced and she had a new man in her life, Andy Stroud, a light-skinned black man, stocky with a neatly trimmed mustache. They had met during the brief, dismal Roundtable job. As she remembered it Andy told Nina he was a bank teller. They visited between sets, and just before she returned to the bandstand, he asked her out for a drink after the show. "He seemed very sure of himself, very unflustered," Nina wrote in her memoir. "I liked that so I said sure." They went to a nearby hotel, and Nina had such a good time over drinks that they scheduled another date. Before leaving, she wrote Andy a short note on a Roundtable business card: "To Andy—How nice meeting you. Most sincerely Nina Simone."

On their second date Andy told Nina the truth about his profession. He was a cop, a detective sergeant in a district that covered Harlem. He'd been on the police force fourteen years. He admitted that he had told Nina he was a bank teller because he thought she'd be put off by the truth. But Nina wasn't. In fact, one of the things she liked about Andy was his strength, nothing overt, just the calm confidence he exuded. Even in her dressing room, with her back to the door, she knew exactly when Andy arrived "because I felt his personality around me." When they were out together, Nina felt safe. She understood his reputation as a no-nonsense tough guy every time they went into a bar or a club. Some of the men who recognized him got out of his way in a hurry. Others who did come to say hello were respectful and quiet.

Andy had been married before and had two sons; Nina didn't mind. She thought this gave him experience in how to treat women, and she loved getting flowers and little gifts. "He understood that I was shy," she remembered. "I opened up to him." A photo taken of the couple a month or so after they met shows two people gazing sweetly at each other. Later Nina sent Andy a more provocative picture: stepping out of the tub wrapped in the shower curtain but with one leg fully exposed. "To My Andy," she wrote.

NINA SPOKE LESS OFTEN now about returning to classical study, though the lessons learned from Miss Mazzy, Friedberg, and

Sokoloff still infused her music. The most tangible evidence of her success with "chamber jazz" came in late spring when she received a $10,000 royalty check from Bethlehem. Nina used a chunk of it to fulfill one of her dreams: she bought herself a car, a 1960 steel-gray Mercedes-Benz convertible with red leather upholstery. After she picked it up from the dealer, she recalled, she put the roof down and "cruised the village for hours, looking so fine." She had bought a red hat for the occasion that matched the interior. A few days later she and Andy drove around the city snapping photos of her and the car along the way.

Nina hadn't expected to see much of Andy when she and the trio left for Philadelphia at the end of June for another week at Pep's. She settled into her room at the tony Bellevue Stratford, but an hour or so after unpacking, she was stricken with an intense headache. Feeling feverish, she called for the hotel doctor. He was concerned enough that he called a second physician, and when her condition worsened, Nina was rushed to Hahnemann Hospital. Max Cohen, her lawyer, was alerted, and later he frankly told reporters, "I'm afraid she's a very sick girl." Doctors first thought Nina had a bladder infection, but when she failed to respond to treatment, they feared that she had polio or another spinal disease. They put her in an isolation ward.

Nina didn't remember much except waking up in the hospital drugged and disoriented and then scared when she saw Andy with a surgical mask over his face. The doctors performed a painful spinal tap and Nina fainted. Andy was holding her hand when she came to, still wearing his mask.

Nina started to cry as her doctor explained his concerns, thinking of her older brother Harold, Carrol's twin, who had been disabled by meningitis. She was sure she would be paralyzed and confined to a wheelchair, a budding career ended. But fortunately, after several days on medication, she started to recover from what doctors said was a mild case of polio. Andy had been at the hospital every evening, driving down after work, staying the night and then heading back to New York early in the morning. He told her that as soon as she got better, they were going to get married. "I laughed and cried at the same time," Nina remembered. "I nodded my head: I loved this man, and needed him, too."

Nina had to cancel all of her July dates, and while Chris, Bobby, and Al were concerned about her, they worried about their own livelihoods. "We didn't know when she's gonna get better and in the meantime we all have families to support," Chris said. Nina's friend Olatunji stepped in to help, hiring the men to play with his group until Nina was back on her feet.

Nina had spent seventeen days in the hospital. On her release she went to North Carolina to recuperate with family, and while she was there she resolved to make some good come from the frightening episode. She had Max Cohen issue a statement on her behalf urging her fans and the public to immunize themselves with polio shots. Her separation from Andy made her realize how much she missed him, and she sent special delivery letters to let him know how much. It was hard to believe, she said in one, "that what I knew was possible between a man and a woman would come to pass for me, anyway. Frankly, I don't think I still believe it. I even try not to believe it, but when you touch my woman's soul with your eyes, or your hands, your mouth or your body, I am moved . . . and I love you." In the next sentence, Nina showed her sense of humor. "Is my baby doing his exercise every day? Every day? NO FLIRTING WITH THE GIRLS ON SATURDAY AT THE BEACH!! (Smiles)" But she closed on a serious note: "I'm quite lonely tonight—Nina."

WHEN NINA RESUMED WORK August 6 in Detroit at the American Jazz Festival, she gave a musical thank-you to Olatunji for the help he had given her sidemen. "It was like we were home again," an African exchange student in the audience told *Detroit News* writer Josef Mossman. "She touches us here," and he pointed to his heart. A *Variety* critic already had picked up on Nina's African stylings, which he dubbed "Afro Simone."

Back in New York the next week Nina got her most extensive television coverage yet. The CBS Sunday morning program *Camera Three* devoted all of the August 13 broadcast to her. She was singing

"Sunday in Savannah" as the show opened, giving a languorous reading to the story about a day in church. When she finished, host James Macandrew gave an introduction that could only have pleased her. "Miss Simone brings to her music, which is definitely jazz, the kind of technique and discipline we generally associate with classical music. She has introduced fugue and counterpoint into the freewheeling spontaneity of the jazz world."

In fact Nina was anything but freewheeling, even though she sported a new look—a pageboy wig fastened in front with a jeweled barrette. This time when she sang "When I Was a Young Girl" she was accompanied only by Al's guitar, which made a song about heartache even more poignant. She barely smiled during the show, though she did perk up during a blues instrumental, and she was clearly pleased to mention Olatunji when she introduced "Zungo." "One of the most beautiful musicians and beautiful men in the world taught it to us," she explained. At the end of the song, she gave a slight nod that seemed to signal her satisfaction. Nina closed with "Work Song," the credits running while she and the trio played. Ironically, it was the most spirited moment of the entire show.

IN THE MIDDLE OF AUGUST, Nina returned to Chicago to play one of the most popular South Side venues, Roberts Show Lounge. Black Chicagoans of means and whites who liked jazz flocked to the place when topflight entertainers were in town— Count Basie, Sarah Vaughan, Dinah Washington, who even ran Roberts for a few months earlier in the year and dubbed it "Dinahland." But Nina didn't like the place, didn't like the fact that some evenings were more social than musical. The sharply dressed men and women were as eager to see and be seen as they were to enjoy the act onstage. They didn't worry much about the schedule, either, sashaying to their tables with shouted greetings even if the music had already started.

One night during the run Brigitta Peterhans, the IIT architecture student who had seen Nina at Lake Meadows, was in the audience with her friends, hoping Nina would sing some of the songs from her latest album, *Forbidden Fruit,* whose title song about the temptations of the Garden of Eden offered a lighter-than-usual touch. But Nina didn't want to sing at all. "You people just can't sit still," she lectured. Then came a threat: "From now on you can only hear me in concert if you don't behave yourself." And she walked off the stage.

Operating on instinct—for if she had thought about it she never would have been so bold—Brigitta got up from her table and rushed backstage. She found Nina in her dressing room changing clothes, still angry. "I don't want to go out there anymore," she mumbled. "They might as well listen to the radio. They might as well listen to the jukebox." She didn't seem annoyed that Brigitta was standing there, and Brigitta plunged ahead with an introduction. "You're fabulous," she said, urging Nina to come back to the stage.

"You seem to be from Europe" was all Nina said, picking up on Brigitta's slight accent.

"Yes," she replied, "I'm German."

After a quick thank-you, Brigitta left. She couldn't recall years later whether Nina came back to finish that night. But decorum apparently improved because she and the trio completed the Roberts engagement. Though Chris understood why Nina got upset, he offered an alternate perspective. "The talking had nothing to do with disrespect," he insisted, reflecting on the moment. "You go to a black club, the closest I can get to it is when you start looking at it socially—homogeneous—next to a musical performance . . . The music is part of the experience. 'We went to Roberts and we saw Nina Simone—and we saw Bobby there and you know Bobby told me about the fact that the car got lost and she sang "I Love You, Porgy." ' It's a total experience—and so disrespect didn't enter into it. You have to take in the cultural context."

At least for now Nina didn't buy the explanation. In October she got into another brouhaha, this time at the Town Hill, a club in Brooklyn. She and the trio were booked for a week, and in a replay of the fiasco at the Roundtable, she cut it short after three days. Nina delivered her complaints in triplicate: the audience was rude, the piano was out of tune, and her dressing-room door did not have a lock on it. But Nina's temperamental side was not enough to dissuade the Schiffman family that ran the Apollo from booking her again as part of another jazz revue November 10–16. And she even got a raise, to $4,500 for the week—$1,000 more than in February, when she chewed out the audience. Nina's higher fee suggested that even with tantrums, or perhaps because of them, she was worth it.

NINA AND ANDY ENCOUNTERED more than just bumps in the road on the way to their wedding ceremony. In her memoir she recounted a story that would lead one to wonder why she got married at all. She claimed that when she and Andy went out to celebrate their engagement, Andy drank much more than usual. He became jealous after a fan handed her a note and didn't believe her explanation that it meant nothing. He struck her in the face as they were getting in a cab to go back to the Central Park West apartment, and when they got home, he beat her in a rage. He pulled a gun at one point and demanded that she read parts of letters from Edney Whiteside that she had saved. He pushed her into the bedroom, she wrote, tied her up, and forced himself on her. It was only when Andy fell asleep that Nina wriggled free and fled the apartment, terrified, bruised, and bloodied.

Though it had been nearly two years since Nina had recorded with Hecky Krasnow, the freelance producer, they remained friends. And in the midst of her terror, she called him to ask for help. It was the middle of the night, but Krasnow came to get her right away. His daughter Judy vividly remembered how her father and mother nursed Nina back to health over the next two weeks, feeding her ample amounts of chicken soup. Krasnow counseled Nina not to marry Andy, incredulous that she was still thinking about it.

When Nina finally left the Krasnows, she tried to relax at a favorite coffeehouse in Greenwich Village. Andy tracked her down there and wanted to know where she had been, according to her account. Noticing her bruises, he asked who beat her up.

"You did," she told him.

"He denied it absolutely," she wrote. "He just stared at me and said, 'You're insane.'"

According to Nina she made Andy see two psychiatrists because he didn't believe that the awful incident had really happened. One psychiatrist told her she shouldn't marry him, and the other said that he'd probably been temporarily insane and that nothing like this would ever happen again. Nina was in a quandary as she weighed the pros and cons. When Andy was around, she didn't feel lonely, and, perhaps more important, she could envision a life with him. They both wanted children, and Nina insisted she wanted to be more than "a performing machine." She worried, too, that without Andy, she'd have "nobody again . . . no one to go home to, no one to tell me funny stories and hold me in his arms late at night when I couldn't sleep."

Decades later Andy told a completely different story about their courtship having nothing do with any beating. He remembered seeing one psychiatrist but not for the reason Nina asserted. She had been seeing a doctor to help her with mood swings, he recalled in a spring 2006 interview with the magazine *Fader*. He told her to end the therapy so she wouldn't have "two men telling you what to do." According to Andy, Nina stopped but only after her doctor analyzed him.

He received a good report: "Feet on the ground, . . . normal, no problems."

That seemed to satisfy Nina, and she stopped seeing the psychiatrist. But Andy was disturbed about something else. Too many women were around Nina. Patti Bown, a jazz pianist and one of Nina's friends, had been surprised when Nina talked about her romance with Andy. At the Village Gate, Patti said, "she had some kind of girlfriend." Andy was clear on this matter, too. "We threw out the gays that were hanging around the apartment. There were some—mostly females. . . . We can't continue this if we're gonna be married," he told her. In later years Nina's brother Sam would speak of affairs she had with women, but she never acknowledged them, talking only—and sometimes boastfully—of the men in her life.

Nina and Andy exchanged vows during a small ceremony December 4 at the Central Park West apartment. Nina's sisters Dorothy and Frances attended—Frances was the matron of honor— and Andy's siblings came, too. Reverend John Ginzell, a Lutheran minister known to be friendly with entertainers, performed the ceremony. Nina looked elegant in a white suit that featured a V-neck jacket collar. It set off the small silver pendant she was wearing. She held a bouquet of white flowers, which were fastened with a large white bow, and the small white hat she wore had a veil that rested just above her eyebrows. All of it was eye-catching next to her ebony skin. Andy wore a dark suit and sported a white boutonniere in his lapel. Standing together, Andy's arm crooked in Nina's elbow, they smiled for the camera like any traditional bride and groom.

"Nina Simone Gives Up on White Mate, Marries Negro Cop," *The Philadelphia Tribune* archly observed in its write-up of the wedding.

Nine days later Nina left for her first overseas trip. She was among thirty-three black artists, performers, and educators headed to Lagos, Nigeria, for a two-day conference sponsored by the American Society of African Culture. "Afro Simone" was about to take on a new and richer meaning.

11. Respect

~ December 14, 1961–December 1962 ~

Langston Hughes brought Nina into the circle of black talent that headed to Lagos December 13. Their friendship had blossomed during the 1960 Newport festival, and ever since the two had kept in touch. Langston periodically sent Nina books along with an occasional invitation to dinner at his Manhattan apartment, these missives filled with the panache of his other writings. She was especially sorry to miss the one that featured homecooked "*coon—not a possum but a COON*," Langston promised, "that a friend brought us from 'Down South.'"

The AMSAC meetings provided Nina entrée to New York's black intellectuals, and it was hardly surprising that she was drawn to James Baldwin. His first novel, *Go Tell It on the Mountain,* had been acclaimed by both black and white critics, and some of the passages reminded Nina of the revival meetings she played for, when she had to keep up with all the testifiers. But Nina also understood the anger that bristled in Baldwin's characters when he described the humiliations they endured every time they ventured from their insular world into the one dominated by whites. Nina found him mischievous and

Nina with, from left, Martha Flowers, Geoffrey Holder, Natalie
Hinderas, and Brock Peters in Lagos, Nigeria, December 1961, for a
conference sponsored by the American Society of African Culture
(Moorland Spingarn Research Center, Howard University)

delightful, but she thought his eyes, large and round, "always made
him look slightly sad."

In addition to Langston, her traveling companions to Africa
included Olatunji; Odetta Gordon, a folksinger whom Nina occasionally saw around the Village; Brock Peters, a singer and actor
with a compelling bass voice; jazz instrumentalist Randy Weston;
the dancer-choreographer Geoffrey Holder; and Natalie Hinderas,
the classical pianist who had the kind of career Nina so often said she
wanted. If Nina was envious, she kept it to herself. She considered
the adventure a party, even though she, like the others, was not getting paid. AMSAC could only cover the performers' expenses. (One
of the biggest problems was getting the headliner Lionel Hampton
released from a booking in New York so that he could join the celebration in Lagos, albeit a day late. It cost the organization $1,000.)

The group arrived at the Lagos airport shortly before midnight December 14 after a stopover in Rome. Spending an afternoon in one of Western Europe's fabled cities and then landing six hours later in a country so rich in the imagination of many American blacks only heightened the anticipation. As the plane braked to a halt at the Lagos airfield, one of the musicians was moved to speak. "Well," he said loud enough to be heard, "it only took three hundred years, but we're back home at last." Given the hour no one expected a big welcoming party, and certainly not any entertainment. So Nina and the others were astonished to hear the unmistakable sound of drums and then women singing songs of welcome when the plane door opened. The group had been waiting nearly three hours to greet the visitors but still looked fresh in ceremonial robes a fashion designer would envy. Nina was so enthralled with the scene that it seemed as though everything was unfolding in a bright noonday sun rather than the artificial lights that bathed the tarmac. "I knew I'd arrived somewhere important and that Africa mattered to me and would always matter," she said.

The trip in from the airport offered an African landscape dotted with symbols of American enterprise: Amoco, Standard Oil, Chase Manhattan, and Pepsi-Cola signs marked the way. The yellow fluorescent streetlamps along the road gave the signs and the buildings they were attached to an eerie cast. AMSAC member William Branch thought it all looked like a Broadway stage set. After the group settled into the Federal Palace Hotel in downtown Lagos and ventured out on their first full day, it was clear that the "bush telegraph" had successfully spread the news of their arrival. Local men and women crowded the streets around the hotel, waving and clapping their hands. Children pulled away from their parents, jostling for a better look at the strangers.

"We had interviews from sunup to sundown," Odetta remembered. "The only thing to eat was chicken salad sandwiches!"

During these rounds of formal welcome, Nina gamely posed for photographs with her fellow musicians and an assortment of African dignitaries. She looked chic in a gray suit with a black blouse and matching shoes, holding a rectangular clutch purse in her hand.

The stated purpose of the Lagos event was to open a new cultural center, and while Nina appreciated the goals of the trip, she focused instead on the camaraderie of the musicians and new African acquaintances and even found time to steal an hour or so at the beach. She posed good-naturedly for a photo in her polka-dot bikini. Mostly, though, Nina was eager for the concerts in King George V stadium to begin.

The concept behind the evenings of December 18 and 19 was to present the music and dance of American blacks together with native Africans. Langston was emotional when he introduced the American performers the first night. "In a sense, we feel we are coming home, to our ancestral home, back to the roots of our culture," he told the crowd of three thousand. "Of course, in the Americas — north and south, the United States, the West Indies, Brazil — other cultures have mingled with those of the peoples of Africa, other bloods have mingled with your blood. But all of us here tonight have in our veins, to some degree, the blood of Africa and in our hearts, the love of Africa."

On this first night Nina was the last to perform before the finale, accompanied by Al Schackman, Olatunji, and bassist Ahmed Abdul-Malik. Their set was called "The Blend." From the musicians' point of view the evening went smoothly, but the critic in the Lagos *Daily Times* seemed unimpressed. He called the entire affair "dull." The second night was anything but. The entertainment started nearly an hour late, and the audience was already restive when Lionel Hampton, who had just arrived, took the stage. Then he set things back further by going far longer than his allotted time, giving the crowd the full Hampton treatment — dancing, clowning, and acrobatics. Scheduled to play next, Nina was angry by the time she came onstage. "This number is a fast one," she sniffed, "and we should all be exhausted at the end of it all. It is about sinners, which we all are." There was no humor in her voice, and the audience gave no indication it knew what to make of her cryptic comment other than a few uneasy laughs. Then the music took over, and the rest of her set went on without incident. When she finished, the appreciative crowd wanted an encore. Nina didn't even consider it. In his *Daily Times* report, reviewer Peter Pan said Nina left the stage "in an undisguised huff."

NINA CAME BACK to the United States on December 22. Though she would have loved to stay longer, Andy wanted her home, but she promised herself she would return one day. Nina also had two jobs lined up. New Year's Eve she joined an all-star bill at Carnegie Hall that included John Coltrane, Thelonious Monk, and Sonny Rollins. Four days later she returned to the Village Gate for the first of three weekend performances with Al, Chris, and Bobby. Before the final evening Chris delivered some surprising news: he was leaving. The sixteen months with her had been great, he told Nina—she "gave me my pass out of the ghetto," he would say years later. But like Ben Riley, he wanted to play instrumental jazz. Dizzy Gillespie had recently lost his bass player, and he offered Chris the job. Chris said yes on the spot, but he promised Nina he would finish the Gate performances.

If Chris had to leave, Nina knew this was as good a time as any. She planned to cut back her work over the next few months because she was pregnant with her first child, who was due in the fall. And she and Andy had moved into a large three-story house in Mount Vernon, a suburb north of New York City. It stood on a large piece of land at 406 Nuber with trees all around and on a slight hill, a setting very much like Tryon. Nina remembered that her first argument with Andy after they married was over furnishing the house. Andy favored a modern look; Nina wanted antiques. Eventually they compromised someplace in between.

They turned the third floor into a nursery, with a room for the baby and one for the nurse. Andy's sons from his previous marriage would use another room when they came for weekend visits; the downstairs had plenty of space for a piano and rehearsals when Nina summoned her musicians to work over new tunes. It seemed like the ideal setup, but strangely, the reality of a new house, a real home, left Nina disappointed. Rather than enjoy these comforts, she worried about the responsibilities. When she wasn't supervising a Jamaican

Nina in her garden in Mount Vernon,
New York, c. 1962
(*Bernard Gotfryd*)

maid, she was watching over the gardener. "I found running a household not much less exhausting than doing all the work myself."

But there were sweet moments, too. Andy had bought a tandem bicycle for the two of them and little bikes for his boys, and on spring weekends they rode around the neighborhood like any happy family. During the week Nina cruised in her Mercedes convertible, top down when the weather permitted. She didn't let anyone else drive it, not even Andy. But when her father came for a visit, she let him drive and he loved it, smiling and whistling all the while. It reminded her of all the times she and her brothers and sisters had watched their father's magic with the old Model-A Ford back in North Carolina.

•

THE FEBRUARY 1962 ISSUE of *Negro Digest*, a magazine of short features published by the same company that produced *Ebony*, profiled Nina as "A Girl with Guts." The theme of the four-page article was Nina's insistence on proper decorum when she performed. Like *Variety* a year earlier, writer Robert Lucas gave her credit for being a trendsetter. "For refusing to knuckle under to audience rudeness or to compromise her art, Nina Simone was labeled temperamental, but all performers share in the dividends of her one-woman crusade," he wrote in his introduction. Citing the Johnny Mathis incident and a similar one involving the opera singer Risë Stevens, Lucas said "it proved to Nina that she was not fighting a lonely battle." He reminded readers, too, that not long after the Roundtable tiff, she had lectured the audience at a Madison Square Garden jazz festival for interrupting her. "You folks are at a jazz festival," she snapped, "not a nightclub where you can tell me all those things."

Nina tried to have a sense of humor about it. "It got to the point when people would come out just to see what I'd do next," she joked. But these were serious matters. "I was taught at an early age to respect any artist in any field—when someone is rehearsing there must be no interruption; at a concert hall one must be neatly dressed and observe proper decorum," Nina asserted. "I grew up assuming that anyone acquainted with the social graces would be aware of these basic elements of good conduct. That's why I could never get over the shock of coming face to face with badly behaved audiences . . . and while all entertainers may not be considered artists, they should be accorded the same respect. That's all I ever wanted—respect."

Three weeks after the *Digest* article appeared, Nina found herself on the front page of the *Amsterdam News*, but it was hardly the kind of attention she wanted. The March 17 story, which called her the "stormy petrel of the piano who has walked out on many a concert," reported that she had "secretly" settled a $100,000 breach-of-contract suit filed by a personal management corporation, most likely General Artists Corporation, which had represented Nina for the past three years. Max Cohen, still Nina's lawyer, would not divulge the exact amount of the settlement or the details of the claims against her, only that the result came after "long deliberation" between the parties. What she thought about this latest imbroglio remained a mystery. "Miss Simone, who is now in her third month of pregnancy, is hiding from public glare," the *News* reported.

That didn't prevent Nina from returning to the studio, however, apparently at the bidding of Colpix executives. They assigned her a new producer, Stu Phillips, who had put together the successful *Nina at Newport* album. He did it from tapes and had never worked with Nina in person. "She wasn't making any money," Phillips said, and his job was to turn that around. "We needed to get Nina into a pop groove." Ray Charles was in the midst of a good run with "Hit the Road, Jack," and two enterprising writers had come up with an "answer" song with Nina in mind, "Come on Back, Jack." Phillips took it to her right away. But Nina agreed to go forward only on one condition: "I've got to know that Ray Charles will OK it."

Phillips argued that Charles had no say over a song he didn't write.

"Well, I don't see it that way," Nina retorted. So Phillips had no choice but to get Charles's permission—and fast. "Every day with a song like this you're losing sales," he said. "But I got very lucky. When I called Los Angeles, they said Ray is in New York to perform the next night at Madison Square Garden." Phillips met Charles in his dressing room before the show and explained the situation.

"I don't give a motherfuckin' thing what she sings. She can sing any fuckin' thing she wants," Charles said.

"So of course I went back and told Nina, Ray said he'd be very happy if she did the song."

They recorded it, rushed the release, and it was a flop.

Phillips had done some advertising work before coming to Colpix, and Roy Eaton, a high school friend now connected to Yuban coffee, thought Nina would be perfect to record a jingle for the product, which Phillips wrote. He asked her make a demo, but she was reluctant. Phillips persuaded her at least to meet Eaton, and "when Nina saw that Roy was black, she felt quite a bit better about the situation. She agreed to make the commercial." The punch line was understated innuendo, Nina calling Yuban "Deep, Dark, and Delicious."

Phillips and Eaton couldn't wait to present the demo to Yuban executives. "We love the jingle," they told the men. "We hate the singer. She sounds like a man. She sounds black." It was a bitter disappointment for Eaton when the company used a white singer for the promotion.

Despite these two setbacks, Nina went forward with a new album under Phillips's guidance. This project would be theirs from the start, in the studio and with none of the vagaries of a live performance. They had settled on a different concept. Instead of Nina's usual mix of genres and tunes by an assortment of writers, she would devote the album to the music of Duke Ellington. Some of the songs were well known—"Do Nothin' Till You Hear from Me," "Solitude"; others were more obscure—"Merry Mending," "Hey Buddy Bolden." Nina "conceived" the arrangements, but Ralph Burns, a Ray Charles arranger, did the actual notation for a session that not only had a full orchestra but for the first time had background vocalists as well, the Malcolm Dodds singers. Dodds was a well-known choral director in the New York area, Nina liked him, and she wanted his group on the album.

On "Do Nothin' " she traded verses with the singers and used them like a horn section for "It Don't Mean a Thing" as she played off their spirited vocals with her own up-tempo piano runs. The combination gave the song the feel of a revival meeting. Nina made room for the dramatic and moody, spitting out the lyrics of "Hey Buddy Bolden" and underlining them with harshly struck piano chords.

"Nina was a very difficult person to get along with—like sitting next to a keg of dynamite," Phillips said. "You never knew when she would blow or wouldn't blow." But he found her to be professional. "She worked quickly. She wasn't a time waster. She knew that if she was late it was costing her."

By the time the album was finished and the cover shot was taken, Nina was eight months pregnant. The photographer tried to disguise her changed figure, but nothing worked. So the label used a close-up of Nina's face cropped from a full-length photograph. She does look plumper than usual, with round cheeks and a full chin. Colpix released *Nina Simone Sings Ellington* in October. It received kind notices in *Cash Box* and *Billboard*, but though the album featured the classically influenced piano and singular vocal interpretations Nina's fans counted on, it was another commercial failure.

NINA HADN'T FELT WELL during much of the pregnancy, but Andy was a calming influence, and seeing his pleasure at becoming a father again made her discomfort much more bearable. When Nina's due date approached in early September, her sister Frances came up from Philadelphia. After one false alarm the doctor ignored, Frances insisted that Andy get Nina to the hospital. She was sure the baby was on the way. Nina let Andy drive the Mercedes, and he put all of his police driving skills to work at the wheel, Frances next to him while Nina was in the back seat hoping the baby wouldn't arrive and mess up the red upholstery.

With Andy by her side, Nina was rushed into the delivery room as soon as they got to the hospital. Within an hour their daughter was born. It was September 12, 1962, three years to the day after Nina's concert at Town Hall. They named the baby Lisa Celeste—the Celeste was for a daughter Andy lost when she had accidentally swallowed poison as a toddler.

As Nina, Andy, and Lisa were leaving the hospital to return to Mount Vernon they stopped for a photo, perhaps taken by Frances. Andy is cradling Lisa in his arm, her head, with a full crown of black hair, just peeking out of the blanket. A smiling Nina is behind the baby, her left hand resting on the blanket. It was the perfect picture of domestic tranquility. Rose Seward, the nurse who had been hired, was waiting for the family when they returned to Mount Vernon. As Nina remembered it, she wanted to breast-feed Lisa, "but Andy didn't want me to—he was jealous." So Nina stopped.

BARELY TWO MONTHS AFTER Lisa was born, Nina returned to work at the Village Gate on a bill that once again reflected Art D'Lugoff's adventurous programming. Nina was third in a lineup that reunited two performers for the first time in a dozen years, harmonica virtuoso Larry Adler and dancer Paul Draper. *The New York Times* called their reunion "a show business triumph," alluding to the difficulties each had faced during the anti-Communist fervor that swept the country a decade earlier. They left the United States for a time, and Adler had been removed only recently from a Hollywood blacklist and hired to write theme music for a new Metro-Goldwyn-Mayer film. (*Camera Three*, the CBS television program, found the Gate lineup so intriguing that the network invited all three performers to appear on November 25.)

Although she was not the main attraction, Art gave Nina equal billing in the Gate's newspaper ads and even ran a small headshot of her in some. This engagement also marked the debut of new sidemen. (After Chris left, Al and Bobby went on to other work, too.) The previous year in Boston Nina had met the hand drummer Montego Joe when he invited her to a party. "I was very fascinated with her singing, and artistry, and musicianship. I was determined to meet her," Montego recalled. He was also determined to play with her, and at the party he seized the opportunity. He asked Nina if he could join her on a job. She was noncommittal but promised to keep in touch. Sometime after Lisa was born Andy called and told Montego to come to Mount Vernon for a rehearsal. The timing couldn't have been better. Nina needed new musicians, and Montego Joe turned into a one-man talent agency. He recommended Lisle Atkinson on bass, impressed with his playing when the two worked a dance together. Montego had promised Lisle that if he got the chance to recommend him for something worthwhile he would. Playing with Nina fit that bill.

Lisle had initially trained as a violinst, but the realities of race prompted him to switch to the bass. "I went to school with a slew of black violinists at the Manhattan School of Music," he said. "I've never seen any of them in an orchestra."

Montego Joe also brought Paul Palmieri, whom he knew from New York jazz circles, to play guitar and drummer Warren Smith, another Manhattan School of Music graduate. Smith was thrilled. "I had all of her records," he said. "I was very familiar with her style. I was an admirer." Playing for her, however, was another matter. "This was big-time for me. I hadn't worked with anyone of her magnitude." Though Nina was cordial when they were introduced, Smith was intimidated. Going over the first tunes he was nervous and restrained, sure the others were, too. "We were very careful not to make any mistakes or fool around."

NINA AND ANDY had not had a proper honeymoon, and even though they had been married nearly a year now and had a baby, they decided to have a long-delayed wedding celebration in Acapulco. It would be a welcome rest before the year to come. The calendar was filling up fast, which was the best evidence that Nina's mediocre record sales were an unreliable gauge of her popularity.

12. Mississippi Goddam

~ 1963 ~

Nina's thirtieth birthday fell in the middle of a two-week engagement at Chicago's Sutherland Hotel. "I'm really quite content," she told the *Chicago Defender* in one of two feature stories promoting the date. "I have a wonderful husband and a marvelous baby . . . She's very pudgy and she has black curly hair. She has an atrocious temper if she's not fed on time, but, all in all, she's a joy." Frances, Nina's younger sister, had come on the road to help—they had just played the Sir John Hotel in Miami and a concert in Atlanta.

Perhaps as a present to Nina Andy booked the family into a new motel in Hyde Park with a beautiful view of Lake Michigan. The place was appropriately called "50th on the Lake," noteworthy because it accepted black guests. Most entertainers still stayed at one or another of the well-known South Side hotels, the Sutherland itself or Roberts Motel, which was right across the street from the Show Lounge. Langston made sure to send Nina birthday greetings, and she replied with one of the motel postcards, the front photo showing off the building's sleek lines and a large, enticing swimming pool.

Chicago's knowledgeable jazz community made it an attractive place to play, and the Sutherland drew a different crowd from Roberts. Nina appreciated their warm response to the fast numbers as well as the ballads. The *Defender's* Bob Hunter probably helped when he encouraged readers to "Dig her, she's the boss." *Down Beat* reviewer Pete Welding made a point of her command of the stage in a laudatory review. "She had the crowd with her all the way on the up-tempo pieces; yet her quiet, more intimate numbers brought an attentive, rapt silence over the audience. Everyone was listening; everyone was sharing." Welding appreciated that her moods furthered a musical end. "Nina's whole approach," he wrote, "is aimed at evoking an immediate emotional response in listeners." He loved the way she melded a Schubert-like instrumental "Where Is Your Heart" and the vocal "If You Knew," calling it "an ardent, luminous performance."

The evening of February 19 Nina and Andy attended a gathering put on by the Lake Meadows Art and Jazz Society. The group frequently used the Lake Meadows club room to host visiting performers after hours. Gloria Lynne, who was playing the Tivoli Theater, was also there, but unbeknownst to the group and apparently Gloria, too, Nina had some kind of beef with her. It may have started a week earlier, when the two shared the bill at an Atlanta jazz concert.

Doris Bluitt, who kept the society's guest book, didn't know the particulars, but Nina made clear she didn't want to be anywhere near Gloria. So as guests mingled in the club room, they saw Nina move as soon as Gloria approached. When Gloria realized what was going on, she made it a game, deliberately going toward Nina, who scurried away. The few guests in the know chuckled privately, but no one wanted an out-and-out confrontation. "Nina was a bitch," according to Doris.

Warren Smith, the drummer, had grown up in Chicago, so he enjoyed returning to the city. He loved the way Nina did Oscar Brown's "Rags and Old Iron," now a staple of every set. "That came right from my neighborhood," Smith said, referring to the story of a junkman trolling for goods, though Brown used it as a metaphor for a broken heart. But as much as he respected Nina's musicianship, Smith wasn't getting along with her. "Nina could be pretty gruff—

sometimes in rehearsals we would have a little spat about something or other," he recalled. But Smith accepted a share of the blame. "I was a smart-ass. It took me awhile to realize the magnitude of the people I was playing with and that I should just shut up." Smith decided to stay in Chicago rather than go back to New York with the group.

A YEAR OR SO into their marriage, Andy became Nina's personal manager. They liked to "evaluate each other's potential," he recalled. He set up a blackboard in the kitchen and wrote in one spot, 'Nina will be a rich black bitch by . . . ' " The last part was always changing, Nina explained, with the eventual end point representing the moment they would retire "fat and rich and never work again." Nina liked the arrangement, appreciating how quickly Andy took to the business. She trusted him completely to protect her from what she called the "thieves" in the music world.

To focus on his work, Andy rented office space in Mount Vernon a few blocks from the house. One of his first deals put Nina in a concert of her own at Carnegie Hall April 12 in conjunction with promoter Felix G. Gerstman, who had presented such stars as Renata Tebaldi and Richard Tucker, the opera singers, Harry Belafonte, and Edith Piaf. As part of the deal, Gerstman paid the $825 hall rental. The musical format was different from anything Nina had done. This time she used two guitarists, Phil Orlando (who replaced Paul Palmieri) and Al, Montego Joe on drums, Lisle on bass, and the Malcolm Dodds singers. The musical selections were drawn from a list of twenty songs printed on the program, which also included Langston's tone poem to Nina, reprinted in full. Colpix released an album from the concert a few months later, *Nina Simone at Carnegie Hall*, and while it garnered a few nice notices, it was not a big seller.

"BLACKBIRD," WHICH NINA HAD PERFORMED at Carnegie Hall, was an original song with only three verses and several repeated lines. On the surface it appeared to be about romantic longings unfulfilled. But it also alluded to the escalating struggle over civil rights, and according to *Jet*, Nina wrote the song "to express her feelings about the current racial crisis." Though she hadn't said anything publicly about the demonstrations going on in Southern states, Nina couldn't ignore them. It wasn't only the black press—the *Defender*, the *Amsterdam News*, *The Philadelphia Tribune*, or Norfolk's *Journal and Guide*—who were paying attention, but mainstream newspapers and television stations, too. Just as Nina was preparing for the Carnegie Hall concert, the Reverend Dr. Martin Luther King Jr. and his associates in the Southern Christian Leadership Conference were bringing other activists to Birmingham for a direct challenge to the city's segregation policies. King himself was jailed on Easter weekend. Black commentators differed about whether and how black entertainers could contribute to the effort. The *Defender*'s Bob Hunter believed they should, and he published a harsh piece April 12 calling them collectively to task. "Negro entertainers and stars could and should do more than they are doing at present . . . How long will it be before they cast off their makeup and mascara and take to the battle fields in both the North and South?" he asked. Yet a commentator in the *Journal and Guide* praised Clyde McPhatter after he joined an Atlanta picket line and noted that such entertainers as Lena Horne, Sammy Davis Jr., Harry Belafonte, Louis Armstrong, Ruby Dee, and Ossie Davis were also contributing.

Nina, however, was on the sidelines, not recognizing yet that she had a part to play in the emerging struggle. She was certainly aware of all that was going on from listening to Langston and Jimmy Baldwin and the political talk that was a staple of the Gate atmosphere, but she hadn't made the effort to put it all together for herself. Part of the reason, Nina thought, was because of how she had been raised: "The Waymon way was to turn away from prejudice and to live your life as best you could." She had dealt with the rejection from the Curtis Institute "the Waymon way," and even the nasty experience at the Raleigh train station had passed from her memory. Nina knew she needed prodding to get more involved, and her good friend Lorraine Hansberry turned out to be the catalyst.

Hansberry's groundbreaking 1959 Broadway hit, *A Raisin in the*

Sun, presented the lives and struggles of a black American family in Chicago, her birthplace. It took its title from one of Langston's poems: "What happens to a dream deferred/Does it dry up like a raisin in the sun?" Nina had been introduced to Lorraine sometime in 1960 or 1961, but she didn't get to know her until she and Andy moved to Mount Vernon. Lorraine and her husband Robert Nemiroff lived a few miles away in Croton-on-Hudson, and after some neighborly visits, Nina found herself inexorably drawn to this woman who was so passionate about the condition of the world around her. She couldn't help but admire her resolve to make it a better place. Though Lorraine would hardly have put it this way, Nina thought she was unnecessarily ascetic. She didn't even wear makeup and had, Nina thought, five dresses, if that. "I'm pretty the way I am. I don't need lots of clothes," Lorraine would say when Nina broached the subject. Nina felt so close to Lorraine so quickly that she asked her to be Lisa's godmother. Lorraine attended Lisa's christening April 7 at St. Martin's Episcopal Church in Manhattan, standing right beside Nina throughout the ceremony. Never indulgent for herself, she gave the baby an elegant silver hairbrush and comb from Tiffany.

Nina didn't know it at the time, but Lorraine provided a case study in the collateral effects of activism. *Raisin*, whose cast included Dee and new star Sidney Poitier, had earned her a coveted honor from the New York Drama Critics' Circle, which named it the best play of 1959. But this new fame only intensified the Federal Bureau of Investigation's interest in Lorraine. The agency had kept her under surveillance since 1952, part of its wide search for individuals believed to be associated with the Communist party and therefore a danger to the country. Lorraine's writings and activities at *Freedom*, the newspaper founded by her friend Paul Robeson—whose passport had been revoked for his alleged Communist sympathies—were well known, and it didn't take long for the FBI to put her on its "security index." When *Raisin* was in development, the bureau was so concerned that it dispatched an informant to a preview so he could determine whether the play "is in any way controlled or influenced by the Communist Party and whether it in any way follows the communist line." He gave *Raisin* the FBI equivalent of "all clear": "The play contains no comments of any nature about Communism as such but deals with negro aspirations, the problems inherent in their efforts to advance themselves, and varied attempts at arriving at solutions."

In their many conversations, Lorraine could see that Nina was a reluctant student. When they talked about politics and current events, Nina protested that she felt disconnected. But Lorraine persisted. Like it or not, she told Nina, she was involved in the struggle by the fact of being black—"it made no difference whether I admitted it or not, the fact was still true." Lorraine had called Nina right after the Carnegie Hall concert, but it wasn't to congratulate her. She wanted to talk about King's arrest in Birmingham. What was Nina doing for the movement while the reverend and his colleagues were sitting in jail?

Nina didn't have a good answer that day. But by the first of June she was ready to take her most direct step yet in the service of civil rights. She headlined what the NAACP billed as a "mammoth benefit" in New York City for all the state chapters of the organization. Ten days later Nina listened attentively to President John F. Kennedy's televised address on civil rights, his boldest remarks yet on the subject, and the speech filled her with optimism. By the next morning her hopes were dashed. Barely two hours after Kennedy finished speaking, Medgar Evers, the NAACP's Mississippi field secretary, was shot to death on the doorstep of his Jackson home. He had just returned from the office after watching the president. "I heard the news with disgust," Nina recalled. "What I didn't appreciate was that while Medgar Evers' murder was not the last straw for me, it was the match that lit the fuse." She didn't yet know how brightly the fire would burn, but everything in her life was now transformed into kindling.

IN THE WAKE OF Evers's murder and Kennedy's speech, plans jelled throughout the civil rights movement for a large demonstration in Washington, D.C. If all went well, six major organizations, led by King's Southern Christian Leadership Conference, would come together under one banner to rally their voices on behalf of new legislation. Harry Belafonte, Lena Horne, Sammy Davis Jr., and Sidney Poitier spearheaded fund-raising drives, though other black artists were also contributing, among them Eartha Kitt, Dinah Washington, and Al Hibbler. By mid-June benefits had been held in Los Angeles, Detroit, and Chicago. By early summer Nat King Cole and Johnny Mathis, who had previously kept a public distance from the movement, agreed to participate. Before a Chicago event where he pledged $10,000 of his own money, Mathis told the *Defender* that he wanted it known that he "is 100 percent behind the fight for equal Negro rights . . . These are not days for anonymous and quiet approval, rather these are days that—it seems to me—each Negro must stand up and be counted."

In a concrete sign of Nina's changed perspective, she met in early July with Lorraine and two officers of the Student Non-Violent Coordinating Committee, one of the groups sponsoring the march, at the home of singer-actor Theodore Bikel, a white activist. (Six months earlier the organization—supporters called it "Snick"—asked her to perform at a Carnegie Hall benefit, but she declined.) Alerted to the meeting, the *Amsterdam News* published a photograph of the five at Bikel's Greenwich Village apartment in the July 6 issue.

There were almost daily announcements now from the entertainment world about new efforts to raise money for the march. One of the most significant came from the American Guild of Variety Artists—AGVA—which had agreed to sponsor a "Salute to Freedom '63" fund-raiser August 5 in Birmingham, with a program as ambitious as it was provocative: AGVA planned to bring the first integrated variety show to the city in the wake of the spring protests. The choice of Birmingham was deliberate. "If Birmingham breaks the segregation barrier, others will fall," said the Reverend A. D. King, Martin's brother, who was working with AGVA. Mathis and Ray Charles were already booked as the headliners, and jazz man Billy Taylor, R&B star McPhatter, and boxing champion Joe Louis had also agreed to participate, as had the Shirelles and the integrated seventeen-piece orchestra from the Apollo. During Nina's late June stint at the Gate, which featured Bobby Hamilton back in the drum chair, A. D. King had come by to ask her to join the lineup. She promptly said yes, encouraged that Jimmy Baldwin was coming, too.

Nina at the Newport Jazz Festival, July 4, 1963, just as her
involvement in civil rights activities increased
(*Chuck Stewart*)

Three weeks before the show Birmingham officials abruptly told
AGVA that the promised city auditorium would not be available
August 5 because it had to be painted and redecorated. Comedian
Joey Adams, the AGVA president, was undeterred. "We plan to
appear in Birmingham on that date whether it be in a ball park, tent,
empty lot, or a street corner," he announced. Within a matter of
days, the group had secured the football stadium at Miles College, a

small black school associated with the Christian Methodist Episcopal Church, and workers promised to have a makeshift stage ready for the event.

AGVA chartered a flight August 5 for the performers and newsmen, which Adams dubbed the "Spirit of 76" because there were seventy-six passengers on board. Max Asnas of the Stage Deli had donated all the food and drink, with enough to be taken to the Gaston Motel, informal headquarters of Birmingham's civil rights movement, where everyone was going to freshen up before rehearsal.

Except for the police, who ominously ringed the plane after it landed at the local airport, white Birmingham ignored the event. When white taxi drivers refused to ferry the performers and others to Gaston's, Reverend A. D. King organized a caravan of cars and buses to get everyone to their temporary lodgings. Worried about security, A. D. King had also organized his own civilian defense force—"the Deacons"—to protect the group.

Although a stage had been hastily erected in the Miles stadium, Adams had to put up the money for lights. Via local black disc jockeys he also asked patrons to bring their own chairs because the college couldn't provide enough seating. Though the event was not scheduled to start until the evening, by midafternoon groups of people were trekking to the small campus, each of them carrying a chair.

When Nina and the trio arrived at Miles, Ray Charles and his band, who had come on Charles's private plane, were already there. Bobby immediately went over to speak with Charles's drummer, an old friend. He tried to relax because the whole setup "was a really scary scene." The two men happened to look up at one point and saw a black man sitting in a tree cradling a rifle. "Don't worry," the man shouted. "We're here to protect you." But Lisle, the bass player, was less sanguine. "Every other person had a gun . . . they're walkin' around with rifles and dogs," he recalled. "It was tense, very tense," and he had to work hard to concentrate on the music once he took the stage with Nina and the others.

She performed in the early part of the show, and at nearly an hour, her set was hardly a cameo appearance. The high point was Oscar Brown's "Brown Baby." Nina's dramatic reading left the crowd "cheering to the skies," according to the *Amsterdam News*'s George

Barner. It was already dark when she and the sidemen got back to the bus to wait for the others, but they could still hear the program. Johnny Mathis was in the second chorus of his first song when he was interrupted by a thunderclap of noise. Then the lights went out. Everyone had the same thought: a bomb had gone off. Shrieks and cries mixed with the sound of splintering wood. But after a few minutes the sponsors said it was only the back of the stage that had collapsed, pulling at the wires that kept the lights on. Several people tumbled to the ground, a few struck by falling timber. One person sustained a broken arm. Dr. King came forward to reassure the crowd, and calm was quickly restored.

Mathis had bolted and didn't surface for an hour, when he quietly boarded the bus, but Billy Taylor, unfazed by the dark and the absence of a microphone, simply pushed the piano to an undamaged part of stage and summoned his drummer and bassist. The trio played until the lights and sound were restored. The rest of show went on as planned. Even a dubious speeding ticket given to one of the bus drivers as the performers were leaving and a bomb threat on their plane didn't diminish the evening. Though later than expected, Nina, along with the others, was back in New York at nine a.m. August 6, tired but committed, just as Lorraine had hoped.

About $9,000 had been taken in from the $5-a-person ticket charge. It was a small amount compared to other summer benefits, but few, if any, could top the Birmingham concert for its significance. Jimmy Baldwin had said so, telling the crowd, "This is a living visible view of the breakdown of a hundred years of slavery. It means that white man and black can work and live together. History is forcing people of Birmingham to stop victimizing each other."

The Washington, D.C., march took place on August 28. Some two hundred thousand people rallied at the Lincoln Memorial, making it the largest political demonstration to date in American history. A. Philip Randolph, head of the Brotherhood of Sleeping Car Porters and the inspiration behind the protest, introduced Dr. King, who was the last speaker, calling him "the moral leader of our nation." King's stately baritone soared out over the crowd as he read from his prepared text. Occasional shouts of "Yes!" and "Right on" filled the air when he talked about freedom and justice and the urgent need to collect on the one-hundred-year-old promise of the Emancipation Proclamation. All was going as planned until King neared the end. Perhaps spurred by the huge audience, he shifted to a preacher's cadence and began to speak extemporaneously. Mahalia Jackson, who earlier had sung a moving spiritual, could be heard by those close by exhorting, "Tell 'em about the dream, Martin." Her words may or may not have reached him, but even if they didn't, the two of them were apparently in sync. "I have a dream," he declared, bringing forward parts of a speech he had given in Detroit, "that one day on the red hills of Georgia the sons of former slaves and the sons of former slaveowners will be able to sit down together at the table of brotherhood." He described a host of other dreams that anyone could wish for, ending each part with the now-storied refrain, "I have a dream today." He recited the first stanza of "My Country, 'Tis of Thee," and then reached back to the church for a final flourish. He hoped for a moment, he said, when "all of God's children, black men, white men, Jews and Gentiles, Protestants and Catholics, will be able to join hands and sing in the words of the old Negro spiritual, 'Free at last! Free at last! Thank God Almighty we are free at last!' "

Surprisingly, Nina wasn't in Washington that day. In later recollections she didn't say why. But she paid tribute to the marchers when she returned to the Gate early in September, dedicating songs in her sets to those who were there. "What I am and what I do are all involved with the underlying fact of color," she declared in a backstage interview with *Newsweek* magazine, further proof that Lorraine's lessons had stuck. "I'm the Blackbird of show business," she said, referring to her own song, perhaps a line in the verse: "You ain't got no one to care. If you'd only understand dear nobody wants you anywhere."

"When I first sang that song, it made me sad. But I liked it, and it expressed the truth. That's how I perform," she went on. "I relate to people. My music is about what they feel. Others could tell the same story, maybe their talent is not as obvious as mine. Music is *my* medium."

Nina was candid about her reputation, too. Yes, she knew many thought of her as "mean, evil, temperamental. I'm all those things, but that's not all I am," she insisted. "I am no more mean or evil or temperamental than anybody else, the only thing is I'm more obvious. I'm a performer. I do it in public. I am in a business that feeds on emotion . . . When you have talent as big as mine, and I don't say this with ego, it can overwhelm you sometimes."

IN THE YEAR SINCE MOVING into the Mount Vernon house, Nina and Andy had built a den over the garage where Nina could write and practice for upcoming performances. She liked the private space, and she kept a radio there so she could listen to music or the news whenever she felt like it. Nina was in her office the morning of Sunday, September 15. She had just completed another week at the Gate and was getting ready for a job in Los Angeles and then a return to the Apollo. It was one of those mornings, a little before noon, when she had the radio on, perhaps listening to a classical music show or maybe a gospel hour. But sometime around one p.m. programming was interrupted for breaking news from Birmingham: just as Youth Sunday at the Sixteenth Street Baptist Church was about to begin, a bomb planted right outside the church exploded. Four girls who had been primping and preparing in the ladies' room—they were going to help lead the adult service—were killed instantly. Denise McNair was only eleven; Carol Robertson, Cynthia Wesley, and Addie Mae Collins were fourteen. In the tumult that followed, another young black, thirteen-year-old Virgil Ware, was shot to death by two young white men who were cruising the city on a motor scooter decorated with Confederate flags.

"I sat struck dumb in my den like St. Paul on the road to Damascus," Nina recalled. "All the truths that I had denied to myself for so long rose up and slapped my face." The church bombing and the slaying of Medgar Evers now fit like the last pieces of a jigsaw puzzle, when the whole picture was completed. "I suddenly realized what it is to be black in America in 1963. . . ." It wasn't an intellectual awakening. Instead, Nina said, "it came in a rush of fury, hatred and determination." Now she knew how the testifiers must have felt during those St. Luke CME revivals: "The truth entered into me and I 'came through.'"

But having "come through," Nina didn't know what to do next. Instinct took over. She was so angry, she went to the garage to see if she could fashion a weapon. She wanted to hurt someone, anyone she could "identify as being in the way of my people getting some justice for the first time in three hundred years."

Alarmed, Andy didn't argue with Nina, but he gently reminded her she knew nothing about killing. "The only thing you've got is music," he said. And then he left her alone.

Nina never liked protest songs because she found most too simple and unimaginative. They ended up stripping the dignity away from the individuals they celebrated. A man like Medgar Evers couldn't be reduced to a few lyrics that fit some melody. But Nina knew Andy was right. She sat down at the piano, and the music "erupted out of me faster than I could write it down." Within an hour she had a song. She called it "Mississippi Goddam." But it was no minor-key lament about the tragedy in Birmingham. The song was incongruously up-tempo with an insistent two-beat rhythm, its biting lyrics more commentary than anthem. "Alabama's got me so upset./Tennessee made me lose my rest./But everybody knows about Mississippi Goddam." The middle of the song cataloged worries: "Hound dogs on my trail/Schoolchildren sitting in jail/Black cat across my path/I think every day's gonna be my last." Then Nina turned defiant: "Don't tell me/I'll tell you/Me and my people are just about due." She shifted to metaphor in one sharp passage: "You told me to wash and clean my ears/And talk real fine just like a lady/And you'd stop call-ing me Sister Sadie"—that name standing in for all the demeaning moments at the hands of overly familiar whites. She ended with a simple prescription: "You don't have to live next to me/Just give me my equality."

Nina could hardly wait to perform the song. She put it in her set the next week out in Los Angeles, where she was booked into Small's Paradise West. "The name of this tune is 'Mississippi Goddam' and I mean every word of it," she said. As Nina remembered it, the song was an instant hit with the audience, and she felt as if she had hurled "ten bullets" back at the Birmingham bombers. Her first week was so successful that she and the trio were booked for another. Though *California Eagle* columnist Chazz Crawford didn't mention it specifically, he could have been referring to "Mississippi Goddam" when he called Nina "our spokesman or spokeswoman when it comes to that earthy 'let's drag it up by the roots' sort of stuff. She tells the TRUTH."

NINA WAS LESS THAN EBULLIENT in her week at the Apollo early in November, likely the result of her new focus on all the racial strife. "Very sulky and difficult" was how the Schiffmans described her, and business was only "fair." But Art D'Lugoff, who had booked that date, kept her busy with bookings that steered her away from controversy. He included her in the "the folk & jazz wing ding" at Carnegie Hall that he was producing with sponsorship by the Ford Motor Company. They styled it the CARavan, and the concert, aimed at students who attended ten area colleges, was a kickoff for a campus tour that also included Nina. Among the first college dates was a performance at Dartmouth November 22. Nina and the group arrived shortly after noon, unaware that tragedy had struck in Dallas. As soon as word of President Kennedy's assassination spread, Dartmouth officials canceled the concert. With the remaining schedule in flux, Nina was free to play a night at the Academy of Music in Philadelphia, and she made a point of dedicating one song to the slain president.

Two weeks later Nina and her trio were in West Virginia for an unlikely performance: the national taping of the television show *Hootenanny,* this installment sponsored by tiny Salem College in Clarksburg. Though geared to a folk audience, the *Hootenanny* lineup frequently included someone from the jazz or country-and-western world. Now it was Nina's turn, and she had a slot on the December 10 taping along with the New Christy Minstrels, a ten-member group with a top-ten hit, "Green, Green," and the Four Preps, a popular quartet that already had put a dozen songs on the charts. Singing to a crowd of several thousand, most of them white college students from Salem and surrounding schools, Nina was nonconfrontational, choosing numbers that featured Montego Joe, especially the Israeli folk song "Eretz Zavat Chalav." The stage setup, perhaps deliberate, put him on a riser right next to the grand piano, so his fast hand action on the dumbeq, his specially made hourglass drum, couldn't be missed. Judging from her broad smile, captured in a photograph as she bowed from the piano, Nina seemed to be enjoying herself. Performing for these well-scrubbed young whites, who seemed like holdovers from another era, provided a brief respite from the weighty matters that were much on her mind now. But *Hootenanny* aside, Nina knew there was no going back.

13. Don't Let Me Be
Misunderstood

~ 1964 ~

Nina's appearance in Summit, New Jersey, on January 22 to headline a benefit for the Congress of Racial Equality (CORE) further confirmed that Andy was right. She *did* have her music. "I played on stage for a reason, and when I walked off stage those reasons still existed," she said, long outlasting the applause. In an odd juxtaposition beyond Nina's control, the *Hoot-enanny* show she taped in Clarksburg was broadcast on television just four days before the Summit concert. Perhaps to piggyback on the event, Andy had taken out a two-column, four-inch-high ad in *Variety* that featured a new, appealing headshot of Nina and proclaimed her "star of the Ford CARavan of Music for 1964." He had even hired promotion man Paul Brown to help, and his name was featured along with Andy's as a contact. But the ad ran in *Variety*'s Vaudeville section, hardly prime space in the weekly.

Although only one of Nina's Colpix albums had touched the charts, that didn't deter Willem Langenberg, the voluble head of

Philips Records, a division of the giant electronics firm, from wanting to sign her. Philips had initially concentrated on classical music but now branched out into other genres as it looked for ways to distribute its product in the United States. When Langenberg, a native of the Netherlands, came across "Mississippi Goddam," he was smitten. He listened to the record nonstop, as Nina told it, and got on a plane to New York determined to make a deal. He found her at the Village Gate and waited in her dressing room until she came off the stage. An imposing man of nearly three hundred pounds, he wasted no time. "I've come to take you back to Holland," he said in his booming voice, "so you can be on the Philips label."

"There was no question I was going to sign," Nina recalled, finding "Big Willy," as she nicknamed him, irresistible. Despite the conflicts she often felt about her music, when she took stock, she knew it was another step forward to be embraced by a label that wanted her so much. She didn't actually have to leave the country to make the switch, but "Big Willy" did set things in motion. Andy worked out the details for her to leave Colpix, and on February 22 an announcement appeared in *Cash Box* that Nina was now recording exclusively for Philips. The label had acquired Mercury Records, the Chicago-based company that once was home to Dinah Washington and Sarah Vaughan, among other notable singers. Mercury president Irving Green released the news. The announcement noted that Nina was going to appear at Carnegie Hall on March 21 in another concert sponsored by Felix Gerstman, and plans were already under way to record the evening for a new live album, this time under the auspices of Philips. But *Variety* suggested that Colpix wanted to piggyback on pre-concert publicity, noting in a short item that the Carnegie event was "in conjunction with Colpix Records promotion for her eight LPs."

Phil Orlando had left the group, never able to conquer his nerves onstage with Nina. "There were times before he would go on that he would go in the men's room and throw up," Lisle said. "So obviously he didn't play his best." This time Bobby recommended a successor, Rudy Stevenson, a multitalented musician who not only played the guitar but also played the flute, clarinet, and saxophone. He was a composer-arranger, too. With a weekend back at the Village Gate in February and then another Ford CARavan performance March 12 at Chicago's Illinois Institute of Technology, Nina had plenty of time to get comfortable with him. He had made an immediate contribution when they rehearsed, fleshing out the arrangement for "See-Line Woman," a new song Nina had incorporated into her live dates at Langston's suggestion. "I think See-Line Woman is particularly suited for you," Langston had told her in one of his regular notes, "custom-made." He said it was adapted from an old island folk tune by his secretary, George Bass, who had a musical bent and was studying the arts at New York University.

In this arrangement Rudy's distinctive flute solo alternated with the vaguely calypso beat from Bobby and Montego Joe. There was no piano, so Nina performed the song—even on March 21 at Carnegie Hall—standing up, dancing as the spirit moved, which was fitting given the lyrics about the vixenish "See-Line Woman dressed in red/Make a man lose his head." For this night at Carnegie, though, Nina wore white, a full-length halter-top dress with the unusual accessory of two silver bands on her upper left arm.

A high point of the opening set was her ferocious reworking of "Pirate Jenny," the Kurt Weill–Bertolt Brecht song from *The Three-penny Opera*. This play with music had been revived in the United States a decade earlier, and Nina captured the bitter pessimism that underlay the work's surface amusement. Assisted by a few well-placed drumbeats from Bobby, Nina shouted, hissed, whispered, and threatened, never more so than when she sang about being "in this crummy Southern town in this crummy old hotel." The audience sat transfixed when she growled that "there's nobody gonna sleep here, honey. Nobody . . . Nobody!" She displayed her softer side in an extended version of "Plain Gold Ring." Bobby thought he gave one of his best performances because the drums were tuned so well and blended in with the piano. "It was almost like playing the timpani," he recalled.

Central to the evening was a trio of songs that reflected Nina's newfound interest in civil rights, although she presented them more as crowd-pleasers than efforts to rally the troops. "Mississippi Goddam" had its same angry lyrics, but when Nina introduced it as "a show tune—only the show hasn't been written yet," it brought a collective laugh that had the effect of letting the audience off the hook. "Old Jim Crow," which she co-authored, was standard blues, but "Old Jim Crow" wasn't a man. The name, of course, was slang for the "separate but equal" laws that had governed Southern segregation for so long. "Old Jim Crow. It ain't your name. It's the thing you do," Nina sang, but her presentation was entirely without bitterness. "Go Limp," in the vein of "Little Liza Jane," was a sing-along folk song and a benign if mischievous tribute to the young protesters. It told of a mother's concerns as her daughter prepares to march with the NAACP. Nina asked the audience to join her at each chorus between verses. "All right now, hootenanny time," she joked.

The song's title was a play on one of the lines that counseled protestors to "go perfectly limp" when the authorities came. Nina turned suggestive when she sang of the protester who told the young girl she should be kissed and how this young girl obeyed "and did not resist." The audience let out an appreciative chuckle. Nina's sly finish alluded to romance and ultimate victory so that if there was later a baby, he wouldn't have to march "like his da-da and me."

A sense of occasion surrounded the entire evening. Irving Green came in from Chicago, a gesture no doubt intended to let Nina know that her new label was serious about promoting her. They held court backstage while she relaxed with Max Cohen, still her lawyer, and Charles Aznavour, the French star, who had come to say hello. Ever attentive, Langston sent a telegram ahead of time even though he was at the concert compliments of Andy. At the post-concert celebration, Langston traded jokes with comedian Godfrey Cambridge, Nina happily sandwiched between them, sharing the laughter.

Lisle had mixed feelings about the concert. It wasn't his place, or any sideman's for that matter, to argue about what was being played. If he did, the solution was obvious: he could find another job. Lisle didn't say anything and didn't discuss his views with Bobby and Rudy, but "Mississippi Goddam" and the other civil-rights-related material made him uncomfortable. For one thing, he didn't think much of "Mississippi Goddam" musically. "It wasn't very challenging at all," he said. He chafed because he felt that his training—and Nina's too—was going to waste. "Here's a brilliant woman—why are you sitting down and composing something like this when you can *compose* something?" Beyond that Lisle wrestled with the propriety of using his talent to make political statements from the stage. "Not that I was against the civil rights movement," he explained, "because everybody knew that things had to be straightened out—or at least an attempt had to be made. But I personally didn't feel the stage was the place for *me* to make the statement—not through any music I'm going to play. If we're up there to play beautiful music, that's what we should do . . . I didn't study all my life to protest when I'm playing my instrument, not with a bass in my hand."

But Lisle kept quiet. "If she called the tune," he said, "that was part of the job."

PHILIPS WANTED TO GET Nina into the studio, and assigned veteran Mercury producer Hal Mooney, well known for his big orchestral arrangements, to a couple of spring sessions. Just like Colpix, the label hoped to get Nina into the mainstream, and while the aim was both laudable and understandable, the results were mixed. Surrounding Nina with the same kind of sound used for, say, Dinah Washington in her final sessions on the Roulette label had the effect of undercutting her distinctiveness. The lush orchestrations, though, did highlight the singular edge in Nina's voice every time she cut through the swooning violins.

One especially notable track did emerge from the session. Mooney was fond of the writer Bennie Benjamin, whose "Wheel of Fortune" had been a hit for Kay Starr but had also done well for other singers, white and black. They had already settled on several of Benjamin's songs; the rest would be show tunes, which were still a part of Nina's repertoire. Although Mooney would be in charge of the eventual album, at Benjamin's suggestion he brought in Horace Ott, a young composer-arranger who had made a name for himself in New York doing demo and session work.

Benjamin and his writing partner, Sol Marcus, wanted one more song for Nina but hadn't come up with anything. Ott told them he had been playing around with a verse he liked, and had found a few chords and the hint of a melody. He confessed that it came to him after a tiff with his wife when he went to the piano to work out his frustration. Although he hadn't turned the inspiration into a full-blown song, he was pleased with the hook: "Oh Lord, please don't let me be misunderstood." Ott suggested that Benjamin and Marcus finish the song, and they'd share the writing credit.

The men agreed, and when all three were satisfied, they took it to Nina, waiting for her backstage until she finished up one of her April nights at the Village Gate. Ott made the presentation "with all the humility I could find." "Don't you know no one alive can always be an angel," he sang. "When everything goes wrong, you see some bad." And then he delivered the hook.

The men could see that Nina was intrigued. "My goodness," she said when Ott finished. "A person would really have to be hurt to sing this song."

"You want us to hurt you?" the men blurted out almost at once, laughing at their obvious joke. Nina was sold.

Though Ott had created an elaborate arrangement, with strings, woodwinds, the Malcolm Dodds singers, and the well-regarded organist Ernie Hayes on the celeste, Nina found her way to the heart of the song, raw but completely without melodrama. The much more spare live versions that came later, with only her piano and two or three sidemen, still packed the same emotional punch.

NINA'S FRIEND LORRAINE HANSBERRY had not been feeling well for some time, and like others close to her, Nina was concerned that she was seriously ill. If she couldn't do anything directly to help Lorraine, at least she could show her that she had taken her entreaties seriously. She willingly returned to Carnegie Hall April 23 for an impromptu performance to benefit SNCC, joining host Dick Gregory, the outspoken comedian, to fill out a program that featured the SNCC Freedom Singers. "Pirate Jenny" this night seemed to elicit a particularly strong response. "As Bertolt Brecht expressed the turmoil of Germany, so do your songs express the terrible ramifications of our oppression," Julia Prettyman, SNCC's executive secretary, wrote in an effusive thank-you note. Not only had Nina agreed to appear on short notice, she also apparently didn't charge anything for the performance. Nina felt most at home with SNCC because she liked the organization's pragmatic attitude: "There was more than one way to skin a cat and whatever means worked to get what you wanted was the right one to use."

Six weeks later Nina performed again for the organization, this time headlining a benefit at the Westbury Music Fair in Long Island. Fund-raising efforts were in such high gear because SNCC, along with other organizations, had just begun a major civil rights campaign in Mississippi dubbed "Freedom Summer." SNCC gave Nina $200 to cover her expenses, and in her thank-you letter, Prettyman apologized for being tardy because of "the incredible amount of work our limited staff has to handle. Right now we are operating as much as possible on getting federal protection promised for the Mississippi people." Prettyman's letter was dated June 17. Four days later the first reports surfaced that three civil rights workers were missing. They would be found two months later, shot to death and buried in an earthen dam several miles outside of tiny Philadelphia, Mississippi, in Neshoba County.

Nothing so grim was on Nina's mind as she prepared for a relaxing summer: a live date here and there in New York scheduled around nearly three weeks at Cape Cod with Andy, Lisa, and Andy's boys. She seemed to be in an especially good mood before they left, and it showed in her pre-vacation stint at the Gate. So much so that the *Amsterdam News* was moved to write about a "new" Nina. "The singer-pianist, who often has been criticized for her surly manner, is in a happy period and has never played better in her life," the *News* declared. "A former press agent who couldn't get along with Nina"—probably Paul Brown—"rushed to her the other night after a performance and kissed her hand," the paper reported. Later, he told the *News*, "She's finally come to a point where she's happy." (The "surly" Nina, though, had been on display a few weeks earlier in Washington. John Pagones, a *Washington Post* reviewer, called her a "benevolent dictator" for her response to fans who shouted requests—which she ignored—during a job at the Shadows, an upscale club in Georgetown.)

Jimmy Baldwin had come to one of the Gate performances, and by coincidence, Bernard Gotfryd, a *Newsweek* photographer and now a family friend, was also there. He rarely went anyplace without his camera, and backstage later he snapped the two of them joyously conversing. "This is one of my friends," she told Jimmy, "the best photographer in the world." "She looked up to Baldwin," Gotfryd remembered. "She was always looking up to people who accomplished something."

Nina particularly enjoyed the Cape Cod vacation because she and Andy had brought along a nanny. It allowed her free time to stroll on the beach, binoculars in hand, and take in the vast seascape or play in the sand with the children. "It's such a change from New York," she wrote Langston in one postcard. "I wish we could stay all summer." But of course they couldn't. Nina was booked at Basin Street East at the end of July and at "John Terrell's Music Circus," a folk and concert series, in Lambertville, New Jersey, on August 9.

IN MID-JULY Philips had released its first Nina LP, from the Carnegie event, titled simply *nina simone in concert*. It took a few weeks to find an audience, but on September 16 the record went on *Billboard's* Top 200 album chart. Though it stayed on the chart for nearly three months, it didn't rise above number 102. The statistics suggested that Nina had a loyal cadre of fans and a certain staying power, but the album was well short of a hit. Philips also released a single, pairing "Mississippi Goddam" with "See-Line Woman." Though Nina had left Colpix in February, the label, still eager to mine her catalog and capitalize on any publicity from Philips, issued a new compilation just days after *in concert* hit the stores. *Folksy Nina* received modest notices from a few music writers but didn't do much commercially.

The new records coincided with Nina's trip to Los Angeles the first week in September. She and the trio were set to play a big jazz show on the fourth at the Hollywood Bowl. But the date seemed like an afterthought because it came in the middle of two appearances on Steve Allen's nationally televised variety show. For the September 3 installment, Allen had reconfigured the studio to create a more intimate atmosphere. The lights were dimmed, and instead of sitting behind his desk, Allen was at a small table, ashtray and coffee cups visible, as if he were at a club. The audience was also seated, club style, around him. Allen introduced Nina as "one of the most original talents in our business—a young lady who has a style all her own." She had chosen "See-Line Woman" for her first number, and like the Carnegie Hall version, it opened with Rudy's flute solo. Perhaps to improve the sightlines for television, he was standing on a small foot-high platform behind her, with Lisle and Bobby just to her left. Nina showed off her dance moves, doing little shuffle steps and twisting her hips as she clapped to the beat, constrained only by her floor-length sheath dress.

When Nina sat down with Allen between songs, he immediately gave a plug to the new Philips record, holding it up for a straight-on camera shot. Noticing "Pirate Jenny," he wanted her to do it, but Nina explained that the song was too long for her time slot. Instead she chose "For All We Know," "but we do it in kind of a hymn-Bach-like way. I think you'll like it."

"Hymn and Bach?" Allen asked.

"Yeah, like a Bach chorale, you know?"

Nina started slowly, playing single notes in her right hand before she sang the opening verse—"For all we know we may never meet again"—and then the piano work got increasingly intricate as she continued. Rudy came in on guitar, playing the same kind of counterpoint that Al Schackman had done so effortlessly when he and Nina first improvised "Little Girl Blue." Then it was Lisle and Bobby's turn. Just before the end they backed off for a few bars, and Nina used her voice to create one of those Bach embellishments she usually played at the keyboard. By the time the song reached its final crescendo, the audience had witnessed the building of a song note by note, layer by layer. When it was over, they erupted with applause and whistles. Clearly pleased, Nina bowed in all directions and whispered "thank you."

Allen returned to his usual format, sitting behind a desk, when Nina came back for the September 10 show. Brought on in the middle, she opened with one of her favorites, "Zungo." As the song wound down, she slowed the tempo and tossed in a lyric she appeared to make up on the spot, confident that her sidemen would recognize a transition: "That's what I tell my old man—every day I tell him that I love him . . . " Bobby had never heard that before, and just as Nina expected, he, like Rudy and Lisle, fastened his eyes on her, waiting for what would come next. She struck a familiar chord and segued into "Porgy."

When Nina joined Allen at the desk before her next song, he told her he wanted her to sing "Mississippi Goddam" because he knew it would provoke a lively discussion about censorship.

"This is kind of an awkward song to talk about," Allen said.

"I memorized what I'm supposed to say," Nina assured him, revealing that they had planned this ahead of time. "So can I say it?"

Allen told her to go ahead.

"This is a song I wrote during the time the four little kids were bombed in Alabama," Nina said, giving perhaps her fullest explanation of its origins, "and it was conceived, though, during the time when James Meredith was finally getting into the University of Mississipppi. And I was beginning to get angry then. First you get depressed, then you get mad. And when these kids got bombed, I just sat down and wrote this song. And it's a very moving, violent song 'cause that's how I feel about the whole thing. It's called 'Mississippi Blank-Blank.' I have to explain that," Nina went on before Allen could say a word, "and this is where the memorization comes in. It's a two-part expression, Steve, ending with the word damn. In other words it's 'Mississippi' "—and then there was a high-pitched bleep that the networks used when they wanted to block out curse words or anything else deemed offensive.

"If I may speak of this entirely without passion," Allen interjected. "The first word is God and the second word is damn, and I think everyone up this late at night who can afford to pay for a television set is adult enough to recognize that one not only hears that expression but most of you say it when you hit your thumb with a hammer."

That made Nina chuckle.

"I figure I might as well lay it on the line so I won't get nine thousand letters." Nina interrupted to assure Allen that she and the trio would only be mouthing the words.

Allen had another idea: "So everybody at home when you get to the words scream them."

"Yes," Nina agreed, "that'll work. Let me tell you something," she added, "since I recorded this song we have had several letters from them—this show doesn't go down South does it?"

In a few cities, Allen told her.

"They're gonna cut you off tonight," Nina warned.

"That's all right."

But Nina had more to say. She wanted Allen to appreciate how strong the reaction had been in some quarters. "We got several letters from Arkansas, Mississippi, Alabama. Well I know about nine of the letters where they had actually broken up this recording and sent it back to the recording company, really, telling them it was in bad taste. How could I stoop to this? They missed the whole point. We also got a letter from the Ku Klux Klan," though Nina admitted she hadn't actually seen the letter. "I heard about it. I'm glad I didn't see it. What astounds me," she continued, "if the song were sung about some other state they wouldn't care."

"You mean Rhode Island?" Allen wondered.

"Yeah," Nina said. "It's when it touches you personally that you have some violent reaction"—and she hit the table for emphasis before getting up and going over to the piano.

Two lines into the song the network censor was activated: "Everybody knows about Mississippi BLEEP BLEEP" though when the camera panned Nina's face, it was clear what she was saying. She improvised the second verse apparently to reflect the latest from the civil rights front: "Alabama's got me so upset/St. Augustine's made me lose my rest"—a reference to the recent arrests in that Florida city during civil rights protests.

The network bleeped the chorus all through the song, but it was obvious from Nina's expression that she was anything but amused. She looked positively angry when she sang, "Don't tell me—I'll tell you," and one could imagine viewers at home flinching on the sofa. Nina did soften one verse, if only slightly. She usually sang, "Oh but this country is full of lies/You're all gonna die and die like flies." Tonight she was more inclusive: "We're gonna die and die like flies." After the final "Mississippi bleep bleep," Nina jumped up from the piano.

"That's it!" she yelled, and took her bow.

NINA GOT BACK to New York in time to perform at a CORE benefit September 12 on Long Island with popular folksinger Pete Seeger. Fortunately the concert was in the evening and didn't interfere with celebrating Lisa's second birthday. Nina loved watching her daughter blow out the candles, marvelling that this adorable little girl was hers. "And Lisa," she mused to a friend not long after the party. "I always wanted to be physically, naturally acceptably beautiful. (I have to work at it.) Hers is all natural, a physically perfect girl." Lisa was light-skinned like Andy and had his delicate features rather than the broad, distinctive nose and lips that all the Waymon siblings shared. Though Lisa could barely reach the keyboard, she wanted to play the piano, too, and it must have tickled Nina to watch Lisa plunk her little fingers over the keys.

By this time Andy had moved Stroud Productions and Enterprises Inc. to Manhattan, taking space on lower Fifth Avenue. He also established an affiliation with the International Talent Association,

Nina celebrating her daughter Lisa's second
birthday in Mount Vernon
(Bernard Gotfryd)

which would help with bookings and publicity. The timing was good, coming just as Philips released Nina's second album on the label, *Broadway-Blues-Ballads*, which had been recorded at those spring sessions. (Compound-genre titles seemed to be a trend. Harry Belafonte had just released *Ballads, Blues & Boasters* and Johnny Mathis's latest was *Ballads of Broadway*.) The first track, the evocative "Don't Let Me Be Misunderstood," fit either the "blues" or the "ballads" referred to in the title. Such an unusual and powerful mix of sound and sentiment could have brought Nina her biggest hit. But four months later the British group the Animals took it away from her. Nina never forgot either. When Eric Burdon, the Animals' lead singer, introduced himself after one of her concerts, she let him know it.

"So you're the honky motherfucker who stole my song and got a hit out of it?" Taken aback, Burdon quickly recovered. "I'll admit that your rendition inspired us to record the song. Besides, the Animals having a hit with it has paved the way for you in Europe. They're waiting for you." Nina took in the comment and then extended her hand. "My name is Nina Simone," she said. "Sit down."

Among the "Broadway" part of this new album were "Night Song" from *Golden Boy* and "Something Wonderful" from *The King and I*. The label also included the live version of "See-Line Woman" that had been performed March 21 at Carnegie Hall. It stood out from the rest of the heavily orchestrated tracks if for no other reason than the absence of strings. Once again Langston allowed the use of his tone poem to Nina, this time slightly revised and taking up most of the back cover.

Though *Variety* called the album a good illustration of Nina's "arty inclinations," and *Cash Box* praised Nina's "rich soaring lyrical voice," this album didn't do very well either. But Nina's record sales seemed to have little to do with her draw as a live performer. She was recruited to be part of a package tour with Harry James and his band that made stops at Carnegie Hall, Chicago's Arie Crown Theater, and a few other Midwestern venues before ending in Nebraska. "Mississippi Goddam" was still proving to be controversial. The

Chicago Defender would not print the title, and Nina told columnist Beatrice Watson that she adhered to a request not to perform the song in Chicago because it was "thought to be in poor taste and not good for occasions of this sort." The suggestive "Go Limp" on the other hand got "quite a response," Watson later reported.

SETTLED INTO HIS NEW Manhattan office, Andy devoted a good part of November to an ambitious project: a thirty-page booklet of photographs with narrative interspersed that presented Nina's story as they wanted it told. While several of the photos featured Nina in performance, including the amusing shot of her in apron and kerchief performing "Pirate Jenny," the most arresting were the family photos: Nina in the garden at Mount Vernon with Lisa, snuggling with her in a chair, Nina and Andy affectionately reclining in the yard, and a casual portrait of the three of them, probably taken in the fall. Nina and Andy are wearing jackets; Lisa, bundled in a thick sweater, is smiling, her head resting just under Nina's chin. The pamphlet projects the picture-perfect world that Nina dreamt of in her loneliest moments, a woman with a thriving career and a happy family. The Christmas card Nina and Andy had chosen this year was distinctly religious. On the front "A Joyous Christmas" was written in Old English script, printed next to a picture of an open prayer book on a stand that rested in a small archway. A page marker with a small cross lay on the book's right-hand page. The message inside in formal script read, "Sincerely wishing you all the blessings of the Christmas Season and a New Year filled with Happiness and Peace. NINA, LISA, AND ANDY STROUD."

The holiday season, however, proved to be anything but peaceful. Right before Christmas, Nina instructed Max Cohen to file a lawsuit against Premier Records, a small independent label, and the R. H. Macy company for the unauthorized release and subsequent sale of an album Premier called *Starring Nina Simone*. When Nina listened to the disc, she realized it was a compilation of old demo tapes made in 1955–56, when Jerry Field had been representing her. Premier claimed Field had signed a contract with them allowing release of the music, a claim Nina found ridiculous. In a lengthy deposition Nina contended that Field had no such right to make a deal on her behalf and that she had never signed anything with Premier.

Though the lawyers clearly influenced Nina's language, her statement nonetheless reflected the fierce pride she took in her work. One can only image the hauteur in her voice as she expressed her resentment that Macy's would display this counterfeit record right next to her releases from Colpix and Philips, as though this album was as current as the others and recorded with the same kind of studio-level equipment. "My professional reputation depends upon the maintenance of a high standard of artistic and technical competence," she declared. "In fact my recording contracts reserve for me the unique and exceptional right to oversee and pass upon the artistic and technical qualities of all records which embody my recording performances prior to the manufacture and distribution of any records." The next sentence was underlined for emphasis in the written transcript: "I am one of the few top Artists granted this very unusual privilege by contract." Nina asked for a million dollars in damages.

No one knew how many of these bootlegged albums had actually been sold, but those who heard the music could recognize the seeds of "Mississippi Goddam" in "Lovin' Woman," which had that same insistent two-beat rhythm.

Nina had agreed to play a jazz show at the Hollywood Palladium in Los Angeles right after Christmas, but the event dissolved into a riot before she and a handful of other acts could take the stage. The promoter apparently had not raised enough money, and when Bobby "Blue" Bland told the audience, "Man, there isn't enough bread to sing for. I'm getting out," some of the fans stormed the box office and demanded their money back. Mirrors and windows were smashed and furniture was torn up before police could restore order.

Much more troubling than the Los Angeles fiasco was Lorraine's poor health. As the new year dawned, Nina realized that her friend might not even make it through January.

14. My Skin Is Black

~ 1965 ~

When Nina returned to the studio early in the new year, Andy asked Bernard Gotfryd, the *Newsweek* photographer, to shoot the session. He found an engaged performer talking over arrangements with Horace Ott, chatting with the backup singers, and studying the music. In one moment, between takes, Gotfryd caught Nina in silhouette, standing against the wall, her head bowed in deep contemplation. Resonant with possible interpretations, the photo offered the kind of intriguing shot to illuminate a future release.

This session featured more varied songs than the previous spring, including two rhythm-and-blues tunes from Andy with provocative titles: "Gimme Some" and "Take Care of Business." The most unusual song, though, was Nina's remake of Screamin' Jay Hawkins's wildly entertaining "I Put a Spell on You," an original full of hollers, moans, and a rat-a-tat sax that in live performances featured Hawkins emerging from a coffin amid swirls of fake smoke like some voodoo prince. Hal Mooney set Nina amid his trademark strings but also added an evocative sax solo from Jerome Richardson that played off

Nina in the studio, c. 1965
(*Bernard Gotfryd*)

Nina's vocals. She interspersed the lyrics with her version of scat singing, as if Bach was a bluesman and Ella Fitzgerald had done her signature moves in slow motion. This strange musical stew took the menace and camp out of the Hawkins original and turned the song into a mood piece. It was nonetheless effective because Nina sang with such conviction. She did the same in another musical departure, Jacques Brel's "Ne Me Quitte Pas," a song that pleads, "don't leave me." Surrounded by strings again, Nina cast herself as a chanteuse.

Philips planned to package several tracks into an album called *I Put a Spell on You*, set for a spring release.

ANDY AND FELIX GERSTMAN had joined up again to present Nina in another solo concert at Carnegie Hall January 15, their most ambitious outing yet. Nina would play the first half with her regular musicians—Lisle, Bobby, Rudy, and Al Schackman, who had temporarily rejoined the group. In the second half she would perform with a thirty-five-piece orchestra conducted by Mooney. Not only that, her parents, Kate and J.D., would be there, and also Miss Mazzy, her beloved first piano teacher. Determined to have a look that matched the evening, Nina enlisted Dorothea Towles to be her fashion consultant. Towles had been the first successful black model in Paris, a regular on the runways of top-tier designers Christian Dior and Elsa Schiaparelli. Having parlayed her success in Europe to help black models in the United States, Towles now found ways to combine her talents with support of civil rights causes. One of her more notable events, "Fashions for Freedom," combined a fashion show that featured Towles and her models showing off their outfits to the music of Count Basie and his orchestra. According to the *Amsterdam News*, Nina snapped up sixty tickets.

Reflecting Towles's influence even before she stepped on the Carnegie stage, Nina arrived at the theater swathed in a luxuriant full-length mink coat with the eye-catching accessory of a silver buckle just below the waist. She had acquired a hairdresser for the evening, a man named Frenchie Casimir, and he had pulled Nina's own hair off her forehead and affixed a three-section circular hairpiece at the back of her head like an elaborate ponytail. Nina had chosen the same evening gown she had worn on *The Steve Allen Show* four months earlier; it had a white sheath skirt, and a top and removable train that were dark but with white appliquéd flowers. Backstage Towles applied sequins strategically on her eyebrows and eyelids that only accentuated the false eyelashes she had already put on. Though not as dramatic as Screamin' Jay Hawkins and his smoke-shrouded coffin, Nina's ensemble sent the message that she, too, could cast a spell.

At her mood-setting best in the first set, Nina took the audience through ballads, folk material, and songs that even when secular in nature seemed like hymns. She might start by idly fingering the piano keys to no apparent purpose, humming a little and then singing a lyric until it all unfolded into a song. The four sidemen, picking up the cue, comfortably molded their parts into a satisfying whole. Nina prefaced "Mississippi Goddam" with a note of optimism, announcing that it was "not quite as urgent as it used to be." She was referring to the morning's news that a federal grand jury had indicted several individuals in connection with the deaths of the three civil rights workers the previous summer.

When Nina came out for the second half, she walked to center stage to introduce Mooney and the orchestra. She seemed tickled to have all these classically trained musicians behind her. "We went high class," she said, showing off the elbow-length white gloves she had put on. Nina sang part of this set standing at the microphone. When she sat down at the piano for other numbers, the gloves now removed, Nina paused to reflect on the moment. "It was the kind of concert I would kill for when I was Eunice Waymon," she thought to herself. She looked up to where Miss Mazzy was sitting, and even though Nina couldn't see her face, she was sure Miss Mazzy, too, understood how much had happened since those first lessons back in Tryon.

But having to mesh with the orchestra made Nina much less comfortable than usual. In the middle of one song, she actually sang a warning to Mooney to slow down. She may have called this second half "high class," but many preferred Nina low-down, Langston (who had also attended) among them. However, he said so with kind circumspection. "Your Carnegie Hall concert was terrific!" he wrote a few days later. "Except that you don't need an orchestra. You YOURSELF are enough for anybody's money."

At the post-concert celebration Nina couldn't wait to see her parents. J. D. Waymon was bursting with pride, but Kate said nothing. Nina was hurt, her disappointment compounded when Miss Mazzy later told her that Kate expressed her pride when Nina wasn't around. "I longed for her to say it just once," Nina confided in her memoir.

IT MUST HAVE BEEN sheer willpower that enabled Nina to pull off the Carnegie Hall concert even with her parents and Miss Mazzy in attendance. Those closest to her knew that she had walked onstage with a heavy heart. Lorraine had died on January 12. Her last days had been difficult. For a time as cancer spread through her body, she had even lost her sight. But by some miracle it had returned, enough so that she could see the gold and amber necklace her ex-husband, Robert Nemiroff, had given her as a Christmas present. (Though they had divorced, they remained close.) He was at the hospital as much as he could be while tending to business with Lorraine's most recent play, *The Sign in Sidney Brustein's Window.* Decidedly mixed reviews and the resulting poor box office were imperiling its run. Lorraine's sister, Mamie, had come from California in October and remained in her room full-time.

Early in January Lorraine had asked for Nina. She went to the hospital with a record player and put on a recording of "In the Evening by the Moonlight." She never forgot her friend's reaction. "They say I'm not going to get better, but I must get well," Lorraine told Nina. "I must go down to the South. I've been a revolutionary all my life, but I've got to go down there to find out what kind of revolutionary I am." All Nina could do was listen and take Lorraine's haunted words as a challenge.

Barely twelve hours after the final applause at Carnegie, Nina performed at Lorraine's funeral at Harlem's Church of the Master. Spent and, beyond tears, she played "In the Evening by the Moonlight" and an Israeli folk song that was one of Lorraine's favorites. She nodded approvingly as Paul Robeson, making one of his rare public appearances, recited a verse from a black folk song he said reminded him of Lorraine. "Sometimes I feel like an eagle in the air, an eagle in the air . . . As Lorraine says farewell," Robeson went on, "she bids us keep our heads high and to hold onto our strength and powers, to soar like an eagle." Nina understood exactly what Shelley Winters meant when through her sobs she told the packed sanctuary, "I am unreconciled to her death. . . ."

Lorraine had mentioned that she was working on a new play, tentatively titled "To Be Young, Gifted and Black." Nina stored that title away, determined to use it in some way to honor her friend's memory.

ANDY AND NINA HAD BOOKED a ten-day Caribbean cruise for January. The timing turned out to be fortuitous; the emotional highs and lows of the last two weeks had drained them. They managed smiles and good cheer at a bon voyage party with friends who toasted them with champagne before the ship set sail, though Nina could hardly wait to relax the minute she got to their room. Her plan for uninterrupted rest went awry on the very first day at sea because of a lifeboat drill. "Some shit!" she grumbled, as she, Andy, and Lisa donned their life jackets and hurried to the deck to await further instruction along with the other passengers.

Eventually settled in, Nina slept most of the first few days, finally emerging for a shore trip to Guadalupe. Andy snapped a photo of her and Lisa holding hands as they disembarked, mother and daughter wearing matching sundresses and headbands, though Lisa's was adorned with a little bow. The family returned to New York January 28. As if to bookend the trip, Andy snapped another photo of mother and daughter as they got off the ship in the cold Manhattan air. Perhaps still inspired by Dorothea Towles's fashion instruction, Nina had put on an animal print double-breasted coat and knee-high boots. Lisa, no less fashionable, wore a jacket with a fur-lined hood that framed her face.

Nina had scribbled some notes to herself during the cruise, and on the last day she committed a confession to writing: "I stole a book about psychic power, which could be of tremendous help if I'd use it seriously. Perhaps I shall." The book might have been on her mind when she gave an interview right after the cruise and mused on the mysteries of her talent. "Music chose me," Nina told a reporter for the Newspaper Enterprise Association, which syndicated feature stories. "I'm learning to control this gift, but I hate it too. It's a tremendous responsibility, and I find myself wondering why I was given something other people don't have. Sometimes it makes me feel guilty."

But only sometimes. At other moments Nina was both proud and protective of her art, the lawsuit against Premier and Macy's serving as ample evidence. Max Cohen greeted her on her return with good news. He had settled the suit for a substantial sum—rumored to be $25,000—plus 5 percent of the total amount from sales of the unauthorized *Starring Nina Simone* release. Cohen told the *Amsterdam News* that the settlement would help protect the rights of other artists against unauthorized release of their early works without their permission.

THE HARLEM BRANCH of the YMCA of Greater New York honored Nina February 28. The *Amsterdam News* billed the benefit evening as "the first time she will be presented in concert in the Harlem community," but Jesse H. Walker, the *News* "Theatricals" columnist, used the event to needle Andy. He was miffed that Andy or one of his representatives had ignored the black press before Nina's Carnegie event—they "decided they didn't need the Negro press to cover her concert . . . 'We have sufficient coverage' we were told." Walker said he would mention the YMCA benefit only once and provide no further publicity.

When Andy learned of the columnist's barb, he hurried to smooth things over. Popular as Nina might be, he didn't want to antagonize the *News*, least of all its influential entertainment writer. "We had no intention of demeaning the name of pianist Nina Simone in the civil rights struggle, an apparently mollified Walker wrote in a subsequent column, "since the North Carolina born entertainer has always—not just lately—been in the forefront of those fighting for the Negro's cause. Our concern was with the manner in which we were handled when we made inquiry in the office which handles Miss Simone." He noted that the YMCA had netted $1,296.12 from Nina's benefit.

BY THE TIME NINA RETURNED to the Village Gate in March, "Alabama's got me so upset," the opening line of "Mississippi Goddam," was both descriptive and prophetic. The civil rights front had recently moved in full force to a voter registration drive in tiny Selma, roughly forty miles west of Montgomery, the state capital. Despite extensive work by SNCC in surrounding Dallas County, only 353 blacks—barely 2 percent of those eligible—had been able to register at the courthouse in Selma. White officials restricted office hours and employed a highly dubious literacy test to thwart the registration effort. Dr. King, who had just received the Nobel Peace Prize, came to Selma, adding immeasurable heft to the effort.

When an order from a federal judge to speed up the registration process proved ineffective, movement leaders prepared for decisive action: a march from Selma to Montgomery to confront Governor George Wallace, the region's most vocal segregationist. On Sunday, March 7, the 525 demonstrators, arms linked as they headed through Selma, were confronted by state troopers at the Edmund Pettus Bridge, which spans the Alabama River. As they started to cross, Major John Cloud told the marchers their protest was "not conducive to public safety." He gave them two minutes to disperse. Hosea Williams, one of King's lieutenants, asked for "a word with you."

"There is no word to be had," Cloud replied.

Two more brief exchanges followed, and when the protesters remained in place, Cloud broke the silence: "Troopers advance." Roy Reed of *The New York Times*, among the reporters gathered to cover the protest, provided a vivid account of the action in the next day's paper, chronicling what citizens across the country had seen on their television sets: "The mounted possemen spurred their horses and rode at a run into the retreating mass. The Negroes cried out as they crowded together for protection and the whites on the sidelines whooped and cheered. The Negroes paused in their retreat for perhaps a minute," Reed went on, "still screaming and huddling together. Suddenly there was a report like a gunshot, and a gray cloud spewed over the troopers and the Negroes."

It was tear gas.

"The cloud began covering the highway," Reed continued. "But before the cloud finally hid it all there were several seconds of unobstructed views. Fifteen or twenty nightsticks could be seen through the gas flailing at the heads of the marchers."

President Johnson had deliberately withheld a strong show of federal force before the march, fearing it would only inflame the situation. But after "Bloody Sunday," as the day became known, he faced enormous pressure to act, particularly because King promised to lead another March to Montgomery right away. After intense negotiations among movement leaders and federal and state authorities, however, King agreed to a delay, though he led a symbolic protest on the ninth. On March 15 the president made a nationally televised address to a joint session of Congress laying out his plans for new voting rights legislation. The signal moment in the House chamber came when Johnson, a Southerner himself, embraced the civil rights anthem as his own, promising the country, "And we shall overcome."

That same day fifteen thousand individuals marched through Harlem to protest what had happened in Selma and to support the voting rights drive. Similar demonstrations were taking place in cities and towns across the country, all of them a backdrop to high-wire negotiations between the president and Governor Wallace to guarantee a peaceful march. Finally on March 21 the last legal hurdles were cleared, and the activists set off on their three-day journey to Montgomery.

The news accounts coming out of Alabama consumed Nina, and when she and Art D'Lugoff, still the Gate's impresario, learned that a concert for the marchers was planned for Montgomery, they knew they had to participate. Art immediately canceled the rest of the week's shows, but he didn't just post a notice at the Gate's door. He took out an ad in the March 24 edition of the *Times* to declare that "Miss Nina Simone will not perform TONIGHT. Instead she will be in MONTGOMERY, ALA helping to make a little history (along with her husband Andy Stroud, musician Al Schackman and Art D'Lugoff)."

Art arranged to fly them to Montgomery, but because they couldn't find a direct flight, they had to stop in Atlanta and hire a private plane for the rest of the journey. "We had a real cracker," Art recalled of the pilot. His plane was so small that it took several tries to spread the weight properly so the plane could get airborne. "We arrived safely," Art said, the unsympathetic pilot notwithstanding.

Alabama's white legislators probably didn't know of Nina's "Go Limp," but the song foreshadowed their claims of inappropriate and lascivious behavior during the march. The day before the concert the legislature passed a resolution declaring "evidence of much fornication" among the demonstrators and asserting that "young women are returning to their respective states apparently as unwed expectant mothers."

The concert was held at a muddy ball field on the grounds of the City of St. Jude, a Roman Catholic parochial school and hospital complex near Montgomery's city limits. The constant rain and wind had blown down a tent intended to provide cover, so a stage was hastily erected from coffin crates donated by Selma undertakers and overlaid with sheets of plywood. Harry Belafonte had coordinated the entire concert and pulled together a stellar cast: Sammy Davis Jr. had canceled performances of *Golden Boy* on Broadway to attend; Peter, Paul and Mary, the popular folk trio, were on hand. Leonard Bernstein came because "I just wanted to be with you." He had wanted to bring the entire New York Philharmonic "but there just wasn't room." Tony Bennett, Tony Perkins, Shelley Winters, Billy Eckstine, Odetta, and comedians Nipsey Russell, Dick Gregory, and Alan King were also on hand. Belafonte told *The New York Times* another 150 performers couldn't get flights.

By the time Nina, Andy, Al, and Art got to the grounds, the music had already started and the atmosphere was surreal. A big army searchlight fastened to the back of a truck lighted the area, picking up the tiny outlines of children perched in trees near the stage. More than fifty individuals already had been treated for exhaustion, worn out by the combination of heat, humidity, and the crush of bodies jammed together in the muddy field. Peter, Paul and Mary had played "If I Had a Hammer," which thrilled the crowd, and then moved into the equally apt "The Times They Are A'Changin'." Tony Bennett's sweetly sung "Just in Time" took on special meaning, too. When Nina's turn came, Al looked for a place to plug in his amplifier and asked Belafonte's drummer, Ralph MacDonald, what to do. MacDonald told him to pull up a canvas sheet that had been laid over the plywood, and he would find an outlet. "Oh, my God!" Al exclaimed when he saw the coffin crates holding up the stage.

MacDonald just laughed: "Welcome to Montgomery."

Nina knew exactly what to play even if in this outing "Mississippi Goddam" had only Al's accompaniment. Her enthusiasm made it work, a moment of revelation as she faced the tired but hopeful protesters. "Those kids out in the backwoods knew I was part of their fight before I knew it myself," she recalled, admiring their courage because they didn't have the comfort and protection of fame as she did and risked harm every day. Nina was convinced she had to join them, finding no other word for it than "destiny."

Not surprisingly the crowd gave its biggest cheer to her improvised line: "Selma made me lose my rest." An otherwise exhilarating moment had only one off-kilter element, the mismatch between Nina's message and what she wore. Dressed in a plaid skirt, white blouse, and dark vest, she looked more like a college coed on her way to class than a civil rights protester.

BILLBOARD'S "JAZZ BEAT" COLUMNIST Del Shields devoted his May 29 installment to Nina, praising her for a "fierce integrity that she will not abandon. She does not try to hide behind the show business façade to keep 'the image.' " Her performance a few weeks earlier at Hunter College illustrated his point. Aggravated by a balky microphone, Nina prowled around the stage herself, looking to fix the problem. When it was finally taken care of, she sat back down and announced, "I'm sick of this concert already; too many difficulties!" But she didn't stop. Instead she wove her aggravation into an extemporaneous lyric. Shields declined to criticize her, trying instead to give perspective to her behavior. "A high degree of honesty can sometimes produce explosive consequences," he wrote. "People who know Nina well realize that her occasional outbursts stem more from pain than anger." Not only had her good friend Lorraine died, but Malcolm X, the Black Muslim leader, had been gunned down in Harlem February 21. Nina was especially close to his widow, Betty Shabazz, and their children because Malcolm had moved them to Mount Vernon for safety after his split with Elijah Muhammad, the head of the Black Muslim movement. The loss of these two individuals only deepened Nina's convictions and heightened her awareness of how race was shaping her own place in the world.

Shields had tied his column to the release of *I Put a Spell on You*, which went on the magazine's Top 200 June 26. It stayed there for two months, rising to number ninety-nine, which made it somewhat more successful than the *in concert* album, but once again not a hit. The single of the title track, however, was more successful, going on the *Billboard* R&B chart July 23 and rising to number twenty-three. It was Nina's best showing on the singles chart since the fall of 1959 with "I Love You, Porgy."

WHEN NINA RETURNED to the studio in May, Philips, as Colpix had, looked for different strategies that might increase her sales. But Nina's best songs still turned out to be those that moved her and took advantage of her own arrangements. Though in later years she would chafe at comparisons to Billie Holiday, right now she paid homage, first with "Tell Me More and More and Then Some," which Holiday wrote, and then with "Strange Fruit," Abel Meeropol's anti-lynching masterpiece, forever associated with Holiday. Unlike the original, Nina's had no introduction. She jumped right into "Southern trees bearing strange fruit." She employed the same dramatics used to such good effect in "Pirate Jenny" so that in her hands "Strange Fruit" became an indictment, not a lament.

The tour de force of the sessions, however, was a ten-minute version of "Sinnerman," a traditional song taken from a Bible verse and arranged by Nina as a frantic plea for absolution. Live versions went on even longer, according to Bobby, who was responsible for keeping the steady beat and recognizing rhythm changes when Nina "would just swing out." The end result once again evoked those St. Luke revival meetings decades earlier, and somewhere in this charged performance, even though she was in the studio with only her musicians and the technicians, Nina had "come through" again and taken the music to another plane.

In an inverview with Doug McClelland, the editor of *Record World*, a new addition to the music trades, Nina reveled in her intensity. "I feel emotion is dying, what we feel is dying, everything is so orderly," she told him. "Raising your voice has become a crime! I want to evoke joy, sadness, pain. . . ."

ON JUNE 26, Nina, Andy, Lisa, and a nanny, along with Lisle, Bobby, and Rudy, left for a six-country tour that started in England the first week of July. The *Amsterdam News* published a photograph of Nina at the New York airport just before she was getting ready to leave. A variation on the theme of the booklet Andy had prepared a few months earlier, the picture showed a sweet family moment of a mother reading to her daughter. Nina wore a stylish gray dress with a capelike jacket and a turban on her head. Lisa had on a checked dress and shiny patent leather shoes, her white anklets matching her little hat.

Arriving ahead of the first opening night, everyone went sightseeing. Nina and Andy rented bicycles with a little seat for Lisa on one of them and "pedaled around town like a couple of kids." A photo of Nina and Lisa on a bike made it back to the United States, where *The Philadelphia Tribune* gave it prominent play on the entertainment page.

Nina was booked into Annie's Room, a club named for the singer Annie Ross, who had been part of the groundbreaking vocal trio Lambert, Hendricks and Ross. She left the group in 1962 and moved to London. Friends suggested she open a club—they would put up the money if she would be the hostess. By the time of Nina's two-week stint, Annie's Room had established itself as one of London's livelier nightspots, known not only for the acts it brought but also for the celebrities in the audience. The actor Peter O'Toole often came by. So did Jimmy Baldwin when he was in town, and occasionally they could be persuaded to join in an impromptu group number onstage. Ross remembered one particularly boozy version of the blues that left everyone in stitches.

The last time Ross had crossed paths with Nina—in Pittsburgh while Ross was still with her singing trio—Nina had been frosty. "She would only talk to Jon Hendricks," Ross recalled. And nobody knew why. Nina was all smiles now and ready to meet an entirely new audience. David Nathan, a young fan who attended opening night with his father and uncle, remembered that Nina stayed away from her more controversial material—no "Mississippi Goddam"—and instead sang such favorites as "Zungo."

The crowd gave her a "rapturous reception," according to *Melody Maker*, though the reviewer found Nina "better on record," as the headline on his story read. "Her music is fine, her piano playing tremendous," he wrote. "But her tortured facial expressions and cabaret-style histrionics don't fit the picture. It's all a bit too 'showbiz' for comfort."

Nina didn't care. She drank in the loud applause and London's cosmopolitan atmosphere. "This place is something," she wrote her younger brother, Sam. "I've done lots of traveling in the states but London doesn't seem to have anything in common with the states." Although everyone spoke English, it was a different kind of English. She got a kick out of "jolly good" or "splendid," or "swiftly" as a compliment for doing something fast, she wrote. "All the music is Negro!" she added. "<u>All</u> the music, mind you."

She went further in an interview with the *Evening Star*. "The nice thing is that they give credit and respect where it is due, something they don't do too much at home," she said. By this time the Beatles and the Rolling Stones were all over the U.S. record charts, and they always acknowledged their debt to the American rhythm-and-blues artists who had influenced them. Two of the Beatles, who had just returned to London from a European tour, had even dropped in one night, Bobby said, though years later, he couldn't recall which two.

Nina, Andy, and Lisa were staying in the Mayfair section of London, just off the city's famous Park Lane. Nina took time in her room one evening to write Langston a letter—long overdue, she admitted—reflecting not only on the trip but also on how much his autobiographical *The Big Sea* had affected her. She was sorting so many things out in her mind now, and deprived of Lorraine's counsel when it would have meant so much, she turned to Langston to fill the void.

"I read chapters over and over again—'cause certain ones paint complete pictures for me and I get completely absorbed: then, too, if I'm in a negative mood and want to get more negative (about the racial problem, I mean) if I want to get downright mean and violent I go straight to this book and there is <u>also</u> material for that," Nina wrote. "Amazing. I use the book—what I mean is I underline all meaningful sentences to me—I make comments in pencil about certain paragraphs. Etc. And as I said there is a wealth of knowledge concerning the negro problem, especially if one wants to <u>trace</u> the many many areas that we've had it rough in all these years—

sometimes when I'm with white 'liberals' who want to know why we're so bitter—I forget (I don't forget—I just get tongue-tied) how <u>complete</u> has been the white race's rejection of us all these years. And then when this happens, I go get your book."

Despite two successful weeks at Annie's Room and a performance on the popular television show *Ready Steady Go!*, Nina closed her letter on a strangely down note. Her melancholy overwhelmed any excitement about playing for the first time in France and Belgium. "No pleasure," she told Langston, "just work."

NINA GOT STAR BILLING at the big jazz festival held in the ancient port town of Antibes Juan-les-Pins on France's Mediterranean coast. Nervous the first night, she quickly found her stride after she sized up the crowd. "I needed the audience to get to know me," she told a reporter later. "The second the audience knew that it could listen to me I had nothing more to prove, and I was more relaxed."

Nina and the trio also played a private party for a wealthy family in Monaco, followed by a dazzling meal on a docked ship that had been turned into a restaurant. Andy was both manager and maestro, coordinating Nina and the band and doing his best to keep her on an even keel. The French jazz press treated her like the toast of the town, and ever mindful of her need to relax—by shopping or chatting poolside at the hotel with friends—Andy orchestrated who could talk to her and when. He put off one persistent reporter, Philippe Carles of *Jazz*, for almost half a day before finally telling Carles he could accompany Nina in a taxi to a late-night job in the nearby village of Valbonne.

Carles found Nina "haughty but courteous." Andy instructed him not to be timid: "Get close to her, and don't be afraid . . . get acquainted." Nina, however, did little to put Carles at ease. "Journalists!" she roared when he tossed her what he considered an innocent question. "But I've met tons of them since I arrived in France! You must be at least the fifteenth." Carles tried to draw her out about her live performances. "I never sing the same way in a cabaret, in a concert hall, or at a festival," she told him. "I change my repertoire according to setting. I know when I need to sing something sweet, sentimental, fast or violent."

Nina was irritated when Carles asked if she worried too much about the kind of piano she played. How well could he get his information with a substandard tape recorder? she snapped. "Of course the quality of the piano is the most important thing. I am first a pianist. When the piano is lousy, I leave." By this time they were at the club, and Nina immediately went over to the piano and struck a few keys. "No," she said, "it's not the worst." Then she played a chord lower down on the keyboard. "But it's not the best either." It would do. The piano bench was another matter; it wasn't a bench at all but rather a wicker chair with extra cushions that matched the club decor. Carles translated Andy's request to the manager to get a real bench. But he waved off the suggestion. On this night neither Nina nor Andy chose to argue.

Nina was more philosophical when she talked with a reporter from *Jazz Hot*, picking up on some of the things she had written to Langston. "I feel my origins very deeply," she said. "My art is anchored in the culture of my people, and I am immensely proud . . . Because of a lack of respect that endures even after hundreds of years, each time I go to a new country, I feel obliged, proudly, to assert my race, and don't fool yourself," she went on, "no matter what I sing, whether it's a ballad or a lament, it's all the same thing—I want people to know who I am."

Pressed about the way she put songs together, Nina could only say, "I make a concentrated effort, even though people have told me that it comes to me naturally. It's the atmosphere of the moment. I'm convinced it has to be that way. Time passes no matter what we do, and it's time that matters, not action. When I sing, there's a moment in my life that passes by."

Asked about her musical influences, Nina's penchant for recasting the past surfaced again. "I know, as people have often told me, that I'm similar to Billie Holiday," she said. "I suppose that's because we have identical lives. In one or two ways I have gone through things that she went through, both musically and personally; always pushed down, rejected. That's the way it is. When you are at such a

point, you sing with a sort of resigned, disillusioned air about you."
That the actual particulars of their lives, from childhood on, differed
greatly was immaterial. In this telling it didn't matter to Nina that
she was never in the grip of a well-chronicled drug addiction like
Holiday's or the legal and health problems that came with it. Emotionally, at least, Nina felt as though she struggled just as much, and
the feeling spoke to the melancholy that could cloud her life.

The European tour ended in Coblenz, Germany, on August 1, a
slice of the performance preserved in a photo of Nina and the trio
onstage that was published a week later in the *Pittsburgh Courier* as
a kind of welcome home.

OVER THE SUMMER CORE asked Nina to join an "Artists
Evening for CORE" to raise money. Andy sent regrets, but he did

Nina relaxing at the Fire Island, New York,
home of Art and Avital D'Lugoff
(*Courtesy of the D'Lugoffs*)

offer Nina's services for benefit concerts in various cities at a reduced cost: $1,000 for weekdays, $1,500 for a Saturday or Sunday. Normally, Nina received $2,500 or $3,000 per concert, he explained. "I am doing this because it will help the civil rights cause, give Miss Simone a chance to do more for the cause and at the same time provide her with enough compensation to prevent her losing money," Andy added.

Right away CORE sent out notices to its California chapters letting them know that Nina was going to be in Los Angeles in October and in San Francisco the first week of November. The Stockton chapter responded immediately, but national CORE officials worried that the local group couldn't cover the expenses. However, East Coast chapters had expressed interest, convinced that Nina would draw well, and discussions with Andy continued about later concerts in the region.

Her latest album, *Pastel Blues,* was released in late summer and showed up on the *Billboard* charts October 16. As measured by the music trade, it was the least successful of Nina's Philips albums thus far, rising only to number 139. The views of *The Washington Post*'s Byron Roberts reflected the *Billboard* tally. He found the album "done with aplomb but with a modicum of Miss Simone's great talent." Except for "Strange Fruit." "Miss Simone," he wrote, "could well be a Pied Piper of Freedom marchers on this one."

At least this reviewer had recognized the passionate intensity that now informed Nina's work. "The first thing I saw in the morning when I woke up was my black face in the bathroom mirror," she wrote later, reflecting on the moment, "and that fixed the way I felt about myself for the rest of the day, that I was a black-skinned woman in a country where you could be killed because of that one fact."

All of this internal turbulence fueled Nina's latest composition. She put it down on vinyl in the next session with Horace Ott. Simply titled "Four Women," it compressed two centuries of black history into four compact verses, as if she was turning in a final class paper in song, the end point of a highly personal course of study and a synthesis of her gifts and her identity, one fueling the other. Each verse described a woman who was an archetype of an era: Aunt Sarah, the mammy; Sephronia, the light-skinned mulatto; Sweet Thing, the young prostitute; and Peaches, a surly street tough. The opening line declared a truth: "My skin is black." And the muscular lyrics talked of slavery, rape, prostitution, and the threat of wanting "to kill the first mother I see."

If "Mississippi Goddam," its biting lyrics aside, had undeniable bounce, no one would confuse "Four Women" with a "show tune." Nina played simple chords and an occasional single-note pattern. Rudy's restrained guitar and few measures of flute counterpoint matched the quiet strokes from Lisle and Bobby, as if all three were whispering, not wanting to interrupt as Nina spun out her story. It made the final two lines, about the street tough, all the more compelling when Nina shouted, "My name is PEACHES!" Up to that moment "Four Women" had been in a minor key. In a musical exclamation point, Nina ended with a triumphant chord in A major.

15. Images

~ 1966 ~

Andy's negotiations with CORE had borne fruit. He and the organization agreed that Nina would do six benefit concerts in the Northeast starting January 21, 1966, in Pittsburgh and concluding January 28 in New Rochelle, New York. Something close to military precision would be required to get Nina and the musicians from one place to another, but Andy knew they could do it. Despite the lack of formal training in management or the music business, he had caught on fast. Some of it was instinct, some was learned from his association with pros like Felix Gerstman, who taught him about scheduling and promotion. Perhaps most important, he knew his star well. He understood what Nina needed at each performance to make her comfortable, from sound checks (at least two hours ahead of time) to microphones (two upright, one with a miniature boom) to a Steinway piano tuned at 440 concert pitch. The dressing room had to be clean and with a mirror, preferably full length. And Andy handled all of the finances; for these concerts, Nina got half beforehand, with the rest delivered at intermission.

Alfred Wertheimer, a freelance photographer who had accompa-

Nina and Andy at an airport terminal in the winter of 1965
(Alfred Wertheimer)

nied Nina and Andy to Buffalo for a December performance, considered Andy "the rudder that kept things moving in the proper direction. He was the businessman, the pragmatist, not the artist who had fifty songs floating through his head. He was thinking about how do we get on the plane, how do we get to the opening. He had to do the nuts and bolts of the business end of things." Wertheimer captured Andy in full command during the Buffalo trip striding purposefully through an airport, a look of pleasant concentration on his face.

Nina hardly lacked for material appropriate to a civil rights benefit. "Mississippi Goddam," "Four Women," "Old Jim Crow," "Go Limp," and "Strange Fruit" were on point. She could also draw on the songs she had arranged with unmistakable allusions to Africa. "Be My Husband," which Andy had written, never failed to catch on with an audience. Nina turned it into a rhythmic chant, performed away from the keyboard with hand claps and a few spontaneous dance moves. When the *San Francisco Chronicle*'s popular jazz critic Ralph J. Gleason saw her do a version at the hungry i, one of the city's popular clubs, he described her as "some exotic queen of some secret ritual" that he was fortunate to witness. The song was even more compelling before an audience that found such common ground with the singer before them.

The concerts might have been more successful artistically than financially, however. The Pittsburgh chapter, facing money problems even before the benefit, failed to earn as much as the members hoped. But chapter president Nicholas Flournoy promised the national CORE office that its debts would be paid with proceeds from "new and more intelligent efforts . . ."

Nina was relieved to get back to Mount Vernon before a big winter storm engulfed the city, wanting to enjoy the heavy snowfall from the warm confines of the house. When the weather let up, she wrote in one of the notes she occasionally made about a day's events, "the whole family got together and we shoveled snow to make slopes for sledding." Andy's sons came to play with Lisa and some neighborhood friends, and Nina joined in. "I felt so relaxed and free of any depressing thoughts."

A HAUNTING SONG called "Images" stood out on Nina's latest album, *Let It All Out*, which was released in February. She had set the poem, by Waring Cuney, one of the many writers acclaimed during the Harlem Renaissance, to music, choosing a minor-key melody that resembled a chant one might hear on the Jewish high holy days. It underscored the poignancy of a woman "who does not know her beauty. She thinks her brown body has no glory." Though the lyrics and Nina's delivery were much less fierce than "Four Women," "Images" was nonetheless a first cousin to her own composition. During one of the first live performances early in February at Haverford College, a small liberal arts school outside Philadelphia, Nina told the largely white audience that she was tired of "having to hear, and see and feel and read about the indignities and injustices" suffered by blacks.

In Philadelphia a few weeks later at the East End, a new supper club that had once housed a radio station, Nina was no less direct.

She made the large room, which seated six hundred, feel like home, "as if she were in her own world," according to *Philadelphia Tribune* reviewer Jake Sherman. The night he attended, Nina performed only a dozen numbers. "And yet the intensity and truth of her often strange songs made every individual in the place an intimate sharer in that world. To hear her sing," Sherman continued, apologizing to his readers ahead of time for his torrent of words, "is to be brought into abrasive contact with the black heart and to feel the power and beauty which for centuries have beat there. It is like a journey to a dark and uncharted nether region of the soul where hate has mated with love and given birth to searing, tortured anguish . . . It was an evening that left us deeply moved and at the same time badly shaken"—precisely the kind of evening Nina wanted.

ALONG WITH HER MUSIC, Nina's stage dress had grown more provocative and had drawn more attention, too, though part of this resulted from a double standard. While it was true that male performers, usually dressed in generic suits or tuxedos, left little to talk about, writers, most of them men, still felt free to comment on what women entertainers wore. Sherman highlighted how good Nina looked in her gold-sequined blouse and "tight black pants," and a few weeks later another reviewer said she stood out in what he described as "gold lamé pajamas." Double standard or not, Nina was probably pleased. She knew that if she wore sequins and lamé, her outfits would sparkle in the stage lights.

Nina actually ended up in fashion stories after she attended a March 18 show in New York put on by Ohrbach's, the well-known department store, and publicized as "Ohrbach's line-for-line copies of Paris fashions." The *Washington Post* story singled out Nina among all the celebrities as being the "chicest" for her suggestive and revealing new outfit: off-white crocheted pants and matching top with see-through holes worn over a dark body stocking. Nina had changed her hairstyle, too. Gone for the moment was the fancy hairpiece from Frenchie Casimir. In its place was a close-cropped cut of tight curls that she called a "freedom cap."

·

Nina sporting one of her new looks at Leo's Casino in
Cleveland as bassist Lisle Atkinson looks on.
(Cleveland Public Library/Photograph Collection)

NINA FOUND MORE REASON to complain about the music
business in May when Colpix, her former label, released an album
called *Nina Simone with Strings*—though only six of the ten tunes
had string accompaniment. The new arrangements had been added
during an instruments-only recording session in Los Angeles the previous June with a twenty-two-piece orchestra: violins, violas, cellos,
and four French horns. Still wanting to mine its catalog, Colpix
apparently thought it could catch a trend and sell some records by

setting these previously recorded vocals amid strings. However, the liner notes were careful to avoid suggesting that Nina and the orchestra had actually recorded together. She must have taken private satisfaction when the album turned out to be little more than a curiosity.

AFTER PLAYING A JAZZ FESTIVAL in Atlanta, another of entrepreneur George Wein's projects, Nina returned to his Newport event in July, a place that always brought out something special in her. Three years earlier, Nina used her forty-minute set to create a half-dozen mini-dramas. A highlight was her version of George Gershwin's "Bess, You Is My Woman Now." She changed it to "Porgy, I's Your Woman Now," but halfway through, she segued into an up-tempo rhythm, shouted a key change to the trio, and took off into Oscar Brown's version of the well-known Paul Laurence Dunbar poem "When Malindy Sings." At the line "I want to listen from the breast of angel's wings/Soft and sweet, Swing Low . . . " she made another segue, this time to a full chorus, a cappella, of "Swing Low Sweet Chariot" and completely changed the mood. She had taken the music—and the audience—from the vernacular to the spiritual and come back one final time with a determined "When Malindy Sings."

This year Nina performed on the second evening of the festival, following what had been, by several accounts, uninspiring earlier acts. While many singers choose upbeat numbers to open a show, particularly on a windy night in an outdoor setting, Nina opened with a ballad, "You've Got to Learn," giving special emphasis to the ripe imagery of overcoming heartbreak and "pocketing pride": "You got to learn to leave the table/When love's no longer being served." The audience seemed to hang on every word of the subsequent songs, transfixed even through a slow and weary "Porgy."

Nina closed her set with "Mississippi Goddam," but on this night instead of the bouncy "show tune," she offered pure swing, the kind of treatment one might hear at the Village Gate with a hot combo. The lyrics, though, had lost none of their bite, and Nina had updated the opening verse once again. In place of Tennessee, it was

Watts that "made me lose my rest," a reference to the troubled neighborhood of Los Angeles that had seen devastating riots the previous summer.

Nina and the trio left the stage to sustained applause and shouts of "more." The MC tried to quiet the crowd, reminding them that a full evening of music remained. He even started to introduce the next act, but the audience wouldn't let him continue. Finally, he announced that Nina, accompanied only by Lisle on the bass, would sing one more song. She sat down and noodled at the keyboard for a minute, tossing a good-natured "shut up—shut up" to a fan who kept hollering. Then she sang another affecting ballad about romance, "Music for Lovers," that was as hopeful in its message as "Mississippi Goddam" was bleak. "There would be a time," she promised, "when the whole world would discover that love's the only thing worthwhile." (*The Boston Globe*'s music critic still talked about the performance months later, citing it as one reason fans should attend Nina's week in November at a local club.)

Just as Nina finished up the summer circuit—after Newport came Pittsburgh and then New York City's Rheingold Festival—Philips released another album filled primarily with songs from the 1965 recording sessions. It was called *Wild Is the Wind* after one of the songs—originally recorded ten years earlier by Johnny Mathis for the film of the same name. Less fussy than earlier Philips productions, the record featured more ballads than up-tempo numbers. "Four Women," which the label also released as a single, was the second track and seemed even more blunt coming right after the rock 'n' roll "I Love Your Lovin' Ways."

Though the controversy in the South over "Mississippi Goddam" was hardly surprising, Nina never expected "Four Women" to provoke conflict—and in the North. But Dolly Banks, manager of WHAT, a white-owned Philadelphia station proud of its attention to the city's black community, was so concerned about the song she took it off the air after reading a copy of "Night Life," a flier distributed at local clubs. The flier called "Four Women" insulting to blacks, noting that some listeners didn't like the last stanza about "Peaches," the street tough: "My skin is brown, my manner tough/I'll kill the first mother I see; my life has been rough . . . " (Critical reaction in print went in the opposite direction. The *Evening Bulletin* correspondent dismissed the song: "If you squeeze 14 or so bland words into four beats without rhythm, rhyme or story content, you get 14 bland words.")

At the same time a program director at WWRL in New York, one of the city's two black-oriented stations, banned the song after one listener complained about the stanza describing "Sweet Thing," the prostitute. And white listeners didn't like the verse about mixed-race "Sephronia," particularly the line "My father was rich and white/He forced my mother late one night. . . . " A spokesman for Nina told the *New York Post* that the lyrics had been read by civil rights activists and by "a cross-section of the community" and no one had found them to be "objectionable."

Supporters in both cities protested with telegrams, letters, and postcards, and a few had even threatened to demonstrate. Both stations ultimately relented and put "Four Women" back on the air.

Nina gave an unexpected live performance of the song in October when she was honored in Philadelphia as the woman of the year by a local jazz club. As the honoree, she wasn't supposed to sing, but the audience insisted, and afterward they gave her a standing ovation.

When the *Chicago Defender* got wind of the "Four Women" controversy, the paper sent its "inquiring photographer" out on the street to interview residents, and the responses reinforced Nina's view that the song was not objectionable at all. Typical was the comment of Thelma Hinkle, who described herself as a beautician: "Some people do not appreciate this kind of song and consider it vulgar. Once you really listen, there can be no conclusion other than that the song is packed with wisdom."

Nina herself described "Four Women" as an homage to black women, their varying skin tones influencing "their ideas of beauty and their own importance. . . . All the song did was to tell what entered the minds of most black women in America when they thought about themselves: their complexions, their hair—straight, kinky, natural, which? And what other women thought of them. Black women didn't know what the hell they wanted because they were defined by things they didn't control."

Andy didn't like this kind of publicity even if it did call attention to Nina. It was one thing for her to sign a biracial petition against South African apartheid, appear at a fashion benefit for the New York chapter of the NAACP, or do benefit concerts, which were seen as acceptable forms of quasi-political activity. But it was quite another to be associated with racial controversy. Andy understood that Nina—and he, too—could be hurt economically because some white promoter somewhere wouldn't want to hire her. "My wife is first and foremost an artist," he insisted. "Her life is her music." But nothing could stop Nina from appearing at a black power rally in Philadelphia convened by Stokely Carmichael, the new head of SNCC, who made no apologies for his confrontational tactics. Moved to tears when she introduced Carmichael, Nina told the one thousand who had gathered that "I have been thinking of some of these things since I was three years old." Nina would take it as a singular honor when Carmichael, referring to her respectfully as "Miss Simone," later publicly praised the lyrics of "Mississippi Goddam."

NINA'S MERCURIAL SIDE surfaced again when she played a jazz concert in the city on November 13 headlined by Herbie Mann. By the time she came out it was almost midnight, but even so she didn't feel like playing right away. Instead, she chatted with the audience about her new outfit, even more revealing than her usual wardrobe. "I wonder what my mother would think if she saw me in this dress," Nina joked before going on to suggest the different things Kate Waymon might have said.

She started "Porgy," but midway through she stopped to talk. She sprinkled her comments with observations about ongoing civil rights activities, drawing applause from some in the racially mixed audience. She got up from the keyboard a little later and danced while she sang a couple of songs. The steps weren't really choreography but rather an integral part of her musical expression, spontaneous, sharply rhythmic, and much more daring now than the few sensuous hip swivels she had done to "See-Line Woman" on *The Steve Allen Show* two years earlier. Introducing what she said was a "Negro spiritual," Nina went from prayerful to playful, announcing "I'm saving my body for God . . . but if God doesn't want it, I hope my boyfriend does." There were audible titters in the audience, the kind that suggest either genuine amusement or the uneasiness that comes from having been told too much. Those apparently in the latter group left. However, most remained, and when Nina finished shortly before one a.m. they cheered and clapped for more.

Stu Chase, a local white disc jockey, had left early. He railed against Nina on the air the next day, castigating her dance moves as "the most disgusting exhibition I've ever seen." The *Tribune* reported that it received complaints about the concert, too. One man, who described himself as a professional musician, said he had seen Nina many times before and was disappointed. She "didn't even put on a show," he claimed. "She wiggled, talked, and dragged everything out until people started asking each other what was going on." Another caller said there was too much talking, especially about civil rights and black power. He didn't like the dancing either. "A girl with her looks," he said, "ought to realize that people are paying money to HEAR her."

Asked for comment, Andy told the *Tribune* the show had been great, that barely a handful of people had walked out, and that Nina's references to a "boyfriend"—even though she was married—were harmless. "That's typical Nina. That's what makes her great. She's at the peak of her career."

He sloughed off any concern about her erratic behavior. Noting the standing ovation she received, Andy said she would have done an encore if it had not been so late.

Nina's fans came to her defense. Several accused Chase of a double standard. William Mathis, head of the local CORE chapter, told the *Tribune* that Chase's comments were not only in "bad taste" but racist, too. While Nina talked about racial issues, Mathis said, she never mentioned " 'black power' per se." Rather, her references to "Negro pride" were central to her performance. "Whenever any black person begins to assert racial pride, there's a great deal of negative reaction by whites," Mathis went on. "With Nina's natural hairdo, it makes some people more uneasy." To emphasize his support of Nina, he invited her back to perform at a CORE benefit December 16—Andy called it "the vindication trip." Another fan noted the racial double standard, citing what he said was the lack of criticism of comic Lenny Bruce, who delighted in breaking taboos in both subject matter and language. "Everybody said he had 'artistic license' to do as he pleased and said he was a 'great artist.' But when a black person does something controversial, it's called 'disgusting.' " The implied criticism of Nina's looks incensed a female fan. "I say Miss Simone is indeed beautiful to those who understand her and realize her aim and mission."

ANDY HAD FORMED a relationship with a new promoter, Ron Delsener, a young man who had co-produced the Beatles' record-breaking concert at Shea Stadium a year earlier. A few months after that event he played a major role in organizing the Rheingold Festival in Central Park, where Nina had done two performances. "She'd be very surly," he recalled. But that didn't faze him. "She knew I could take her—I was gentle to her and made her laugh. That broke the ice. You know I felt kind of bad for her. She wasn't a great beauty, but she had a lot of talent," he added, confirming, perhaps unconsciously, that at least in the world of entertainment, artistic gifts counted for only so much.

Just before Thanksgiving Delsener presented Nina in her first solo appearance at Philharmonic Hall at Lincoln Center. But she would be performing with new musicians. In the space of a few weeks, two of her sidemen had left. Lisle was first. Sometime in the spring Nina, at Andy's urging, had pestered him to play the electric bass. Lisle resisted in no uncertain terms and the matter was dropped. But when they got to Chicago in May for a job at the Plugged Nickel in the city's popular "old town" area, Andy started in again, and apparently worn down by the entreaties, Lisle agreed to give it a try. Andy rounded up an instrument so Lisle could practice for a half hour. "I played one tune," he recalled, "I put it down—and then he asks me to play it again. He had me up to three or four tunes. At that point," he went on, "I must have snapped. I took the instrument, broke it, smashed it into the wall and it splintered."

Enraged, Nina yelled at Lisle and called him names. He shouted back. When they finally stopped fighting, Lisle walked out of the club, went to the hotel, packed his clothes, and was paying the bill in the lobby when Andy found him.

"Where are you going?" he asked.

"Wasn't I just fired?" Lisle said.

Andy reassured him that it wasn't the case at all and promised he would smooth things over with Nina. Lisle was temporarily satisfied, but he threatened to quit if Andy mentioned the electric bass again. For the next several weeks, calm prevailed. But then Andy started in again. "That's when I said 'OK, that's it,' " Lisle recalled. "I wasn't going to do that for nobody."

Bobby's subsequent departure was more amicable. He simply told Nina he needed more work. "She'd play two weeks and then be off a month. I can't pay no rent that way," Bobby recalled. He wanted more stability, and he had already done jobs with Dakota Staton. More were lined up with Hazel Scott.

Rudy Stevenson was staying on. If he and Nina didn't click as easily as she had with Al Schackman, musically they got along well. He was also composing, and Andy had even proposed a deal to represent his music. The new sidemen for this Philharmonic concert were Lloyd Buchanan on bass and Charles Crosby on drums.

Ever the thoughtful friend, Langston sent Nina a good-luck telegram before the concert. This one had special resonance because the evening marked the introduction of a new song, Langston's penetrating poem "Backlash Blues," which Nina had set to music. Much more blunt than many of his other poems and stories, which so often delivered their pointed message with devilish humor, "Backlash" dovetailed with Nina's growing passion for civil rights. "You give me second-class houses/And second-class schools/Do you think that all colored folks are just second-class fools?" was just one of the verses.

Amsterdam News reviewer Raymond Robinson admitted that he was not an avid fan of Nina's. Aware of her "unstable temperament," he wrote after the event, "I approached the concert with a tongue-in-cheek attitude." But he was won over the minute she walked onstage in a "stunning African motif hat and gown ensemble." The program credited it to Khadejha, a Philadelphia-born designer who was known for creating unusual designs in colorful African, kanga-cotton material and most likely provided the caftan and turban Nina had worn two months earlier, when she received her jazz society honor. Raymond also noted that most of Nina's musical selections wove in African rhythms, suggesting a new synthesis intended to make her music and her image match.

Yet for all the controversy over "Four Women" and the obvious message of "Backlash Blues," Nina still had plenty of mainstream appeal. Right after the Philharmonic concert, she appeared in the annual Thanksgiving Day parade in Manhattan on a float, "Autumn Splendor," dressed up like a butterfly with enormous wings protruding from her back. She was supposed to be "a butterfly upon a wheel" in a paraphrase of Alexander Pope's "Epistle to Dr. Arbuthnot." When "Autumn Splendor" approached the reviewing stand, Nina sang out "Blue Skies." Two weeks later she headlined a Brooklyn College concert, the overwhelmingly white audience filled with fans.

"You know all my music," Nina exclaimed at one point, "and I'm glad."

On this night she wore another of her eye-catching outfits, a white sarong with large blue, yellow, and red dots and a matching turban. To Alan Mitchell Nadel, who reviewed the concert for the school newspaper, she was not so much an entertainer as "a West Indian sorceress."

16. My Only Groove Is Moods

~ 1967 ~

Andy and Nina signed with RCA at the end of 1966. It was a step up to one of the majors that already had demonstrated a commitment to black artists, among them Harry Belafonte and Nina's good friend Miriam Makeba. Andy had also formed Ninandy Music as the publisher for the couple's compositions and expanded his management duties by signing a handful of new acts. Most important, he had negotiated Nina's four-city tour with Bill Cosby, a young black comedian and actor and right now one of the hottest acts around. He was a co-star in the popular *I Spy* television series with Robert Culp and had already earned four gold records, the first comedian ever to do so. Eager to build on his success, Warner Bros., Cosby's label, had recently launched "Bill Cosby month" with a goal of selling a million albums in a six-week period.

The tour started in St. Louis on February 13, swung east to Baltimore in Cosby's private plane, made a stop at Howard University in Washington, D.C., and at Philharmonic Hall in New York. In Baltimore, Nina drew as much attention for how she looked in her see-through fishnet outfit as for what she sang. Several Baltimore Colts football players in the front rows blushed with embarrassment when she sauntered onstage to catcalls and whistles. A few whispered that maybe she didn't have anything on underneath. (She did.) Perhaps the distracted audience wanted to look more than listen, and the crowd's tepid response irritated her. She chided them for living up to the city's reputation as "tough to move."

Although Nina seemed happy and pleased when Howard University students in Washington, D.C., presented her with a gift after her performance there, offstage she was coming apart. The strange performance in Philadelphia in November was, in hindsight, a symptom of a much more serious problem, as was the melancholy she expressed in that letter to Langston a year and a half earlier, when she should have embraced her overseas success. Nina loved working with Cosby and appreciated how well he treated her, but none of this, including a responsive audience, could ward off the private turmoil that left her distracted, fatigued, and, in the worst episodes, delusional. Even though she was exhausted, she couldn't sleep, "and my head was filled with music and snatches from speeches or conversations from the past two years," she recalled in her memoir. In some moments she went blank, losing all track of time until a noise broke the disconcerting trance.

When the tour got to New York, Nina was hardly functioning. Andy found her in her dressing room at Lincoln Center staring into the mirror while putting brown makeup in her hair. "I was wearing a white gown, and all I could think about was how the color of my gown should contrast with the rest of me, which had to be the same all over," she wrote.

Andy had never seen Nina like this, and he was frightened.

"Don't tell Bill!" she pleaded.

When Andy tried to talk to her, she insisted he was her nephew and not her husband "and we were going to fly back up to heaven together and he'd better do what I said because I was Grandma Moses." In Nina's retelling, her behavior got even more bizarre. "I looked over at Andy and for a moment I could see right through his skin, right through as if he were covered in plastic . . . And then it was gone, and I was my normal self again."

Rudy sensed a problem even if he could never have imagined the fantastical scene that Nina described. She was late, which she never was for an event as important as this one. She was supposed to go on first, and when it got close to showtime and she still hadn't arrived, Cosby opened. Nina finally came into the hall, offered no explanations, and performed with no apparent difficulty. But her behavior was the most obvious clue yet that she might be suffering from a mental illness. For now, however, she and Andy were grateful the troubling moment had passed.

THOUGH NINA HAD ALREADY MOVED to RCA, Philips still had one more album to release. *High Priestess of Soul* included material from recording sessions several months earlier. The cover featured a cartoonlike drawing of Nina in profile and wearing a gigantic headpiece that evoked tribal royalty. The song selections mirrored earlier records—such tunes as "I Hold No Grudge," with Nina set again amid Hal Mooney's strings, and a wittily suggestive "Brown Eyed Handsome Man," the Chuck Berry tune. But the music was less important than the image presented on the album jacket. "High Priestess of Soul" reflected how Nina saw herself now in performance, and the "priestess" part did capture the otherworldly way she sometimes behaved in private. The moniker also evoked the mysticism and the dash of the exotic Nina sought to impart from the stage, helped by the turbans and flamboyant earrings routinely a part of her dress. And on those nights when everything worked, she swept up an audience, even the doubters. No less than Leonard Feather, a producer and a music critic for the *Los Angeles Times*, pronounced her "one of the most hypnotic performers on any stage today."

This last Philips album provided a clear contrast with the first record RCA planned to release, *Nina Simone Sings the Blues*. As the title suggested, it featured Nina in a musically intimate setting. Rudy was the only one from her touring trio on the sessions. Two highly regarded studio musicians, Bernard Purdie on drums and Ernie Hayes, who had played the celeste on a Philips record, joined him. Purdie had known Andy since his detective days, and Andy had asked him to recruit the rest of the band. "When she sat down to play, we could easily get into what she wanted," Purdie recalled, especially Hayes, who made sure his organ work was a complement to Nina's piano, not her competition.

The sessions flowed amicably, according to producer Danny Davis, with moments of spontaneity that would please any record executive, especially on "Backlash Blues"; "Blues for Mama," words by Abbey Lincoln, music by Nina; and "I Want a Little Sugar in My Bowl," a playful throwback to the bawdy blues of an earlier generation that Nina flavored with sultry good humor.

"My Man's Gone Now," another Gershwin tune from *Porgy and Bess*, turned into a surprise. At the end of one session, Nina stayed at the piano. She played a few chords, perhaps to wind down or maybe to stoke an inspiration. After a moment, she sang the opening Gershwin line—the same as the title—the huskiness in her voice appropriate to the moment and the sentiment. Ray Hall, the engineer, had come out of the control room. But as soon as he heard Nina and then heard the bass player catch her groove, he hustled back to run a tape. "From somewhere," Davis said of the bewitching moment, "she called up the stamina to deliver with even more intensity and spirit a rare, perfect performance in one take, which could not possibly be improved."

High Priestess of Soul registered briefly on the *Cash Box* album chart. The RCA blues album didn't show up at all, nor did it crack the *Billboard* Top 200 albums. But as Nina had proved from the beginning, her success came more from an intense connection with her live audiences than record sales. "My music is so much me that people who like me aren't much affected by what else they hear," she told the *Washington Post*. "My only groove is moods."

THE SECOND WEEK IN APRIL Nina left for England for two weeks of concerts with comedian Dick Gregory. She apparently liked the singer-comedian formula—in addition to the Cosby shows, she'd also done a couple of jobs with comedian Flip Wilson. But the tour got off to a rocky start. When Nina and Gregory arrived at Colston Hall in Bristol, only thirty tickets had been sold, a sure sign of lackluster promotion. Nina was outraged, "and the screams could be heard from far away," according to David Nathan, the young British music enthusiast whom Nina and Andy had recently befriended. Andy summoned Nathan to go for a walk and unburdened himself to the teenager, leaving Nathan alternately flattered and embarrassed that Andy confided in him about such personal matters. "Sometimes, David, I just don't know what to do with her," he admitted. Now he feared that Nina's odd behavior during the Cosby tour was only one episode in a worrisome pattern of moodiness and occasional tantrums that showed Nina sinking into a depression. At her most beleaguered, she'd even lose interest in Lisa, leaving notes around that asked, "Why did I have the baby?"

Nina managed to pull herself together to perform for those thirty ticket holders, and as Nathan remembered it, she ordered everyone to move to the front of the hall so they could experience the full Nina Simone treatment: singing, dancing, lecturing, laughing through a mix of her well-known songs and a few from her latest album. The crowd at Portsmouth Guildhall a few days later was larger—about a hundred audience members—but still a disappointment. The reviewer for *Melody Maker* made a point of praising Nina and Gregory for going all out despite the turnout, and gave a special nod to the trio, Rudy, Charles Crosby, still on drums, and bassist Gene Taylor, the newest addition, for providing "sympathetic and vibrant accompaniment."

During an evening at the Ram Jam club in Brixton, south of London, Nina got upset when the crowd, primarily West Indians, hollered for "My Baby Just Cares for Me." They had adopted her uptempo version as something of an anthem, and they couldn't wait to hear it, interrupting her with so many shouted requests that she stopped in the middle of a song. Nina couldn't understand what they were saying, and finally she stood up from the piano to tell them to be quiet. When shouts for the song persisted, she slammed down the lid, hollered "Shut up!" and walked away.

The worried promoter, afraid the excited fans would riot, begged Andy to get Nina back onstage to sing "My Baby."

"I'm not singing that piece of shit," she yelled. "I don't even remember the words."

Andy finally convinced her to go back out after a few slugs of gin, and she sang the song, glaring at the audience the whole way through.

The final concert of the trip was a welcome turnabout. Nina and Gregory performed for a celebrity-filled crowd at the sold-out Royal Albert Hall in London. Gregory remembered that Nina was supposed to open, but he insisted that the order be reversed "so I could introduce her." Nina loved the challenge of winning the audience over in a short span of time. "I have to get more out of myself," she told a *Washington Post* interviewer a few weeks after the London performance. Recalling the Cosby tour, she added, "I had to call on every resource. I had to give on a huge scale. When it's my concert, I may stick with a mood, but when you go on and off in thirty-five minutes, you have to project emotions and do it immediately. If you can establish intimacy in a concert hall," she added, "then you've really done something."

LANGSTON HUGHES DIED on May 22. His friends knew he had been in the hospital, but none of them realized how ill he was. Deeply affected by his death, Nina turned her set at the Newport Jazz Festival July 1 into a tribute. "Langston used to sit on the Newport festival board," Nina told the audience when she introduced "Backlash Blues." "He was here when it began, you know, and he wrote this tune . . . and gave it to me to put some music to. It was his final slap in the face of the white backlash of his country," she went on. "So we're going to do his tune, and of course he's gone from us, but not really. He's out there somewhere." She played a little blues progression, hit the turnaround, and then delivered a potent version, jumping on the last line: "I'm gonna leave you with the backlash blues."

Nina announced that she would close her set with "Four Women," but first she needed to give one more salute to her friend. "We want to say hello to Langston again and hope that you remember him. Keep him with you always. He was beautiful, a beautiful man, and he's still with us, of course."

Now Nina was ready. "Four Negro women. I had to go into all

kinds of bags to be able to compose it," she explained, sadness in her voice as she told the story of Aunt Sarah, the "southern mammy" tired from working so hard. And then she moved on to Sephronia, the mulatto; Sweet Thing, the streetwalker; and finally the angry Peaches. That triumphant final chord was the perfect way to leave the stage, all the more so because she had conquered a crowd easily distracted by the outdoor elements. "I could feel it," she said later. "It's your most dramatic moment."

ANDY STILL WORRIED when Nina talked about race. He threatened to end one interview on the spot when he thought the writer was baiting her. "What kind of thing are you doing?" Andy demanded. "We're not interested in the race issue." But Nina was. In March she bluntly told *Sepia*, which had featured her in a five-page spread, that "Negroes are entirely too apathetic concerning civil rights. They get aroused only when something happens like a church bombing or a mob lynching. What is needed is everyday commitment by the rank and file, not just the dedicated leaders." In Los Angeles to perform again with Dick Gregory at a fund-raising event, she struck the same theme with *Billboard*'s Eliot Tiegel: "I'm going to sing about the race problem. It's needed. I know it does good because I feel my audience knows I'm not just an entertainer. I'm a colored woman! Don't you think bringing things out in the open is good?"

But Nina was at her most provocative in Detroit August 13 at Jazz Festival '67, another George Wein event that nearly fell victim to circumstances beyond his control. In the early morning of July 23 the city had erupted in a riot after police raided an after-hours club—a "blind pig" in local parlance. A day later President Johnson sent in troops to help quell the violence that already had resulted in nineteen deaths and $150 million in damages from fire and looting. Despite the chaos, calm had been sufficiently restored by August 13 to go ahead, and several thousand patrons packed Cobo Hall to see an all-star cast: Nina, Herbie Mann, Miles Davis, Dizzy Gillespie, Cannonball Adderley, and Woody Herman. Among the handful of whites was Bill Smith, who was working a summer construction job in the city and was grateful that an area-wide curfew had been suspended.

His brother had gotten them tickets through a couple of his black friends, and they all sat together.

Miles Davis came out first, setting a chilly tone when he pointedly refused to shake hands with Wein, who waited to welcome him to the stage. Dizzy Gillespie, by contrast, smiled nonstop, the showman eager to please. When her turn came, Nina sensed an opportunity. Newark had just exploded in violence and so had Cambridge, Maryland, where her SNCC friend, H. Rap Brown, had been shot. Her opening tune, the one she had started with at Newport, too, was a meandering version of "Just in Time" that started in contemplation and ended in the prayerful thanks of one who had been rescued "just in time." But tonight, Nina gave the song a twist. "Just in time," she sang, "Detroit—you did it . . . I love you Detroit—you did it!"

The audience roared. They knew exactly what she meant. Bill looked at his brother, each of them sinking a little lower in his seat. "Whoa—this is heavy," he whispered. Later, *Detroit Free Press* reviewer Harvey Taylor noted dryly that Nina's improvisation met with approval "among, presumably, the arsonists, looters and snipers in the audience." "Backlash Blues," not surprisingly, received the same loud cheers. Calling attention to the city's racial divide and, perhaps, Nina's candor, Dale Stevens of *The Detroit News* said "Backlash" "reveals more clearly than speeches and burning stores what her people are thinking and what the white folks had better understand quickly, that the blues can be a two-way street."

Nina found another avenue to express the blues through "I Wish I Knew How It Would Feel to Be Free." The song was written by Billy Taylor, who had performed in Birmingham four years earlier undaunted by a broken stage and no lights, and it was included in Nina's latest RCA release, *Silk & Soul*. In her hands Taylor's trenchant lyrics echoed Eunice Waymon and Tryon when she sang, "I wish I could break all the chains holding me," and he captured the essence of the civil rights movement in a single line: "I wish you could know what it means to be me and then you'd see and agree that every man should be free."

"All my life I've wanted to shout out my feeling of being imprisoned," she told one interviewer. "I've known about the silence that makes that prison, as any Negro does."

One of Nina's favorite gifts that she carried on the road served as a constant reminder. It was a poster made and given to her by Sister Mary Corita, an artist who also ran the art department at Immaculate Heart College in Los Angeles and had gained fame for her provocative serigraphs. Two years earlier one of her works commenting on the Vietnam War had caused such controversy that IBM, which had displayed the art, made her amend it. On the poster she gave Nina, Sister Mary had incorporated a quote from Albert Camus: "I should like to be able to love my country and still love justice."

DESPITE HIS CONCERN about Nina's outspokenness, Andy remained determined to "eliminate certain barriers," he told Leonard Feather, that arose because of her "tendency to use controversial material. She'll play Las Vegas yet. When she does," Andy declared, "it'll be just the way it's been everywhere else she's worked: Wild, cheering crowds, standing room only, replays—and then, of course, they'll let her sing anything she likes."

Nina got her chance in Las Vegas the first week in October. Only it didn't turn out the way Andy had predicted. She was booked into Caesars Palace, but she was in Nero's Nook, not the main room. And she didn't have the stage to herself either. She had to alternate sets with Xavier Cugat and Charo, and the comedian-actor Paul Gilbert.

Rudy considered himself a veteran musician who had seen it all, but he was not prepared for the hostile reaction Nina got from the Nook's technical staff. It had nothing to do with the songs she sang. It was her attitude. They thought she was haughty, and they took it out on her when she came onstage. "She would start to sing something, and the mike would go off," Rudy explained. "She'd tap the microphone, and it would come back on. When she got ready to sing, the mike would go off."

The frequent interruptions destroyed any kind of mood Nina tried to establish. "That was a joke," she recalled in her memoir. "I lasted four days in Vegas and then walked."

·

A BRIEF TRIP to Los Angeles boosted Nina's spirits. She performed at a sold-out concert at UCLA where the crowd bathed her in cheers and delivered the now-customary "oohs" and whistles when she appeared in the fishnet outfit. And she was a guest on Pat Boone's local talk show along with George Jessel, a singular combination that raised more than one eyebrow. Then she came back to New York in mid-November to the welcoming environs of the Village Gate. But sometimes even the Gate crowd failed to meet her expectations.

"You're not giving one thing tonight," Nina complained on the evening that John Wilson, the *New York Times* critic, took in a show. "What bag are you in?"

All she heard back were a few murmurs and a chuckle or two but no answer.

"So I'll have to guess," Nina announced, looking out in the darkness. "I just want you to know that I know. All right." She turned to the keyboard. "I'll take you down—down—down." And she began to play what Wilson described as a "lazy, sinuous rhythm. She hummed along to the beat, vocalizing a low, keening sound." Rudy caught her mood, plucking starlike accents on his guitar. Charles Crosby and Gene Taylor found the beat. Within moments, Wilson said, "she filled the room with a budding, spreading sense of tension."

Sitting at a table in the rear of the club, Andy shook his head in wonderment. "I never heard *this* arrangement before," he said. "In the seven years I've been with her, I never heard it."

"Sometimes the audience sparks the mood. Sometimes the guys get the mood and take it away from me," Nina said later, referring to the sidemen. "If I know I've got to make it happen, I won't quit— unless the rapport is just not there, and it's taking too long. This is what creativity is to me. There's no end to the varieties of depth of feeling when you're creating a mood." Away from the music, Nina admitted those moods could be trying. "I'm not the easiest thing to live with," she told Wilson during a December interview. "But if I can't make it with him," she said, crediting Andy's patience, "I can't make it with anybody."

It had been thirteen years since Eunice Waymon declared herself to be "Nina Simone," and most of the time she didn't consciously look back. But recently, she said, "Eunice Waymon has come alive in many more ways than I'd expected. Eunice is extremely soft and frightened to death of almost everything. She has to be handled extremely gently. . . . Nina," she went on, "Nina takes care of Eunice. Nina was always there, but now I think she'll relax a little and not have to fight so hard. Andrew," she added, "takes care of them both. He always brings me back to myself."

17. Black Gold

~ 1968 ~

Nina's return to Carnegie Hall January 6 was as much coronation as concert. Undeterred by a snowstorm and blustery winds, her fans filled every available seat, lined the balconies, and even spilled out onto the stage where space permitted. They got restless during a half-hour delay that Nina gamely explained was caused by the theft of Rudy's guitar. But they came to attention when she went ahead without Rudy and her brother Sam, who had joined the band, while they searched for a replacement. She barely skipped a beat when applause announced their arrival onstage in the middle of a song.

Nina started the evening in churchlike fashion with "Draw Me Near." "This is a nice groove to get into," she said, "but let's do the important ones first." Those who knew Nina understood that meant "Backlash Blues," "Strange Fruit," and now "Turning Point," with Nina in the guise of a white child asking her mother if her friend, who "looks just like chocolate" and sits next to her in school, can come over to play. The mother says no. "We could have such fun!"

Nina and her brother Sam at Nina's
Mount Vernon house, spring 1968
(*Courtesy of Sam Waymon*)

the child pleads. "Why no?" Nina paused for effect and lowered her
voice. "Oh . . . I see."

It was her custom when she finished to look across the lights and
ask in an offhand, almost lazy way, "Did you get it?" The emotional
current running through Carnegie Hall left no doubt that the audience did. A few weeks earlier in San Francisco, Ralph J. Gleason, the
Chronicle's critic, had seen her perform the same magic, marveling
that "she had people from Georgia and Alabama in the crowd and
still put over her message songs."

Andy's company and Ron Delsener co-sponsored the Carnegie
concert, evidence that Delsener's initial instincts about Nina were
right: they *could* get along, and she was a good draw. *Variety* reported
that the sold-out performance brought gross receipts of $11,000. But
Andy still worried that Nina's provocative material could cost her.

Gleason had actually addressed the subject of controversial black artists in one of his recent columns and cited Archie Shepp as one who believed an economic boycott existed against him and others who spoke up. One of Gleason's friends said he found "a lot of hate" in Nina, and while the observation didn't surprise him, Gleason wrote, he was saddened. "It struck me that this is the kind of reaction a great many people in this society have when someone makes them think or face an issue. The jazz musicians are and always have been wave makers by their implicit stance (their very existence brings you face to face with the problem of color) but they have played it rather than said it out loud." Nina and the other artists "who are newly speaking out in the jazz world and the pop world," he added, "are going to make it hard for any of us to avoid facing up to the reality behind the American dream."

ON FEBRUARY 29 Nina opened a two-week stint in Vancouver, British Columbia, at Marco Polo, a supper club owned by one of the city's prominent Chinese families, whose manager had a penchant for booking some acts that hadn't yet made it, those on the downside (a literally staggering Bill Haley), and on special occasions genuine stars like Nina. The club's full-time MC, Harvey Lo, combined fluency in Cantonese, Mandarin, and English with the skill of a world-class yo-yo champion. He opened every night by singing a song and doing a few yo-yo tricks before introducing the main act. Nina hated it. "Andrew," she complained, "do I have to follow this every night? Is there any way we can get him off?"

But there wasn't, so Nina usually arrived onstage in mild disgust, letting those with the best seats see "a look that could stop a truck with no brakes," according to Henry Young, a popular local guitar player who was in the house band. "But when she took the facade off," he added, "you could see all these beautiful features." Henry felt a deep connection to Nina's music because, as the son of a Ukrainian woman and a Chinese man, he, too, had faced discrimination. "You gotta remember," he explained, "I'm not white. I suffered the same prejudice as Nina did. You really know what she hits," he added. "It's not about show business. It's about emotional life."

Henry wanted to meet Nina, and he thought Rudy was his best route to an introduction. One night he simply asked if he could sit in. Rudy took the request to Nina, and perhaps recalling the immediate connection with Al Schackman when he had appeared out of nowhere, Nina said yes. "But you don't know the songs," she reminded him. Henry told her not to worry. His ear was good enough to pick them up.

"She looked at me with these glaring eyes," Henry recalled, seeing them still after forty years. "She scared the shit out of me."

"Are you black?" she asked him.

"I'll be whatever you want me to be," Henry replied.

It didn't take long for Nina to render her verdict. "You play like a brother," she told him. "You have black blood in you." Henry didn't say anything, but he silently thanked Rudy, who whispered the right key if something got tricky and encouraged him to relax. Late one evening Nina and Andy went to hear Henry at the Elegant Parlour, an after-hours club owned by the future comedian Tommy Chong and a favorite of R&B musicians. By the time they left for the Troubadour in Los Angeles, neither Nina nor Andy knew how fortuitous their meeting had been.

"THE GREAT THING about Miss Simone is that she rarely makes a mistake on stage," *Variety* said of Nina's week at the L.A. club. "She gives the audience everything they want while clicking it off with superb pacing." The reviewer also doled out praise to the sidemen, who now included Buck Clarke, the New York drummer who had played some dates with Nina a few years earlier. But more change was coming. When the L.A. job was over, Rudy announced he was leaving for The Fifth Dimension. The band's offer was too good to pass up. Nina was going to miss him—she often introduced Rudy as "our rock of ages"—but she and Andy remembered how much they liked Henry. So Andy called him up and invited him to join the band in New York when they returned the first of April.

"I canceled all my jobs and left," Henry said. "When somebody like that phones you, you don't say no." Andy sent him a plane ticket and a contract with terms that were the best he'd ever seen. Not only that, when he arrived in New York Andy was waiting for him at the airport and had arranged a room for him at a YMCA not far from the Fifth Avenue offices of Stroud Productions. He handed Henry a sheaf of arrangements and told him to be ready for a rehearsal. Nina was scheduled to play the Westbury Music Fair on Long Island on Sunday, April 7, and RCA planned to record the evening live for Nina's next album.

Rudy's wise counsel aside, Henry was a nervous wreck when he showed up for the rehearsal. But Nina put him at ease: "You know what, child, throw the music away, and let's just play from the heart."

Their first performance together scarcely went according to plan. On April 4, the Reverend Dr. Martin Luther King Jr. was gunned down at his hotel in Memphis as he prepared to address striking sanitation workers. Though devastated, Nina professed no surprise at King's killing. "It was the traditional white American tactic for getting rid of black leaders it couldn't suppress in any other way," she wrote in her memoir. "Stupid, too, because the thing that died along with Martin in Memphis was non-violence . . . It was a time for bitterness. . . ."

President Johnson had declared Sunday, April 7, to be a day of mourning, and Andy considered canceling the Westbury date right up until the last minute because Nina was so distraught. But he found a way to put her at ease, and she found comfort in talking to the band members one by one in the dressing room. She told Henry she was sorry his first job was under these circumstances. Finally onstage, Nina offered a subdued welcome to the audience. "We're glad to see you, and happily surprised with so many of you. We didn't really expect anybody tonight, and you know why. Everybody knows everything. Everything is everything . . . but we're glad that you've come to see us and hope that we can provide . . . " and Nina paused to look for the right word but all she could come up with was "some kind of something for you, this evening, this particular evening, this Sunday, at this particular time in 1968. We hope that we can give you some—some of whatever it is that you need tonight." She didn't say so explicitly, but Nina needed something too, and drawing on every bit of her talent in the charged moment, she expressed her sorrow the best way she could, through her music.

For twenty minutes Nina wove a tribute to Dr. King through three songs, starting with "Sunday in Savannah," one of the first songs she had recorded, about going to church. Tonight, she said, the audience should think of it as Sunday in Atlanta, where King's funeral would take place. Then, she explained, Gene Taylor had written a song just the day before to honor the slain leader: "Why? (The King of Love Is Dead)." "Course, this whole program is dedicated to the memory of Dr. Martin Luther King. You know that," Nina added.

"What's gonna happen now to all of our cities?" she cried out. "Our people are risin'—they're living at last even if they have to die." She was chanting now more than singing, striking a chord here and there, Henry following her lead on the guitar. Then she swung into a gospel rhythm: "He had seen the mountaintop, and he knew he could not stop, always living with the threat of death ahead." What would happen, she asked, when the king is dead?

Then Nina stopped. She wanted to talk, and while Sam played the organ softly behind her, she spoke of those who had already died: her dear friend Lorraine Hansberry, Otis Redding, John Coltrane. "We can go on—it really gets down to reality, doesn't it? We are thankful, but we can't afford any more losses," she continued. "Well, all I have to say is that those of us who know how to protect those of us that we love, stand by them and stay close to them. And I say that if there'd been a couple a little closer to Dr. King he wouldn't a got it, you know—really. Just a little closer then," she added quietly, "stay there, stay there, we can't afford any more losses."

"Mississippi Goddam" was the final piece, updated to reflect current events: "Alabama's got me so upset./Memphis made me lose my rest." Midway she stopped again to talk, and this time Buck Clarke kept up the marching beat behind her. "If you've been moved at all, and you know my songs at *all*, for God sakes join me! Don't sit back there! The time is now! You know the king is dead—the king of love is dead. I ain't 'bout to be non-violent," she shouted.

The audience cheered.

"Whoa!" Nina exclaimed, perhaps startled by the ferocity of her own words and the crowd's reaction. And then she picked up the song: "All I want is equality for my sister, my brother, my people, and me."

Three weeks later, when she performed for the New York Urban League—and President Johnson attended the gala evening—the *Amsterdam News* reported that Nina's passionate delivery of "Why?" had "wrung tears from the eyes and hearts of her audience."

NINA HAD GIVEN SPECIAL ATTENTION to Buck at rehearsals, sensing his discomfort if she went on one of her improvisational jaunts. "When the show actually starts, Buck, when we're up here, you keep your eyes on me," she told him. "Whatever happens, just keep your eyes on me. Breathe with me . . . you'll be all right."

Buck took it to heart, but Nina remained unhappy with his appearance. Most of the time she didn't mind that he dressed like of a dandy, but when he showed up for a job in Boston in a khaki safari jacket, top hat, riding boots, and carrying a switch, Nina had enough. He looked like a cartoon, or worse, a lawn jockey. "Tone it down," she instructed. "Don't embarrass me."

Lester Hyman, a Boston lawyer, happened to stop by the club, Paul's Mall, during Nina's week there, though he didn't know anything about her. "She just blew my mind, just extraordinary," he said. Hyman was head of the state Democratic party and in the planning stages for a major fund-raising event. Although he had already booked society bandleader Peter Duchin and his orchestra, he thought Nina would be a terrific addition for the program.

He went back to the club another night to talk to Nina, but this time he found a completely different person. Two white men were talking constantly at one of the front tables, and Nina was perturbed. Finally she blew up. "You!" she shouted at them. "I get bad vibrations from you, and I don't want you in here!"

The men must have been stunned, and perhaps choosing to avoid further confrontation, they left. Club owner Fred Taylor let it ride, figuring it was better to keep Nina in good spirits than tell her not to insult the customers. "You were always on pins and needles," Taylor admitted, but he credited Andy with keeping "fairly good control of her."

Hyman worried that the outburst didn't bode well for him, and he asked Andy what to do. But Andy played it hands off: "You're on your own buddy. You picked a bad night." Hyman decided to forge ahead anyway. How much angrier could Nina get? He approached the dressing room cautiously, took a deep breath, and walked in hoping that a little humor would help.

"Miss Simone, I just"—and he stammered for a second or two. "I just would hate to be on the wrong side of you."

Nina apparently thought this was hilarious. "She started to laugh," Hyman recalled, and from then on they were fast friends. She readily agreed to do the fund-raiser.

NINA'S BUSY SPRING started with a concert at the Brooklyn Academy of Music sponsored by Soul East Productions, noteworthy, if nothing else, for the way it billed a Nina performance: "An Evening in Black Gold." She returned to the Village Gate the next week with RCA hosting an opening night reception and springing for ads in several New York newspapers promoting her albums. After a trip to Chicago to play three shows at the Civic Opera House with Flip Wilson, Nina and the band headed to Europe the second week in June. It was Sam's first overseas trip with her, and he couldn't have been more excited, not only to see new places and meet new people but also to witness the tumultuous reception for his sister. In Amsterdam June 8, an overflow crowd of 2,500 applauded for a full minute when she walked onstage, and she hadn't said or sung a word. Ben Bunders, a Dutch reviewer, noted later that the audience knew her from her previous trips and a few television appearances on the Continent. Promoter Paul Acket had added extra rows of chairs in the hall, but he could have sold hundreds more tickets if there had been space.

Though Nina made sure to sing some of her best-known songs, she used the occasion to introduce others that she and the band had worked up in the spring, notably "Why?"—to honor Dr. King—and another instant crowd favorite "Ain't Got No—I Got Life" from the hit Broadway musical *Hair*. After listing the things she lacked, Nina sang with infectious energy about all that she did have: "I got my hair on my head, got my brains, got my ears, got my eyes. . . ."

Nina played the piano with such gusto during the evening that the other musicians, according to Bunders, had a hard time getting a note in edgewise. Only Henry found a moment to let loose with a long bluesy guitar solo, which earned him appreciative applause and a nod from another reviewer in the *Amsterdam Daily News*, who said Henry played with "a blues tonality of T-Bone Walker and the warmth of Kenny Burrell," referring to two respected American guitar players.

Nina and Sam reveled in their time onstage. He had lived on and off with her, Andy, and Lisa in Mount Vernon, but performing together had an intensity all its own. "The truth is I reminded her of her daddy," Sam said. "I look like my father. I could also see that she was lonely. She was very lonely for family." Henry thought of Sam as a safety valve. "When she couldn't see eye to eye with Andy," he recalled, "she turned to Sam."

Lisa had come on this trip, too, accompanied by a new nanny, a white woman named Cheryl whom Nina and Andy met at the Marco Polo. She was one of the hostesses but was eager to shake up her life and have an adventure. She hit it off with Andy and Nina perhaps because of her easygoing attitude. "She was such a charming honest person," Sam said. Henry called her Nina's "Sigmund Freud, 24/7." "She would listen, listen, listen and never talk." Sam joked that maybe Nina got along with Cheryl so well because she was Canadian and not an American. It was certainly high praise when months later Nina dropped Henry a note and told him that Cheryl "is working out very well—says she's never coming back to Vancouver."

Cheryl's presence made it easier when Nina used a private concert in Morocco as an excuse for a four-day holiday. With Lisa taken care of, Nina relaxed at a seaside resort, even posing for photographs with some fans. The good time was diminished briefly by an episode at a hotel they were visiting, when some white people walked in and, in Nina's view, acted in a way "that showed their prejudice. So we got up and walked out." But that moment was forgotten by the time the group arrived in Switzerland, where they were among a handful of Americans in a largely European lineup at the Montreux Jazz Festival. Nina played the evening of the sixteenth to a crowd so large that some had to watch the performance from another room on closed-circuit television.

RCA had released Nina's version of "To Love Somebody," the torchy Bee Gees' song, and now she sang it in her shows. The studio version had backup singers and an orchestra. Onstage Nina had only her piano, the guitar, bass, and drums, and Sam to harmonize. But this spare arrangement had an intimacy unrivaled by the record, Nina introducing the sweet melody of the chorus, "You don't know what it means," with soft chords that would not be out of place in church.

Though she and Sam meshed well musically, she chided him if he irritated her. When he played the tambourine too close to her during "Just in Time," she looked at him and said, "Click click click," prompting laughter from the audience. But Sam got the point and backed off.

Nina turned "See-Line Woman" into an audience participation number, giving the crowd a primer on how and when to shout "See-Line" as she strutted about the stage. At the end of the eleven-song set, everyone cheered for more, and Nina obliged with her revival-styled "Gin House Blues," the old Bessie Smith tune. "Don't stop now!" she shouted, exhorting the audience to keep clapping. A few bars later, when she thought the drummer was slowing down, Nina hollered encouragement: "Come on, Buck!"

Michael Smith, reporting for the British paper *Melody Maker*, was among those who had to watch Nina via the television hookup. But it did nothing to diminish the power of her performance. Like Ralph Gleason a few months earlier, he acknowledged Nina's focus on race and marveled how she could take "a predominantly white and initially indifferent audience and by sheer artistry, strength of character and magical judgment drive them into a mood of ecstatic acclamation. This was Black Power in its most dignified and enriching sense."

The news that Senator Robert F. Kennedy had been assassinated in the midst of his presidential run dampened all the good feeling from the tour. Nina was still grieving over the death of Martin Luther King, and Kennedy's murder upset her even more. She recalled the moment years later with such intensity that in her mind she had barely been able to perform at Montreux and Andy had to help her off the stage. But a recording of the concert and contemporaneous accounts indicate that she was in a good mood and in terrific form. "Thank you very much for having us," she told the crowd. "We enjoyed it very much. And you've been a beautiful audience."

NINA FREQUENTLY STARTED her concerts by letting the band play an instrumental before she came onstage. But with the deaths of Dr. King and Robert Kennedy so much on her mind and the memories of Lorraine and Langston always with her, Nina changed things up June 28 at the Hampton Institute in Virginia. The histori-

Nina with Gerrit DeBruin at a television studio
in Hilversum, the Netherlands, in 1968
(*Courtesy of Gerrit DeBruin*)

cally black school was celebrating its centennial, and when Nina saw the ten thousand people packed into the campus athletic field, she walked right out to the front of the stage. "It's so wonderful looking out here and seeing all of you beautiful black people!" she exclaimed. The audience, which did include a sprinkling of whites, responded with a robust cheer.

Though Nina rarely, if ever, opened with "Four Women," on this night it felt like exactly the right thing. After she had worked her way through a few blues numbers, she ended on a somber note with another gripping presentation of "Why?" She and the band were rewarded with a standing ovation. *The Christian Science Monitor*'s Amy Lee noted afterward that Nina "let the whites present know unmistakably where things stand." At Newport on July 4, in Philadelphia the next day with Ray Charles, and in New York in Central Park July 6, Nina elicited identical responses: rapturous applause from her fans and riveting attention when she slowed things down to remember Dr. King.

For the moment Nina said she yearned for tranquility. "I'm kind of tired of being controversial," she told a reporter right after Newport, her song choices and some of her commentary to the contrary. "I want to settle down and be quiet. People come here expecting me to walk off the stage. But I enjoy Newport. It's wonderful to play here before so many people. I love music," she added, "it's my life. It is the very foundation of my existence. I haven't even begun to use half of my ideas."

NINA AND THE BAND went to London in September to film an hour-long special, *Sound of Soul,* for British television. The studio audience, some two hundred individuals, most of them white and under thirty, sat arrayed in a circle around the bandstand. Nina made her entrance dressed in a variation of her fishnet outfit—white body stocking underneath the black see-through outer layer and dangling earrings at least five inches long that swayed to and fro as she walked around the stage. She bowed every few feet and extended her hand to audience members close enough to reach her, as though she was visiting royalty awaiting her subjects' obeisance. "She was almost quite lovable," Henry recalled, the most relaxed he had seen her.

The opening numbers elicited respectful if restrained applause, but soon heads bobbed to the music as the camera panned the room. By then it was time to change clothes. Signaling Nina's return to the stage, Buck Clarke started rhythmic drumming on a set of bongos and kept it up as she entered in a bold print jumpsuit with billowing sleeves that whisked the floor when she bent over in an interpretive dance. She kept it up for a good five minutes, speaking only to tease an audience member who was trying to hand her the long microphone cord. "Get it, baby! Get it," she chortled. All of this had turned into her elaborate introduction to "See-Line Woman."

The final costume change came after a few more numbers. Now Nina reappeared in a sarong with a matching turban. The dangling earrings were replaced by pearl studs, all but ensuring that nothing distracted from the hat-and-dress ensemble. Striking a few chords familiar to anyone who had paid attention to the pop charts, Nina told the audience, "As you know, the Animals had a hit with this tune." A hint of a smile was on her face. Then she presented a measured, compelling version of "Don't Let Me Be Misunderstood," suggesting, without actually saying it, that *this* was how the song should be performed.

Rather than explaining the origins of "Backlash Blues," Nina improvised a verse in the song about what Langston had told her before he died: "When you finally made it, and the doors are open wide/Make sure you tell them exactly where it's at/So they'll have no other place to hide."

"What I hope to do all the time is to be so completely myself," Nina said, explaining such improvisations, "to be so much myself that my audiences and even people who meet me are confronted when they—oh wow! they're confronted with what I am inside and out, as honest as I can be," she continued. "And this way they have to see things about themselves, immediately. It's like for instance, if I have a conversation with somebody, I can be honest every minute, and they're forced to be honest. Whatever you get from my music," she went on, "whatever you feel from my music is real, and it comes from me to you. Whatever it is, if it's disturbing, eh, OK, but you're part of that disturbance. If it's love, whatever it is, and you get it from the music, then you got it from me . . . you can get your answers about me from my music."

AFTER THE LONDON TRIP Henry returned to Vancouver to take care of family matters, and at roughly the same time, Gene Taylor and Buck Clarke went their separate ways. In a stroke of good timing, Al Schackman was back in New York and available. By happenstance, Nina and Andy found a new bass player, Gene Perla, whom they heard when they dropped in to a café in New York's St. Marks Place. Impressed, Andy asked Gene afterward if he would come to a rehearsal October 21 at an Upper West Side studio. He made the date and was hired in time for a two-day trip to the Midwest: first a concert October 26 at Lake Forest College outside Chicago and then Detroit's Ford Auditorium the next night.

After a subsequent four-day swing that took them from New York to Miami and Atlanta, Gene could see that Nina was unhappy with the drummer who had replaced Buck. Though he didn't know Nina and Andy that well, he stepped forward anyway and told them to hire his talented friend, Don Alias. Nina said OK, and after the first rehearsal, she knew it was the right decision. She had also picked up a new organist who composed, too, Weldon Irvine. He had graduated from Hampton with a degree in English and music and had built a name for himself in New York music circles since arriving in 1965. The band was set for the foreseeable future.

Unbeknownst to the musicians, Andy and Nina had decided to change the group's uniforms. They showed up at the next rehearsal with a couple of big bags, and instead of handing out new dinner jackets, they gave each of the men dashikis, one type of traditional African shirt. Gene's eyes opened wide in disbelief when he saw the next thing: long gold chains with large medallions in the shape of Africa.

He held his tongue but only for a moment. "I'm not going to wear this," he blurted out.

"Why not?" Nina asked, her irritation obvious.

"I'm Italian, not African."

"You're fired!" she snapped.

But Andy rushed in before the situation escalated. He calmed Nina down, and she and Gene reached an accommodation. He would wear the dashiki but not the medallion.

THE THIRD WEEK IN OCTOBER Nina had returned to the *Billboard* pop and R&B singles charts. RCA had released a record from a June recording session, "Do What You Gotta Do," backed with "Peace of Mind," and "Do What You Gotta Do" caught on, if modestly, staying on each chart for just over a month. The label had also released Nina's third album, *'Nuff Said*, with most tracks coming from the live performance at the Westbury Music Fair in April, right after King's assassination. "Why?" though, had been redone in the studio to eliminate Nina's impromptu comments. It made for a shorter, more cohesive track but one that was nearly devoid of the emotion in the original. Perhaps RCA was uneasy about putting out something so raw that even Nina's fans would blanch. Henry remembered the work in the studio as "cleaning up" some rough spots in the entire performance, and perhaps that's all it was. It would take a generation before the full scope of Nina's artistry and her pain that evening became available, when RCA released another record containing the entire tribute to Dr. King.

Shortly after *'Nuff Said* RCA put out another single, "Ain't Got No—I Got Life," the song from *Hair*, backed with "Real Real," an upbeat tune that Nina had written. Though "Life" wasn't doing much in the United States, it hit the charts in the United Kingdom, which prompted RCA to dispatch Nina to London for a round of publicity appearances, including coveted spots on two popular television shows, *Top of the Pops* and *The David Frost Show*. She agreed to do a meet-and-greet at Soul City, a small store in the middle of London, and took great pleasure in the sight of so many fans lined up to get in. "Well, it's good to know they finally dig me," she told one of them. True, she had to work and travel more, but "I'm having a ball, and at least this time I'm getting paid, and it's about time, too."

Nina reflected further on her career in an interview with *Melody Maker*, making sure to express her satisfaction with European audiences. "They seem to know all my records and when they were made," she said. "I suppose the civil rights thing does come into it and has some bearing on their response, but in a lot of cases, I'm sure it has nothing to do with it." Nina professed a disdain for politics and declared she was "not a politician. But when I'm on stage, of course, I'm conscious that I'm colored. I feel that I am upholding the prestige of my people and most of my songs are about the problem. I never forget that my first purpose is to bring art to the people," she added. "Any social feeling I have must not overwhelm my music or be taken to extremes."

18. To Be Young, Gifted and Black

~ 1969 ~

Nina's latest album, released early in February, featured only her and her piano. The title was direct: *Nina Simone and Piano!* The jacket copy emphasized that Nina had done everything at the RCA sessions three months earlier, including overdubbing vocals and playing a little tambourine and organ. One of the most affecting tracks, "Compensation," consisted of Paul Laurence Dunbar's two-stanza poem, which Nina surrounded with the gospel progressions she had played since she was a child. It fit perfectly with Dunbar's meditation on a divine power that first gives the gift of song and later as "the master in infinite mercy, offers the boon of death." Those spare dramatic words seemed to capture the burdens that so often now accompanied her success.

"I've been called bitter, sharp, hotmouthed and moody," she had said in a recent interview after a Miami performance. "But there is nothing superficial about me. There is no fakery . . . Most people have their own thing to fight with. I am fighting just for honesty and to grow by singing and being black."

The release also put Nina in the unusual position of having her newest record represent a musical moment she had already passed. Her live performances now featured a new sound and new material — a dollop of Bob Dylan, a white singer-songwriter from northern Minnesota; a taste of Canadian writer Leonard Cohen; and the Beatles, represented by Nina's take on "Revolution"—"Some folks are gonna get the notion—I know they say I'm preachin' hate/But if I have to swim the ocean—well, I would just to communicate." But one track on this new album, "Who Am I?" written by Leonard Bernstein, spoke to Nina's otherworldly moments. Woven into the lyrics were ruminations on reincarnation: "Someday I'll die—will I ever live again as a mountain lion, or a rooster or hen?" she asks. "Were you ever here before?" At times Nina acted as if she had been. When a white music writer in London told her that he had discovered rhythm and blues fifteen years earlier, she cut him off before he could explain. "Well, you've been a negro for fifteen years—so you know little of what it's like. I've been one for nine hundred years."

Though it showcased Nina's dual talents, the piano album turned out to be more of a collector's item than a commercial success.

Nina traced her music to the same source despite this new eclecticism. "The blues and jazz come from my people for one reason," she told *Time* magazine. "We are the ones who had the misery of being slaves in this country. We're the ones who had to be invisible. We're the ones who had to devise different means of staying alive. We did it. It's a bore just to talk about pain per se unless something can come out of it that's constructive," she went on. "I want an easier life, and I want an easier life for my people and for all people that are oppressed. But before you can have that, the pain and the injustice have to be exposed, and that's very painful in itself, because nobody wants to look at it."

Nina could have been talking about her life offstage. The good-natured understanding with Andy she had described eighteen months earlier in *The New York Times* had eroded. "Distracted by everything else going on, we'd let our relationship slide to the point where we never talked about our feelings or ambitions anymore," she wrote in her memoir. During one outburst that Sam witnessed at the Mount Vernon house, Nina threw dishes around the dining room, and Andy tossed a chair. Sam stepped in to help but only incurred his sister's wrath. "What are you doing getting in the middle of my business?" she snapped.

Even Gene and Don witnessed the couple's troubles. Backstage at the Gate one evening they could hear Nina and Andy arguing. When they opened the dressing room door, they were astonished to see that Andy had pinned Nina against the wall, her feet several inches off the floor. "Buddha! Buddha! Buddha!" she hollered, her nickname for him ever since he had developed a noticeable paunch. The men abruptly shut the door and walked away, chuckling once they realized Nina was not in danger. Nobody spoke of the moment when they all went onstage.

In an interview for a planned television documentary, Nina had hinted at the source of their arguments: she was tired and being pushed too hard. Granted, Andy took care of all the arrangements—booking, travel, paying the band—but she still found it taxing to hopscotch around the Midwest on consecutive days or fly down South and then make several dates in a row on the way back to New York. "I think nineteen people who depend on me for their livelihood—that's a helluva lot of people," she said. "Because I know that if I say, 'Well, look I'm too tired to work tonight' I'm gonna get it from both ends. Nobody is going to understand or care that I'm too tired. I'm very aware of that. Now I would like some freedom somewhere—where I didn't feel those pressures, and I think that some songs would flow out of me—they really would have to come."

When she spoke to the *New York Post* March 15—it was a story pegged to the U.S. airing of the *Sound of Soul*—Nina reverted to her divided self to drive home the point. "Eunice is a woman who doesn't get enough time off," she said. Nina Simone? "She's the machine who must perform every night. The one that goes to work. The woman is Eunice." The large photo that accompanied the article reflected Nina's unease. In a story intended to celebrate her, she offered no trace of a smile.

Andy saw things differently. Nina's complaints mystified him—

she'd only done thirty dates the previous year. Yet she wanted a swimming pool and other upgrades to the house costing several hundred thousand dollars, he recalled in 2006. He asked her point-blank, "Where are we gonna get the money?"

NINA'S RECORD SALES in the United States still failed to reflect her popularity as a performer. But in England she had three songs on the charts—"Ain't Got No," "To Love Somebody," and a Philips re-release, "I Put a Spell on You" backed with "Don't Let Me Be Misunderstood." Hoping to piggyback on her overseas success, RCA released a version of "Revolution" as a single in the United States. "Nina Simone. She's making News in England," declared a full-page ad in *Cash Box*. "Today she's starting a revolution in America." The single was also released in England just as Nina and the band left for an ambitious three-week trip to the United Kingdom and Europe to take advantage of her foreign hits.

The first stop was in Dublin, followed by seven more concerts, one right after the other, that took the group, this time including two backup singers, from Belfast to the Netherlands, then to Scotland and Wales, London, over to the Continent, and finally back to London. It was precisely the kind of schedule that Nina hated, even though she understood it was both efficient and economical. Still, she blamed Andy for her fatigue. "You go out there, go out and tell them *I'm tired*," she hollered in her dressing room before one concert. "You think I'm a machine, you're just like all the rest. You just want me to perform, you don't give a damn." Andy's efforts to soothe her seemed only to fuel her anger. Finally, she gathered herself and calmed down when she noticed Sylvia Nathan, David's sister and now also a friend, who had come to greet her. "But I'm telling you," she warned, "you better ease off me, man. . . . I'm not gonna keep doing this shit forever you know. I'm human, too."

Once Nina got onstage, she managed to transform her anger into a set that mirrored her emotions. Derek Jewell told London *Times* readers that some songs were "declamatory sermons driving straight ahead into the dilemmas of our age, or quiet personal cries of joy and lament about the business of living."

Nina admitted that the venue could influence her feelings, too. "I've done things like count seats, try to get into the mood of the place," she said. "I'll know what kind of people come here if the seats are very lush. I'll check the position of the stage, the intelligence and education of the light and sound men, the mood I'm in, the mood my musicians are in and what I want to say. All that is influential and will certainly determine what I'm going to play." Sometimes she didn't make those decisions until a half hour before she went onstage or even less, counting on her musicians to adjust.

At the Olympia Theater in Paris, Nina changed moods between sets. The first wove through gospel, blues, and ballads. The second, according to *Figaro*'s Paul Carriere, was "all about 'pop music,' vehemence and racial protest sometimes clothed in poetry." He loved it. So did the music critic Maurice Cullaz of *Jazz Hot*, who called Nina "absolutely incapable of compromise . . . she will enchant you."

On many nights her musicians felt the same way. Gene particularly liked the setup at the Hague. Though not exactly theater in the round, the audience essentially surrounded the musicians. At one point, Nina chose a ballad, "and she sang it with such delicacy . . . like crystal glass. Man, during that tune, we could have heard a pin drop." More than the critics, Gene and the other musicians knew Nina's private turmoil, and that made it all the more compelling when they saw her deliver onstage.

During the second day of a two-day stop in Munich, Nina and the band taped a television program. "This is a very rare evening," she announced. "Are you enjoying the show? Are you really?" she asked, letting the subsequent applause give her the answer. As was her habit now, she scanned the crowd for black faces and usually found them, though in far fewer numbers than in the United States. "I'm singing only to you," she often said. "I don't care about the others." It didn't seem to offend the white patrons, who gamely clapped along. "I see about ten soul brothers out there," Nina announced, and then gave them a special hello. An appreciative audience had lifted Nina's spirits so much that she shouted "Hello Buddha!" to Andy right in the middle of the last song, their personal problems diminished by the temporary thrill of a good performance.

The final stop was back in London April 4 with a concert at the

Palladium, another storied venue. Nina announced that the night was dedicated to Dr. King, given that it was just a year since he had been assassinated, and on this evening she had changed from her usual stage outfit of black satin pants with a light top to one of her bold print robes. The combination of this solemn anniversary and Nina's particular look seemed to create a special energy. The audience couldn't get enough, and Nina happily came back for multiple encores. "The spirits of my African ancestors were there—I could feel them," she bubbled afterward, "and they really took hold of me. Ha! Even I got a bit scared of what they may do to me. The crowd felt it too. . . . Shit, it was everywhere, man! Yes, it was deep, man!"

Only a few months earlier Nina had reminded a reporter that she had set her heart on a classical music career. "Ten years ago I thought if you had the talent you could make it. But I was discouraged and was told of my inferior education." At moments like these, however, when everything clicked, those negative thoughts fell away, and Nina not only accepted the musical choices she had made but took immense pride in her unique creations. "When I die," she told *Melody Maker*, "I want to have left some particular mark of my own. I'm carving my own little niche in the world now."

DESPITE COMPLAINING OF FATIGUE, Nina had no respite. As soon as she and the band returned from Europe, she performed at Hunter College, went back to the studio for another recording session to finish an album due out in June, and then traveled to California to play back-to-back dates in Berkeley and Los Angeles. But no rest came after this long trip either. She and the band went immediately to suburban Boston for a three-night stand at a club called Lennie's.

Finally Nina had a few days off before returning to work, this time right in New York with a week at the Apollo that started May 9. She cast herself now as a proud black woman, but she often sang to a largely white audience. If, in other contexts, she hoped to instruct, during this week at Harlem's most exalted theater, she could inspire. So it was disconcerting, to say the least, that her final evening took a bizarre turn even before the performance started. She and the band were onstage ready to play when a woman's high-pitched voice from the back of the hall distracted her. "Get her together!" Nina shouted to the Apollo staff. "Get her out of here!" A couple of men hustled into the auditorium to remove the offending patron but not fast enough for Nina's liking. Annoyed, she gestured to the band to leave the stage. A few patrons pleaded with Nina to change her mind.

"We love you Nina baby! Don't leave us now!" Apparently satisfied that she had everyone's attention, Nina returned to the piano and played her first song. Perhaps rattled by what had just happened, she inexplicably fell off the piano bench before she could start the second number. The audience gasped and then grew quiet, not knowing what would happen next.

Nina got back up. The audience rose to its feet to cheer when they saw she was not hurt. Some in front tossed red, white, and pink carnations onto the stage. Momentarily flustered, Nina recovered. "You know, being black lends to one's paranoidness," she said. "I fall on my face, and you give me flowers. Since this is my last night," she went on, "if you want, we can start this all over again—all night!" An appreciative cheer signaled their assent, and by the end of the evening it was as though that strange beginning had never happened.

IF SHE HAD a hit record, Nina mused to *Melody Maker,* "I know that I'll be able to reach more people, but what to say? I don't know." Nina did have a message, though, and her late friend Lorraine Hansberry provided the inspiration for her to craft it. Earlier in the year, Robert Nemiroff, Lorraine's former husband, had finally mounted a montage of her unfinished writings under the title *To Be Young, Gifted and Black.* Though it got off to a fitful start in spite of appreciative reviews, the play was still running off Broadway. This was all Nina needed. She had already collaborated with Weldon Irvine on "Revolution," and now she asked his help for a new song with the same title as the show. "To Be Young, Gifted and Black" wasn't as sophisticated as some of Nina's other compositions either in its lyrics or its melody, but it communicated purpose and for Nina—and Weldon, too—the sound of autobiography. The June 22 jazz festival at Morgan State College, the historically black school in Baltimore, couldn't have been a better place to try out the song, and Nina was gratified when the students leapt to their feet, applauding the last line: "To be young, gifted and black—that's where it's at." The theme of the festival was "Music with a Message," and ahead of time several musicians in the lineup had given thumbnail views on the subject, which were printed in the *Baltimore Afro-American* under their photographs. "You might keep us off the radio," said saxophonist Roland Kirk. "But you can't keep us out of the air." Nina had addressed religion: "I don't believe in Jesus, but I believe in God. Tonight we'll call him Jesus. And as long as he's black, he's all right with me."

As it happened, the band had literally changed complexion by the time Nina arrived in Baltimore. Gene Perla had lined up other work that would allow him to play instrumental jazz, his true interest. Al cycled out again, and Nina replaced each of them with black musicians, guitarist Tommy Smith and bassist Clint Houston. Don Alias, who was also black, remained on the drums, occasionally joined by another percussionist, Jumma Santos.

The producers of *Black Journal*, the public television show, wanted to film Nina on a college campus, and they worked out an arrangement with Andy to cover her at Morehouse College in Atlanta, the alma mater of Dr. King. Nina's hairstyle and stage dress had long reflected her various moods. For this date, she dressed all in black, her slacks stuffed into knee-high boots so they billowed out like pantaloons, her sweater adorned with a long silver necklace. She wore her hair in an Afro, now the style on many college campuses. (Howard University had even devoted two pages in one student publication to the various-sized Afros that could be seen around the campus.) During "Black Is the Color of My True Love's Hair," one of Nina's earliest songs, the camera caught the young men in suits and ties and the women in their Sunday best stealing glances back and forth while Nina sang. "To Be Young, Gifted and Black" enraptured both performer and audience. At the line "there's a world waiting for you," she took one hand off the keyboard and without missing a beat pointed to the audience for emphasis. The camera picked up row after row of heads nodding in agreement.

"Oh, I'm feeling good now!" Nina exclaimed. When she got to

the end, she didn't want to stop, so she threw her arms in the air like a sprinter who had just crossed the finish line. Then she gave the crowd, already cheering, one last chorus. "Hold on! Hold on!" she shouted, repeating the instruction five more times, milking the last note, neither embarrassed nor self-conscious at demanding more attention. Finally, she jumped up from the piano, bowed to the audience, and headed to the dressing room.

"My work completely takes all my energy," Nina said later, "but when there are kids who come backstage afterward who want to talk, or who are moved to the point sometimes, they're moved to tears and want to know more about it, they shake my hand and kiss me and want to talk about their problems, I find the time to do so. I discourage breakfasts and speeches because I don't make speeches," she continued, "but I will go out of my way in spite of the fact that I'm too tired to do it, to talk to them at least five minutes or so, to sock to them the same message that I just finished singing onstage and perhaps to get some of their grievances off, just to make them feel that they are not alone. I feel a responsibility—they're so glad to see me. I represent something to them, and I can't give them enough. They need me, and when I'm needed, I have to give, and the most important thing is they are our future." Nina understood that her gifts came with responsibilities, even burdens, not just for her but for the recipients of her message as well.

"I try to make my songs as powerful as possible," she explained, "just to make them curious about themselves. We don't know anything about ourselves," she continued. "We don't have the pride and the definition of African people. We can't even talk about where we came from. We don't know. It's like a lost race, and my songs are deliberately to provoke this feeling of who am I, where do I come from, you know? Do I really like me, and why do I like me? If I am black and beautiful, I really am, and I don't care who says what."

NINA'S POINTED MESSAGE to black America had not precluded appearances in mainstream outlets. On July 15 British talk show host David Frost, who now had a program out of New York, invited her to perform. Perhaps seeking common ground, she chose

"Ain't Got No—I Got Life." In keeping with the play from which it came, Nina wore an elaborate headdress that fit snugly over her own hair and featured a circular design of braids. It complemented her African sarong, and the combination provided a striking image for viewers. They first caught sight of her sitting regally at the piano bench. Only when she got up at the end could those at home and in the studio see that she wasn't wearing any shoes.

Nina started out this version with a few bars that evoked Bach and continued solo as she listed all the things she didn't have, pausing for dramatic effect at some of them—no home, "no guy." Then she raised her right hand and snapped her fingers to cue the house band, which joined her as she sang the litany of what she *did* have. This vibrant arrangement featured horns, though with the camera trained on Nina, none of the band members was visible. Perhaps band and singer meshed so well because Billy Taylor, the jazzman, was Frost's conductor. Nina had done him a good turn in her recording of "I Wish I Knew How It Would Feel to Be Free," and now he could do the same for her. She seemed delighted with it all, jumping up from the piano after the last long note and dancing a few steps before she took her bow.

JAZZ IMPRESARIO GEORGE WEIN regularly put Nina on his expanding festival circuit. One current lineup included Miles Davis and Hugh Masekela, the African trumpeter, and for the Longhorn Jazz Festival in Dallas July 18, Wein and the local promoter added the jazz-rock group Blood, Sweat & Tears.

Henry Young had rejoined the band, and Tommy Smith was glad to have him onstage. He admitted that Nina intimidated him, so Henry gave him blunt advice: if Nina barks, "you bark back." Henry remembered that everyone was on edge after their arrival at the Dallas airport. It was taking longer than usual to load their equipment into the waiting cars, and a surly airport cop didn't help matters with a tasteless joke to hurry them along: "You better behave. We shoot presidents here." They were a room short at the hotel, too, which was uncharacteristic given Andy's attention to detail. So Henry stayed with Miles Davis's piano player. Henry could see that Nina herself

Nina at the Longhorn Jazz Festival in Dallas on July 18, 1969, with her band:
from left, Clint Houston, Tommy Smith, Henry Young, and Weldon Irvine. Two
drummers who are not in the photograph are Don Alias and Jumma Santos.
(Tad Hershorn/Getty Images)

was out of sorts, otherwise she wouldn't have come to ask him to get
her a drink. He told her he couldn't. Andy had a strict policy: "The
first one who gives her any booze or any money to buy it, you're history." Nina didn't argue.

"That's OK," she told Henry. "I was only testing you."

Later everything went surprisingly well onstage. The *Dallas Times Herald* called Nina "proud and dignified." One photograph captured her at the microphone, on this day wearing a long white dress and a favorite crocheted cap that had been a gift. The band members, dressed in the prescribed dashikis, were attentive behind her. By the next morning Nina's mood had changed. All the performers were at the airport awaiting their planes, and although those nearby didn't know what started it, Nina and Miles Davis had gotten into a tiff. Nasty names could be heard tossed back and forth. In the meantime, David Clayton-Thomas, the lead singer for Blood, Sweat & Tears, had been visiting with Henry, chatting about their native Canada. He asked if it would be all right to speak with Nina, whom he admired. Henry said sure.

Clayton-Thomas took his cue, but the moment was hardly what he or Henry expected. He barely got out his greeting before Nina gave him an earful. He and his band were just like a bunch of other white musicians, she thundered, exploiting the music of black artists. The band had just recorded "God Bless the Child," a song long associated with Billie Holiday, and in Nina's view, it amounted to stealing. Clayton-Thomas didn't know what to do except listen until Nina finished her harangue. It would have done no good to remind her that she sang and recorded white musicians' material. All she saw were the racial inequities. It aggravated her no end that white groups doing covers of songs first done by black groups got more publicity than the original singers. "I resent that! I deeply resent that," she told one interviewer, the Animals grabbing "Don't Let Me Be Misunderstood" never too far from her mind. "It makes me very bitter and very mad, and it has for years."

The angry Nina had disappeared by the time she performed at the Antibes Juan-les-Pins festival in France ten days after Dallas. The reviewer for *Jazz Hot* barely found enough superlatives to describe her blazing set and its hold on the crowd. Nina spread the credit around. She enthusiastically introduced the band, now back to one guitar player because Henry had had to return home for an emergency. She called out the musicians one by one, dancing a little in front of the piano and speaking in rhythm to the beat of Jumma Santos on his conga drum.

Nina during the Schaeffer Music Festival in Central Park, August 1969
(*Gerrit DeBruin*)

•

SINCE TALKING to *Melody Maker* in December 1968, Nina had sharpened her views about the relationship between music and politics. Then she insisted that nothing, especially politics, should get in the way of her art. But in a long interview with *Ebony* published in August, she declared that "the most important thing these days is to make certain that I make some statement on the stage about how we feel as a race. That's more important than anything." She regularly spoke now of books that influenced her, several written by black men with different viewpoints of the struggle: Eldridge Cleaver's collection of essays, *Soul on Ice*; John A. Williams's autobiographical novel, *The Man Who Cried I Am*; and *'Sippi*, a novel by John Oliver Killens. "To me at this point," she said, "the subject of love between men and women is not as important as getting our people to become completely unified, to forget about their arguments with each other, to come together and see what they can do about getting their rights as human beings."

Two months earlier at the Hampton Jazz Festival, Nina had chided the crowd for its lack of enthusiasm for her message. "Hampton is full of Negroes!" she exclaimed. "I can't hear you singing."

Recognizing the popularity of "To Be Young, Gifted and Black," RCA put out a single, and Weldon expanded the studio arrangement to include a ten-member choir behind Nina. The label released the record early in October, in plenty of time to push it for a rapturously received concert at Philharmonic Hall on the twenty-sixth. As was her habit now, Nina closed the show with the song, but this evening she wanted to talk about her friend Lorraine. She missed her "more and more every day, every day," Nina told the crowd. "I think that very soon now, maybe four or five weeks, I won't be able to sing it anymore for each time I do it, she comes a littler closer, and I miss her a little bit more. It is on 45, RCA Victor," she went on, snapping out of the momentary sadness. "It is not addressed primarily to white people, though it does not put you down in any way. It simply ignores you." A collective cheer mixed with laughter erupted, the whites in this audience, too, either not offended or not inclined to protest publicly. "For my people need all the inspiration and love that they can get. So, since this house is full and there are twenty-two million blacks in this country," Nina added, now in the role of sales-man, "I only want one million to buy this record while it's spinning."

THE *BLACK JOURNAL* SHOW that included Nina's Morehouse concert had aired earlier in October. Along with Nina in perform-ance the segment included a long interview with her and scenes of the family together. They presented an image of contentment, par-ticularly when Nina played hand games with an obviously delighted Lisa. But the reality was something else. When Nina and Andy went overseas again in November for a few concerts, the arguments about fatigue and too much work started again. "You just want me to be a work horse! Nina sing, Nina play, Nina smile," she shouted at Andy before her London date at the Palladium November 16. "Well, I'm sick of it. . . . You can't keep working me to death. I've had enough. I need a rest, man, and you better let me rest or you'll be sorry, really sorry. . . . You better back off!"

Sylvia Nathan, Nina's English friend, had come to see her back-stage and was startled at the ferocity of the outburst. She'd seen Nina angry before, but not like this. Andy couldn't calm her down, and he decided it was best to leave Nina alone. He motioned to Sylvia and her brother David, who had just arrived, and they left. Away from the dressing room, he expressed his frustrations. "It's just hard with the record company screaming for product, trying to keep her in the public eye and taking time," he said. "I'm trying to sort things out, but it's hard." Andy's goal was financial independence, so that Nina could be "highly selective in what she does," as he put it, "you know, you call your shots so you can work about four months a year." But he knew they were not yet there despite the several thousand dollars Nina now earned for each performance.

THE COUPLE SMOOTHED OVER this most recent dustup and returned home to good news: "To Be Young, Gifted and Black" had not only reached the *Billboard* R&B singles chart, it had climbed to number eight, Nina's best showing since "Porgy" a decade earlier. Nina took it as a gift from Lorraine, a sign that her friend approved.

Nina with Michael J. Pollard and Janis Joplin at the
Fillmore East in New York City, December 1969
(*Chuck Stewart*)

Solace still came from a live performance that went well, and
Nina found it again during a two-night stand December 12 and 13 at
the Fillmore East in lower Manhattan. (The unusual bill also
included folk-pop star Richie Havens and Isaac Hayes, a former Stax
session man now on his own and soon to be famous for writing the
soundtrack to the movie *Shaft*.) Nina again aimed her set at the
black patrons in the racially mixed audience, emphasizing African
themes and explaining that she chose one number because "Miriam
Makeba told me to sing it." Nina was in constant motion, "stalking
the stage with the exhortative passion of a female shaman," according to Donald Heckman in *The Village Voice*, "bending and twisting
her sensuously full body in response to the driving rhythms of her
super rhythm section." For a moment she was in a world of her
own making, free from the workaday pressures that so often brought
her low.

19. I Have Become More Militant

~ 1970 ~

Nina and Andy split up early in 1970. On February 14 *Amsterdam News* columnist Jesse H. Walker reported in his *Theatricals* column (usually at least a week behind events) that the couple had separated "and a divorce may be in the works." A front-page story in *The Philadelphia Tribune* February 21 announced that "Nina Simone Leaves Mate Who Earns $100,000 as Her Personal Manager." Andy had moved to a midtown Manhattan apartment, and though he did not comment on his income, he insisted there was no "love triangle" involved. "It's simply a matter of personal difference." Rumors of his infidelities persisted nonetheless.

Years later Nina might have forgotten exactly when she left Andy, but she did not forget the reason. "As usual he refused to accept that I needed rest," she wrote in her memoir, "and I realized he wasn't even sure I meant it. That did it." Lisa was staying with Andy's mother, leaving Nina to do as she wished. "So I walked out on Andy. I left my wedding ring on the bedroom dressing table and caught a plane to Barbados." Nina maintained that she didn't mean her abrupt departure to signal an immediate end but only that she needed "a vacation from my marriage for a while."

Andy described a different scenario. He had been understanding and attentive even in the most troubled times, and now he had had enough. When Nina worried about her mood swings, he readily agreed to pay for medical testing at a prominent New York hospital even though, he remembered in 2006, the doctors "came up with zilch." He maintained that Nina wanted as big a career as he wanted her to have and that she blamed him whenever they came up short. During one argument Andy could barely contain himself. He told Nina that unless she wanted to "turn tricks," there was no money if she didn't perform. "You gotta do the mathematics." He did agree with Nina on one thing: she left abruptly, and he had no idea where she was.

Nina was surprised that Andy didn't track her down. "I assumed he was being proud—just like a man—and wanted me to make the first move. So I caught a plane back to New York," she wrote. "I got home to Mount Vernon and found the house dark, nobody home." Even that blackboard where they had charted her career had vanished. "I'd left Andy in order to make a point about our marriage, and now he'd put up his hands and said, 'OK, if that's the way you want it, I quit.' " At least temporarily the house was hers.

Neither Andy nor Nina apparently stopped to think about the effect of their separation on Lisa. The confusion of that moment stayed with her for years. One day her father was there, "and the next day he wasn't," she recalled decades later. "No one explained anything to me." For the short term, she went to live with relatives in North Carolina.

"TO BE YOUNG, GIFTED AND BLACK" was still riding the charts, and a radio station in Baltimore even sponsored a contest inviting anyone between the ages of eighteen and twenty-five to write an essay or poem about what it means to be young, gifted, and black. The winner, Roland E. Slocum Jr., received an all-expense-paid trip to New York and a ticket to see Nina in a weekend performance at the Gate. They met later, a moment captured in an *Amsterdam News* photograph and reprinted in other black newspapers. Nina liked the way the symbolism connected her to Lorraine: she had taught Nina, and now, through her music, Nina passed on those lessons.

While she sorted out the breakup of her marriage, RCA released a new album drawn from the Philharmonic Hall concert the previous October. Borrowing from that Brooklyn Academy of Music evening nearly two years before, the label called it *Black Gold* and created a cover modeled from the original publicity poster, which had shown Nina in a silhouette profile, her hair in a full Afro. Her name and the album title were within the outline of her Afro, suggesting not inaccurately that the person and the music were one.

"I'm very proud of this one," Nina told the *Philadelphia Bulletin*. "It captures the electricity that can develop between audience and performer that is rarely gotten on records. From this standpoint, this is the best of all. It developed into sort of a love gathering, that concert, and the medium [RCA] was able to capture it completely." Just how completely was evident on "Westwind," the percussion number that Miriam Makeba had given to Nina. "This is a good time to introduce you to the heartbeat of our organization, the pulse of anything we do that centers around the drums," she had told the audience. "And of course you think about that. Really, seriously, we know that your entire life is centered around your heartbeat, and that's written, is it not?" Jumma Santos and Don Alias picked up the signal to weave their intricate rhythms together as Nina started to sing. They modulated their sound, getting softer or louder to blend with her vocals. Though *Black Gold* provided only audio, it took little imagination to conjure up Nina bobbing and weaving about the Lincoln Center stage, carried away once more by the power of her own creation.

To Hollie I. West, a *Washington Post* reporter who happened to be black, the Nina captured on vinyl did not so much perform as engage in a communal act between herself and her audience. "It is almost as if her listeners rededicate themselves during her concerts to the social and cultural revolutions in a cleansing rite or exorcism . . . It must be said," he wrote, "that this is her time and many of us are her people."

Black Gold found an audience quickly, hitting the *Billboard* Top 200 March 14. Although it stayed on the chart for three months, the record didn't rise above number 149. *Black Gold* also registered on the *Cash Box* charts for two months, both magazine tallies suggesting once again a committed if modest-sized contingent of Nina Simone fans.

NINA SPENT MOST of the long break before her next job with her brother Carrol in San Diego, her confidant when they were younger and at her side when a nervous Eunice Waymon, hastily rechristened Nina Simone, took the job at the Midtown in Atlantic City. Now he provided a temporary haven while she contemplated the future. In the middle of March, Nina told the *Philadelphia Bulletin* in a long-distance interview—a setup for two shows in the city March 29—that she felt refreshed. "I've had chronic laryngitis, but it's all better now. I guess partly it was from the pollution. But I had been working too hard, too. The voice needed rest."

Though Nina had been on national television several times, she said she'd like to do more. "I guess they're scared of me," she added, only half joking. But if the networks were reluctant to book her, Andy always thought she was to blame. "You can't scream and holler about killing white people and think they're going to have you as an entertainer," he told Nina, recalling years later how she would go into a rage when she saw Aretha Franklin or Nancy Wilson on a show and holler, "Why ain't I?"

But the last week in April comedian Flip Wilson, a friend and a guest host on NBC's *Tonight Show*, invited her to appear. On the day of the taping, Nina and the musicians arrived at the studio in plenty of time, waiting in a dressing room like the other guests. Wilson mentioned at the top of the hour that Nina would perform, and when he got to her spot, he did his introduction and waited with the audience for her to appear. Nothing happened. The "ad lib" sign flashed, and Wilson vamped for another few minutes.

Still no Nina.

Finally the producers sent out another guest, a beauty consultant, who chatted until it was time for Wilson to wind up the program. After the sign-off, as the audience was leaving, the stage curtain suddenly parted. There was Nina. Surprised to see people heading out the doors, she got up from the piano and started toward them. "Where are my people?" she asked in a loud voice. "Who is with me?" Some thirty-five or so—all but one of them black, according to *Jet* magazine—followed her as she walked off the stage and went to Wilson's dressing room.

"What happened, Flip?" she asked.

Wilson was as baffled as she was and told her he had no idea. But Nina refused to let it drop. Admittedly susceptible to paranoia, she was sure this was a deliberate snub, which only further justified her mistrust of whites in authority. She grabbed Wilson to track down a producer to get an explanation. When they finally found him, he claimed that Nina had been given a thirty-second call before her time slot but asked for five more minutes to get ready. Apparently no one came back to get her, and by the time she came out, the show's top brass said it was too late for a taping that could be inserted for the later broadcast.

Nina didn't buy it. "Several times Miss Simone angrily told off the producer and the assistant," *Jet* reported. Finally the two sides reached an agreement: NBC would issue a statement preceding the actual broadcast that it was not Nina's fault that she did not appear as had been advertised. But Nina insisted that a white announcer make the statement. "I don't want the monkey on Flip's back," she declared. Later Wilson told *Jet*, "There should be no doubt in anyone's mind how I feel about Miss Simone's talent as a performer. It was through my invitation that she was there, and for every time I am asked to fill in as host, I'm going to try and get as many black artists on the show. It's unfortunate that this incident occurred."

Andy, described by *Jet* as Nina's estranged husband, told the magazine the snub was deliberate. Nina had not been properly cued because NBC didn't want her to come out and sing "To Be Young, Gifted and Black." When Skitch Henderson was musical director of the *Tonight Show* in 1965, Andy added, "NBC refused to permit her to perform 'Mississippi Goddam.' "

NINA'S MODEST SCHEDULE provided the best evidence that Andy no longer managed her career: a Chicago concert May 23, a return appearance at the Fillmore East a week later, and then a concert in Nassau. But even with the reduced work schedule she said she wanted, Nina was still unhappy, not only about her personal situation but also because of the disillusion she felt over a civil rights movement that in her view had stalled. She found little to cheer in the progress that had resulted from the landmark federal laws of 1964 and 1965, even if more open public accommodations and a surge in black voting were transforming American society. "Optimists talked about advances we had made, but all I saw were lost opportunities," she wrote. And to her the truth was plain—"we were in retreat . . . The attitude was no longer 'What do we want?' but 'What can we get?' "

Nina seemed determined to make a statement, literally, when she landed in Nassau June 28 for her concert the next day. Bahamian children waiting at the airport presented her with flowers, and though she willingly smiled for photographers, her comments contrasted with the gentle picture that appeared on the front page of *The Nassau Guardian*. The concert the next night, she announced, "will be aimed directly to black people. I suggest that everyone come to the concert to judge for themselves what kind of singer I am," declining to spell out what material she would present.

Nina had been invited by Mafundi Bahamia, a relatively new organization whose goal was to promote the varied culture of the Bahamas. The Bahamian actor Calvin Lockhart, who had appeared in the movie *Cotton Comes to Harlem* and was a friend of Nina's, had urged the organization to bring her to Nassau to help the group raise money.

The June 30 evening got off to a rocky start when Nina kept the racially mixed audience at Le Cabaret Theatre waiting an hour and offered no explanation for the delay. Despite advance publicity, the auditorium was half-empty. She sang one song and then stopped, insulted at the vacant seats. She had been promised an audience of eleven hundred, she said. "I'm used to playing to an audience of five thousand on college campuses."

Nina returned to her program, interspersing the music with provocative observations about black power. The lukewarm response only incited her, and she chided the audience for being "too royal. If you weren't so royal, you could relax and respond," she asserted, instead of being "the coldest audience I've ever sung to. I'm used to playing to those in the front line—those who back Stokely Carmichael . . . You knew what you were inviting down here, Calvin, didn't you?" she shouted, concerned, if briefly, about how all of this might affect her host. "I want to see the black people down front," she went on, pointing to some empty seats near the stage. "The white people are only here because they think it's the thing to do. The white people are accidental and incidental." The embarrassed silence didn't faze her. Turning again to the black patrons, she insisted the English had stolen their land. "You've got to take it back!"

This was too much for one of them. "We've already got it!" he retorted.

The evening degenerated into more argument between Nina and audience members until she announced that "To Be Young, Gifted and Black" would be her last song.

"It's a good thing and about time," hollered one young man, identified later as P. Anthony White, a public relations executive.

When she finished, Nina left the stage, but as people were making their way out, she unexpectedly reappeared. Lockhart raced up and gave her a bouquet that was to have been presented by the president of Mafundi Bahamia, Timothy McCarthy. But he was nowhere to be seen. He had bolted from the auditorium and issued an immediate apology to all who had attended: "I will state categorically that our organization did not dictate or influence Miss Simone's remarks, which were part of her own culture and emotional experience." By that time John Lambert, Mafundi Bahamia's publicity director, had already announced his resignation.

Over the next few days, concertgoers, both black and white,

vented their anger in *The Guardian* and *The Tribune*, another Nassau paper. A few expressed dismay that Nina had the gall to demand full payment—$5,000—for what they regarded as a fiasco. Local radio commentator Mary Kelly said Nina should donate her fee "to the very organization you nearly destroyed. Money alone," she added, "will not erase the memory of this disappointing evening. . . ."

Though Nina would be loath to admit it, had Andy been around, he could have calmed her down before she went out to perform, just as he had done on Long Island right after Dr. King's assassination. Failing that, he surely would have gotten her offstage sooner. But on her own and unmoored, she went wherever the moment took her.

Albert Goldman, a music critic known for his florid style, wasn't in the Bahamas, but he had recently seen Nina when she was in a lecturing mode. And he didn't like it either. "She still pollutes the atmosphere with a hostility that owes less to her color than to the rasping edge of her pride," he wrote in *Life* magazine. "She has still to learn that the humility of the true performer is based on the drastically simple fact that he owes his life to the public." Like Nina's other detractors, Goldman was missing the point, though perhaps it wasn't his fault. He could only see the performer before him, and his harsh comment emphasized the change that had come over Nina. She could be elegant and purposeful onstage, even in the midst of admonishing a noisy crowd. But her anger now was less about an overweening pride that put Goldman off and more a sign of mental illness that left unattended might grow to disabling proportions. Nina didn't see it this way, even when her own words provided the evidence of instability.

"I have become more militant because the time is right," she declared. "I know I am being watched and that in the end, when the deal goes down, I'll be taken seriously; for in many ways I have not been taken seriously by the white world until now. Time is running out, though, because I am sick and tired of my people being beaten and stepped on. I'm sick and tired of my people thinking they are nothing. So I'm just a blind person saying, all right you did this and that, well, you're going to pay for it. Life is a balance and justice is blind. Whoever it hurts, I'm sorry, and I may have to die feeling like this. When it comes to black people in the white world, I would rather die at the hands of a stupid black. Let me die for a simple reason, an argument between blacks or an argument over five cents as happens sometimes when they're gambling in Harlem. Let me die for something stupid as that, but don't let me be killed by the establishment."

THE CALM NINA who took the stage July 11 at the Newport Jazz Festival bore no resemblance to the angry woman in Nassau. She even sounded hopeful—*Washington Post* reviewer Hollie West described one selection as looking to "a brighter future for man." In Nina's immediate future was rest. She left right away for Barbados, where her vacation took an unexpected turn. She struck up a friendship with a hotel porter named Paul, and it turned into "a short uncomplicated affair which made me feel good about myself again . . . Paul gave me all the attention and affection I'd been missing and I loved it—loved it! He took me riding on his motorcycle every day, took me to the movies, went swimming with me, everything—all the fun things I hadn't done for years."

Nina knew she couldn't stay in Barbados forever, and she returned to the United States sometime in the fall to plan for the next year. But even if she wasn't performing, the public saw her in September on a television special, *& Beautiful II*, which traced black music in America over the past century. Though she was not the only star, Nina couldn't have asked for more from the production. In the opening scene the camera homed in on a woman's feet in bejeweled sandals. It proceeded upward to show Nina in a purple robe with metallic stripes that glistened in the light. She looked like an African princess, silver rings on every finger of her left hand, her trademark long earrings swinging as she moved. She stood in front of an eight-person choir, each of the men and women wearing a black robe, singing "To Be Young, Gifted and Black" a cappella following Nina's direction. Then the camera cut away to begin the narrative.

Halfway through, the program returned to Nina, now dressed in a sarong with a matching turban. She stared directly at the camera to deliver Aunt Sarah's story from "Four Women." By the next frame, she had jumped ahead to the final chorus and changed her clothes, now menacing in a long black dress with a black hood pulled up over her hair. The gold band across her forehead was the only hint of color. She spit out the words of the angry street tough, and then as the song neared its end, she pulled down the hood, stared at the camera, and announced with a mixture of joy and defiance, "My name is Peaches!"

The program had highlighted the biggest names in music—Louis Armstrong, Count Basie, Duke Ellington, Billie Holiday, B. B. King—but it was Nina in the final frames. She was back in front of the choir, standing still to preach the blend of hope and pride that is the last exuberant line of her song. "To be young, gifted and black, that's where it's at," she sang as the image faded and the credits rolled.

As if to confirm the message, a group of sixth-grade students at P.S. 92 in Harlem honored Nina a month after *& Beautiful II* aired. Their teachers had worked with them for weeks to create a program about blacks in America using Nina's music to tell some of the story—the tough material ("Backlash Blues") as well as the inspirational ("To Be Young, Gifted and Black"). "I had no idea the seeds I have planted have taken such roots in so many hearts," a tearful Nina said afterward. "I shall never forget this day as long as I live, for I know that you mean it, you must mean it for it is what's happening."

MAINSTREAM AMERICA remained interested in Nina despite her pronouncements about race. *Redbook*, the women's magazine, profiled her in November. The poet Maya Angelou wrote the impressionistic piece, and the editors couldn't have selected a better interviewer. Here was another talented black woman, born poor and raised in rural Arkansas, who had transformed herself into a cultural force through her talent as an actress, dancer, and writer with a deep feeling for Africa and the cause of American blacks. In the early days of the civil rights movement, she had even been a senior coordinator for Dr. King's Southern Christian Leadership Conference. Nina knew she was in capable, empathetic hands as Angelou prodded her to look back on her life. In this telling, Nina highlighted the disappointments rather than the triumphs. "To watch people in church meet and greet their God was like watching a reunion between old friends. But at the same time I felt left out, included in the general happiness but left out from the deeper secrets. I was afraid when my mother spoke in tongues or when she became silent. Especially when she became silent and went into her private place. I feared that the very thing that provided me with joy could also bring about my alienation."

She hadn't talked about Edney Whiteside, her first boyfriend, in a long time, but now she did, though she didn't mention his name. "I found a youthful love and lost it," she said. "That was the turning point. I lost love and found a career. To me I'm a long way from compensating for what I gave up."

Redbook's main appeal was to white America, but Angelou didn't shy away from race. "Did the Black experience press down on your fingers, forcing those peculiar Simone harmonies from the keys?" Angelou wanted to know.

"No Black person can be unaware of the climate in the United States," Nina replied. "But during my early years I was no more aware than most. My sense of responsibility unfolded slowly. Slowly. It's not enough to be a 'great artist,'" she went on. "If I have the power to convince, I am bound to use it. At this time I must stretch to reach my fullest potential. I must address myself to the needs of my people. My people need inspiration."

Inspiration—and confirmation—of a different sort came just three weeks after *Redbook* appeared. *Essence*, an eight-month-old magazine its publisher frankly said was aimed at the modern black woman, featured Nina in a four-page spread. She was thrilled. "I told you it had been a dream of mine for fifteen years to be featured in some fashions," she explained to a friend.

"That's a woman's thing. Black women have to feel beautiful, and it's very bad when everything around you says that only blue-eyed blonds are beautiful. It's an intense interest of mine because it's directly related to what people think of as beautiful."

Nina modeled three long knit dresses by three different designers, in separate poses and with distinct hairstyles. A fourth photo presented a side of Nina rarely seen, as a mother. She posed with Lisa, now eight, nestled against her, the two of them wearing identical cornrows.

Though she couldn't be sure how Lisa was handling her parents' separation, Nina believed her daughter was resilient. "She adapts well," Nina told the magazine. "Whatever country we visit, Lisa quickly picks up the accent and the mood. I'm so proud of my baby. I only wish I had more time for her . . . I want to prepare Lisa for a life in a natural unaffected way," she added. "Being a celebrity's daughter can prove pretty unhealthy when you're on your own." She hadn't fully worked out the parenting arrangements with Andy, but he had made one thing clear. He would pay child support, but only when Lisa was in the United States.

Lisa herself appeared as the normal child Nina wanted to raise, unfazed by her mother's militancy. "My mommy is the greatest person in America," she said. "I like all Mommy's songs except 'Love You Porgy.' I can't stand that song. Everywhere I go people want me to sing it, and I sing it just the way Mommy sounds and they all laugh." But Lisa admitted she really liked the Jackson 5, the youthful singing group. "Could you ask the Jackson 5 to call me sometime?"

20. Definite Vibrations of Pride

~ 1971 ~

On a trip to Holland a few years earlier, Nina had befriended a young Dutch man, Gerrit DeBruin, perhaps impressed by the ingenuity he showed in getting backstage to meet her. He had offered to help some musicians who were playing the same night, and once inside the theater, he found Nina and announced that he was her biggest fan in Holland. Instead of shooing him away, she invited him to pull up a chair while she rehearsed a few songs. She introduced Gerrit to Andy and then told him to join them at a post-concert party at the Amsterdam Hilton. From that moment on they stayed in touch, and Gerrit made sure to attend Nina's return concerts in 1968. He and his wife subsequently named their daughter after her. Gerrit finally came to the United States to see Nina and Andy in the fall of 1969 before returning home early in 1970.

A few months later, just before Christmas, Gerrit received a phone call and was surprised to hear Nina on the other end. She was in Paris, she explained. She had left Andy and had no money. Could she scrape together enough to get to the airport? Gerrit asked. Nina said she could. So he bought her a ticket to Amsterdam, met her when she landed, and then put her up at the American Hotel at the Leidseplein, a popular square in the city. That suited her fine. Not long after the breakup, she had written Gerrit that she wanted to return to Holland anyway "to relax and refine the tuning of myself."

Safe and comfortable for the moment, Nina was still broke, but Gerrit had an idea. He contacted one of his musician friends known as Boy Edgar, and the two agreed that Nina could sing during a special television concert January 8 for the band's twenty-fifth anniversary. In the meantime, Nina had asked Sam if he would become her manager. He was only twenty-six, but he was already an experienced musician and, more important, she trusted him—"truth, dialogue that only blood could have," Sam explained. He flew over to Amsterdam to help with the concert, even sharing a room with Gerrit at a hotel near the Concertgebouw. Money was tight, and there was no time for rehearsal, only the chance for Nina to meet Boy Edgar and his musicians beforehand to sketch out the program.

Nina swept onstage at the appointed time in a new dress, red and trimmed with fur, that was distinctly different from the bold African

Nina with Boy Edgar, a Dutch musician, and his band, before her
performance in January 1971 in Amsterdam.
(*Gerrit DeBruin*)

prints she had worn so often the last couple of years. She opened with a jazzy version of "Compared to What," which the young star Roberta Flack had recently recorded, and then offered a spare "Suzanne" with only modest accompaniment. So far so good. But when she turned to "My Father," written by Judy Collins, the lack of rehearsal with the band was obvious. She started to sing but immediately realized something was off. She started again and willed her way through the rest of the song. Then she got up from the piano and hurried off the stage after barely ten minutes. The audience booed.

For nearly a half-hour Gerrit and Nina's old friend Big Willy, the man who had signed her to Philips, cajoled and prodded to persuade her to continue the performance. She finally agreed to do so after forbidding Boy Edgar's band to make a sound, according to Gerrit. Then in her boiling state she sang a heartbreaking version of "Strange Fruit." Nina was so used to improvising even in the best of circumstances that she decided to go on with "To Love Somebody." When she got to "See-Line Woman," she enlisted the crowd as her backup singers and won them over so completely that they cheered for more. She had saved the night, and she walked offstage to loud applause, carrying the bouquets that had been tossed her way in appreciation.

Two days later Nina saw television footage of the concert and got angry at Boy Edgar all over again for what had happened onstage. "You are right," he screamed back, "but in the end this film is the most beautiful 'Strange Fruit' you ever can do." "Nina started crying," Gerrit remembered, "and they fell into each other's arms. I went to get a bottle of wine and three glasses. Friendship was restored again."

NINA'S FANS IN NEW YORK who tuned in to WNET, the city's public television station, on January 6 saw a completely different performer from the woman who would flounce off the stage in Amsterdam. This Nina had been filmed more than two years earlier for an independently produced documentary, and footage from that project made up a segment in the debut installment of *The Great American Dream Machine:* gentle scenes of Nina with Andy and of Nina at the Village Gate in that white fishnet outfit, rousing the crowd when she jumped up from the piano to do an interpretive dance. Intercut with a performance of "I Wish I Knew How It Would Feel to Be Free" was an interview done at the Mount Vernon house, the images of a life now changed only underscoring the piquant comments that by most any standard were timeless.

"What is freedom," a voice off camera asked.

"I'll tell you what freedom is to me—no fear," Nina declared. "I mean *really*—no fear! If I could have that half of my life, no fear. Lots of children have no fear," and here Nina put her hand to her forehead as she thought for a moment. "It is something really, really to feel—like a new way of seeing something." And then she chuckled, no doubt realizing she couldn't have said it better.

Independent producer Peter Rodis, who was finishing his degree at New York University's film school, provided the footage. A longtime fan, he had gotten permission from Nina and Andy to follow them around to live dates, rehearsals, and an RCA session for the documentary. Rodis knew that if Nina had known the circumstances behind the airing of this segment, she would have been enraged—at least until she realized it was nothing but good publicity. The producers of the new show, according to Rodis, came to him when they realized that a program advertised as showing American culture—art, politics, business—had segments with only white individuals. They had heard about his Nina project and made a deal to license the footage. As it turned out, Nina was not the lone black featured. The show included a segment with Ron Dellums, a civic activist from Berkeley, California, who had recently been elected to Congress.

THE BREAKUP WITH ANDY did nothing to change Nina's contract with RCA. The label brought her back in the studio in February, probably spurred by news that *Black Gold* had been nominated for a Grammy as the Best Rhythm and Blues Vocal Performance— Female. (Aretha Franklin would ultimately win.) This time Nina worked with two new producers and two new musicians. Jumma Santos, whose percussion work she liked so much, had left, but she wanted to keep that sound and turned to Leopoldo Fleming. He had played percussion on and off with her good friend Miriam Makeba. Leopoldo never forgot the first time he met Nina, coincidentally at Makeba's house. She had lent Nina a fur coat, and Nina returned it when an afternoon barbecue happened to be under way in the yard. Leopoldo watched wide-eyed from the driveway as Nina handed the garment back.

"This is not the coat I gave you," a startled Makeba said.

"I had it restyled for you," Nina replied, giving her friend what was now a mink jacket and acting as though it was the most natural thing in the world to have altered the coat because she thought it was a good idea.

"Miriam was gracious," Leopoldo recalled, and accepted the "restyled" mink in silence.

Shortly before the February session, Nina called Leopoldo and asked if he would work with her. Of course, he said, but he told her that he had just been initiated as a member of the Santeria, an Afro-Caribbean religion that required its initiates to wear only white for a year. He was relieved when Nina said that was no problem.

Nadi Qamar, the other musician, specialized in unusual African instruments: the valiha, a Madagascan bamboo harp, and what he called the "mama-likembi," which resembled a square-shaped xylophone. Nina had met Nadi some weeks earlier when she attended a production of an Ed Bullins play at the New Lafayette Theatre in Harlem. Nadi was in the band that provided incidental music. He had no idea she was in the audience until he went into the lobby afterward. "I just put the mama-likembi in her face and said, 'This is what I do,'" he recalled. "I just put it up under her nose." Nadi hadn't known that Nina enjoyed the music so much she wanted to hire the entire band. But only Nadi joined up.

Leopoldo and Nadi had been recruited to play on the selection of pop-rock songs that Nina and RCA hoped would keep her current. Among them was George Harrison's "Here Comes the Sun," "Mr. Bojangles," by Jerry Jeff Walker with vocal harmony from Sam, and "My Way," which turned out to be the most distinctive number, largely because of the double-time bongo beat underneath the entire song. Leopoldo came up with the idea, and nobody in the studio flinched when he suggested it. His brisk counterpoint to the sweeping strings that had been ordered for the session kept the track from descending into melodrama. Nina sang with conviction, never treacly even in her hushed tones.

RCA packaged these tracks along with five others into an album called *Here Comes the Sun*. The record jacket, though, reversed the customary presentation. Instead of a photo or some kind of likeness of the artist on the front, it was on the back, and instead of a shot of Nina, the label used a photo of twelve-year-old Eunice Waymon wearing a neat schoolgirl's blouse, her hands resting primly in front of her. She had inscribed that picture with a long passage about music and the sounds of various instruments. It was as inexplicable as any other marketing decision, and not a word of explanation about the photo was offered on the record jacket.

When *Here Comes the Sun* was released in the summer, it found a month-long niche at the bottom of the *Billboard* Top 200 but never got above number 190.

NINA HAD GIVEN SAM a credit as the "production coordinator" on this latest album, and he had earned it. Coordinating Nina was no easy task. The first date after the recording session provided another reminder of his sister's mercurial nature. The event was a benefit concert in Dallas for one of the AME churches, and she kept the audience waiting two hours. Tad Hershorn, a white teenager with a zest for photography and jazz, made certain to be at the concert as soon as he heard about it, and he stationed himself precisely to capture Nina in performance. He had long forgotten the reason she gave, if any, for being so late, but he remembered her performance, especially a duet with Sam on "Let It Be Me" that moved the entire auditorium. If anyone inside had been irritated by Nina's tardiness, all was forgiven after this number.

Nina was a good hour late for a concert February 27 to celebrate the first-ever black culture week at St. Louis University, but she blamed the delay on heavy traffic for a Harlem Globetrotters basketball exhibition under way across the street. She offered no explanation a few days later in Chicago when she kept a packed Orchestra Hall waiting an hour at the Black Arts Festival '71. But like the crowds in Dallas and St. Louis, the audience forgave her as soon as she came onstage, on this evening in an eye-catching black gown cut low at the top and slit high up one leg. She wanted "to talk to my people," in both word and song, she said, and intended or not, the performance demonstrated how much her music had changed, even in the last year, from what still fit the traditional jazz format—piano, bass, drums, and sometimes guitar. Now she had an altogether more unusual and percussive sound and a show that allowed her to sing, chant, and dance and almost as an afterthought sit at the piano and play.

"Yeah, I feel it . . . don't you feel it too?" she exulted at one moment, the crowd cheering while she moved around the stage.

"Teach!" someone yelled out. "Tell the truth!" came another cry in a hall more accustomed to the sounds of Mozart and Beethoven now turned into the church of Nina Simone.

NINA'S PERIODIC BLOWUPS were so well documented that her official press release noted them, although with some explanation: "Unfortunately business relationships in the past, coupled with the built-in problems of a Negro-American, have made her susceptible to hurt and impatient with ignorance." But to Nina it went even deeper. "This is the dirtiest business I've ever heard of. They try to make a slave of you," she declared to *The Philadelphia Inquirer's* Jack Lloyd right before an April 2 concert at the Academy of Music. "It is the dirtiest and most immoral business in the world. It can be beautiful, too, of course," she said, abruptly changing direction. "You can move the whole world with music, and this is beautiful." Then she made another U-turn. "But people make you into a robot. I'm not a robot because I protest. I protest all the time. . . . "

Nina's actions the night of the concert proved her point. The starting time came and went, but she remained backstage. When one of the promoters finally asked about the delay, he was told "Miss Simone will go on at her convenience." Onstage fifty minutes late Nina insisted the delay was not her fault. She "adheres to the starting times of show business," she said, "but the engineers were late getting their job done, and so I am late." The loud applause suggested that the crowd forgave her. She elicited the usual appreciative response to her material over the next hour, but on this night it brought her little joy. "Just because I belong to you is no reason for you to think you own me," she said, leaving the audience to wonder what had prompted the tart comment.

When Nina was late again for a Mother's Day concert at Carnegie Hall, Sam simply shrugged his shoulders. "Lateness . . . tardiness, that was her nickname," he lamented. Her musicians thought that mostly it boiled down to Nina coming onstage when she felt like it. Period. But at this event she told the audience that her dress needed last-minute repairs before she could make a proper entrance. Perhaps that was the case. But even if it was just a story, this late arrival, like the others, reflected Nina's complicated relationship with the audience just as her snappish comments did. Albert Goldman had chastised her for a lack of humility, but Nina understood as well as anyone that an artist needs her public. Her resentment at this immutable fact occasionally boiled over, and the resulting behavior could fairly be seen as her way of trying to rewrite the rules for performer and audience.

WHEN NINA AND SAM arrived in Cairo, Illinois, for a concert to benefit a civil rights group, they knew this was different from the usual fund-raising events. Cairo is a small river town in the southernmost point of the state, with a racial history to rival the Mississippi Delta. During the Civil War, Union soldiers used it as a headquarters and brought freed slaves there. But bounty hunters eager to round up the ex-slaves and return them to their Southern owners also called it home, much to the relief of many white citizens. "Free Negroes Are Over-Running Cairo," blared one local headline at the time. By the early twentieth century blacks made up roughly 10 percent of the population, but the relationship between the races was rarely smooth. It was no surprise when tensions spiked after blacks held in the local jail were lynched. Decades later the city's black residents felt as though the victories of 1964 and 1965 had bypassed them altogether. Federal law may have mandated desegregated public accommodations and voting rights, but in Cairo blacks could not get a library card, swim in the public pools, or use the city's parks. The local banks and department stores, among other institutions, still refused to hire them.

After a jailed black soldier was found hanging in his cell in the summer of 1967, the subsequent rioting prompted the governor to send the National Guard. Authorities labeled the death a suicide; black residents insisted he was a victim of police brutality. After two years of futile negotiations with white leaders to improve economic conditions, the black community began a boycott of certain white businesses. The principal organizers banded together as the United Front and were sustaining their effort by regular marches and demonstrations that featured visiting civil rights leaders and entertainers who wanted to show their support. Invited to be part of the "Black Solidarity Day for Survival" on June 20, Nina jumped at the chance to participate, a perfect forum to meld her music and her message.

Sam realized that this year alone he had played five events with Nina to benefit black enterprises, but he had never performed in the heart of a protest. Walking around in Cairo, he took note of the "goon squads," as he called the whites who stared menacingly at the protesters, but any uneasiness vanished when he saw the looks of appreciation on the faces of the black residents who had tangible evidence once again that they were not alone. Sam's resolve only deepened when the Reverend Ralph Abernathy, one of Dr. King's lieutenants, told the Solidarity Day crowd that President Richard Nixon "sent the vice president of the United States around the world to hand out moon rocks to heads of state when he should have sent loaves of bread to the poor people of Cairo."

As Sam remembered it, Nina offered much of the same program from a few weeks earlier, first at Illinois State University in Normal for the college's black fine arts festival and then in Columbus, Ohio, where she had done a benefit for the East Central Citizens Organization. "With rare exceptions," *The Columbus Dispatch* had reported, "all her songs were rendered for black listeners and black participation": "Black Is the Color of My True Love's Hair," "Westwind," "To

Be Young, Gifted and Black," and one that Sam thought was particularly effective, "He's Got the Whole World in His Hands."

"Miss Simone won the hearts of Cairo's Blacks and other participants in Solidarity for Survival," the *East St. Louis Monitor* wrote later. (Cairo's white-owned paper did not cover anything related to the protest.) It wasn't only her singing, the *Monitor* explained, but her participation in a fifty-block march that took the protesters through the black community and past the boycotted stores. One of the many *Monitor* photos showed Nina with the head of the United Front, the Reverend Charles Koen. Sam knew there was more to the photo. Nina and Koen had taken an instant liking to each other and embarked on a brief affair. "They got along quite well at the very beginning," Sam said. "But he couldn't meet her demands — couldn't keep up with her. He couldn't be flying to New York or meet her in Chicago. He couldn't afford it, couldn't afford it emotionally."

BY LATE SUMMER Don Alias had left the band to join Miles Davis. Nina was furious, and she let Davis know it in a blistering phone call that was so loud Leopoldo could hear her from another room. Nina also blamed Gene Perla, convinced he had encouraged Don to leave. She gave him a tongue-lashing he remembered long after.

Leopoldo told Nina to hire Warren Benbow, a young Manhattan drummer he liked who had recently worked with the singer Betty Carter. Nina followed up and told Warren to be at the band's next rehearsal at the Mount Vernon house. Determined not to be late, he showed up on the appointed day, walked up the front steps, and rang the bell. "She opened the door with a silk outfit on — the whole Nina Simone outfit," Warren recalled. "Yes," she told him, "the rehearsal is a little later. Please come back."

Warren wasn't offended. He guessed that no one else was home and that Nina was uneasy with a stranger, even one who came recommended. "She didn't know me," he said, "and I came back." Nina kept a snare drum and a high hat at the house, which were sufficient for a rehearsal, and when everyone had assembled, they ran through a few songs. Only later did Warren realize that this was his audition.

He knew he had passed when Nina told him to be over at RCA a few days later to rehearse with Leopoldo, Weldon Irvine, and Nadi Qamar.

Warren expected the same easygoing atmosphere he had found at the house, but Nina kept her distance in the studio. "Tell the drummer to play softer," she told Weldon at one point.

"You can tell me," Warren piped up. "I'm sitting right in front of your face."

Momentarily startled, Nina said, "OK."

Even though he was the youngest one in the room by at least a decade, Warren wanted Nina to know he wasn't afraid of her. "Betty Carter told me to respect myself," he said. But Warren's brashness covered the fact that he was tickled to be playing with Nina. "She was a genius," he said, recalling with great clarity a moment they had together talking about music. "You know Warren, I can play anything," she said, and then she reeled off a couple of intricate runs on the keyboard. "I don't have to think about this." He believed her. "Wherever she wants to go, she can go."

FIVE YEARS AFTER their first collaboration, Ron Delsener still got along well enough with Nina to book her again. This time he sponsored her at Philharmonic Hall for the evening of October 10. Twenty minutes after the announced starting time, eight p.m., Nina finally came onstage to cheers from the crowd, roughly two thirds of them black patrons. They could not have known that an unusual night, even by Nina's standards, lay in store. At her request Nadi did some of the piano work, though he protested that the audience had come to hear her. He also assisted in a new feature, Nina's short playlet in which she acted out the part of a junkie. She deliberately mumbled as part of her character, but her mumbles got lost in the fuzzy amplification, leaving the audience more confused than enlightened.

When she finally sang, she ventured into gospel, the Beatles ("Come Together"), the James Taylor hit "You've Got a Friend," and saved "To Be Young, Gifted and Black" as an encore, inviting the audience to join in. But she darkened the mood at the end with a pointed "Let My People Go" and a discordant version of "God Bless America." "Miss Simone's message doubtless was disturbing to some of her audience," *Variety*'s reviewer wrote, noting the minority of whites, "but she meant to disturb. Her prime target was white subjugation of blacks in the U.S." "We know where you've been," Nina had announced to no one in particular. *Billboard* reviewer Radcliffe Joe, himself black, found the evening troubling. Not only had Nina kept everybody waiting, he wrote in the October 23 issue, she "then subjected them to an exercise in black militancy. That Miss Simone is concerned with the social and political problems facing America today is commendable, but the arbitrary use of her entertainment as a political forum was hardly acceptable." Joe worried that Nina could alienate enough of her audience to damage her career.

But Nina was clear in her objective. Two weeks later she performed at a benefit in Harlem to raise money for research on sickle-cell anemia, a hereditary disease that struck with particular force in the black community. Billed as "Operation Get Down," the event was put together by a man named Barry Hankerson, identified in the program as the spokesman for the Liberation Church. According to a brief biography, "His main ideas center around the use of self-awareness and complete black unity," concepts long embraced by Nina. The evening also featured Nikki Giovanni, a poet, and Myrna Summers, who led a choir known as the Interdenominational Singers. "Tonight we are presenting three women representing three different aspects of the black community and black femininity," Hankerson said by way of introduction, which must have pleased Nina, given how the message of "Four Women" echoed through his comments. From Nina, he added, "one gets definite vibrations of pride, black sorrow, and spiritual release."

One aspect of that pride was the way physical beauty could be defined to embrace shapes, sizes, and colors beyond white America's usual standard. Nina had taken a short vacation to Jamaica in July, and in a letter to her friend Gerrit DeBruin, she mentioned how much she loved the beach. "I've been sitting in the sun and am very much blacker," she wrote. "I love it." What Nina had enjoyed about the *Essence* feature was the chance to make a statement about beauty with her own image. So it should have surprised no one that a photograph from the *Essence* shoot a full year earlier showed up as the cover photo for the Philharmonic concert and the Operation Get Down benefit. Nina wore a floor-length gray knit gown with a deep V-neck that set off her elaborate, dangly necklace. She sat on the floor, her right hand used as a brace and her knees tucked into the folds of the dress. She stared straight ahead with a look of alluring determination. Twenty years after the shoot, Nina would approve this photo as the cover of her autobiography.

NINA CONTINUED TO PURSUE her agenda in a show for servicemen November 18 just outside of Fort Dix, New Jersey. It was part of the mischievously titled "Free the Army" tour that Jane Fonda and fellow actor Donald Sutherland had created to entertain disaffected soldiers at bases around the country. Nina, with Warren and Sam in tow, met with Fonda and Sutherland November 16 at a Manhattan restaurant to talk about the program. Warren could hardly believe it when the agreement was written out right there on the tablecloth. Nina recalled that she specified the show would be for black GIs just back from the war "so that I could play at least once for my own people." And while black soldiers were certainly included, the free program at the Town Theatre in Wrightstown would be open to any soldiers.

Before the meeting ended Sutherland grabbed a paper napkin to execute his own deal. He scrawled out the promise that in one of his upcoming films "Nina Simone shall sing at least one special title song." The gesture was well-meaning, even if the promise never became a reality.

The day of the concert Fonda said several soldiers had told her that Fort Dix officials threatened to restrict everyone to the base so that they couldn't attend the show. But no such order materialized, and the theater was standing room only by the time the program started. The men and women left no doubt about how eager they were for the music. "We want Nina! We want Nina!" they chanted until the MC came out and announced, "Brothers and sisters, the High Priestess of Soul, Nina Simone." The emotional peak of the set came with a dramatic rendering of George Harrison's "My Sweet

Lord." The Bethany Baptist Church Junior Choir from South Jamaica, New York, sang behind Nina, Weldon directing the choral arrangement he had written for the group. RCA technicians were recording the performance.

The choir set the mood with a harmonized "Hallelujah!" "Oh my I really want to see you—I've got to see you," Nina responded, and then she went on for another ten minutes, alternately singing and talking, at one point trading phrases with Sam about searching for the Lord. "I've been waitin' all my life," she sang, "so you got to bring the truth."

Then she stopped playing, and chanted her way into a poem, "Today Is a Killer." "Nobody has taught us any patience, Lord," she lamented. "Hope it's not too late now." She paused and returned to the song, Weldon cuing the choir at just the right instant. She quieted everything down again to talk about dreams and wishes and embracing "a stolen moment of happiness" only to see it crumble away. She found her way back to praise the Lord but ended on a somber note. "Today, who are you, Lord," she asked, and then declared, "You are a killer," the choir rising behind her in an oddly buoyant "Hallelujah!"

Years later Nina remembered that "The GIs—only kids, most of them—sat quietly and listened." But the *Trenton Times* reported the day after the event that the soldiers were anything but reserved. If they had been suffering from malaise, the paper indicated that Nina jolted them out of it. They gave her "a standing, shouting ovation."

ON PAPER Nina's date at the Academy of Music in New York, December 11, looked like it would be a continuation of the good time she had at Fort Dix. A promoter she knew handled the booking, the venue was local, and because there were other acts on the bill, she didn't have to perform too long. Her contract called for two shows, and except for an overlong intermission between acts, the first went fine. "Nina is the only artist I have seen hold an impatient audience quiet while one of her musicians tunes his instrument," one reviewer wrote later.

The theater manager needed to clear the house for the second show, which took nearly two and a half hours, but finally it got under way. After Labelle, a trio of women headed by Patti LaBelle (who would go on to a successful solo career), it was time for Nina. But none of her musicians returned to take their places. Instead a man came out and read a statement Nina had apparently written backstage:

> Ladies and Gentlemen, I would like to say that I will not appear in the second show because these people have no money with which to pay me. You have my heart, as you know, which I have proven in the past fifteen years, the climax being "Young, Gifted and Black," which is now recognized as the Black National Anthem all over the world. With the song "Mississippi Goddam" it was apparent to all blacks that I was unequivocally dedicated to the struggle of my people, and since then have consistently shown this dedication. So do not ask me for more. I deserve payment for my work just as you do—be it $35 or what, there is no difference. I leave you with love and peace to lift your level of consciousness so that you, too, may live a life of which you are proud.

The grandiose tone of Nina's comments was beside the point. Her fans understood her position and aimed their anger at the management. They bolted from their seats and raced to the box office, shouting demands for a refund. Those closest to the ticket window beat on the glass so hard that it broke in three places, but they soon realized no money would be returned. When the police arrived, it took some thirty officers to restore order.

21. This Ain't No Geraldine Up Here

~ 1972 ~

Washington, D.C.'s Constitution Hall was nearly filled to its 3,800-seat capacity February 12 for Nina's first performance in the city in several years. It was not lost on her that three decades earlier the Daughters of the American Revolution, who ran the hall, had barred Marian Anderson, the heroic contralto, from singing there because she was black. It was equally well known, like spring following winter, that First Lady Eleanor Roosevelt had stepped in to ensure that not only could Anderson sing in Washington, she could have her concert at the city's prized outdoor venue, the steps of the Lincoln Memorial. So Nina's departure from her usual opening number on this Saturday night in 1972 was especially noteworthy. She walked briskly onstage toward the piano, but instead of sitting down to play, she stopped and asked everyone to sing "To Be Young, Gifted and Black," which she again proclaimed the black national anthem. Her spirits were not diminished because the majority black crowd seemed unsure of the words. She simply spoke each line first and then conducted the singing.

Nina tried to balance every performance now, seeking to apportion her art and her anger into a workable whole. She might miss the mark, but her calculation showed in the songs she chose, the musicians she brought with her, what she wore, and what she said. "You have to know when to push, and, you know, when to not," she observed. "No one can tell you, though."

At Constitution Hall she put plenty of bite in her program, crystalized by "All Hid." Nina transformed a rhyme that black children chanted while playing hide-and-seek into pointed commentary on the tensions between the black community and local police departments. Instead of twenty-four robins knocking at one's door, as the chant goes, she put twenty-four policemen at the door and the people inside ending up "in a cooling bin."

Though the audience gave Nina a standing ovation at the end of the night, MC Bob "Nighthawk" Terry, a local black disc jockey, worried that she might have gone too far. "I just want to tell my white brothers they should not feel excluded," he said. The crowd booed, but *Washington Star* reviewer John Segraves, a white man, understood. If not feeling entirely excluded, Segraves was disappointed. "Oh, Nina Simone, what has happened to one of the most distinctive styles ever to keep a crowd in awe?" he wondered. He missed the Nina "who used to sit, half hidden behind her huge grand piano all murky and mysterious, doling out the lush lyrics and the pretty single notes as if they were special gifts to her hushed audience." Segraves conceded that when Nina turned militant, when she got up from the piano and danced her sultry steps, the audience "bought it all." The evening "became more crusade than concert," Segraves said, "which I consider sorrowful because I came prepared to hear one of the truly fine pop vocalists and pianists in America."

Nina hardly saw the two as mutually exclusive. "I've always thought that I was shaking people up, but now I want to go at it more," she explained in one interview. "I want to go at it more deliberately. I want to go at it more coldly. I want to shake people up so bad, that when they leave a nightclub where I performed, I just want them to be to pieces, and we're all reelin'. That's my idea of a great performance, when I have pleased me and pleased them, and everybody's feeling like everything's all right."

Nina's reception March 31 at the Rainbow Sign in Berkeley, a new social center for the area's black community, proved her point, the crowd only too happy to be part of her plan. Before the first show, the mayor had even proclaimed "Nina Simone Day," citing her "stunning influence over black people" and "her resolute convictions to do something about what's wrong with the world." A member of the Bay Area Urban League announced he was starting a campaign to make "To Be Young, Gifted and Black" officially declared a new black national anthem, though the lack of such a proclamation did not deter Nina.

By the time the second show started, it was already Easter Sunday. "We never used to sing gospel out of church," Nina told the crowd, "but now that a white girl's made a lot of money from a recording, it's all right to sing 'Amazing Grace' in public." She was referring to Judy Collins, still bristling over RCA's reluctance to let her record the song. Then she led the audience in an a cappella version.

NINA PLAYED to a responsive crowd April 29 during the New Orleans Jazz and Heritage Festival. She filled her sets with what *Down Beat*'s Dan Morgenstern called her "prancing and shaking in that mixture of political preaching and sex that is uniquely hers." She exited to appreciative applause, and then B. B. King and his band came on, all of them black musicians except for keyboard player Ron Levy, who was white. King was introducing his sidemen with a slow bluesy vamp behind him when Nina suddenly appeared at the back of the stage and walked toward Levy with Don Pullen, her keyboard player, in tow. (Sam was temporarily away working in Hollywood.) She tapped Levy on the shoulder and motioned him to leave. Levy didn't know what to do. He wanted to keep playing, but he didn't want to cause a public scene. So he got up, assuming that Nina had worked something out with King ahead of time but hadn't told him. Nina took Levy's place and then grabbed Pullen, who was obviously uncomfortable, to sit down next to her. She played a few chords and signaled Pullen to take over. Then she left.

Backstage, Cato T. Walker, King's longtime equipment manager and good friend, had seen everything. "Get your butt back up there," he told Levy. "You want to give your gig away?" So Levy returned to the stage and whispered to a relieved Pullen to get up. He sat back down just as King's introductions were ending and barely had enough time to get settled for the next tune. Later, Nina confronted Levy. "You're a white boy. You shouldn't be playing with B. B. King," she snapped. Levy absorbed the swipe in silence, but those who had witnessed the bizarre moment were united in their view that Nina had inexcusably crossed the line. Though he kept it to himself, Leopoldo was aghast. "I thought she was wrong," he said. "I was not amused."

ARETHA FRANKLIN, whose blend of gospel and rhythm and blues propelled her to stardom, had released a new album in February that was partly an homage to Nina. Franklin called the record *Young, Gifted and Black*. Her version of the title song had the churchy fervor of Nina's treatment mixed with a hint of syncopation that allowed Franklin to put in her trademark exhortations—"Isn't that a sweet thing? Yes it is!"—when she felt like it. The best news for Nina and Weldon as co-writers of the song was that Franklin's album sold very well. It rose to number eleven on the *Billboard* Top 200, number thirteen on the *Cash Box* tally, and stayed on both charts for more than six months. Nina and Weldon could hardly begrudge her a success greater than theirs, given that they were entitled to a share of the proceeds from the sales, though artists often complained they never received the money due them.

When Chicago's Malcolm X College awarded Nina an honorary degree June 9, it provided more evidence of her role as an exemplar of black culture. The honor was gratifying, too, for someone whose formal education had stopped abruptly when she was still a teenager. But now she stood onstage at the college's West Side gymnasium alongside the provocative writer Amiri Baraka (formerly LeRoi Jones); Robert J. Brown, a special assistant to President Richard Nixon; and the civil rights lawyer Clifford Alexander, who would go on to become secretary of the army under President Jimmy Carter.

That her longtime friend Betty Shabazz, Malcolm's widow, helped bestow the degree only added to the occasion.

Nina reveled in the moment only briefly. She had to rush out to San Francisco to perform the evening of the tenth at the Bay Area Jazz Festival, another George Wein production. Any good feelings left from Chicago dissipated when Nina learned that *Chronicle* reviewer Dennis Hunt was at the event, and onstage she didn't hide her anger. She informed the audience that Hunt had published a negative review about the Rainbow Sign shows two months earlier, and, apparently unconcerned about any future ramifications, she admonished him in front of the crowd never to write about her again.

To any neutral observer Hunt's earlier comments reflected more disappointment than criticism, falling well short of the evisceration that could be doled out by a dissatisfied critic. Hunt had said that he was a fan of Nina's, but "I am now somewhat immune to her spell, and, frankly, annoyed that she continues to squander her formidable gifts on dated material." Her protest songs, he argued, were reaching the wrong audience because "the kind of people who might profit from her barbed social messages would never bother to attend a Simone show . . . Certainly blacks do not need Miss Simone to tell them what is happening," he went on. "Miss Simone should branch out and not concentrate so heavily on archaic protest songs. If she were someone with limited talent, it would not matter. But it is criminal for a performer of obvious versatility to linger in such a rut," a notion that would be echoed later in the summer by other reviewers, usually white men.

Ignoring Nina's command, Hunt needled her once more after the jazz festival. "Apparently Miss Simone is of the opinion that if a critic has nothing complimentary to say about her then he should say nothing at all." As he saw it, much of the audience "seemed disinterested in her," but according to Doris G. Worsham, who covered Nina's set for the *Oakland Tribune*, she had engaged them. "Her protest songs have pervaded her repertoire more and more of late, and the audience Saturday night gobbled them up."

It wasn't only the California crowd. Nina found a similarly receptive audience at the Hampton Jazz Festival June 24 and again at the

Schaeffer Music Festival in Central Park a week later. Critics might not like it, but Nina's music, not only the lyrics but the presentation, too, continued to strike a special chord with black audiences. Just as Hollie West had written three years earlier, by giving vent to her feelings onstage, Nina invited fans to do the same with theirs, and in the process she became a catalyst for examination or perhaps a reexamination of their own anger.

A less appealing side of Nina's rage emerged in Cincinnati July 22 at the Ohio Valley Jazz Festival during what was usually her best moment, "To Be Young, Gifted and Black." But instead of a joyful coming together, the song turned into an embarrassment that revealed Nina out of control. First she coaxed the crowd to sing with her. Then she berated them for singing too loudly and told them to quiet down, leaving everyone bewildered. She was no stranger to faulty sound systems, especially at big outdoor venues, and most of the time she handled the problems smoothly. But on this night, impatient with the balky microphone, she swore audibly from the stage.

Nina was still angry the next night in New York, where she opened an ambitious two-week music and culture program at Lincoln Center, "Soul at the Center," designed for the region's black community. Now her target was RCA, and before she sang a note at Philharmonic Hall, she lashed out at the label for not promoting her properly. She also claimed that overall "suppression" of black artists had diminished the careers of Diana Ross and Dionne Warwick, two established black singers. Nina took off after white music critics and even some black writers, too, who she felt had been unfair. Then she shifted gears to bemoan the scourge of drugs and exhorted the audience to "Kill the pusher! Kill the pusher!"

Nina's erratic behavior must have alarmed friends, who worried that it signaled another period of instability. She was outwardly calm when she returned to Lincoln Center three nights later to attend an all-gospel program. But at the end of the concert, she behaved strangely again. Apparently moved by the music, she jumped up from her seat shouting, "Yes, yes, yes, oh my God," went up onstage, and sat down at the piano. She played and a man she brought with her sang as anxious producers eyed the clock, worried about union overtime. One hundred or so patrons stopped to listen until she was finished, no more than five minutes after she started.

"What can you say? That's Nina," lamented Ellis Haizlip, one of the festival's producers, knowing he had been powerless to stop her but now grateful that her burst of inspiration had been a short one.

FOUR YEARS AFTER much of his footage was shot, Peter Rodis found a local taker for his documentary project, WOR television. The Nina who showed up on the screen August 24 was far from the angry woman who had been at Lincoln Center a month earlier, not only in hairstyle and dress, but also in the way she sounded. This Nina was gentler and resolute as she spoke about her sense of mission.

"I can't tell you in words what I want," she said at one point, sitting on a couch in the Mount Vernon house. "But I am wise enough to tell you that life doesn't give us the dreams as we dream them, and so I don't know what's going to happen. But all I know is that the force inside me is pushing me toward something," she continued. "It's very frustrating to find you're not moving as fast as you'd like, and sometimes I get afraid that I won't be able to do all I'm supposed to do before I die. But I don't know where I'm supposed to go—and I'm on my way—slowly, but going."

The final frames of the documentary featured Nina performing, each one showing her from a different angle. Over the footage she was singing Billy Taylor's "I Wish I Knew How It Would Feel to Be Free," her exotic and exuberant moves suggesting how the freedom Taylor wrote about might look.

NINA MAY HAVE publicly chastised RCA, but that didn't stop the label from releasing another album early in September, *Emergency Ward*. The distinctive record jacket was a collage of newspaper articles about the Vietnam War, clipped short and pasted every which way and covering the front and back. The words "Emergency Ward" were set diagonally over the collage in large red letters, like a banner headline announcing a cataclysm. Nina had picked the title, explaining ruefully in one interview that "the times are desperate and America is one big emergency ward with everybody in the hospital."

The record had only four tracks. The long version of "My Sweet Lord/Today Is a Killer" from the Fort Dix event filled the first side. The flip side included "Poppies," a lushly orchestrated anti-drug song. "Take a deep breath if you're reaching for truth," goes one line. Then comes a knock at the door "and death takes another youth." The last track was another George Harrison song, "Isn't It a Pity," which Nina improvised to twice its original length. "Until we concentrate on giving, giving, giving/Mankind don't stand a chance," she sang, accompanied only by her rolling piano chords. One reviewer called it "cosmic exasperation," a release of pent-up sadness that lay beneath the anger that was now so frequent.

"I wish that it had not been necessary to become socially and politically oriented," she said shortly after *Emergency Ward* was released. "I don't want to be Jesus Christ. I don't know beans about politics—I mean technically. But I had to choose this way. My people were in trouble . . . I believe in evolution, which to me is God," Nina went on. "I'm always thrilled when I hear of some fantastic thing that happens with the weather—something destructive. This is nature rising up and saying to man, 'I'm bigger than you. I can save you or I can destroy you.' On that occasion, man is brought to his knees."

"I WANT TO GO in that den of those elegant people, with their old ideas and smugness and just drive them insane," Nina had said in the Rodis documentary. On October 28, she found herself in just such a place, the two-year-old John F. Kennedy Center for the Performing Arts, Washington's state-of-the-art concert hall. But she could not have predicted the circumstances surrounding the event. They were anything but joyous. Nina would be forty years old this coming February 21. Her beloved older sister Lucille was only forty-eight, but she had been stricken with cancer and died October 2. At the same time, their father, J. D. Waymon, lay desperately ill in a convalescent home not too far from Tryon. Nina had gone back home, but it wasn't to see him. Instead she spent much of the time practicing for the Washington date under the tutelage of Miss Mazzy, her first piano teacher. She found it therapeutic, especially, as she recalled in her memoir, because she had been estranged from her father for the last eighteen months. Immersing herself in the piano helped keep the complicated feelings at bay when she refused the family's entreaties to go and see him.

The break between father and daughter came during a visit when she overheard J.D. telling Sam that he was the one who had provided for the family all through the years. Nina was astounded. "I stood there in the dark and listened to Daddy tell lie after lie after lie," she wrote. Not only had J.D. diminished everything Kate had done to help provide for her children, but he had also completely disregarded the help Nina had given her parents as soon as she started earning money. "It was being able to make up for the sacrifices they had made for me which made me glow inside," she wrote. And now her father claimed none of it ever happened. Nina vowed right then that she would never speak to her father again, banishing in one stroke any memory of all that she once had cherished, even their special time together when J.D. had been so ill and the private "real" music they made whenever Kate was out of earshot.

J.D. died October 23, while Nina was still in Tryon. His funeral was Saturday, October 28, the day of the Kennedy Center concert. She refused to cancel the date. That evening she purposely wore all black. She told the audience about her loss and then performed a new song that wove the circumstances of her father's death into the lyrics—how he had wasted away to eighty-eight pounds, was nearly blind, and just "when I needed him most, he was already a ghost." She took the song's refrain, "alone, again, naturally," from British rocker Gilbert O'Sullivan's hit of the same name. Nina performed with surprising disengagement. But her coolness only served to draw in the audience, and the moment seemed to be "an apparent purgation for her," according to Hollie West, who attended the concert.

Nina didn't leave out politics, however muted her message was musically and otherwise, compared to past performances. From John Lennon's "Woman Is the Nigger of the World," which some radio stations were refusing to play, Nina took one of the lines—"a woman is the slave of the slaves"—as the impetus for a short sermon on second-class citizenship. The mostly black crowd leapt to their feet, cheering.

Though Nina didn't say so explicitly, she missed having Sam around, especially during this time of loss. By the force of his personality and experience, Nadi had become something of a spiritual adviser, introducing her to yoga and, when they were at the Mount Vernon house, policing the refrigerator to get rid of greasy food he considered unhealthy. On the job, Nadi made sure the piano was tuned in sync with the mama-likembi and that no microphone cords were in the way when Nina made her entrance. It surprised him that after all this time, Nina still got nervous before a performance. So sometimes while she sipped a glass of champagne, he gave her a kiss on the cheek and a smile as he headed out to play the introduction. These gestures seemed especially important at the Kennedy Center, given the circumstances.

NINA ADMITTED that she could miscalculate a performance, that she could go too far with her lectures. Occasionally her thoughts escalated into worry about the backlash that others feared. "I was about to be crucified. I can't say by whom," she told Hollie West while she was in Washington. A sense of foreboding and alienation, too, clouded her observations. "I am not in my country," she said. "I was born here, but this is not my home. I may leave this country soon." She didn't elaborate, but her appearance December 17 in Chicago indicated that she wasn't ready to leave the United States just yet.

Before the concert, Eugene Harvey, described by the *Tribune* as her producer, told the paper she was "trying to win back her white audience." But when she stepped onstage at the Auditorium Theatre, Nina dispelled any notion that she was going soft. "I'm not allowed to preach anymore," she announced. "But for all you little white folks out there, this ain't no Geraldine up here."

The reference to her friend Flip Wilson's campy alter ego was a deft touch. The audience chuckled, but Nina had made her point.

22. Where My Soul Has Gone

~ 1973–1976 ~

Despite her disparaging comments now and then about their marriage, Nina and Andy maintained a relationship beyond their common interest in Lisa. She even expressed her gratitude to him on the jacket of *Emergency Ward* "for encouragement and proper handling of this album." In December Andy had taken his business interests one step further, forming Stroud Records. The first album he put out confirmed that Nina's music was the linchpin of the enterprise, *Nina Simone Sings Billie Holiday — Lady Sings the Blues.* Andy was no doubt hoping to capitalize on the recent movie about Holiday starring Diana Ross. The album consisted of eight songs cobbled together from Nina's live performances and studio sessions, though there were no dates given nor or an explanation of how Andy had gotten the tracks. The cover featured a picture of Holiday — not Nina — and the music represented a Nina of the past.

The album appeared just as Nina received good notices for her part in an all–Bertolt Brecht program at the Brooklyn Academy of Music January 14. If nothing else, the two things together reminded fans of Nina's versatility as well as her contradictory nature. Not every singer could pull off a convincing "Gimme a Pigfoot (And a Bottle of Beer)," which Holiday had taken from Bessie Smith, and "Pirate Jenny."

Though Nina later waved off comparisons to Holiday, right now she accepted the notion of common musical ground between them just as she more readily talked about her interest in Smith. In fact, Nina made it known that she wanted to be considered for the lead role in a planned movie about the singer, vying publicly for the part with Roberta Flack. She hadn't liked the Holiday movie because it put too much emphasis on the singer's drug problems. Nina expressed hope that a Hollywood treatment of Smith's life would do better by the singer.

The much-discussed movie never happened, but Nina was part of another project that celebrated black culture, *The Majesty of the Black Woman*. It was a book of photographs of one hundred thirty black women, from the ages of eight to eighty-nine, some famous, many not, taken by Arthur Tcholakian. Nina's full-page portrait has none of the affectations one might expect from the self-proclaimed high priestess of soul. She is staring straight ahead, bare-shouldered, without any apparent makeup, her hair in a short Afro. She looks calm and serious, elegant in the simplicity of her pose.

Nina's portrait was among those selected for the opening of a show March 2 based on the book. The hosts had selected the New Yorker Club, which was housed in the Time-Life Building on the Avenue of the Americas, and as the name on the building suggested, the epitome of mainstream America. Nina had been negotiating the worlds of black and white for decades, and in a way this was only the latest version of the concert eight-year-old Eunice Waymon performed for Tryon's white elite at the Lanier Library. But it remained as true now as it was then that outward success could not erase the turmoil and conflict inside. Only now Nina found it harder to hide her distress, which may have been why she had so few jobs during the spring and no new recording sessions.

RCA didn't know what to do with her. While Nina remained proud of *Emergency Ward*, essentially a concept album, the commercial payoff was minimal. Perhaps because *Black Gold*, which was taken from a live performance at Lincoln Center, did well, the label decided to record Nina again in concert at Philharmonic Hall July 28 with two musicians she had known since the beginning of her career, Al Schackman and Olatunji. Only the three of them were onstage on the twenty-eighth, and Nina's loping "Sugar in My Bowl," the saucy old blues, reflected her good mood. She ad-libbed, drew out phrases on the piano with the trills she liked so much, and accentuated the many double entendres to the crowd's delight. Her mastery of the dramatic moment showed in the haunting "Dambala," a chant-song that talks of God and Satan, slaves and "slavers" who themselves will know of bondage "and remain in your graves with the stench and the smell." When Nina finished, no one doubted this was true. Moments later she changed the mood with "Obeah Woman." "You know about the holy roller church—ain't that where it started?" she exclaimed, as Olatunji tapped out a syncopated beat. "We got to take our time gettin' this one started," Nina added. Then she spun out a tale, half sermon, about the mystical "Obeah woman" from beneath the sea who "can eat thunder and drink the rain . . . kiss the moon and hug the sun."

Variety's reviewer found Nina's "simple and uncluttered" performance a refreshing change, noting an absence of "the sullenness and ill-temper that has marred some of her recent appearances in the N.Y. area." RCA eventually pulled together songs from the evening and three tracks from 1971 sessions into a new album darkly titled *It Is Finished.* But the company didn't release it for nearly a year, and in fact it was Nina's last record for the label.

NINA WAS LISTED as a performer for the August 16 Black Expo '73 in Philadelphia, but she didn't show up. Max Cohen, her long-time attorney, gave no explanation except to say her refusal to perform "is complex, but it has nothing to do with Black Expo." Cohen added that he was quitting as Nina's attorney; he gave no further explanation for this either, though he implied that he was tired of the incessant conflict.

Nina had more serious problems than standing up a promoter or disappointing fans. The Internal Revenue Service was looking at her tax returns, and she professed to know very little about her finances.

Andy had taken care of everything while they were married, and once they split up, various individuals—Sam, Max Cohen, personnel at RCA—looked after her career. She had taken an apartment in a building adjacent to Lincoln Center in Manhattan, though she still owned the Mount Vernon house. By August, however, her circumstances had changed significantly. A for-sale listing for the suburban property, advertised as "Nina Simone House," showed up in *The Wall Street Journal* August 17 with the cryptic line "extended European tour."

Nina, though, remained in the United States. On October 4, she opened at the Troubadour in Los Angeles and kept the audience waiting fifty minutes. She chided them for being indifferent, though she admitted she was rusty because she hadn't performed in a club in quite some time. According to Dennis Hunt, who had moved from the *San Francisco Chronicle* to the *Los Angeles Times*, it showed. "She was so miffed by the noise," Hunt wrote, "that she ended the 45-minute set after a long half-hearted rendition of her best song, 'Porgy.' " This kind of performance was hardly a good omen for her most ambitious foreign booking yet, two weeks in Japan right after the Troubadour, followed by a week of concerts in Australia, accompanied by Al and Nadi.

Whatever her irritations in Los Angeles, Nina could hardly have asked for more to prepare a Japanese audience for her shows. Her records had been re-released there as *Nina Simone Collection, Vols. 1–6*, and a double album pegged to this trip, *Golden Hour of Nina Simone*, showed up in stores just before she arrived. But on opening night in Tokyo October 18, her Japanese fans failed to meet her expectations. Nina had planned a varied repertoire that included Bob Dylan, the Beatles, African-themed chants, and her audience participation numbers. One of these in the early going so disappointed her that she abruptly got up from the piano and headed offstage. "I'll see you later," she said. "Good night." The crowd, though surprised, intuited their role and cheered loudly enough to bring her back for another thirty minutes. The *Japan Times* reviewer, Don Kenny, later admonished Nina for not understanding local mores. Japanese "lack of demonstrativeness does not mean coldness or lack or interest," he wrote.

The Australian dates went so well that a reviewer in Sydney declared that "a Nina Simone cult has now been firmly established" in the country. But the appreciative crowds in both places were no barrier to the bouts of melancholy that still gripped her. During one of her London trips, Nina had poured out her feelings in a letter to Langston Hughes, but he was gone six years already. Now she found an unlikely pen pal in Warren Benbow, even though he was no longer playing with her and they had been out of touch for a year. Despite the age difference—he was eighteen years younger—they had had a brief romance, and she apparently still felt close to him. In her letters she talked about feeling lonely and in a few earthy passages left no doubt how he could make her feel better.

WITH LISA IN TOW, Nina retreated to Barbados early in 1974. The Caribbean country had become a refuge, both spiritual and physical. She loved the warm weather, the beach, and the overall surroundings, which defined relaxation. "Empty afternoons were filled by Paul, his motorbike and his undemanding loving," she wrote in her memoir. "I thought I had all I wanted at least until I felt strong enough to go back out into the world again."

But the romance with Paul ended after Nina met Prime Minister Errol Barrow. As she remembered it, he invited her and Lisa to stay at one of his personal estates and then began making late-night visits after his work was over but before he went home to his wife. "We had to be discreet," she wrote, but for the moment "we both had what we wanted—an easy fun relationship with no particular future in mind, just the present to enjoy." Nina got used to the perquisites that came with essentially being Barrow's mistress. On occasion when she let herself want more and talked about marriage, he reminded her he was married. And Nina replied, "Well, divorce your wife," even though she knew that would end his political career. Nonetheless she held on to the hope that she could have a permanent relationship with Barrow and a stable life in Barbados, so much so, she wrote, that despite the uncertainties, she moved her belongings from New York to set up a home there. Because she didn't have the necessary papers as a resident, however, her personal effects were held at the airport. On top of that, Barrow ended their affair, so Nina not only had to find storage for her things but also a place to stay.

A bright spot amid this turmoil was May 11 in Washington, D.C., when the city honored Nina during the third annual "Human Kindness Day," an event that promised to draw a largely black crowd to the National Mall for a variety of activities. This year several thousand individuals turned out for a concert on Nina's behalf that was sandwiched between an honorary breakfast at the Kennedy Center and an evening tribute at the Smithsonian Institution. Beyond the performances, which featured Herbie Hancock, the Pointer Sisters, and Nina's friend Dick Gregory, the boxing champion Muhammad Ali was on hand to bestow one of the many tributes Nina received. The homemade gifts from an assortment of young people moved her to tears.

Any doubt Nina may have had about her importance to black women, in particular, should have been erased by poems written for her, each of them printed on a huge honorary poster. "I'll hold my own mirror/to reflect my dignity with my heritage wrapped around it/so that all the world can see," wrote Roscoe Dellums, one of the hosts of the celebration, who was also the wife of U.S. Representative Ron Dellums of Berkeley. "She was our goddess," Mrs. Dellums said, remembering how Nina had influenced her and her friends when they were teenagers, not only through her music but through her appearance. It was affirming, Mrs. Dellums said, to see a prominent black woman so proud of her heritage, making it obvious by wearing an Afro or jewelry and gowns inspired by Africa.

Touched as she was by these personal tributes, Nina was even more thrilled that her mother, now seventy-two, had come for the celebration. Nina knew that Kate had never entirely approved of her career even if she had benefited from it. Now Nina could see that Kate had a new appreciation for what her daughter had become, and the realization thrilled her. Finally, she saw that "our blood was a bond between us which rose above our differences to bind us together."

After the celebration, Mrs. Dellums and her husband took Nina out for a final dinner. The couple had chosen the restaurant carefully—the red-carpet supper club at Pitts Motor Hotel, one of the favorite spots of Washington's black elite. Cornelius Pitts, the owner, showered Nina with attention when they walked in. Grandly, she turned to everyone at the bar and announced, "It's Nina. Drinks on the house!" This elicited the expected cheer, and only later, after a pleasant dinner, did confusion reign when Pitts quietly approached Nina with the very large bar tab.

"You expect me, Nina Simone, to pay?" she exclaimed. "You should be delighted I came here! You could not pay for the publicity you've received." Then she turned to her escort, a friend of the Dellumses, and pointedly said, "Are you going to take this bill?" His astonished look gave her the answer.

After a few minutes of hushed conversation, the Dellumses told Pitts they would handle the tab. Mrs. Dellums never forgot how Nina took umbrage at the thought that she should be responsible: "She was thoroughly insulted."

DURING HER WASHINGTON VISIT, Nina told the *Post* what had become obvious—that she was cutting way back on her performing. The entertainment arena, she declared, "is full of hypertension." All she wanted to do, she added, referring to Barbados, was "stay near the sea," spend time with Lisa, who was now eleven, and just "gather myselves together," that plural invoking Nina's divided persona.

But Nina did have one more engagement, a performance June 29 at Avery Fisher Hall, the recently renamed Philharmonic Hall, in conjunction with the Newport Jazz Festival. The auditorium was packed with her fans on this last Friday of the month, and for them Nina could do no wrong even when her performance veered away from the music and into self-indulgence. Sometimes she could harness the turmoil to give a song an entirely different shape and meaning. But sometimes, as *The New York Times*'s John Rockwell wrote of the evening, "the music bends and sags and threatens to snap altogether."

Just like her mood: close to the breaking point. She was even more disillusioned with the civil rights movement, and still mourning the loss of her father and sister. Devotion to the church had sustained

Kate; it was not the answer for Nina. "The truth was," she said, "I had no home any more."

By the end of the summer of 1974, as Nina recalled, she had left Barbados behind and was in New York at her apartment with Lisa, feeling despondent and rudderless. Her association with RCA had come to an end, and though she still technically had the house in Mount Vernon, there were mounting financial problems having to do with unpaid taxes. The city would eventually foreclose on the house December 31, 1975, putting an irrevocable end to that chapter of her life. With nothing but worry hanging over her head, she wondered what to do next. Her friend Miriam Makeba, apparently long since over the restyled mink coat, offered a solution. She insisted that Nina and Lisa join her on her upcoming trip to Africa. Makeba would be performing the third week in September in Kinshasa, Zaire, at a three-day music festival, but her first stop was in Liberia, where Nina and Lisa would stay. That suited Nina just fine. The small West African country had been founded in 1821 by free blacks and freed slaves returning to settle in the home of their ancestors. "It was a good place to start at for any Afro-American to reconcile themselves to their own history," Nina wrote in her memoir.

In Nina's memory, her arrival in Liberia was as thrilling as the first time she touched down in Africa thirteen years earlier for the AMSAC program in Lagos. She recalled an airport reception in Monrovia and another at the presidential palace with President William R. Tolbert and other dignitaries. It didn't really matter if these events hadn't taken place precisely as Nina described them (Tolbert was on a European trip when Nina, Lisa, and Makeba and her group arrived). What was more important was the opening of a new chapter in her life that had nothing to do with making music onstage or off. "I was just a mother with her child happy in school and nobody looking over my shoulder telling me what to do," she wrote.

On one of her first nights in Monrovia, Nina got drunk at a club, dancing nonstop as night turned into morning and in the process shedding her clothes. Leopoldo, who was traveling with Makeba, recalled Nina's escapade as the talk of the town. She didn't mind. "I was so happy to be home, so happy to be in a place I could do this where everyone laughed and clapped rather than having me arrested," she said. Later she wrote a song about the evening, "Liberian Calypso," one line capturing her unbridled joy: "You brought me home to Liberia/All other places are inferior."

Lisa loved the country, too, recalling an unimaginable freedom, not to mention the chance to stay in one place for nearly two years. "I was twelve, and I'd drive the car to parties. My mother treated me as if I was grown up," she said, "sending me on errands with $100 bills." But Nina made sure she knew who was in charge, especially when they were arguing—"like rams crashing into one another," Lisa said. "My mother was the kind who would want you to heel, no matter what. Once, I wouldn't back down in an argument and ran off. By the time I came back, my mother had changed the locks."

NINA HAD DONE VIRTUALLY no performing while she lived in Liberia—in her memoir she wrote of this time as a period of romantic adventures with local men, one of them a high government official. But when Claude Nobs, the founder of the Montreux Jazz Festival, invited her back for the 1976 event, Nina was ready to return to the public eye. She came out onstage the night of July 3 shorn of the turban, jewelry, and dramatic makeup that once helped define the high priestess of soul. On this night Nina wore only a sleeveless black dress and black high-heeled Mary Janes. She had no makeup on, and her hair was in a short Afro. The only accessory was an antique silver choker from Greece that was a pre-concert gift from Nobs. She walked purposefully to the piano and bowed deeply to acknowledge the lusty applause that greeted her. She stood up and looked straight ahead for what seemed like an eternity. Then she looked to the left and then to the right as if she was sizing up the crowd but rendering no verdict despite such a hearty welcome. She knew it must have unnerved them, and a few titters and a smattering of applause punctuated the air. Then Nina finally sat down at the piano and smiled. "I haven't seen you for many years since—1968," she said. "I have decided I will do no more jazz festivals. That decision has not changed. I will sing for you—or we will do and share with you a few things. After that I will graduate to a higher class

I hope and hope you will come with me. We'll start from the begin-ning," which was her oblique introduction to one of the first songs she had recorded, "Little Girl Blue." It was clear that Nina had lost none of her facility at the piano and none of her improvisational tal-ent during her absence from the stage. The intricate phrases, the unusual rhythms, the rolling chords were all there—the things that had amazed Henry Young, the guitar player from Vancouver, when he realized that with all that going on, she was singing melody above it.

Over the next hour Nina kept the audience on tenterhooks, the joys and torment that filled her daily life on full display. She hop-scotched from the jocular to the testy, airing a grievance in one moment with enough force to startle. "I made thirty-five albums. They bootlegged seventy," she declared with some hyperbole and mentioning no names. "Oh, everybody took a chunk of me." That put her in mind of the previous day, she said, when she went to see a movie featuring the late Janis Joplin. "What distressed me the most—and I started to write a song about it—but I decided you weren't worthy—because I figured most of you were here for the fes-tival—anyway . . . " and her voice trailed off as she began "I Wish I Knew How It Would Feel to Be Free."

"Everybody should be free," she announced in another of her pointed improvisations, "'cause if we ain't, we're murderous."

Nina used Janis Ian's "Stars," a meditation on the vicissitudes of fame, to describe her current status in the media's eyes: "She used to be a star—she's gone on her way to the bottom and all kinds of crap. It doesn't bother me," Nina insisted. But any lack of decorum still set her off. A few bars into "Stars" she stopped, annoyed at a young woman who had gotten up. "Hey girl!" Nina yelled. "Sit down . . . SIT DOWN!" she yelled even louder, and then repeated it a third time, finally satisfied that she had prevailed and could finish the song.

Nina ended the show with variations on an African theme. "Let's just give 'em some of what it feels like to be in the bush," she told her two drummers. "Maybe it will work, and maybe it will not. You will know where I'm trying to come from," she continued, "where my soul has gone, and thank God it has gone there." She sat down at the piano and played a minute of rippling chords until the drummers found the beat. Then she was off on her bush dance, returning to the keyboard for one last flourish and a final wave goodbye.

LISA WOULD TURN FOURTEEN September 12, and Nina had decided she should have a more structured school than was available in Monrovia. Nina wanted to send her to a boarding school in the Ivory Coast, "but I wasn't feeling that at all," Lisa recalled. This time Nina relented and instead enrolled Lisa in a school in Switzerland, launching her daughter on a new path and, as it happened, marking another turn in the road for her. She wanted to live in Switzerland herself, enamored, she told the Montreux audience, "of your terrible wonderful peacefulness. It permeates everything that is here. It attracts me and holds me, and I hope that I'm permitted to stay amongst you for a little while."

23. I Am Not of This Planet

~ 1977–1978 ~

Nina's move to Switzerland complicated Lisa's life. "Everything was fine as long as she wasn't around," Lisa recalled, "and then she decided to come and turn my world upside down." Lisa resolved to visit her father and find out once and for all if he loved her. Maybe he didn't, but whatever the case, she told Nina, "we gonna get this straight." When she arrived in New York, Lisa didn't tell Andy she had no return ticket to Switzerland. He thought she was staying three days. On the fifth, she told him she wasn't leaving.

Lisa's separation from Nina had been building over time and marked the beginning of occasional estrangements between mother and daughter that would last more than a decade. A full-fledged teenager now, Lisa had ricocheted between intense love for her mother and anger, especially in the immediate aftermath of the split with Andy. Nina was "not the same person I remembered living in Mount Vernon," Lisa said. "I remember thinking she had turned into a monster. Mommy was selfish in a lot of ways, and I often felt that if she had taken two seconds to consider people around her, especially me, who depended on her 100 percent, she would have made a different decision with her behavior."

Lisa's departure came at a fortuitous moment given the uncertainty in Nina's life. She had almost no work, but at the end of January sponsors of MIDEM, an organization of European music executives, invited her to perform before a thousand members at the group's annual convention in Cannes. In theory, any number of these individuals might help her career, but Nina was in no mood to curry favor. She showed up forty-five minutes late to the gilded Les Ambassadeurs Room of the city's casino, and instead of opening with a song, Nina asked the restless crowd to join her in a sing-along. They were having none of it. She spoke in English, which probably hindered communication, but even if many couldn't understand her precise words, they caught the irritation in her voice. "Loosen up!" she hollered. "Are you all dead or something? The only ghosts I ever saw were white . . . you asked for that. Come on now," she went on, her agitation growing. "Let's have you all a lot less tight. I guess you people are from the inside track of the music business, and I was supposed to be dead in 1970."

"SING!" someone shouted from the audience.

"You can't pay me enough money to sing when I don't feel like it," Nina hissed back at the anonymous provocateur. "I will never be your clown. God gave me this gift—and I am a genius. I worked at my craft for six to fourteen hours a day, I studied and learned through practice. I am not here just to entertain you. But how can I be alive when you are so dead?"

"SING!" someone else shouted.

"Come up here and and say that," Nina retorted. "No you won't because you are a worm, a spineless worm without spine in your body. I sing when I am ready."

Nina's good friend James Baldwin, who was in the audience, hurried onstage to embrace her, realizing that something was terribly wrong even if he didn't know what had set her off. His comforting gesture temporarily relieved the tension in the room, and Nina started to sing, glaring at the audience much of the time. Before her final song, Bertolt Brecht's "Alabama Song" from *The Rise and Fall of the City of Mahoganny*, Nina declared, "The inside track of showbiz is deadly. It denies everyone the right to have fun." Not only that, according to *Variety*'s reporter, Nina charged that some of her unreleased tapes had been acquired from record companies by unscrupulous operators; tapes had been pirated by crooks and reissued on their own labels; and she had gotten no publishing money for seven years. "You are all crooks!" she thundered. "You owe me. . . . I don't wear a painted smile on my face, like Louis Armstrong," she said as she left the stage, lobbing her last insult, this one aimed at a beloved music legend.

Those who had not already departed applauded, exhausted by an evening that had been extraordinary in its bizarre spontaneity, "and because we stayed," one fan said, "and because we loved her, it was sheer agony."

NINA HAD NO PLANS to return to the United States until she received an invitation from an unlikely place. Amherst College, the prestigious school in western Massachusetts, wanted to present her with an honorary doctor of music degree at the May 29 graduation ceremony. She could hardly say no to such an award, which was, considering Amherst's reputation, even more unexpected than the honor from Malcolm X College in Chicago. Amherst was taking care of everything. All Nina had to do was show up.

By long-standing custom the board of trustees made the annual selection in private and pledged to secrecy those few individuals who had to coordinate the graduation ceremony. No one knew Nina was an honoree until just a few days before the event. The proclamation that accompanied her degree recognized the range of her public life: "Nina Simone, a singer, pianist and composer, who has recorded many performances with RCA Victor Records. She has also spoken out about drug abuse and the political rights of black Americans." The honor thrilled Nina. From that moment she took to calling herself "Dr. Simone."

She went back to Switzerland after the event, but it wasn't a very long stay. George Wein had invited her to be part of the Newport Jazz Festival in New York City and had scheduled her for a midnight performance at Carnegie Hall Sunday, June 26. He either hadn't heard about the MIDEM flare-up, or if he had, he went ahead any-way. This would be Nina's first performance in the city in three years, and the press coverage suggested that she would be warmly welcomed. Her program with Lukas Foss at the Brooklyn Academy of Music early in 1973 had been a success, and the plan was to pair her again with Foss and the Brooklyn Philharmonic.

Nina arrived back in the city in time for rehearsals, but they went poorly. "She just freaked 'cause she wasn't comfortable," said Dar-lene Chan, one of George Wein's associates, and with Carnegie full of expectant fans Sunday evening, Nina went missing. Wein had known earlier that something was wrong and sent Chan and his wife Joyce to learn whatever they could. "Joyce Wein and I called all the hotels at the airport. We found her at the Ramada Inn," Chan recalled. "And then we went up to her room. We kept knocking on the door. She had the chain on the door. She would say, 'What do you want?' We told her the hall was sold out, people are upset. . . . She just wasn't going to let us in. We made enough commotion that security came up," Chan added. "They thought we were like prosti-tutes! The bottom line—she didn't come."

Ticket holders received refunds, and the next day, Wein spoke gra-ciously when reporters wanted to know what had happened. "She has a fear and unhappiness when she is in America," he said. She had stayed a week after receiving her honorary degree, "but then she couldn't stand it and went back to Switzerland. We tried to sur-round her with love, but there's no understanding her unless you live with it on a day to day basis. . . . Nina hasn't had much of a career lately," he added, "and we wanted to help. I just feel sad and sorry. I have great respect for Nina. I think she is a fantastic artist."

Wein had advanced Nina $8,000, and though he told *Jet* he didn't intend to sue her, he nonetheless retained the option to file a claim for another $15,000 in related musicians' fees.

The day after Nina's no-show, Gino Francesconi, who worked in the Carnegie Hall box office, took the most unusual call he could remember. It was one of Nina's fans, distraught at her failure to show up. He just wanted someone to know, he told Francesconi, that he was breaking all of her records, and over the phone Francesconi could hear the sound of splintering vinyl before the man hung up.

•

NINA'S DEBUT ALBUM on Bethlehem Records, *Little Girl Blue*, now almost twenty years old, was reissued once again in the summer, this time by a British company. "Porgy," "Plain Gold Ring," and "Love Me or Leave Me," among others, were a reminder of Nina's originality, which sometimes had gotten lost when she became, as one foreign reviewer put it, "a more mannered and stylised singer." The release served another purpose, too: keeping Nina's name in front of the music-buying public during another long absence from performing.

Nina did a job in Amsterdam October 1 and then returned to the London stage early in December, her first show there in six years. She played solo before a packed house at Drury Lane, no sidemen at all. Perhaps anticipating the question of where she had been, she provided a simple answer. "The music business punished me," she announced, an interpretation of her troubles that revealed just how much she felt the victim.

Even her most controversial compositions, "Mississippi Goddam" and "Four Women," still had power with the piano as her only accompaniment. "Elton John can't play piano worth a damn," she sniped at one point, putting some distance in her mind between his pop success and her classical training. The evening, however, had a dark tone. Derek Jewell of the London *Times*, an admitted fan, wrote afterward that Nina seemed "to be carrying the cross of some great personal tragedy." She occasionally lost her way during a song but just kept going, he noted, "and made up free-form ballads as she went."

Spending Christmas in Israel before a New Year's Eve concert in Jerusalem "was exactly what I needed," Nina recalled, "to go to the Holy Land, get in touch with myself and with God." But she didn't like Bethlehem, she told *The Jerusalem Post*, even on Christmas Eve—too commercial for her taste.

Nina's solo concert December 31 was at Binyanei Ha'ooma, one of Jerusalem's main halls. These outings required a good deal of audience participation to make them work, though not every effort succeeded. On "Zungo," which had been a staple of her earliest performances, she exhorted the audience as only she could in Israel.

Nina on a beach in Tel Aviv, January 2, 1978,
after a concert two days earlier in Jerusalem
(*Associated Press*)

"Come on," she shouted, "you've got two thousand years of spirit with you!" But it failed to achieve the desired effect, and Nina abandoned the effort. By the time the evening was over, however, her fans had forgotten the botched "Zungo." The audience tossed bouquets her way, a few rushed the stage for a handshake, and one fan even handed her a bottle of liquor, all of it proof that even by herself, Nina could still move an audience.

VETERAN JAZZ PRODUCER Creed Taylor, who ran his own label, CTI Records, thought Nina might be a good fit with his catalog, so he had flown from New York to London to see her at Drury

Lane. By the end of the evening he was ready to make arrangements for a studio in Brussels to record what would be Nina's first album since 1974, when RCA released *It Is Finished*. In mid-January Taylor brought in a top-notch rhythm section along with CTI arranger Dave Matthews, and he put Nina up at the Brussels Hilton, which was near the studio. But by the time they started work on the seventeenth, the compelling performer he had seen in London had all but vanished. "Nina didn't want to record," Matthews remembered. "She wanted to hang out. The vibe was very, very uptight. It was tense."

Even if he couldn't hear the conversations, Jimmy Madison, the drummer, could feel the unease during several impromptu conferences among Taylor, Matthews, and Nina in the control room. The only bright spot on the first day came when Eric Gale, the guitar player, started fiddling around with a reggae beat, a sound he had mastered during visits to Jamaica, and the other musicians joined in. Matthews tried to build on this spark, though Nina, to his surprise, didn't get it. "What is this corny stuff?" she asked. Matthews paid her no mind, believing the reggae concept would work for some of the tunes.

Nina was still out of sorts by the third day in the studio, and no one could figure out why, including Al Schackman, who had come over for the sessions. Taylor was fed up and told Matthews he was going skiing with his sons in Switzerland. If Matthews could get anything from Nina on the fourth and final day, fine. If not he should pack up and return to New York, and they would figure out what, if anything, to do then.

The musicians' work was done, and that evening Nina invited them to her hotel room for what they thought was an informal going-away party. She had drinks ready and then decided she wanted to have some food sent up. When a hotel employee came to tell her the kitchen was closed, she was furious. As soon as the young man left, Nina picked up her glass and hurled it across the room, "and it smashes into a million bits," Madison said. "For a great grand pause nobody says anything. Then Eric Gale says, 'Well, it's gettin' kind of late. I got to leave.'" The other musicians, understandably unnerved, took their cue, and within thirty seconds, Madison added, "the entire room leaves."

Nina's behavior didn't bode well for the next day's session, but Al promised Matthews she would be ready to do her vocals. When Matthews came to her hotel the next morning, however, he realized Al had been overly optimistic. Nina greeted him "saying all this crazy stuff," Matthews recalled. "I said 'good day' and went back to my room." Al didn't want to give up, understanding, even if Nina couldn't, that her career would continue to suffer if she bungled this opportunity. He called Matthews and assured him Nina really would be ready. Matthews said OK. Finally in the studio, Nina sat down at the piano and reminded him of why Taylor had wanted to do the album in the first place. She ran through her songs in just over an hour—"brilliant vocals," Matthews thought to himself, and maybe in the end, when they had a finished product, worth all the trouble. A day later he was on his way to New York to work on the arrangements with a full complement of strings and backup vocalists.

Matthews had picked some of the city's most respected session players. By coincidence, John Beal, one of three bass players, had seen Nina at the very beginning of her career. He was playing in Atlantic City with Woody Herman's band and late one night stopped in at the Midtown. He was captivated by the young woman playing the piano in a way he had never heard before in a nightclub. He asked the owner who it was. "Oh, that's Nina Simone." "What she was doing was unique," Beal said, and now, twenty-two years later, here he was on one of her recording sessions. Chuck Israels, another of the bassists, was more bemused than anything to have been called for the session. He had played a few dates with Nina fifteen years earlier when Lisle Atkinson was not available. "She was arrogant, a self-important person with a lot less ability than she believed she had—that's just one man's opinion," Israels said. But he wouldn't refuse the chance to work with the top-notch musicians Matthews had assembled.

The new album was called *Baltimore*, taken from the song of the same name by Randy Newman, performed here with the reggae beat that Eric Gale had first laid down. Fans who had been waiting four years for another record from Nina would be pleased to find the drama that always infused her vocals as well as her distinctive piano work. Other selections were songs by well-known pop writers, among them Daryl Hall of Hall & Oates with "Rich Girl," and Judy Collins with "My Father," a somber counterpoint to several midtempo tracks but one that gave Nina freedom at the keyboard.

After its March 15 release, *Baltimore* drew attention from a number of music writers if for no other reason than Nina's long absence from the studio. But it didn't do much. The record registered on the *Cash Box* pop album and "Black Contemporary" album charts for a month in May, and it didn't crack the *Billboard* Top 200. That hardly mattered to Nina. She professed to be unhappy with the entire thing, and her comments after the fact helped explain her unprofessional behavior during the sessions.

"The material was *not* my personal choice," she declared, "and I had no say *whatsoever* in the selection of songs. It was all done before I could make *any* decisions." According to Nina's friend Sylvia Nathan, however, Nina herself had chosen "My Father," and had tried to record it for RCA but was too overcome with emotion after the death of her own father to do it properly. Taylor had loved the studio they used, a historic barn that had been restored, but to Nina it was "a basement in Belgium where I was forced to sing songs in order to get out of there. This went on for three days," she claimed, her perceived slights now escalating to match her distress. "There was no sleep and there was no water and there was no release." She was unmoved that Taylor had hired the best musicians. The way she saw it, "he took the tape to New York, put voices on it without my consent, put orchestrations on it without my consent, and I have not seen the president [Taylor] since that day." Nina didn't like the cover either—a three-quarter-length shot of her smiling, wearing a headdress and wrapped in white fur. It was reminiscent of Ma Rainey, the great blues singer, in top form. "Some of the photos taken were infinitely better than those used," she sniffed.

NINA KNEW SHE HAD money problems, not simply the lack of funds to cover her personal needs but more serious matters involving taxes the Internal Revenue Service claimed were due on previous years' income. Fear of U.S. government action against her was one of the reasons her part of *Baltimore* was recorded in Brussels rather than New York. As she recalled, it was at this moment that a smooth-talking Liberian man, Winfred Gibson, came into her life and invited her to come to London, where he promised to provide lodging and work on her career—for Nina both an escape and a rescue. She trusted him but made clear that this was a business relationship only.

Things hardly turned out as she hoped. Not only did Gibson fail to do the things he promised, he beat Nina when she finally questioned him about his plans, hitting her so hard she lost consciousness. When she came to, she struggled to call for help at the hotel and asked for the police. But as she remembered it, hotel personnel refused so she sent them away. When they left, she reached for her bottle of sleeping pills. "I counted out thirty-five and took them one by one."

Fortunately for Nina, someone had come back to her room, found her, and got her to the hospital. The hotel was discreet when reporters came around, telling United Press International only that Nina had "collapsed in her room" and was rushed by ambulance to the hospital. A hospital spokesman was equally evasive: "We are not prepared to say what the nature of her illness is . . . The medical staff feels she needs plenty of rest."

Nina found it at a spa outside of London before she moved in the middle of May into a friend's apartment in the city. And she called Andy, the one person she thought might help her out of her predicament. After several entreaties begging for his assistance, Andy agreed to help. But he insisted on having a business relationship only, nothing personal. Any new work, especially in the United States, however, would have to wait because Nina still didn't feel like herself. She had even had a CAT scan on her brain May 18 to determine if there was any new medical problem.

In spite of her precarious health, Nina agreed to do a solo concert July 18 at Royal Albert Hall for $2,000. Her hesitant gait when she walked out onstage shortly after eight p.m. signaled that something was amiss. At the piano she bowed and folded her hands in front of her, a gesture that could have been a thank-you for those who came and a silent prayer to make it through the evening.

She spoke but slurred her words, as if she was drunk, but it soon became clear that her condition was more serious than mere tipsiness. She played a few songs, meandering around a melody as she usually did to find a comfortable groove. Then she got up from the piano and walked offstage. She returned almost immediately, aided in the first few steps by a nurse who had been waiting in the wings. She sat down at the piano and played some more, this time distinctly somber melodies. And then she left again for a much longer period, ignoring the loud applause. In the meantime, two fans had jumped onstage and left her notes at the piano. When Nina returned, she read them, tossing one aside, and then after re-reading the other, which said "Are you all right?" asked for the author. The person came onstage and clasped hands with Nina as they visited.

Nina started to leave the stage again as members of the audience rushed forward. One woman grabbed the microphone and exhorted the crowd on behalf of "Women Against Rape." Nina reclaimed the mike, invoking Judy Garland and Billie Holiday as she talked about her own struggles. "Talent is a burden not a joy," she said. She asked all those who considered themselves her friends to write down their names and addresses and leave them with her attendant at the stage door.

But Nina hadn't finished. "I am not of this planet," she said. "I do not come from you. I am not like you." She tried to discuss her artistic pain but gave up when she couldn't find the right words. She went back to the piano for one last song, a dark rendition of "I Put a Spell on You" sung as a dirge. And then she left the stage for good.

Five days after the concert Nina returned to Switzerland, taking up residence for nearly a month at the Clinique Medico-Chirurgicale in Genolier, a municipality north of Geneva.

NINA'S FINANCIAL PROBLEMS were mounting. She hadn't paid the bills for her stay in the London apartment or at the Swiss clinic, nor did she pay for a week's stay at a hotel in Geneva in October. She hadn't paid the bill for the CAT scan either or for a shopping trip eleven months earlier before she went to Israel (among the purchases a Dior purse and scarf and a pair of Italian-made boots). And she owed roughly $10,000 on her American Express credit card. But more important than all of these, the Internal Revenue Service claimed that she owed back taxes for 1971, 1972, and 1973 on income respectively in dollars adjusted for 2009 of $194,102, $393,669, and $446,984.

Her complicated feelings about the United States aside, Nina knew that if she wanted to come back for any reason, she risked arrest. She also knew she needed help. Though Max Cohen had announced in the summer of 1973 that he no longer represented her, he couldn't let her flounder. He was not a criminal defense attorney, but he stepped in and initiated discussions with Alan R. Naftalis, an assistant United States attorney in Manhattan who had been assigned to Nina's case. Cohen didn't know ahead of time that Naftalis was a fan. But as the discussions proceeded, Cohen realized that Naftalis would work with him so that the tax matters could be resolved with as little embarrassment to Nina as possible. Cohen wanted to avoid the spectacle of Nina stepping off a plane from Switzerland and being arrested and handcuffed on the spot.

Naftalis didn't want such a spectacle either and sought to assure Cohen and Patricia Murray, another lawyer Cohen had brought in, that he would handle the case both fairly and delicately. From what he understood of the record, Naftalis believed that Nina had been badly served in relying on others to handle her business affairs. This didn't excuse her from the duty to pay taxes, but the circumstances informed how Naftalis went forward. "I assured Max that if Nina came back she would be treated with great gentility," and the goal would be to find the best way to resolve all the issues, he said.

The first week in November Nina returned to the United States, and as Naftalis promised, she was not arrested. The authorities set bond at $10,000, which Andy co-signed. Instead of going to a grand jury for an indictment, Naftalis filed an "information" that laid out the allegations. Nina admitted in her first meeting with Naftalis that she was nervous and told him that she had had a drink the previous night. This made Naftalis uneasy, and before he went any further he needed to make sure that Nina was fully aware of what was going on and that despite her benign description of the evening, she didn't have a hangover.

No, no, she assured him. She had only had some orange liqueur, a rare brand, she said, that few in the United States knew. But Naftalis did. Her face lit up, he recalled, and she calmed down at the connection the two of them had just made. She tossed out a few words of French, and Naftalis, who could speak the language, answered back. Nina was delighted. From that moment on she insisted that the rest of the meeting to discuss a plea bargain be conducted in French.

"I don't think your lawyers understand French," Naftalis told her.

"It only matters that you do," she replied, so Naftalis found himself in the awkward position of speaking to Nina in French, translating in English for her lawyers, and then waiting for Nina to reply in French to start the process all over again.

The lawyers worked out a deal to allow Nina to plead guilty to one count of failing to file her income taxes for 1972. The other two counts would be dropped. All that was left was the actual proceeding in front of the judge. Beforehand, Nina had dictated a formal statement and then signed the transcribed version. She was led to believe that her affairs were in order, she said. When she learned this was not the case, she hired a well-known New York firm, Phillips, Nizer & Blumenthal, to resolve her problems. "I engaged them because I believed deeply that they would take care of the matter. They wanted a lot of money, at which time I informed them that my funds were limited because I was not receiving any royalties from any source," Nina continued. "Let me clearly state that I had already worked for my money but had not been paid."

She asked the firm to accept what she could spare, and at first they did. But then, she went on, after she had already left the United States, "they wrote me that they would not represent me anymore unless I paid more money." It was likely to be more than $10,000 all told. "I wrote them that in view of my still nonexistent funds and their knowledge of same that I thought their dropping me was unfair and cruel . . . I was also bewildered by this abruptness and confused as to what to do next."

Nina asked Al Schackman for advice, and he put her in touch

with his accountant, who "told me to get on with my concert work and he would take care of the matter. I was greatly relieved and did not know that my taxes had not been filed until approximately one month ago. I believe that I have been reckless in not insuring that my return was filed," Nina concluded, "and I am deeply sorry."

She signed it Madame Nina Simone, which she often alternated now with "Dr. Simone."

Naftalis arranged for Nina to appear in front of one of the few black women judges in the United States, Constance Baker Motley, who had had a distinguished career as a civil rights lawyer. Naftalis had to miss one of the preliminary sessions and sent a colleague instead. But Nina threw a fit when when she saw that Naftalis was not in the courtroom. Judge Motley immediately wanted the plea withdrawn, fearing that Nina didn't understand what was going on despite having signed the relevant documents. The judge appointed a new lawyer for her, Elliot Sagor, who had more criminal defense experience than Murray.

On December 22, the parties reconvened, Naftalis back representing the government and Nina now represented by Sagor, a former assistant U.S. attorney in private practice who Motley knew understood tax matters. He had warmed to Nina enough so that he gave her his home phone number. A day or so before the proceeding, she had called at six-thirty a.m. and wanted to talk.

"He's running now," Sagor's wife said.

"He better be," Nina replied and hung up, leaving both Sagors to ponder the ominous-sounding message.

In court for the final resolution of the case, Naftalis's hopes for smooth sailing were dashed when Motley innocently referred to Nina as "Miss Simone."

"I am Dr. Simone," Nina shot back in a loud voice. The judge was known for running a tight courtroom, and for a moment Naftalis worried that an irritated Motley might decide right on the spot to impose a much harsher penalty than everyone had agreed to. But she didn't. And she didn't press the matter when Nina refused to give her age during the plea proceeding. Motley accepted the government's recommendation and imposed a jail sentence of ninety days, which was suspended, and ninety days' probation. No fine was levied, Naftalis noting years later that it would have done little good given Nina's financial straits. She had liabilities of nearly $290,725 in current dollars adjusted for 2009 and assets just over $35,500 in the most generous reading. She told Motley she didn't even have enough money to pay her hotel bill in New York.

Speaking to reporters after one court date, Nina acted oblivious to the effort that went into helping her. "When one gives so much to millions," she said, "why?" and then walked away.

NINA'S RETURN to the American stage after nearly four and a half years came right in the middle of the tax proceedings, Sunday evening, December 10, at Avery Fisher Hall. She dressed for the concert like visiting royalty, in a multicolored ceremonial robe with a long train, golden disks glistening around her neck. "I heard you wanted to see me," Nina teased. "And so I roller-skated on home and said I must see all my children who want to see me in spite of everything."

24. Loving Me Is Not Enough

~ 1979–1981 ~

Nina returned to the Village Gate February 22 and kept the opening night audience waiting an hour. She groused in her dressing room about the financial arrangement she had with owner Art D'Lugoff and a crowd not big enough to suit her. She finally came out and did an uneven forty-five-minute set. Though she included her biggest hits, she offered only snippets, breaking off a couple of them in favor of talking to the audience. "I must get my money," she told them. "I will get my money."

She was supposed to perform two shows, but she did only one. Her most committed fans chalked it up to opening night kinks. But a week later she was even more erratic. She came on two hours late for the first show and then took such a long break that the second show didn't start until two a.m. "I want to apologize to all of you because I don't know how long you have been waiting, but we played a very long first show," she said, "and we didn't know we were supposed to play a second show. The reason we are late, however, is that the big boys don't know how to count tickets, and I haven't gotten a proper count yet. We played a very long show," she repeated, "and if you detect a slur in my speech, those of you who hate me will say that I was drunk, but I am not. And those of you who love me, do not let anyone judge me. If some critic judges me, shoot him."

Most of the audience applauded.

As she had on opening night, Nina sang in fits and starts, rarely completing a song, even those that had begun with so much musical promise only to fade after several bars. She complained about the lights and complained about Art, their friendship and his support for her career now buried under accusations of shorting the ticket count. Nina was getting a percentage of the door, and lowballing the crowd would reduce her pay. She started to sing "Porgy" and then stopped. "We are still used here like black and brown horses!" she lamented. "It has not changed." Most of the blacks in the audience—perhaps 30 percent of the crowd—clapped. "Since most of you are white," Nina went on, "I don't expect you to clap."

A white man in the audience, apparently frustrated by the declamations, shouted that if she was a performer, she should perform.

"You see," Nina retorted, "here is an example of what I'm talking about." The man hurled something else back, and Nina cursed. "I will sweep the street with you and get everybody in here to help me," she shouted just as the Gate staff escorted the man out, a move that also drew applause.

Art, whose patience with Nina rivaled George Wein's, watched with sadness as Nina unraveled before him. He let her rage run its course and shrugged off her attack. "She offended people regardless of race, color, creed, or anything else," he noted. "So I didn't get too excited about that." But he was grateful that Jimmy Baldwin happened to be in the audience on this night, and Baldwin once again proved to be a calming presence. Every few minutes, he sidled onstage and whispered in Nina's ear, encouraging her to sing a song, which she did. At one point the two of them danced, accompanied by Al on guitar and rhythmic clapping from the audience. It took the edge off the evening until the show came to a close in the middle of the night.

"We love you, Nina," one fan shouted.

"Loving me is not enough," Nina shot back. "I want my money."

The critic and essayist Stanley Crouch was at the second show,

Nina with James Baldwin at the Village Gate in New York, February 1979
(*Deborah Feingold*)

and he lamented in *The Village Voice* not only about the demons that had apparently taken hold of Nina but also their larger effect. "I suspect that shows of this sort feed the terrible backlash against black people that is again starting to form in this country," he wrote without specifying any particular incident. "Simone played into the hands of those who would, again, disenfranchise us, using incompetence, irresponsibility, and inordinate arrogance as excuses." As Crouch understood it Nina received "a very large percentage of the door each night, and her salary was far higher than what most artists—as opposed to Las Vegas entertainers—earn from two one-hour sets." If Nina didn't earn enough money for her shows, he added, then she shouldn't have taken the job.

Finances still concerned Nina when she arrived in Philadelphia for a June 2 performance at the Shubert Theatre and an extended stay in the Northeast. "I don't do interviews anymore," she told one reporter who pressed her for an appointment. "I don't need the publicity. What I need is my money." Nina was hardly alone among musicians in claiming that she hadn't been paid proper royalties. But four decades after her recordings, it is all but impossible to determine the validity of her claims. It remained evident, though, at least as measured by industry sales charts, that however popular Nina was as a performer, she didn't sell that many records. The fallout from her income tax problems also rankled. Nina was spared a jail sentence and fine, but she did have to make restitution, and for a period of time all her royalties from record sales and public use of the songs she wrote went directly to the Internal Revenue Service.

To make matters even more difficult the tentative agreement with Andy to book concerts had fallen apart, and now she claimed that not only had he deserted her, "he has taken my baby." She said Lisa's continued stay with her father amounted to kidnapping. But Andy found her impossible to deal with, "bitchy, problematic, upset for no reason. You could never satisfy her." The audience at the Shubert Theatre got its own taste of her contrariness. When they repeatedly asked for "Four Women," Nina finally consented but not before complaining, "Why won't you let me grow?" She chastised her black fans for not being proud enough. "Y'all are fickled [sic]. You used to be talking about being natural and wearing natural hairstyles. Now you're straightening your hair, rouging your cheeks and dressing out of Vogue."

Nina was so sure the world was against her that when she misplaced the antique necklace Claude Nobs had given her, she immediately assumed it had been stolen. She called the Philadelphia police, and they initiated an investigation. But before it got very far, the necklace turned up in the crease of the living room couch at a friend's house, where it apparently had fallen after Nina herself took it off.

WHEN SHE RETURNED to the stage at Royal Albert Hall in London September 18, Nina wanted to clear up any confusion about her bizarre concert fourteen months earlier. "Hey, I'm well again," she said, guessing that many fans had returned for the occasion. Her subsequent smooth performance provided evidence at least on this night that she had spoken the truth. But Nina's fragile temperament re-emerged in her rambling reflections to Karl Dallas of *Melody Maker*. The public hadn't supported her after the incident at the London hotel, she complained, "and I had no idea until that year that when you're on top, there's a whole public out there waiting to shoot you down, and it's real. When you fall from that little pedestal where they keep you, they're as anxious to see you crumble as they are to see you up there. They enjoy it. People enjoy the macabre, the horror of life. I've had traumas, traumas, traumas. But now I am well," she insisted again.

The peace that Nina claimed to feel had taken her back to her musical roots. Two months earlier, still in Philadelphia, she had told the *Inquirer's* Mary Martin Niepold she wanted to talk only about her own mother and her "white mother," as she called Miss Mazzy, her first piano teacher. "These ladies are phenomenal. They have never been featured. They wanted me to be a concert pianist. They never wanted this show business." Now in London, Nina amplified the theme with a riff on her musical history that rivaled her flights over the keyboard. "I don't like blues. And though I am known as a blues singer and a jazz singer in the states, I'm not really . . . I associate with Vladimir Horowitz, with Rubinstein, with Maria Callas, everything to do with opera, Wanda Landowska, Marian Anderson, Leontyne Price, Oscar Peterson, Ray Charles, certainly, Thelonious Monk, the masters of jazz and the masters of classics, including Bach. Let's not leave him out."

Even though she had recently come onstage Billie Holiday–like with a flower in her hair, Nina nonetheless distanced herself from the late singer. "The only way that I associate with her is that I haven't got my royalties, and that's only a matter of time," she asserted. "I don't smoke. I barely drink a little bit of champagne. I'm certainly not in love with anybody, and he certainly hasn't left me out in the cold and all that junk," Nina added, alluding to Holiday's well-chronicled troubles. "But it is true I got swindled a couple of times. I don't know why they keep comparing us in the press. They love to create monsters and they love to create sorrow and they love to create causes—but they don't know, seemingly, how to accept joy and enthusiasm and a lust for life, which is what I have."

Nina conceded she still worried about her finances. "If things don't get easier for me, if I don't get my royalties I'm going to Las Vegas and become a shake dancer. You think I'm joking?" she exclaimed. "Josephine Baker's one of my most wonderful inspirations." Nina was referring to the American expatriate who became a sensation in France with her exotic dancing—sometimes with only a string of bananas tied around her hips. "She started in bananas. I may end in bananas. It would break completely the impression that they have of me. But it wouldn't mean that I couldn't play."

NINA CONSIDERED SWITZERLAND HOME even if she had hardly been there during the year, what with her extended stay in the United States and then the stop in London for the Festival Hall date. She didn't stay home long in the late fall either before returning to the States in December. But she went to San Francisco, not Las Vegas, and given her caustic remarks about Billie Holiday, few could have predicted that she would join a tribute to the late singer at the Oakland Coliseum December 14. Though a hefty paycheck could have been the inducement, Nina showed her distaste for the event with another tardy arrival. "I have no idea what's going on," she announced. "I also want to say hello to the band because I have never seen them before in my life." She had missed the rehearsal— the program featured a large orchestra led by Ray Ellis that performed first and then a second part made up of Nina and singers Maxine Weldon, Gloria Lynne, Morgana King, and Esther Phillips. "I'm here to get my money," Nina said, and then launched into an extemporaneous monologue, described by one observer as alternately "self-pitying, comical, and defiant" that she interspersed with snatches from Holiday's "What a Little Moonlight Can Do."

When a fan in the audience pleaded "sing, Nina, just sing," she snapped back: "You think I have unlimited energy. You think I'm twenty feet high . . . you're wrong!" Then she rambled some more, urging the crowd to buy her records and support her. "Please give applause for the broken lady when she's down."

In the past the *Examiner*'s Philip Elwood had overlooked Nina's more troubling moments, but this time he couldn't contain himself:

"She made a fool of herself and worse she made a fool of the show's concept, her colleagues and worse the audience."

Hannibal Means, a young singer whose strapping physique fit his name, was not at the concert, but he had been a fan of Nina's since he was a teenager. Some friends who knew she was in town invited him to meet her a day or so later at their house. "We looked into each other's eyes and knew each other immediately," he said. "She told me I was her son from Atlantis and that I could prove it by singing an aria." He sang "Comfort Ye My People" from Handel's *Messiah*, and Nina started to cry. Hannibal insisted that Nina come to his house for dinner before she went to Los Angeles on the twenty-first for two nights at the Roxy Theatre. She accepted, and they, along with friends he had invited, were in the middle of eating when the doorbell rang. Hannibal opened the door to find three or four men standing there with Nina's suitcases, which they promptly tossed on the floor with enough force that the latches came undone. Her clothes and shoes spilled out all over. Nina had refused to pay the $200 bill to get her to and from the Coliseum, Hannibal recalled, and the drivers kept her suitcases hoping to get their money. Instead, Nina threw a fit and started throwing dishes against the wall like Frisbees. Somehow Hannibal calmed her down. "I don't know what possessed me, but I took her by the hand," he said, and got her out of the apartment to his car and drove her around until her rage passed.

Nina brought Hannibal to Los Angeles for the Roxy shows, and he proved to be a steadying hand there, too. "She decided to stay in bed," he recalled. "I had to dress her and put makeup on her, fix her hair, put her shoes on and lead her to the stage." Nina rewarded Hannibal with a few minutes onstage, where he reprised "Comfort Ye My People" to an audience not expecting such traditional religious fare in one of her sets, though before Hannibal came out Nina had talked about the trip to Israel eleven months earlier and proclaimed her love for Jesus.

ON THE SPUR of the moment early in 1980 Nina decided to return to Barbados. She insisted that Hannibal come to keep her company. He agreed to go, but when they got to the airport, he changed his mind, concerned about how strangely she was acting. She was furious, "and she slapped me across the face. With that hand that played those runs and fireworks, I saw stars."

"God damn you," Nina said before boarding the plane.

Not long after, she mailed Hannibal a photo of himself, but with the eyes punched out. "You're dead," she wrote. Hannibal shrugged it off. "I learned that when she screamed that I could just let it pass through me. I knew that it had nothing do with me." So he was not surprised that Nina tracked him down in Washington, D.C., where he was temporarily living, and asked him to meet her in Philadelphia in May for two shows at the Locust Theater. Music critics noted this return to the United States as they had the previous ones, wondering in their stories which Nina had come back. Her comments suggested that the unsettled version had reappeared. "I don't know how long I can stand it," she told the *Inquirer*'s Jack Lloyd. "Mostly it's a culture shock. And I wish you would print that. It's different. Everything is so fast. People are all running as fast as they can to get to one place. There's the pollution, the madness."

Nina offered her own culture shock to readers of *The Philadelphia Tribune* in a provocative photo published right before the May 11 concert. In what could have been Nina's allusion to Josephine Baker, she was topless, an African-print scarf wrapped once around her neck and then lazily hanging down her left side. Her right hand decorously held one end of the scarf so that it slightly obscured her breasts. The *Tribune* made no comment in its caption other than to identify Nina as the "high priestess" and to announce the day and place of her show.

By the time she got to Washington in June for a concert at the Warner Theatre, Nina indicated she wouldn't be in the United States too much longer. "This country is going down the tubes," she declared to Hollie West, who had written about Nina several times over the years in *The Washington Post*. "You're asking me what's wrong with your country, man? Nobody thinks anything of this country, nobody in the world. I love Khomeini," she added, referring to the religious leader of Iran who had fomented a revolution against the shah that also resulted in the taking of fifty-two American hostages, who were still in captivity. "This ain't my country. I claim

Africa. I'm not going to stay here and be an Aunt Jemima," Nina added flippantly.

West understood that Nina was troubled but hadn't realized how much. He and *Post* photographer Fred Sweets had arranged to meet her in the coffee shop of her hotel, Harambee House near Howard University, assuming that she would be most comfortable in this setting. As she expounded on her disappointment with black young people in the United States, West asked what he thought was a reasonable question. Why didn't she come back to the States more often and in some way address this issue?

Nina didn't answer. Instead she grabbed a knife from the place setting, stabbed it into the Formica tabletop and bolted from the restaurant. Dumbfounded and rattled, West and Sweets left in a hurry, and though it was barely noon, they stopped at a bar for drinks to settle their nerves. West knew he didn't have enough material for the kind of feature story he and the *Post* wanted, so with some trepidation he called Nina back and they spoke by phone. She had plenty of grievances, starting with her royalties. She had been bilked out of millions of dollars, she asserted. "I came over here to see if could live in this country again and to see if I could get some of my money." Remembering Andy, she claimed that he had turned Lisa against her: "I didn't know he harbored such hatred for me. He told her I had abandoned her. I feel a sense of loss at not being with my daughter. I miss her. I love her." But moments later, Nina recanted. "I can't stand teen-agers. Do you know what I mean? I can't stand being around my daughter. I can't be close to her emotionally. I may go to her [high school] graduation. She wants to see me this summer. But she needs some help."

She brought up another sore point: slights because of her appearance, and from fellow blacks, too. Wade Henderson never forgot how jealous Nina seemed to be when she shared the Howard University stage with Jean Pace and her husband Oscar Brown Jr. Tall and elegant, Pace was the center of attention, which, as Henderson recalled, prompted Nina to prance around, whispering, "Look at me! I'm beautiful, too."

Nina knew she was a hero to many young black women for how proudly she adopted an African look and her fierce independence.

But still, she said, "I never got the Hollywood thing. People never recognized me in airports. People like Diahann Carroll get designer clothes free. I was never on the cover of *Ebony* or *Jet*. They want white-looking women like Diana Ross—light and bright." It was not the first time Nina had measured herself against Ross, who seemed in her mind to be both arbiter and epitome of beauty. "I'd be more popular if I looked like Diana Ross," she had told Warren Benbow during their brief fling, as much irritated as resigned.

And not long after the Billie Holiday movie came out, Nina coolly dismissed one audience doing its best to shower her with applause. "But you have Diana Ross," she said and then repeated it, suggesting that this spontaneous affirmation still fell short. Nina even tangled with her daughter about the subject. "She would traumatize me at times for having lighter skin," Lisa recalled, "and I'd remind her that she had chosen my father. I didn't."

Given Nina's volatile mood, the Warner concert could have gone badly. But she pulled it off, though reviewer Geoffrey Himes noted later that Nina "ladled out both joy and anger in generous measure."

LESTER HYMAN, who had booked Nina for that 1968 Massachusetts Democratic party event, now lived in Washington and invited Nina to stay at his house when she came through town. On one occasion Hyman had to be away on business but left her with another houseguest, a young man from Hawaii who was a friend of the family. While in Korea on this trip, Hyman received a call from home. His young friend was at wit's end.

"I'm a slave," he cried. "She makes me do all these things!" "She had him doing errands," Hyman said, chuckling at the memory and also his own recollection of the telephone bill he got after Nina had left. "I almost had a heart attack—calls all over the world!"

Nina's current stay in Washington overlapped with a road company version of *Bubbling Brown Sugar*, the Harlem revue, which was at the Warner and starred Cab Calloway. Nina asked Hyman if he would take her to see the show but only, she said, if they had the best seats. Hyman assured her they would because he knew the choreographer.

"So we sat down and the show started, and all of a sudden she starts talking to the people onstage. I was mortified," Hyman said. "And of course now everybody knew Nina Simone was there. Throughout the show she would make comments. 'Oh, that's wonderful . . . pretty girl,' you know. Then after the show she says, 'Now I want you to take me back to see Mr. Calloway.' She said she did know him from the past. She said, 'You do not introduce me as Nina Simone. I am Madame Simone.' I said 'OK.' "

Backstage, Calloway was as gracious as he could possibly be. "Oh Nina, it's wonderful . . . " but before he could finish the sentence, Nina interrupted.

"It's MADAME SIMONE."

"So he had to 'Madame Simone' her. She just prattled on and on," Hyman recalled. Finally Calloway asked Nina if she would excuse him for a moment, and he took Hyman over to a corner of his dressing room.

"Would you get her out of here?" Calloway pleaded. Of course, Hyman said, doing his best to shield Nina from Calloway's annoyance.

IN MONTREAL at an outdoor jazz festival July 18 Nina made no attempt to paper over the tribulations of the previous months, announcing in song that it might take her a few minutes to get her voice, noticeably husky, and her set going. "If you don't mind my fumbling around and doing these strange things, if you don't mind my fumbling around, I'll come up swinging for you," she chanted. "My first time in Quebec you know—I'll come up singing for you even though they say that I'm down," and she pounced on that last word as she delivered a burst of chords. This was her very personal introduction to Janis Ian's "Stars," her anthem now, as if she were the pop-jazz version of the "Unsinkable" Molly Brown. She presented the song with undisguised defiance and then segued into "That's All I Want from You." At the line "show me that you care," Nina paused ever so slightly and the audience got the message. They gave her a round of applause. "A love that slowly grows and grows," she whispered at the end. "That's all I want from you, *merci*," which elicited another cheer.

Nina was using the occasion to practice her French, and she alternated between French and English to introduce the songs and prompt the crowd to join her during "Be My Husband" and "See-Line Woman." "*Exactement!*" she exclaimed when they finally got the groove. Nina had brought Hannibal with her, and during "Let It Be Me," he sang Sam's part. On this night his tenor soared during a brief solo before he joined Nina to harmonize.

Nina's introduction to "Mississippi Goddam" became a history lesson for an audience not only foreign but also years removed from America's civil rights upheaval. "Do you remember Dr. Martin Luther King and Malcolm X?" she wanted to know, before naming other civil rights leaders and several musicians. "I said Martin Luther King and I said Malcolm X," she asserted more firmly. "That's better, familiar. More, more, more, more!" she shouted before signaling her two sidemen."Give it to me!" And then she began the familiar refrain about Alabama, Tennessee, and Mississippi.

An improvisation midway through bore the sound of autobiography: "I can't stand this pressure much longer . . . The whole damn world's made me lose my rest. *C'est vrai. Vraiment! Vraiment! C'est vrai!*" she said, slipping into French.

"They keep on saying go slow—*lentement, lentement, toujours lentement!*" Nina exclaimed.

At the end, she worked in the upcoming U.S. presidential election between incumbent Jimmy Carter and challenger Ronald Reagan. "Everybody knows about Reagan. Everybody knows about Carter. Everybody knows about the whole thing. Goddam! Goddam! GODDAM!"

A more mellow Nina attended a small dinner later on for some of the performers who were on a blues bill the next day. Among them was Big Mama Thornton, already a legend. Nina was moved to serenade her. "You're once, twice, three times a lady," she sang with a quiet passion that could come from no other place but the heart.

NINA CLOSED OUT 1980 on Manhattan's Upper West Side at the aptly named Grande Finale. Even her friend David Nathan, who happened to be in New York, admitted in a *Blues and Soul* review that she was below par. She was hoarse, more so than in Montreal, and talked the songs as much as sang them. She displayed the edginess, too, that *The New York Times* had mentioned in its brief announcement of her appearance: "one of jazz and black popular music's foremost singers, compromised by an unduly overt bitterness of attitude." Even Nina's most loyal fans recognized the irrefutable: her career was in decline. She was all but invisible over the next year in the United States and in Europe. She needed an infusion of energy, which she hoped to find in France.

25. Fodder on Her Wings

~ 1982–1988 ~

The day I discovered Jacques Brel was one of the most exciting days of my whole life," Nina wrote in her memoir. "So Paris seemed to make sense." She knew the city had a large African community with residents from several countries, "so I would be able to create my own Africa in the heart of Europe, Africa in my mind." She found a small apartment and decided to book herself into small clubs until she got established rather than work with a promoter. She distrusted them all. She liked the New Morning, one of the city's popular jazz spots despite its out-of-the-way location (northeast Paris, not the trendy Left Bank), and she brought her old habits with her. On the night that *Jazz Magazine* reviewed a show, Nina arrived more than an hour late, but she looked fetching, combining Indian-rose pants, a black leotard and a dashiki with several bracelets and silver chokers as accessories. She gave the impression of being a new-age African priestess. But she sang spottily, announcing a song and then changing her mind, or starting a song and then brusquely changing the key in the middle. "*Vous êtes seuls*" (You are the only ones), she sang in French, repeating the line over and over in a rhythmic chant. *"Je desire être avec vous."* (I want to be with you.) For many in the audience, however, the evening was, as Nicole Cerf-Hofstein wrote, "a missed rendez-vous."

Nina found enough creative rejuvenation to return to the studio in January 1982 for her first album in four years, this time on the local Carrere label. She recruited three musicians—two African percussionists, Sydney Thiam and Paco Sery, who between them played congas, bells, woodblock, and timpani, and bassist Sylvin Marc, who also did backup vocals. This eclectic mix accounted for the calypsoreggae feel to most of the tracks. With songs in English and French and some that alternated between the two, the entire project felt both international and deeply personal. "I Sing Just to Know That I'm Alive" reflected Nina's belief in her art, and "Liberian Calypso" celebrated her African adventure. And if "Alone Again Naturally," her improvisation about the death of her father, still seemed overwrought, it suggested, a decade after J.D. died, that Nina was still coming to terms with the loss. She thanked her father on the record jacket.

The album took its title, *Fodder on My Wings*, from a somber track. "It's about a bird that fell to earth and was crippled when it landed in fodder and other human debris," Nina explained. "Although it was able to survive, it couldn't fly. So it walks from country to country to see if people had forgotten how to live, how to give. As it went, the bird found that most of the people had forgotten."

Nina was especially proud of the record. Except for borrowing from Gilbert O'Sullivan on "Alone Again," she composed, arranged, or conceived every song, and she insisted that the liner notes say so. "What I did on this new album was to try to get myself deep into joy." But that joy was short-lived. When she came onstage May 7 at Barbican Hall in London, she gave another disjointed performance of unexpected exits from the stage followed by hasty returns, bits of quasi-African dancing, a tête-à-tête with a chattering fan, and a smoldering exchange with a few in the crowd who asked her to sing "Baltimore." She offered the first chorus and then stopped. "Randy Newman gets the money from this," Nina said. "We are not going to sing it tonight."

"Why not?" someone yelled.

"Because I said so."

"Those who had paid to hear music walked out in droves, laughing incredulously," Richard Williams told London *Times* readers after the concert.

But this evening was nothing compared to the embarrassment in Pamplona, Spain, on July 23. Raymond Gonzalez, a promoter in Paris who was artistic director of a festival there, had booked Nina, but the day before the event, he couldn't find her. He knew she was temporarily back in Geneva, and he finally tracked her down. After much argument, he persuaded her to get on a plane for Pamplona via Madrid. Nina changed planes for Noain, the airport near the event, but she arrived without her luggage, and she had been drinking. This made her even more tired, and she demanded a wheelchair to take her to the terminal, then changed her mind and tried to get back to the plane. Guards stopped her. Finally, after a heated discussion through an interpreter, she agreed to take a taxi to her hotel—but she insisted that a case of champagne be sent to her room. "I talked her into half a case," Raymond recalled.

Barely settled in and completely untethered now, Nina went out in the hotel hallway naked and announced that she was going to the pool for a swim. She was stopped before she could get too far. Event personnel thought about canceling her performance but didn't want to disappoint the two thousand people who were at the festival grounds. In the meantime other individuals raced around to gather suitable clothes for her and managed to get her dressed and delivered backstage. She finally came on a half hour after the appointed time. She started to sing Bob Marley's "No Woman No Cry" but abandoned the idea. She left the stage and came back, repeating the routine three times. "I don't sing for bastards. I don't like white people," she said during one of her interludes in front of the audience. "I believe that your race is ill. . . . You are stupid." She insulted the organizers, too, calling them a bunch of thieves, though she had been paid an advance as her contract required.

Then came an abrupt farewell. "Thank you. I love you. You will never see me again." The audience jeered and booed, and most of them went for the hastily offered refunds. One spectator offered a piquant summary: "To see Nina Simone hallucinating and improvising, a lost drunkard on stage, is a unique spectacle."

Raymond couldn't get her out of town fast enough. He drove her three hours to Biarritz, France, for a train back to Geneva. "You are not going to say a word," he ordered. But Nina was all smiles when they parted, as though nothing had happened. "You were great," she told him. "I love you."

"Well, I don't love you," Raymond replied, thinking, incorrectly as it would turn out, that he would never work with her again.

NINA'S FINANCIAL WORRIES likely contributed to her distress. She was livid that she was not receiving royalties owed on her compositions, which were supposed to be protected by the two publishing companies she had set up with Andy, Ninandy and Rolls Royce Music. Her frustration was palpable during a meeting with a British lawyer when she laid out her bill of particulars. She hadn't seen any money from Aretha Franklin's album, which not only featured Franklin's version of "To Be Young, Gifted and Black" but used that title as the name of the record, too. From a cover of "Four Women," "I never got a dime." Most aggravating of all were the bogus explanations from a purported business manager in the United States. She found them insulting. "They must think they're talking to an idiot," Nina told the British lawyer, her words mixed with tears. As she poured out her feelings, her language became even more extreme. "I feel I've been made a fool of, that somebody doesn't appreciate my intelligence. I am one of those angels, and there is no braggadocio in that. I expected money and honor for what I did well. Now I have no shame for that. The fact that I am dealing with pigs and hogs and slime—they're not human beings—is beside the point. My initial reason in being in this business and putting my talents here was because I expected the world to compensate me for what I gave to it." What she wanted, she told the lawyer, was someone like the late impresarios Sol Hurok or Mike Todd, someone with "money and the power and the guts to do a godfather job because he must be a man who has those three qualities. He must not hesitate to cut off legs if it comes to that to get what's coming to me, be that literal or figuratively. He must have power and authority so that when he speaks he's listened to, and he must have money of his own so that he will not supine or bow to the temptations of ripping me off or sell me short as he works for me. Where is such a man?" she asked plaintively.

The lawyer must have been nonplussed. In any case, he had no answer, but Nina didn't seem to mind. She said she felt better just getting this off her chest. "I haven't got any money," she added, "but I've got power, which means people think I got tons of money, and I continue to let them think that. I live like I've got money. I act like I've got money. That is the way I am. I've always assumed money as long as I can remember." She was not about to sell herself short now. "I will live with two pair of pants and no clothes to keep my house," she declared. "I am very strong-willed, and I will pick potatoes like the farmers here. . . . I can get down and lie down on the ground and sleep with the pigs, but it doesn't make me any less than what I am because of what I think of myself."

Though the meeting produced no resolution, Nina thanked the lawyer just the same. It would be far from the last time she was caught up in a tangle over money.

WHEN NINA RETURNED to Los Angeles in the fall, fans at the Roxy Theatre cheered as the curtain rose and they saw her sitting at the piano. "You like me still?" Nina teased. But after this pleasant beginning, the evening degenerated. She talked her way through some songs, failed to finish others, and snidely asked an under-rehearsed sideman, "Do you know how to play, boy?"

Nina had spiraled into such turmoil by the end of the year that she went to the Los Angeles county hospital for what was obliquely termed "a nervous disorder." On her release, she moved to Montreal, perhaps hoping a change of scenery would help. She was turning fifty on February 21, 1983, and she hardly expected to find herself in these circumstances after a quarter-century career: unmoored and the prospects for her future uncertain at best. "When I die," she had told *Melody Maker* a decade earlier, "I want to have left some partic-ular mark of my own." That she had done so musically and by the force of her personality was inarguable, and if at times she was her own worst enemy, it was just as obvious that she couldn't help it. More than one friend or acquaintance — Gerrit DeBruin, Hannibal Means, Art D'Lugoff, Warren Benbow, even Andy and her own daughter Lisa — could recall moments when Nina erupted for no apparent reason, and no one yet had the magic formula, let alone appropriate medication to help her. Sometimes, Warren said, when Nina acted out in a restaurant, he just took her firmly by the shoulders, got her outside, and shook her with a strong hand, not enough to hurt her but enough to say without words, "Snap out of it."

In this bleak moment Nina looked to her brother Sam. "I need help," she wired him in Nyack, New York, where he was living.

When they spoke on the phone, she asked him to get her career going again. He wanted to know why she was in so much trouble.

"Because I've been a bitch."

Sam told Nina he had to think about the situation. "I didn't want to throw myself back into that unless I had some assurances, some guarantees," he said. Though he knew it was a leap of faith, Sam convinced himself that his sister would cooperate, and he agreed to help her. "She desperately needed me. She was sinking, lonely — very scared and she needed money. I was still close to her," he went on. "I still had a lot of love for her. She was family. But I let Nina know I would not take any bull from her, any BS."

WHILE SAM WORKED on a European tour for the summer, Nina returned to New York in June for a two-day stand at Swing Plaza in lower Manhattan. Before the date she took the occasion of a phone interview from Montreal with Stephen Holden of *The New York Times* to reframe her musical journey once again. "Though I include jazz in what I do, I am not a jazz pianist at all," she emphasized. "African-rooted classical music is what I play. I play jazz and blues, but they are not mine. The root is classical."

And she renewed her grievances about her compensation, now calling it "the straw that broke the camel's back" in her decision to leave the United States nine years earlier. "I made thirty-nine albums, and they've pirated seventy," she insisted, the villains unnamed and the high numbers commensurate with her depth of feeling. Hannibal Means remembered that one night Nina had screamed about her royalties "until there was no voice left, only hissing air."

Nina made one of her more unusual entrances on opening night at Swing Plaza, walking through the audience waving a bouquet until she got to the stage. Once there she carefully separated the roses from the baby's breath so she could pull the heads off the roses. Then she scattered the petals on the floor around her and kicked the stems offstage. This floral minuet had nothing to do with the music, but it entranced the audience with its strangeness.

The ramifications from Nina's tax problems were evident after her four-show booking was over. Federal agents confiscated most of her pay, though they did not disturb the bucket out front for $5 contributions to the Society for the Preservation of Nina Simone.

THE EUROPEAN FESTIVAL SWING started at the Hague July 8, and given Nina's precarious finances, Sam expected her to be on her best behavior, especially for such a good deal. She was to receive $11,500 for two shows. But Nina was in middling form, and before the first show was half over, the disappointed audience started to boo. Nina shouted back and then stormed off the stage. She told Sam and the musicians to pack up and get in their car. The promoters had no choice but to provide refunds for the second show. They were not about to let Nina get away with their money without a fight, however, and they chased her down the highway, unsuccessfully as it turned out. "There were flowers flying out the window—it looked like a wedding," Sam recalled, describing the scene as Nina's limousine sped away from the pursuers. "It sounds funny, but it wasn't at the time."

Raymond Gonzalez, willing to put the Pamplona fiasco behind him, had negotiated a $10,000 paycheck for Nina's next date, a return to the Antibes Juan-les-Pins festival July 18. Onstage Nina announced that she wouldn't perform any covers, even "Porgy": "I gave enough but received nothing in return. And so I sing my songs, and I'm at peace," though for Nina such claims were both temporary and illusory at best. No one knew that better than Sam, and he was taking no chances with Nina's performance in Pompeii July 30. The promoter put him in touch with Maria Carneglia, a young Italian woman who spoke English, and Sam paid her $100 to stay with Nina in her hotel room in Sorrento before the concert. At first Maria felt overwhelmed when Nina insisted on having a few drinks and got angry if they didn't arrive fast enough. But she quickly relaxed, enthralled to hear Nina playing the piano in her room until Sam and Roland Grivelle, a friend from Paris and an occasional road manager, picked them up to drive to Pompeii. Maria could tell that Nina liked her, so much so that she promised to dedicate a song to her at the concert. Nina told Sam she wanted Maria to stay on, and when Sam vetoed the idea, she threatened not to perform. To placate her, Sam said Maria could stay, but they had secretly arranged for her to slip away before the evening was over, Sam willing to face the consequences. Perhaps that accounted for his loving gesture midway through Nina's performance, when he strolled onstage and wiped her brow so gently that she barely noticed.

After the show, Sam hoped that once Nina realized Maria had left, her anger would be assuaged by a sightseeing tour Roland had arranged back in Rome. Sam's main concern anyway was returning to Geneva. He and Nina had left so quickly that they had not paid their hotel bill. Sam made sure to wire the Hotel Intercontinental from Italy promising they would settle their account as soon as they returned from Pompeii.

This temporary glitch aside, Sam was using Nina's contracts to help her get a loan from a Swiss bank to pay off her debts. He told the bank that he had already booked dates totaling $30,000 in American currency and expected to double that amount with later bookings. He promised Nina would make monthly payments on the loan. "The personal and business affairs are now in order, I am happy to say," he wrote in a letter that would prove to be unduly optimistic, though he recalled later that the loan eventually came through.

Nina herself took another step to improve her financial situation. In September she signed an agreement with a New York agency, the Artists Rights Enforcement Corporation, to collect royalties on her behalf. In exchange for their work, which covered all manner of investigation, the organization, known as AREC, would keep half of any amount recovered.

·

HENRY YOUNG WAS SURPRISED and pleased to pick up the telephone one day in November and hear a familiar if deeper-sounding voice. "I'm Dr. Simone calling," she said. Sam had worked out a deal to bring her to Vancouver for a concert at the Queen Elizabeth Theatre, one of the city's better venues, and she wanted Henry to play with her. By coincidence he was working with an African percussionist with the mellifluous name of Albert St. Albert. Nina said to bring him along. Henry was scarcely prepared for the woman he saw when he arrived at the theater for their rehearsal. "She was—like, how to describe it—hunched over. You know, you watch old movies, like black slaves in the cotton fields. She looked like that. I was really, really almost in tears."

Nina perked up when she saw him. "You look very good, very handsome like you were before," she said, and then offered a hug. Her mood changed quickly. She told Henry she wasn't comfortable with the promoter Sam had lined up, so Henry immediately called a black entrepreneur he knew in Vancouver, Darren St. Claire. He came right over, and Nina liked him instantly. He told her he would handle the evening and out of respect to her would take no fee. But Nina was still uneasy. She apparently had overheard a racist comment or seen some ugly graffiti—Henry wasn't sure which. But whatever the case, she refused to perform until "Ricardo," a muscular man with a Fu Manchu mustache whom Sam had hired as a bodyguard, arrived. Fortunately Ricardo made it to the Queen Elizabeth by five p.m., and after St. Claire assured Nina that he had her money in hand, she agreed to go onstage.

She walked out to a half-full auditorium, which Henry blamed on poor advance publicity. But those who came were die-hard fans, and they cheered her arrival, more, it would turn out, for simply being there than for her performance. The evening focused on *Fodder on My* Wings, the album she had made in Paris, and on a couple of songs she asked the audience to sing with her in English and French. But the effort degenerated into confusion. The concert ended abruptly when she couldn't manage "Ne Me Quitte Pas."

"I felt that Nina's spirit had been broken," Henry said later.

But she soldiered on. She had two shows a week later at the Colorado Women's College and asked Henry to fly to Denver and join her. He was surprised that once again Nina feared someone might do her harm even though Ricardo was never more than a few feet away and plainclothes policemen stood on either side of the stage. An enthusiastic welcome from the crowd failed to boost her spirits. She gave another middling performance, and the write-up later in *The Denver Post* typified the kind of notices Nina could expect from those who came with high hopes but left disappointed and not inclined to make excuses for her. "She comes on like an African priestess in her own secret world owing nothing to no one — not even a smile to the people who shelled out big bucks and dared a predicted snowfall to see her," wrote Arlynn Nellhaus. "With her unemotional persona she has evolved into the Yuri Andropov of the entertainment world," a reference to the stolid Russian leader. "Idi Amin put on a better show." Worse, Nellhaus wrote, Nina's voice

Nina with Roland Grivelle and Henry Young before a December 9, 1983, concert at Denver's Colorado Women's College
(Courtesy of Henry Young)

"was in shreds," so much so that the best part of the evening was a duet performed by Henry and Sam. "For a few moments there was electricity in the air—and warmth everywhere."

AN ENTIRELY DIFFERENT and more sociable Nina opened an engagement January 9 at one of London's premier jazz spots, Ronnie Scott's, named for the tenor saxophonist. Her lightened mood might have come from relief at being out of the United States and staying at a London hotel with a swimming pool. She found the water relaxing, and though she preferred the ocean, a pool would do for daily exercise. Nina announced she was tired at the end of her first evening, January 9, but everyone was so glad to see her that even this observation elicited applause.

Except for a brief trip to New York to perform at the Blue Note, Nina spent most of the year in London, with two-week stints at Ronnie's. On November 17, the last night of her engagement, the club allowed cameramen to film the performance. It was only Nina and Paul Robinson, a new drummer with whom she had found instant rapport. The extra lights for the filming made the club even warmer than usual with a full house, and rivulets of perspiration dripped down Nina's face onto her chest—she was wearing a low-cut strapless gown. But the music absorbed her so completely that she paid no mind. Every now and then she wiped her brow with one hand, but quickly enough never to disrupt the song.

"Mississippi Goddam" remained a reliable gauge of Nina's mood. Her introduction to the song, her improvisations, and how she sounded were clues to how she felt and what she thought of the world in a particular moment. She presented a spirited version on this night, but her slight shifts downward in a couple of passages and an uncertain pitch were reminders that she was not the thirty-year-old woman who first sang it in 1963 but a fifty-one-year-old with a deeper voice of more limited range.

Nina had always said she wrote the song in memory of the four black girls who were killed in Birmingham when their church was bombed. Now, she said, "Mississippi Goddam" was in memory of Dr. King "because no one really commemorated or remembered in my opinion, enough, Martin Luther King, and 'Mississippi Goddam' brings him back. . . . The youth need to know the history of America. They need to know what we did there," she went on. "That's my contribution."

Nina had ended the previous year with a dismal performance in Denver. She finished 1984 embracing the limelight and her audiences anew. "Well, I love them to love me," she said during the filming, "and if they're going to have an idol, they should have a good one, and that's me."

ROUGHLY SIX MONTHS EARLIER Nina had agreed to work with Anthony Sanucci, a self-styled entrepreneur from Los Angeles, and Eddie Singleton, an associate. "Sanucci liked money," she wrote in her book, referring to him from the beginning, in a not unfriendly way, only by his last name. "He regarded managing me as a two-way bet; if he couldn't win commercially he was going to have fun trying." Sanucci wanted to get Nina back to the United States, and perhaps because of his West Coast connections, he thought Los Angeles was a good place to start. He booked her into the Beverly Theatre on February 22.

By now there had been so many strange, erratic, and even awful performances that Nina's most loyal fans didn't know what to expect. To their pleasure she didn't disappoint, reaching into her repertoire on this night for Brecht, the Bee Gees—her still-haunting "To Love Somebody"—and a couple of new tunes from a record she was making on this trip to California. Among the songs was one written by Sam and his friend Bill Gunn, "Saratoga," a ballad about romantic longing with a melodic resemblance to "MacArthur Park," the 1968 hit for the actor Richard Harris.

BY THE TIME Nina got to New York in March, this latest album was almost ready for release. *Nina's Back* included remakes of "I Sing Just to Know That I'm Alive," "Fodder on My Wings," and "Porgy," all of them, including the latter, in up-tempo highly orchestrated arrangements. In addition to Sam's "Saratoga," the new material included "For a While," which had been written for Frank Sinatra. The album cover took the title literally. It was a photo of Nina, facing away from the camera, that had been taken on a rock in Central Park. She had no clothes on, and it showed her bare back.

Apart from heralding this latest return to the United States, the album title also marked Nina's return to New York—and to Town Hall—where she had announced herself to the world of popular music nearly thirty years earlier. Then a shy and nervous performer had taken the stage in a white silk gown that would have been perfect for the evening of classical music she had dreamed of. Now Nina was all glitter, from her gold lamé dress to her gold eye makeup. She was in such good spirits during the March 8 concert that she improvised a line from the ballad "For a While" to say, "I'm still in love with New York." (Two days later, at the Warner Theatre in Washington, D.C., she changed it again to incorporate Washington into the song.) Afterward Nina greeted fans and signed autographs, even posing for a photograph standing between Sanucci and Singleton. Her career hadn't been on such an orderly path since Andy had run the operation.

SOMETIME IN EARLY SUMMER Nina purchased a condominium in Hollywood and settled in before a mid-July week at the Vine Street Bar and Grill. Plans were in place to record a live album there. As she had done in the past, she used a long interview with a newspaper, this time Don Heckman in the *Los Angeles Times*, to update her story. Yes, she had berated audiences in the past, she admitted. "But I'm not doing that anymore. The country has treated me entirely different this time, and my attitude *about* the country is completely different. Now, there's no question but that when I'm booked to do a show, I'm going to be out there. I'm not going to walk out on anybody, and I'm not going to curse anybody out."

If the anger was gone, she went on, it was "replaced by a lot of nervousness. A lot of it had to do with the way I looked at things then. I think I never knew how much my audience loved me, and maybe I just never knew how to interpret that love. But I'm more accepting now. I'm ready to accept what the public has to give me. And they're

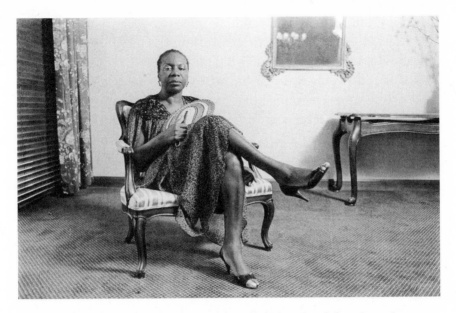

Nina in her new apartment in Los Angeles, July 1985
(*UCLA Charles E. Young Research Library Department of Special Collections,*
Los Angeles Times *Photographic Archives, © Regents of the*
University of California, UCLA Library)

giving me a lot. . . . I wasn't ready for that before, but now I *want* recognition in this country."

Nina said that she also wanted her royalties, the anger that had diminished in other areas still boiling here. She'd never been able to enjoy the fruits of her labors in the studio, she said. "Most of those albums have been pirated in this country, and I'd like to be paid for them." She paused for a moment. "But getting angry about it hasn't gotten me anywhere. So maybe a more reasonable approach will work."

There had been previous reports about an autobiography, and Nina said the project was still in the works, tentatively titled "Princess Noire," a conceptual trifecta with its allusion to royalty (though modestly one step below queen), to her love of things French, and to her pride in being black. Nina hoped the book project would take her mind off music. "I want to be happy—*that's* as important as music to me. Music hasn't made me happy. It makes *life* happy. I think the world would be a terrible place without music. But it has to be balanced with other things." That prompted her to talk about Lisa, which she rarely did publicly.

"I've got a twenty-two-year-old who's never forgiven me for the lack of time we've spent together," Nina said. "That was the result of touring so much and giving so much of myself to music." Not only that, she continued in a new variation, "I've lost five other children because of this business. I was always on my feet so much, traveling so much, that I just couldn't keep them in my belly."

Those closest to Nina had never heard this before. Sam interpreted the comment with a broad perspective. "Her soul was split," he said. "She wanted very much to be a pariah. I could understand it. She already felt underappreciated. Being on the front page of all the newspapers—having all the press, all the adoration. That's only one aspect of the outer Nina. . . . She felt ugly inside. And the only way the ugliness could possibly be justified is through pain. The ugliness, the non-beauty of her life, her spiritual life had to come from pain. To have five miscarriages is pain. That's what she's trying to say. She has pain—pain related to her work. She hated to work. She loved to work."

In a way the miscarriages represented an updated version of Nina's bleak reveries on Tryon, which now could be seen as her justification for a lingering private melancholy that on the surface seemed inexplicable for such a favored child.

Nina ended her interview determined, she said, "to make sure I'm not so blind from looking back at what happened to me in the past, that I fail to see what I can get by just living in the now." But by the time Nina got to Chicago to perform in mid-November, the equanimity she professed to have in Los Angeles had dissipated. "I can't stand it here too long," she told the *Tribune*, her comments suggesting that she was becoming unmoored again. "I don't like the mentality of black Americans at all, of black Americans in general. I mean that. . . . I found my roots in Africa and that's where they belong. People in America don't even want to think about it, because they never ask any questions about it. They just assume I'm a blues singer, and I did 'Porgy' and I'm their sister," she went on. "Black America and white America has its own problems. That tends to put me in the middle. Blacks think because of my skin I'm their sister; whites think because I'm black I'm either their servant or maid, and I'm neither one."

She had exiled some of her most recognized songs, she added. "I will avoid doing the protest songs because that era is dead in America, as far as I'm concerned. I gave ten years to the civil rights movement, and that era is dead now. Ain't seen no movement, have you?"

NINA RETURNED TO LONDON to start the new year with another two-week engagement at Ronnie Scott's. Because she continued to be a good draw, Sanucci, as she remembered it, signed her on for a third week to begin February 3. But Nina said he didn't ask her first. "I was furious," she wrote. "Never mind that I was tired out and my voice was suffering, never mind that I was the one who actually had to go out and do the work." She and Sanucci immediately parted ways—barely six months after she had gushed to a reporter that she finally had managers "who love and take care of me."

Nina's performances had in fact started to disintegrate by her second week at Ronnie's. She got into a terrible fight with Sam over money, demanding that she make more than she was getting, roughly $20,000 a week. She required that flowers and Cristal champagne, top of the line, be in her dressing room every evening, and during their argument she picked up the bottle and smacked him in the head. Fortunately for both of them, the bottle didn't shatter and he was not injured, but he was angry. "I slapped her," Sam said, "and that scared her."

E. A. McGill, who had gone to Ronnie's January 21, was so irritated by Nina's lackluster performance that afterward she wrote Scott to tell him that she and her husband "did not feel we had had anything like our money's worth." Nina was an hour late, and when she finally came onstage, McGill said, "she appeared, then disappeared, reappeared again and sang 'My Baby Just Cares for Me.' She insisted the audience sing it for the third verse. She more or less managed to get through another couple of totally forgettable numbers then stormed off the stage." The sidemen waited a good long while, she added, until it became clear that Nina was not coming back.

Ronnie and his partner Pete King had no choice but to cancel the third week. King told *Billboard* he had to refund more than $20,000 in advance bookings: "It is very sad that such a great artist, who has been responsible for some of the most enthusiastic reactions we have ever had from audiences at the club, should let herself and her fans down so badly just as she was re-establishing her career. I can never book her again after this."

IN THE AFTERMATH of the London incidents Sam had taken Nina to Paris, a city she loved. But at their hotel she began acting more strangely than he had ever seen before. She walked the hallways half-dressed, cursed at the hotel management, and refused to pay her bills. "She was out of control," Sam said. "She knew she needed help," but she resisted so much that she had to be put in a straitjacket to be taken to a hospital for treatment. "You're going to go to hell for doing this," she screamed at Sam as a medical team took her away.

Among the diagnoses was multiple personality disorder, and anyone who was close to Nina had no trouble believing it. "She had many different personalities," Hannibal said. "One was an army general," he added, recalling the military garb Nina donned one day when they were together and she was deep into the part of a dictatorial soldier. And Nina often proclaimed herself to be royalty from some past millennium. Sam did his best to keep this episode from becoming public as Nina recuperated before a planned trip to the United States. Her March 16 performance at Boston's Symphony Hall reflected the recent turmoil. It was tense, uncertain, and marked again by multiple exits from the stage. Many of her fans shared the sad wonderment of Bob Blumenthal, who wrote afterward, "It was hard to believe that the shaky, self-absorbed woman on the Symphony Hall stage once exhorted us to demand freedom now."

Nina's turmoil remained on display at the *Playboy* Jazz Festival June 15 in Los Angeles, an impatient crowd that refused to heed her demands only fueling her irritation. When they continued to chatter

Nina during a March 16, 1986,
performance in Boston
(*John Blanding*, The Boston Globe)

after she told them to quiet down, she threatened to play a Bach fugue. "I'm a classical pianist, you know." Darlene Chan, still one of George Wein's top associates, helped run this festival, and she knew right away that something was amiss. "It was like one hundred degrees and she came in with this coat—sort of a raggedy fur coat . . . She was a fantastic artist. She definitely had highs and lows. We caught her on a low." People were yelling for her to sing, Chan added, but Nina refused. "No, you're going to listen to me." Chan was relieved when she left the stage. "We paid her, you know. She came. She showed up."

Nina was anything but gracious to the *San Francisco Chronicle*'s Edward Guthmann, who interviewed her before her concert July 19 at the city's Masonic Auditorium. "Is there any money in this?" she wanted to know. There wasn't, but Guthmann tried to smooth the way by telling her he had loved her music for years. "Love me, my ass! I

Nina talking to the audience during her performance
at the June 1986 Playboy Jazz Festival in Los Angeles
(*UCLA Charles E. Young Research Library Department of Special Collections,*
Los Angeles Times *Photographic Archives,* © *Regents of the*
University of California, UCLA Library)

need somebody to protect me," she snarled, adding that she wanted a bodyguard. "I don't want no chokin' kind of love, sir. It ain't never fed me, and it ain't never took care of me."

Nina was doing the Masonic date, she said, "just to get out of a contract, and you can print that. I dare ya to . . . I regret singing protest songs for ten years," she went on, warming to the subject of her financial worries. "That's what got me in the bind I am, and that is why my records were boycotted in this country," though this explanation ignored the changing musical tastes that affected so many artists. "And I want my money! I am not one to mince words, and I never was. I'm known all over the world, and I have to come back here and be punished like a slave just to get my money." She added

Nina at a July 1986 solo performance
in San Francisco
(*Frederic Larson*, San Francisco Chronicle)

that she expected to be suing people over her earnings "until I die. Thank God it's makin' me very nice and cool and crisp and direct."

Guthmann reported later that the Masonic concert was poorly attended and that Nina, appearing solo, "seemed unprepared and unfocused." The fans who showed up, though, did their best to cheer her on.

CLAUDE NOBS WAS AS LOYAL to Nina as George Wein and Art D'Lugoff. He invited her back to Montreux July 10, 1987, at what turned out to be an auspicious moment. The makers of Chanel No. 5 had just revamped their marketing, replacing Catherine Deneuve, the perfume's representative for eight years, with a new model and a new theme song, Nina's very first recording of "My Baby Just Cares for Me."

"This song is popular all over France with Chanel No. 5 perfume—unfortunately of which I have none, and not the money either," Nina said to audible chuckles from the crowd. Her performance of the song was as intense as the original was lighthearted. She started with perhaps a minute of counterpoint, evoking Bach, and then rolled out the phrases about "high toned laces" and such as if she were giving a dramatic reading. The formal presentation contrasted with her casual dress—a tight-fitting halter top tucked into a long black skirt. She was wearing no makeup, and that coupled with her stern visage kept the entire performance at a remove, which seemed to be just what she wanted.

Sometime later, Hannibal Means recalled, "she came to me in Vienna wearing the most beautiful light blue polka-dot jacket with a miniskirt and matching high heels. 'Where did you get this outfit, Nina?' I asked."

"I walked into Chanel in Paris and took it and told them, 'You people owe me millions of dollars!' "

Hannibal had no trouble believing that Nina was telling the truth.

"I WAS PROBABLY A MASOCHIST," Raymond Gonzalez said, recalling with good humor why he agreed to work with Nina after the Pamplona disaster. "When you see someone you've admired in such a state, you can only do one thing and try to help them. Simple as that." Al and Leopoldo had come back to play with Nina early in 1988 for several dates in Europe, where Nina had a loyal following. Raymond found her a couple of bookings in Brazil, too. Gerrit, her devoted Dutch fan, was now an invaluable confidant, so much so that she liked him backstage at her concerts as often as possible. When she left the piano to smoke a quick cigarette offstage, "she would ask me, 'Gerrit, did I make you cry?' And when I said 'yes,' she would kiss me and whisper things like 'I know. I felt like crying, too.' "

With Gerrit's steady hand, supplemented by Raymond, Nina was generally the mild-mannered performer she said she wanted to be all through the year. But money was still on her mind. In Barcelona, she got up from the piano, walked to center stage, and told the audience that "Nina's Back" buttons were available after the concert, "and they cost two hundred pesetas, which is not too much money, and I'd appreciate it if you'd buy them." At Hamburg's Fabrik, a factory turned club, she wanted everything "nice and easy" and briefly admonished the drummer, "Now don't speed up!" She did complain, midconcert, however, that the room was "hot and hateful." At the Dominion Theatre in London, she declined to chew out the woman who chattered between verses of "Pirate Jenny." "Be quiet, honey. I want to hear my heart beat" was all she said.

Sam left by the end of the year to return to Nyack, on the verge of a breakdown himself. But Al, Leo, and Raymond were staying, and of course she could count on Gerrit. For all her idiosyncrasies, Nina had to realize she inspired great loyalty. She was not alone.

26. Nina's Back . . . Again

~ 1989–1992 ~

Al called Chris White, Nina's former bass player, in the spring of 1989 and asked him to join Nina in Europe. Chris was surprised. Based on the last time he saw her, he didn't think she was up to performing. They had been at a party in Newark at the home of Amiri Baraka, the poet and writer formerly known as LeRoi Jones. "I said to her twice, 'Hello, Nina. How are you? This is Chris.' And she looked at me and said, 'Hello, dahling. How are you?' She didn't know who the fuck I was. I could have been the man in the fucking moon. She was totally out of it." Later he learned from two young friends, Darryl and Douglas Jeffries, who had been recruited to look after her for a day, that she had been impossible. Promoters just getting started, they hoped that time spent with Nina might help their new business. They arrived at Baraka's house, where Nina was staying, expecting to meet jazz royalty, but the woman they saw looked like a homeless street person. She was unkempt, dressed in an old black poncho and high-topped sneakers, carrying a peanut butter and jelly sandwich in one hand and a fifth of vodka in the other.

A musician friend had asked the brothers to come by with their portable video machine so Nina could play a European tape she had. But the tape and their equipment didn't mesh, and she couldn't watch it. The Jeffrieses tried to make up for it by taking her to a well-established soul food restaurant in the area. Things went pleasantly enough until Nina announced that she had to get to Waterford, Connecticut, for a meeting, and she ordered them to drive her. The brothers told her they had to stop at home first to get a few things. Nina apparently thought they were taking too long at the house, so she got out of the car and banged on the front door. Their mother, a registered nurse, answered to find an angry woman bellowing, "Do you know who I am?"

"Do you know who *I* am?" Mrs. Jeffries yelled back, and the shouting escalated until Darryl and Douglas got Nina back in the car. They arrived in Connecticut just before midnight. "She was ranting and raving" almost the whole way, Douglas said. "She was spewing at us. We hadn't done anything. We had just met the lady." But right after she found her friends and sat down at a piano, "all of that turbulence went away," Douglas went on, the memory of this miraculous transition still vivid. "She was now in a safe harbor, and she came to herself. She was a living walking hurricane until she got to sit down at the keyboard, and then the serenity came over her."

"She wanted me to stay the evening and comfort her," Darryl added, which he declined to do. He and Douglas drove back to New York in a daze. "We thought we had found a mentor," Darryl said, "and we ran into a tsunami."

Al assured Chris that these kinds of episodes were few and far between. Nina was on medication for what had now been diagnosed as schizophrenia, and it kept her on an even keel more often than not. Several dates were booked, and besides that, Al told Chris that Nina had asked for him because she believed he understood her.

Nina had also relocated once again, this time to Nijmegen, the Netherlands, an inland city southeast of Amsterdam where Gerrit lived. He had put the move in motion when he realized that Nina needed a stable base. Over the last year he seemed able to handle her intermittent rages better than most, and he wanted her nearby. He never argued with her even when he was tempted to yell back.

Instead, he listened patiently and then suggested possible solutions to whatever problem had set her off. On occasion, when he sensed that it would work, he first ignored her rantings and then looked right at her before sticking out his tongue. She dissolved into laughter, and the moment passed. Perhaps most important, though, Nina knew that Gerrit would not judge her. She must have sensed that it saddened him to see so much talent accompanied by so much pain. "I thought, 'Poor Nina. You're having an attack. How horrible for you.' . . . Can you imagine if you can't behave yourself. You wake up the next morning and ask 'What have I done?' " Nina's pointed humor, he added, revealed that she understood her own problems. The once-popular song "What Have They Done to My Song, Ma?" included the line "Look what they've done to my brain, Ma," and Nina would sing it with gusto.

In Nijmegen Nina bought a small apartment and had the help of the self-styled "A-team" to assist her: Gerrit and Al along with Raymond, who was still booking her concerts. Roland Grivelle, Nina's

Nina with percussionist Leopoldo Fleming in her apartment in
Nijmegen, the Netherlands, May 1989
(Gerrit DeBruin)

friend from Paris and the occasional road manager, also stepped in to help, and Leopoldo arrived just as Nina was setting up the place. "We took her out shopping and bought her furniture and dishes," he said, and also a shopping cart, which Nina insisted she didn't need. "You may not need it," Leo explained. "That's for whoever does the shopping for you." Nina chuckled at the truth of the matter.

Gerrit knew that Nina appreciated all he had done even if she rarely showed it. He had rescued her from an embarrassing incident at the Grand Hotel in Paris a year or so earlier when, for no apparent reason, she was about to strike a complete stranger who was in the lobby. "I dragged her outside into the street and managed to push her into a taxi," he explained. They drove around until she calmed down, and nothing more was said. A couple of months later back in Nijmegen, "she turned to me and said, 'Gerrit, thank you for getting me out of that situation in the Grand Hotel.'" He was hardly prepared for the more extravagant gesture that came a few months later. He picked up the phone at his office one day to hear Nina demanding that he stop what he was doing and come to the apartment—immediately. She refused to take no for an answer, so Gerrit closed up the day's affairs in his wine import business and headed over. When he walked in, Nina was standing by her piano in full concert makeup, pointing him to a chair nearby. "I'm so grateful," she said. "I'm doing a private concert for you." "She played for four hours," Gerrit recalled, "and then she asked if I wanted an encore."

NINA'S APARTMENT WAS CONVENIENTLY located next to the Hotel Belvoir, where Leo and the other musicians stayed. "It was very pleasant, a nice experience," Leo remembered. Chris agreed. A photo from one of their first dates after his return, a concert in Oviedo, Spain, shows the camaraderie among the musicians and Nina. Everyone, to be sure, was older now. A much plumper Nina was wearing a tailored suit with a floral pattern that would be as suitable for dinner at an upscale restaurant as for the stage of a jazz club. Al's hair was salt-and-pepper, and Chris, dapper in a double-breasted suit, still looked young, though not quite as boyish as the twenty-something who had played with Nina years earlier.

A handwritten set list, c. 1989
(*Courtesy of Gerrit DeBruin*)

The distance had given him perspective. The first time, Chris said, "part of what was interesting with the band was the fact that Nina was inventing herself. And when I came to her the second time, she was a known entity both to herself and to the public, and her intent was to attempt to be whoever she felt that was." In the beginning, he went on, "I felt I was helping to create along with her. The second time I was there to provide just whatever it was she needed. So it was a different approach. The second time required a much more mature player."

Chris had a birthday July 6, and he was touched that Nina threw him a party in Barcelona, not far from one of their festival dates. "It was just magnificent," he recalled, the icing on the cake coming from a solo during an instrumental later on at their sold-out concert at the Lycabettus Theater in Athens. A reviewer singled him out for his "expressive bass."

Nina's model behavior onstage, however, was nowhere to be seen offstage when the antidepressants weren't working. Just before Athens, when they were in Freiburg, Germany, Nina became so angry at Raymond—and no one knew why—that he and Gerrit decided that Raymond had to get out of the hotel for his own safety. She was still mad at Raymond when they got to Athens. In one wild moment, she grabbed a knife from a food trolley that was in her hotel room and went out in the hallway naked, determined to find Raymond. Gerrit had been unable to stop her, but he cried out, "Nina, you are naked. You better get dressed first." Nina realized Gerrit was right and came back for her bathrobe. Then she stormed out again, and he went after her to ask that she listen to him if only for a moment. Hoping he could dissuade her from even more embarrassment, Gerrit told her that the Athens police would not take kindly to her stabbing someone and that if she was going to hurt Raymond, better to do it in London, where she would have more protections under English law.

"Well, Nina's enthusiasm to kill Raymond cooled off," Gerrit recalled, "and that evening we—Nina, Raymond, and I—had a wonderful dinner together." Later, back in Nijmegen, Nina was perturbed that Gerrit had let her go out of her hotel room naked. He simply told her that as long she had a knife in her hand, he'd rather let her run around with no clothes on than get cut.

"Yes," Nina said. "I understand."

NINA'S CONCERN over her royalties had not abated. In the fall a San Francisco lawyer she had hired, Steven Ames Brown, whose specialty was royalty recovery, sued a California distributor, Street Level Trading, and the British-based Charly Records for breach of contract in a licensing deal made in 1987 for Nina's Bethlehem recordings. The lawsuit charged that the two defendants were in breach of the deal and had committed fraud in the way they executed the arrangement. Nina claimed she was owed $200,000. She had been so outspoken in criticizing Charly for failing to pay her proper royalties that the label filed a defamation suit against her in a London court and added Brown to the litigation, too, after he spoke

out on her behalf. All the legal maneuvering tied up any royalty payments until Nina's suit was settled for an undisclosed sum in the
summer of 1990. As part of the settlement Charly dropped the
defamation claims.

(Brown also filed a separate lawsuit for Nina against Ron Berenstein, who ran Vine Street Records, alleging that he owed her
$50,000 for the records that were made from her appearances at the
Vine Street club. This lawsuit was settled, too.)

CLAUDE NOBS INVITED NINA back to Montreux for the 1990
festival, and at her performance July 13 she couldn't resist mocking
her reputation. Introducing "Four Women" and "Mississippi Goddam," Nina announced, "These next two tunes are dedicated to the
blacks of America, the blacks of Switzerland, the blacks of the Middle East, the blacks of Africa—and we're all very happy that Nelson
Mandela is free, right?" She was referring to the release in February
of the black South African leader who had been imprisoned twenty-
seven years. "They thought that I wasn't political anymore and what
a mistake to think that." Nina smiled ever so slightly.

Leo, who was playing a host of percussion instruments on this
date, remembered that a woman from Ghana was helping her now.
In contrast to her two previous Montreux appearances, Nina was in
full high-priestess makeup, heavy liner setting off her eyes, just the
right shade of lipstick and rouge to pick up the reddish stripes in the
dress she was wearing, which was made out of kente cloth. Her hair
was in cornrows, and to finish off the look she had returned to those
long dangling earrings she used to like so much.

Successful as this date was, it couldn't match the delight of a four-
city swing through Italy in the fall with her good friend Miriam
Makeba, and Odetta, the folksinger from the United States Nina had
known since her first days in New York. The tour was the brainchild
of Roberto Meglioli, an Italian promoter who had been working
with Miriam Makeba. He knew Raymond and knew Nina's music
and approached them about doing a joint project. "We would love to
have a third point of view," he explained, "and that's where Odetta
comes in." Fortunately she was in Europe at the time and agreed

right away to join the two other women. They called their tour "Three Women for Freedom."

Roberto knew Nina could be temperamental, and he asked Raymond for advice. "I am very white. I am very Italian, not even American, I know what I am. She is famous. Is there anything I might say or do that could make someone uncomfortable?" Raymond had nothing specific to tell him, so Roberto relied on his own instincts. He would make sure she and the other women had first-class accommodations, and he would be very respectful, especially at their first stop, which was in Catania, Sicily. He had picked a lovely hotel that was near the water, and right away that endeared him to Nina. She was already swimming when a photographer from *Corriere della Sera*, one of the major Italian newspapers, arrived to take pictures. Roberto asked her if she minded being photographed and asked if she would like time to change.

Why on earth should she, Nina wanted to know. She liked the way she looked in a bathing suit, even at fifty-seven. She put on a big pair of sunglasses and posed "like a real diva," Roberto said. "That was funny. Everything went smoothly."

The evening of the concert seven thousand Sicilians packed the spectacular grounds in front of a centuries-old castle Roger the Norman had built to protect against Saracen invaders. With a combination of joy and relief, Roberto watched Nina's set from behind the stage, grabbing Miriam for a giddy minuet while Odetta took a spin with the local police chief, who happened to be standing nearby.

Most of the time, Odetta said, Nina was "in a good place. She trusted both of us." She was convinced, too, that Nina found some special peace in the water. "Everywhere we went on the Mediterranean, the vacation belt, we got there, we would hear a splash. It's Nina in the water. She swam and just played. It was a joy to see she got so much pleasure in the water." At other moments, when Nina was at the keyboard, Odetta sensed the darker moods. As a listener, she said, "all of a sudden you were within a storm on that piano."

Roberto further endeared himself to the women with the accommodations he booked in Cagliari on the island of Sardinia. Each of the singers had her own villa that was equipped with a kitchen, and Roberto remembered that they cooked meals for one another just like great friends would do. He couldn't be sure, but he thought because he had taken such care with the details of the tour Nina never said no to anything he asked of her, and he saw only her calm side.

Odetta had hoped the trio could tour the United States—Miriam was "modern Africa, I was what we bring from Africa to the United States, and Nina represented jazz, where it went, but there was no financing."

AFTER SEVERAL FALSE STARTS and a bevy of possible co-writers, Nina's autobiography finally appeared in England at the end of 1991. It wasn't called "Princess Noire" after all but *I Put a Spell on You*. Her co-writer was Stephen Cleary, a British man who had co-produced and directed the filming at Ronnie Scott's in 1984.

The book was less a reliable guide to Nina's life and career than a window into her feelings about all that had transpired. To her faithful fans it mattered little that she mixed up the history of Tryon and surrounding Polk County, described events in her career out of sequence, some with considerable embroidery, and made a few individuals with whom she crossed paths more villain than the record warranted. She barely gave Sam a mention, and though she gave a nod to Al, she took no note of Chris, Bobby Hamilton, Lisle Atkinson, or Rudy Stevenson—her sidemen in those critical early years when she established her career. Regardless of its literary merit, the book brought a new wave of attention that overshadowed some less than stellar performances earlier in the year.

I Put a Spell on You was released in the United States early in 1992, and Lester Hyman was delighted that Nina was coming to Washington June 18 for a concert at George Washington University. He got tickets for himself and friends who were visiting from California. One of them was a big fan, and Lester promised he would take his friend to meet her. After the concert at Lisner Auditorium, he went to the stage door, told the security people who he was, and handed one of them a business card for Nina. "Miss Simone says she will see Mr. Hyman and no one else" came the reply.

"So I went back," Lester recalled, "and I said, 'Won't you just say hello to my friends?'"

"No!" Nina exclaimed. "I just want to see you."

Disappointed, Lester could only deliver the rebuff to his crest-fallen friend and explain truthfully, "That's Nina."

George Wein sponsored Nina at Carnegie Hall the following week as part of the JVC Jazz Festival. The theme was a variation on her past returns to the city. Instead of "Nina's Back!" it was now "Welcome Back, Nina," along with Al, Paul Robinson, and Leopoldo. A hall filled with fans gave her all the appreciation she could want, even if she was once again in middling musical form. She found the energy, though, to give "Mississippi Goddam" enough bite to inspire the raised fists of the black power salute among the many blacks in the audience.

I PUT A SPELL ON YOU had prompted a French film crew to make a documentary about Nina, *La Légende*, with her full cooperation. Gerrit by her side, she went back to Tryon for a tearful reunion with Edney Whiteside, her first love. She wondered aloud whether her career had been worth it, wiping her eyes as he tried to console her. Holding her hand, he gently reminded her that this was what she had always wanted. Nina revisited the disappointment over her rejection from Curtis, declaring that she was still not over what in her mind was a case of obvious racial bias.

She spoke with passion about her most controversial songs of the 1960s. "I felt more alive then than I feel now because I was needed, and I could sing something to help my people, and that became the mainstay of my life. That became most important to me," she said. "It was not classical piano, not classical music, not even popular music, but civil rights music. All my friends had either left the movement or were exiled or were killed," she went on, "and so I was lost, and I was bitter, very bitter, paranoid. I imagined someone was out to get me, out to kill me every minute of my life. . . . " As if to buttress this point, Vladimir Sokoloff, the Curtis professor who had taught Nina privately, was interviewed on camera, and he lent credence to at least some of her fears. He said that the CIA had come to ask him if there was any evidence that while she was his student "she was mixed up in all this rebellious uprising."

"When the civil rights movement died," Nina said, "and when there was no reason to stay and there was so much racial prejudice, I couldn't bear it, and I didn't think it was my home. I had to get out of there."

The documentary didn't shy away from Nina's angry side. Excerpts from a tape of her swearing at a promoter were included over a still photo of her face contorted in rage. She demanded that he get her contracts to her hotel or she would destroy his event. "I know you're a rich son of a bitch," she yelled into the phone.

"Yes," Nina said, smiling at the camera. "I guess I am a little capricious. I'm not easily aroused." Then she took it back. "No, that's not true. I am very emotional. I'm very disciplined, but I'm very emotional. When I don't like something, I say it immediately. So I think people would say I've got a hot temper. I think so."

Nina spoke of the estrangement with her father. "I wish he was here now," she said, breaking into tears. She dismissed Andy, her former husband, in cutting terms: "I never enjoyed him in bed. He told people I was his sleeping pill."

Perhaps the most significant element of the fifty-minute program was the apparent reconciliation between Nina and her daughter. Only a few years earlier she had spoken of her with disdain, after Lisa had her first child. "I don't see either one of them," Nina had said. "So as far as I'm concerned I don't have a daughter Lisa. That's good enough for me." Now, in the opening frames of the documentary, she cried as she told Edney she had never seen her grandchild, who was now seven. "I wasn't able to raise Lisa very well. I'm sure that we'll make it up as months go by. We will make up for what we didn't share during those years. She seems to think we can, and I think we can."

Then Lisa, now an aspiring singer, had her say. "She wasn't with me or around me. She was always with me musically. So I want to sing her songs. I would love to be able to do that and have her in the wings or in the audience or on the stage knowing that she's appreciated, that she's loved, and knowing that it has not been for naught."

The documentary ended with a segment called "The Dream." Nina wore an orange caftan and played a grand piano in an outdoor setting framed by neoclassical columns. Guests dressed in formal attire watched attentively from a garden. She spoke over strains of Tchaikovsky's Romeo and Juliet Fantasy. "It haunts me," Nina said. "Especially when I'm alone at night. I do still wish I had been a classical pianist, but I don't look back now. I am what I am. Who am I? I am a reincarnation of an Egyptian queen."

27. A Single Woman

~ 1993–1999 ~

Michael Alago, who worked for Elektra Records, had been a fan since he was a teenager. During one of Nina's New York appearances, he stopped in at her sound check to introduce himself. He thought she knew he was coming, but she didn't and her displeasure showed. She demanded to know who he was and what he was doing there. Michael politely explained that he was with the record company and that he wanted to sign her. She started to laugh. "How old are you?"

Twenty-eight, he told her, and she laughed some more.

"Man, do you have the money?"

"I said to her I don't walk around carrying money," Michael recalled, worried that a difficult moment was getting worse. "Then I just started gushing about how much I loved her music over the years and what a great honor it would be to make music with her." Michael knew he had rescued himself when Nina offered him some of her tea. He graciously took it and immediately choked. Nina had a special concoction that called for lemon and cayenne pepper. "Oh, please, cayenne that could kill us—enough cayenne that if you took a sip you really couldn't breathe for a few minutes. I was sweating, my head was on fire, and I thought I'm going to die from drinking tea."

Nina just laughed again.

Michael didn't give up on his idea, even though he didn't know what kind of songs Nina might want to sing or how her voice would hold up. He only knew that he wanted to make a record with her, and his enthusiasm carried the day with the Elektra executives. By the beginning of 1993 he had signed her to the label, and just as she turned sixty, Nina was in a California studio to record a new album. When she and Michael had talked about it ahead of time, she told him she wanted to work with a black producer, so he brought in

Nina with Michael Alago during the 1993
recording of *A Single Woman*
(*Carol Friedman*)

Andre Fischer, who was married to Natalie Cole and had worked with Tony Bennett and Diane Schuur. Michael was on tenterhooks when Fischer and Nina had their first meeting, but it couldn't have gone better. Fischer swooned as soon as he walked in the room, and Nina lapped up all his attention. "He spoke to her with reverence," Michael recalled. "He was going to treat her like a queen, with the ultimate respect. It was a done deal when he walked in the room because she liked him."

This new record was Nina's most ambitious effort since her RCA days—along with Fischer, two dozen orchestral musicians had been hired for the sessions. Nina and Michael picked the tracks together, including three by Rod McKuen, whom they both liked. They modeled the record after Frank Sinatra's *A Man Alone*. One of the McKuen songs was "A Single Woman," and with her husky voice and stately delivery, Nina gave it autobiographical punch: "always alone, at home or in a crowd," she sang, "a single woman in a world few people understand."

Nina's own "Marry Me" seemed like an answer song not only in subject matter but in the light touch. There were no strings and lots of piano, only it wasn't Nina. Instead, except for one track, Michael Melvoin, a well-regarded Los Angeles musician, played. "To be perfectly frank at that point in time her piano playing was spotty," Michael said. "She did do a lot of the basic tracks, and then in the end they weren't to Andre's liking." So Melvoin was brought in.

Twenty years after her father's death, Nina was still sorting through her feelings. She chose "Papa, Can You Hear Me?" from the movie *Yentl* as another homage to him, arranging the song to begin with the recognizable melody of "Swing Low Sweet Chariot." "Nina and I had both lost our fathers," Michael said. "I knew then that the record was going to be about love, loneliness, and loss." He told Nina that *A Single Woman* was the perfect name for the album, but she resisted: "I don't want people to think of me as a single woman in her sixties." Michael refused to back down. The words expressed freedom, he told her. "You should be proud to say 'I'm a single woman who's lived this life, and I'm still standing strong.'" Nina finally agreed.

With a summer release scheduled, Nina spent the spring promoting the album during concerts in the Midwest and the Northeast, but she wasn't happy about it. She insisted on being paid for every appearance, even those that had nothing to with performing. Michael patiently explained that Elektra would cover her travel and hotel and pay for good food, too, but not simply for showing up. He refused to be cowed by her occasional rages and used his own buoyant personality and taste for the bravura gesture as a cushion. "When she got mad, I would say, 'Listen, girl, don't talk to me that way. Kiss me right now!' Then I would kiss her . . . She became like a child and loved it."

Five of Nina's earlier songs were in a just-released movie, *Point of No Return*, as *A Single Woman* was hitting the stores. It was the kind of moment to be cherished, a new album *and* Hollywood exposure. But instead of riding the wave, Nina canceled upcoming concerts and fled the United States in July to a new home she had just bought in the south of France. Though it put a crimp in Elektra's promotion plans, Michael tried to be understanding. "She hates the pace of the United States," he said. "From day to day it changes with her." His motto became "Expect the unexpected."

A Single Woman was released to generally favorable reviews, and music aside, it had handsome packaging. The cover photograph was a close-up of Nina looking thoughtful but with no hint of anger. The photograph inside was stunning. Nina was dressed in a fuchsia Christian Dior gown that billowed out around her and partially covered the gold wire chair she was sitting in. Her head was wrapped in a white-and-gold turban whose color matched her stylish high-heeled shoes. The entire package seemed to say that the high priestess had gone high style.

Though Nina agreed to a midsummer telephone interview with James Gavin of *The New York Times* that had been set up weeks earlier, her testy responses suggested she'd changed her mind about the whole thing. When Gavin referred to the unsmiling performer so many fans saw in past years, Nina cut him off. "How the hell was I going to smile in the United States when I'm black? Come on!" She refused to talk about current politics though she said she kept up by watching television and reading international newspapers. "*J'attend*," she said. "That's French for I'm waiting."

Was there anything she missed about the United States? Gavin asked.

"My money."

Michael knew better than most how the subject still consumed her. Nina had agreed to come back for an appearance on *The Tonight Show* on November 17, and he was there to make sure that everything went smoothly. She was going to be last on the show and sing "A Single Woman." He could see that she was nervous, and he did his best to keep her calm in the greenroom, reserved for guests before they went on. Nina asked several times what she was going to get paid and when she was going to get her money. Michael told her she would get paid through NBC the same as any other performer who came on the show. It was about $750, and a check would come in the mail.

Nina shook her head. She announced that she would not perform unless she got her money first. "I had to leave the greenroom," Michael explained. "I went and found Jay Leno and the producer and had to tell them. They looked at me like I was crazy." The show was starting in twenty minutes. "But they came back with the money. I was shocked. They were furious."

Nina went on as planned. "There was a world-weariness to the performance," Michael said, but she had made it through.

STEVEN AMES BROWN, the San Francisco lawyer, still represented Nina. In the liner notes for *A Single Woman*, she had given him thanks as "my hard-working attorney," and early in 1994 Brown went to court on her behalf again. He sued the San Juan Music Group and its associates to end a licensing agreement on fifty-five of Nina's recordings and to get back her masters. In exchange for his work, Nina had agreed to give Brown 40 percent of any royalties recovered, and they would be joint owners of the masters. Nina had told Raymond Gonzalez that she would rather have 60 percent of something than 100 percent of nothing, which she said had been the case for too many years. San Juan and Brown settled the case in December, and the final order also required the defendant to pay $15,000 to Nina for all the associated costs. (A year later, Brown filed suit against three other companies and after nearly three years of wrangling won a judgment that ended licensing on some of the same recordings as the San Juan litigation as well as an additional forty recordings.)

NINA'S NEW HOME was in Bouc-Bel-Air, about halfway between Marseilles and Aix-en-Provence. The move had surprised Gerrit. After two relatively peaceful years in Nijmegen, she had gotten restless, finding the town too provincial. So Gerrit found her a furnished apartment in Amsterdam in the home of a couple she knew. But that still wasn't enough to keep her satisfied. Late in 1992 Nina decided she wanted to move to the south of France, and one day Gerrit received a phone call with the news that she had bought the house in Bouc-Bel-Air. He tried to dissuade her, but he knew it was useless. "Nina is a reckless person, looking for happiness after the next hill," he said. "We always had to show her that the grass is green enough here." In this instance, however, he couldn't convince her. So again he helped her move, though he worried how she would do on her own, especially without someone to monitor the antidepressant she was still taking.

Gerrit had been alarmed a few months earlier when she called him from Amsterdam and told him she had stopped taking her pills altogether. "I see the world so clear now," she asserted. "I bought a paper. I am interested in reading the paper, going out to sit on the bench and reading the paper. I am not ever going to take those pills again." Concerned about her well-being, Gerrit hustled from his house in Nijmegen to stay with her for a few days. He did all the cooking and slipped her pills into the food until he could convince her to resume the medication. Hannibal Means knew firsthand what could happen without it. He and Nina were at lunch one day when she visited him in Vienna "and the plates started flying. She flipped out," he said. It could have been the look on the waiter's face or perhaps a dish that arrived too late for Nina's liking. Hannibal was never sure.

Within six months of the move to France, Nina's life started to unravel, just as her friends had worried. First came the incident with broken glass. Nina cut herself, and the initial news reports said the accident occurred when she tried to put out a fire on an overheated fax machine. Michael read an account in one of the New York City papers and immediately called. Someone other than Nina answered and relayed a message: "Nina says it's your fault."

"I'm in my office in New York, Rockefeller Center. How is it my fault?" Michael wanted to know. Nina got on the phone and complained that he had faxed too many pages of documents, which she had to sign for the Elektra album. "I'm not a white businessman. I'm an artist."

That may be true, Michael replied, but she still needed to sign the papers. He insisted she tell him what really happened. Nina finally confessed that she had been smoking, and on her way upstairs to the bedroom, she dropped the lighted cigarette on some linens underneath the stairs, and that had started the fire. Glass was broken when firemen doused the flames.

Then came the incident with her car. Nina was ultimately fined $4,000 and given a two-month suspended jail sentence for a hit-and-run accident with the 1991 Volkswagen Gerrit had gotten for her. Though she had left the scene after striking two young women, neither of whom was seriously injured, the police had no trouble finding her. "Everybody knew the black crazy woman," Gerrit said. But neither this nor the fire rivaled the incident in July of 1995 that nearly sent Nina to jail.

The modest house in Bouc-Bel-Air was on a quiet street at the foot of a hill. The dark interior in the main first-floor room gave way to a sunny sitting area entered through glass-paneled doors. On one wall Nina had hung her two honorary doctorates, a signed photo from Miriam Makeba, a casual shot of Bob Dylan, and a signed photograph of Little Richard. (Little Richard's brother Mark was Nina's longtime accountant.) A high metal gate had been installed at the entrance, and the house was surrounded by a hedge. But the gaps in the greenery allowed Nina to see her neighbors, and they could see her. The villa next door had a swimming pool, and on one summer evening, two teenage boys were making too much noise for Nina's liking. Her brother Carrol was visiting, and Nina was having a party for him. She had worked all day on the garden, "and at six o'clock they started their bullshit," she recalled. "Yeah, I'm a comin' to your partee," they heckled. Nina was convinced she heard racial insults in their snide imitation of a black person from the United States.

"Quit it! Quit it!" she yelled, but they persisted, so she got a gun she kept at the house and fired buckshot over the hedge, striking one of the boys in the leg. Carrol had been in town and returned to a scene of great commotion with angry neighbors and the local authorities. He later accompanied Nina to the police station where charges against her were processed, but he returned to the United States before the matter was resolved. Nina eventually was fined $4,600 and ordered to undergo counseling. Her lawyer told the court officer that Nina was "fragile and depressed." The subsequent report determined that she was "incapable of evaluating the consequences of her act."

Nina remained unrepentant. "He went to the hospital, but he didn't die or nothing," she said of the victim. The thought of speaking to the adults next door had not crossed her mind. "I'm not friendly with the neighbors," she said. "The neighbors here are not friendly. They keep to themselves, and so do I. But that one day was too much." She was irritated that she had to pay a fine, but if she hadn't, "they were going to put me into jail. But I'm not sorry. They don't bother me anymore."

Sometime after the French court proceedings, Nina returned to the United States, in the view of her sister Frances well before any counseling could help her. She stayed for a time with her brother John Irvin and his wife Carolle in Sacramento. Then she went to her apartment in Los Angeles, where she promptly got into a nasty fight with a neighbor. The police were called, and Frances said she, too, was summoned from the East Coast "because Nina needed help." Nina was subsequently hospitalized, though she insisted in a letter to Gerrit that she had not been sick. She blamed this stay in the hospital—erroneously, according to Frances and to Steven Ames Brown—on her sister. "I was in the hospital for my protection because my sister tried to kill me literally, guns and all," she wrote in her dramatic rendition of events. One of Nina's caretakers in the L.A. hospital was a young man named Clifton Henderson, tall and slender and with enough of a resemblance to Nina that he could have been a Waymon. They took an instant liking to each other, and Nina asked him to return to France with her as a nurse/assistant. She told Gerrit she had moved everything she had to the house in Bouc-Bel-Air.

"She being an artist as she is, and me being just a simple person, our relations clicked together, and at the time both of us were looking for someone first to be friends with when we met," Clifton said. "A sense of humor and a positive attitude, I think the positive attitude is what makes it," Clifton added. "We laugh all the time. We spend a lot of time together, and the relations just grow from there, and I think continue to grow."

PROFESSIONALLY 1996 WAS a lost year, though Nina asked Gerrit to help her find work—but subject to her conditions: "no less than $30,000 (cash), no taxes" for a one-hour set. Gerrit would earn a 4 percent commission. She returned to performing in the middle of 1997 with six concerts in Europe and two in Brazil—precise terms unknown. Her last was December 14, 1997, back at the Barbican in London. Al, Leo, Paul Robinson, and Tony Jones, a bassist who had worked with Nina a decade earlier, backed her. Chris White had departed when he took a teaching job that left too little time to play overseas. What you came for at these concerts determined how you felt when they were over. If you bought a ticket, sat in your seat, and waited expectantly for a live version of a treasured recording, you were likely to be disappointed. Nina didn't sing the way she used to, and her piano work, which could be fierce and inspiring, sometimes did not approach either. But if you came simply to be in the presence of Nina Simone—Dr. Nina Simone, the high priestess, the self-proclaimed creator of classical jazz—you more than likely came away satisfied.

On this night Nina offered some for each. Swaddled in a full-length silver fox coat, she came onstage walking hesitantly and assisted by two men. Those familiar with Nina's stagecraft were not entirely convinced that she needed help getting to the keyboard, but no one could argue that this appearance of great vulnerability wasn't effective. "Like my coat?" she asked, interrupting the ovation that greeted her. "Yes," came the roar, even among those who in other circumstances would have disdained this particular display of opulence.

Phil Johnson, a reviewer for *The Independent*, gave a clear-eyed account of the evening. He stated frankly that Nina's voice was gone, and to him, she "had seemingly forgotten how to play the piano. Indeed by any objective standard, Simone simply can't do it anymore." But he knew most in the audience didn't care. They stood and cheered anyway. When Nina got to "Baltimore," which she now agreed to perform, and "Pirate Jenny," he admitted that the power and musical presence that had defined her shone through. Still, Johnson wrote, "It was the legend we were continually standing up for rather than the actual performance." Nina offered the clenched-fist black power salute by way of thanks and ended the evening with an auditorium full of Britons joining her in "We Shall Overcome"—"no mean feat in any circumstance," Johnson conceded.

These evenings could be tense affairs for the musicians. They had to watch Nina all the time, and if they couldn't anticipate her, they had to catch up as quickly as possible. "I matured musically in those years," Paul recalled. "What I mean is that I was able to go on to major concert halls around the world, do a pretty average performance, and come off and not feel bad. Nina was very good at theater," Paul added. "With the minimum effort she could actually create quite a lot of effect—I got used to that. She could get them going," he said of the audience, "just by giving them a nice smile."

IN MAGAZINE INTERVIEWS DURING 1997 Nina repeated her criticisms of the United States—"I call it the United Snakes of America"—and her disappointments with the civil rights movement. "Desegregation is a joke," she told *Interview*. "I do not believe in mixing of the races. You can quote me. I don't believe in it, and I never have. I've never changed my color, I have always been proud of myself, and my fans are proud of me for remaining the way I've always been. I married a white man one time," Nina added, "but he was a creep."

Nina was not so angry that she refused to return to the United

States in 1998 for concerts in Seattle and Newark. The evening of August 21 three thousand people jammed Seattle's Pier for the outdoor event, and she made her entrance with a combination of elegance and resolve that not every sixty-five-year-old could pull off. More stocky now than feline, Nina wore a glittery evening gown, her hair woven back off her forehead into a tight crown, a look at odds with the black power salute she gave in response to the cheers. Clifton, dressed in formal evening attire, guided her gracefully to the piano bench. He sent the message that he was there to serve Nina. The audience should, too.

She started with gospel tunes, one or two unaccompanied, and then moved into her best-known songs. Then she took a short break while the band played an instrumental dominated by the drums. After a few minutes, Nina could be seen in the wings, perhaps deliberately, Clifton next to her holding a cigarette up to her mouth. She took a long, dramatic drag and then exhaled. Eric Hanson, who had booked the date for Nina, found the moment mysterious, even sensual. "It was a cool thing," he said. "The percussion thing was carrying on. But all eyes were on her."

In Newark August 30 Nina hinted that she wouldn't be returning to the United States anytime soon. "If you're going to come see me again, you've got to come to France because I ain't coming back," she told the crowd at the New Jersey Performing Arts Center. "How old do I look?" Nina teased at one point. "I'm five thousand years old"—an observation to remind fans that the high priestess had not entirely vanished. Few, if any, in the packed auditorium cared that most of the performance was subpar. Nina elicited her usual standing ovations. "You're beautiful," she shouted during one of them. "Stay strong."

By the time Nina got to London in December for another performance at Royal Albert Hall, her view of the States had soured once again. "I went this year, and it was very hard," she told *The Daily Telegraph*. "I'm not going back there anymore."

Nina was spending most of her time at the house in Bouc-Bel-Air. In addition to Clifton, a woman named Jackie Hammond helped out, along with Javier Collados, a young musician she had met in Paris, who was an all-purpose assistant, bodyguard, chauffeur, and anything else that Clifton didn't handle. But none of them, individually or all together, could ward off chaos. One fall day a writer from London witnessed the disarray firsthand. Javier was on a short vacation, and Nina was raging at Clifton when Precious Williams, the writer, arrived for an interview. "You have no idea what I can drink, you damned fool! I once drank five bottles of champagne in one afternoon. Gays like you ought to be lined up and shot. You go against God," she yelled. "I'm itching to get my gun again. Next time I'll use it on him because of his incapability."

Clifton, if a little nervously, brushed off the insult.

According to Williams, the house was unkempt and so was Nina. Her face was puffy, her eyes were bloodshot, and she moved around unsteadily. Nina said she hadn't slept well, worried over the past few days about money, though a half-dozen concerts were already scheduled for 1999 with handsome fees. Jackie confided to Williams that the house looked messier than usual because Nina had told her to fire the cleaning person to save money. Jackie painted a distressing picture of the current moment: "Her and Clifton drink all night and all day. Her voice is gone. She just croaks along in time with the piano music. She still plays the piano like a dream, though. It's the only time she looks happy."

"Please tell my public that there aren't many of us geniuses still living," Nina said as she bid Williams goodbye. "Hardly any of us left at all. It's down to Bob Dylan, Stevie Wonder, and Frank Sinatra, except Frank's already dead."

Shortly before a July 1, 1999, appearance in London, Nina agreed to another interview with a British newspaper. She was going to be on the cover of the June 26 London *Times* magazine, which she considered fitting. "I compare myself to a queen," she declared. "I don't want to deny that. A black queen. After all, I have to go everywhere. I'm in Africa, in the Third World, the United States, France, Sweden, Germany, England. . . . I have to be a queen all the time, and to make sure that I look the part and act the part. Isn't that a strain? Of course it is. When you leave today," she told Ginny Dougary, the writer, "do you know how long it takes to remove all this make-up?" And then she started to laugh. Jackie had given Nina Nefertiti eyes, amber and bronze with dramatic black contours, and applied gold

Nina in the garden at her house in
Bouc-Bel-Air, France, June 1999
(*Graham Wood*)

lipstick that shone brightly against her dark skin. She was wearing a cream-colored cape with a large hood and several homemade amulets on her arms.

It tickled Nina that Lauryn Hill, a popular rap star, was a fan. She had made overtures about recording some of Nina's music and already had woven her into a rap: "While you imitatin' Al Capone, I'll be Nina Simone," which Nina took as a nod to her reputation for being tough. But she really didn't think much of rap. She always turned the conversation to classical music. Two months earlier, during a BBC television interview, she had asserted again that there were no black classical pianists. "All we have is André Watts," she said, discounting the well-established performer. "But they don't accept him very much because he's part German. But they would have accepted me."

Speaking now with Dougary at her house, her deep feelings on the subject were on display again. "Music has nuances, silences, pianissimos, fortissimos, crescendos, and when you put all the sounds together, my music, which I create, gives me as much of a sense of God as I ever have," she said. She illustrated with a spiritual, starting tentatively until she gathered strength to finish with a confident "I have heard thy voice."

"Obviously," Nina said, "I'm a Christian."

28. The Final Curtain

~ 2000–2003 ~

I continue to believe in God, and when I put myself to sleep at night, I sing a song called "Jesus Paid It All." I chant it. "Jesus paid it all. To him I owe. Sin has left the crimson stain. He washed it white as snow." I sing that over and over and over again until I fall asleep.

NINA SIMONE, c. 2000

By the middle of 2000, Nina had changed her life around again. She moved to Carry-le-Rouet, a seaside town west of Marseilles and near Sausset-les-Pins. "You love the water," Clifton told her. "Why not live like a star?" Not only was Carry much prettier than the nondescript Bouc-Bel-Air, the new house was much nicer, too. The one in Bouc was more like a cabin, while the spacious new house came with a small pool and a terrace off Nina's upstairs suite that allowed her to see the ocean. Her improved financial situation helped make the move possible. The decision to sign

Nina's home in Carry-le-Rouet, France
(Carolle Waymon)

Javier Collados and Juanita Bougere,
Nina's assistants, c. 2001
(Carolle Waymon)

an agreement with the Artists Rights Enforcement Corporation and then, even more important, to hire Steven Ames Brown, the San Francisco lawyer, was paying off. Money came in now with regularity, though the amount each year varied with Nina's record sales and use of her music in other ways. By the mid-nineties, Nina could count on at least $100,000 annually from this source of income. By 1999 she received more than $200,000, and during the year of the move more than $1,000,000 came in.

Moving wasn't the only change. Nina had also fired Raymond Gonzalez, the ever-loyal booking agent, after a new disagreement. She asked his associate, Juan Yriart, to take over his duties. She designated Clifton as her manager, a gesture Juan saw as Nina's way of saying thank you for caring for her over the previous four years. She also had let Javier join the band when she performed, which irritated Leo and Al. But Nina had confidence in Javier's ability because he worked with her all the time, especially when they were getting ready for a tour. Javier's first instrument was the guitar, but to avoid further aggravating Al, he usually played the keyboard.

Nina with Clifton Henderson, c. 2001
(Javier Collados)

This new regime spoke again to the qualities in Nina that inspired great loyalty in spite of the furies that could make her so difficult. But resentments, even jealousies, remained among those who had been close associates in recent years, now replaced by Clifton, Javier, Juan, and a young woman Nina had met in Los Angeles, Juanita Bougere. A hair stylist by trade, Juanita became a personal assistant, accompanying Nina for a time before returning to L.A. to pursue other work. Far from being angry at a middle-of-the-night call, Juanita took it as high praise when she answered the phone at three a.m. one day and heard Nina's voice on the other end from France. "I threw a chair at the bitch," she said, referring to a young Frenchwoman who had replaced Juanita. "Baby, I want you to come back home." Juanita agreed to return and was welcomed with a higher salary.

The old regime was convinced that the new was incompetent or worse. Al griped that Clifton was giving Nina her medication too close to a performance, which left her without energy onstage. As he remembered it, he got the routine changed. He also complained that Clifton had usurped too much authority and that he and the others were closing Nina off, even from people like him. Hannibal felt that, too. "He blocked the connection with Nina. He would not let me speak to her," Hannibal said, though Clifton, at Nina's behest, had called to see if he could come to Carry to help her when she was having problems with her voice. Hannibal said he would charge $1,000 for four days and would need a hotel room. However, he told Clifton that if Nina was still smoking, there was nothing he could do. The trip never happened, though Nina left Hannibal an angry phone message, aggravated that he would think of charging money to help her when it was *he* who owed her for all she had taught him.

Hannibal found it odd that Clifton pumped him for information about Nina, and he was uneasy when Clifton bragged—at least that's how Hannibal interpreted it—about how he kept Nina under control by adjusting her medication.

Even Gerrit was closed off, which only reinforced his conviction that these new assistants couldn't care for Nina properly. "When she was still in Bouc, I had power. But now in Carry," he said, "that power was diminishing. I was a danger to those guys."

Juan, who tried to monitor things from Paris, where he lived, waved off the outside criticism. "There are people out there who consider themselves friends of Nina, but they weren't doing anything to help her," he said. Clifton and the others, he asserted, allowed her "to go home and live a normal life." Javier put it this way: "My main job was to keep Nina safe from people, do whatever she needed, always to make sure that nothing happened to her. In the house it was funny—a lot of people, but it was a family." It was true he and the others were paid, "but it was not a job. It was dedication." Why else would they stay when Nina went into one of her rages? Clifton had weathered many, especially when he tried to keep Nina from drinking so much.

Juanita had felt the sting of Nina's anger shortly after she returned to France, when she accompanied Nina on a trip to Africa. Nina's doctor had not given her enough pills to last the entire time, and without the medication, Juanita said, "She was a raging bull." Nina flailed at Juanita during one outburst with such force that Juanita's thumb was injured as she tried to defend herself. The moment left her not only alarmed but confused. Nina had declared her affection, begging her to come back to France only to turn on her. Juanita realized Nina's illness had caused the wild behavior, but she still needed time to regain her equilibrium. "I had to make sense of it in my head," she said, especially when Nina berated her for being too light-skinned. "I said, 'Nina, what are you talking about? I'm the same color as you!'"

Javier didn't escape either. "I got fired every day," he said. At times, he admitted, neither he nor Clifton would put Nina on the phone if someone called and she wasn't doing well. "We could tell in the morning what kind of mood she was in." Regardless of what others thought, Javier believed he was looking out for Nina's best interests. Besides, he said, if he and Clifton were so bad, "why did they not call the police or take us to court for kidnapping?"

THOUGH NINA STILL PROFESSED a distaste for the United States, she would speak fondly of such things as having a hot dog from Pink's in Los Angeles. Juan thought that was enough incentive to work on getting American bookings, though he understood they would have to be planned carefully. Each date would probably end up being a five-day excursion: a travel day, a rest day, the concert day, another rest day, and then travel to the next stop.

Working through Eric Hanson, who had helped set up dates in 1998, Juan put together a tour of a dozen cities to start in Atlanta on May 26. Al, Leo, Paul, and Tony Jones would back up Nina. A few days ahead of time, Nina, Clifton, and Javier flew from Marseilles to Paris to meet Juan for their nonstop flight on Delta Airlines, one of the tour sponsors. Nina remained uneasy about returning the States, Javier said, and never failed to remind them about the country's discrimination against blacks. She worried someone would do her harm, though once she arrived she calmed down and pleasant memories emerged, at least for a time. They boarded the plane in Paris, Nina in first class with Clifton and Juan nearby and Javier in economy. Nina was taking longer than usual to arrange her carry-on bag and other belongings, and twice the pilot came to tell her to sit down. When he came a third time, he gave Nina an ultimatum: sit down or leave the plane. She chose the latter. Javier had no idea there was any problem until he heard an announcement that a passenger was being removed from the plane and the departure would be delayed. When he saw Clifton walking down the aisle, Javier knew it was Nina.

After security officers escorted the entourage through the concourse, Juan had to scramble to find hotel rooms and seats on a Delta flight for the next day. Clifton got Nina's attention by taking her credit card and convincing her that another problem like this was going to cost her lots of money in rebookings. In the meantime, Juan reassured anxious promoters in the United States that while Nina would arrive a day later, she was coming and nothing would be canceled. This time his promise came true.

BY NOW NINA had thoroughly refined her musical narrative, and it gave shape to her performance. "Porgy" notwithstanding, she had divorced herself completely from Billie Holiday, insulted to be compared with her "because she was a drug addict. They only compared me to her because we were both black. They never compared me to

Maria Callas, and I'm more of a diva like her than anybody else. She was temperamental like I am. She did what she wanted to do except when she was pushed," Nina said. "What we share is music and the passion. She had a passion for opera. I have passion for all kinds of music."

She resisted the notion that she sang from anger. "No," she said, "I sing from intelligence, letting them [the audience] know that I know who they are and what they have done to my people around the world. That's not anger." "They," she explained, "were the white people around the world."

Nina aligned herself, too, with Bob Marley. "He was the same protest singer I am. There is no difference except they killed him, and they haven't killed me yet," she declared, brushing by the fact that Marley had died of brain cancer, which he fought for two years. She was moved most deeply, she said, by Marian Anderson. "I listen to her every morning. She wakes me up and gives me inspiration every day."

Nina disdained the idea that she played jazz. "To most white people, jazz means black and jazz means dirt, and that's not what I play. I play black classical music. That's why I don't like the term 'jazz,' and Duke Ellington didn't either. It's a term that's simply used to identify black people."

Before each concert, Nina reminded Javier of a boxer with his cornermen. She would sit in a chair backstage and bark orders:

"Cigarette!"

"Glass of champagne!"

"How much time do we have?" "A half hour," might be the reply.

"Goddammit!" And then she was ready.

A Nina Simone evening still began with the dramatic entrance, enhanced now by an African fly-whisk she carried that Paul thought resembled a donkey tail on a stick. Others thought it was a feather duster. Nina waved it as a signal for applause, and the audience never failed to respond. The program itself almost always started with "Black Is the Color of My True Love's Hair," a dedication, with "Every Time I Feel the Spirit," to Paul Robeson and Lorraine Hansberry, among others, and then some combination of all the songs her fans loved. She usually wore a sequined evening gown—one uncharitable observer sniped that she was "stuffed" into the garment, given that she was noticeably heavy. On many nights the music was more disappointing than not, as had been the case over the last decade. But it was just as true that these evenings were an homage to the personality Nina had created, and it was rare not to find a moment or two when that mysterious power shone through and Nina cast her spell once again.

"I'm so glad you know my songs," she cooed to the audience in Washington, D.C., when she heard applause at the opening notes of one of her chestnuts. When fans in Boston shouted, "We love you, Nina," she was gracious. "I'm so glad. I don't seem like an angry old woman, do I?" Nina had invited Lisa to perform with her the previous July in Dublin at a blues festival. On June 18 in Chicago, where Lisa now lived, she brought her out to sing a few numbers. To the *Tribune*'s Howard Reich, the daughter suffered by comparison. "The younger singer's treacly repertoire, shrieking high notes and Whitney Houston–inspired bleatings proved as artificial as the elder singer's style is real."

When Nina and the group got to Austin for an October 30 concert, she announced that she wasn't feeling well and declared that she might be having a heart attack. Javier thought it was another gambit to get attention, but he and Clifton didn't argue and took her to a local physician. The doctor couldn't find anything wrong but suggested she go to the hospital to be examined further. The two men left her in the emergency room and went to get something to eat. When they got back, they were told that Nina wasn't there. Panicked, they raced back to the hotel and found her.

"Baby, I'm fine!" she exclaimed. Her concerns assuaged at the hospital, she had hailed a taxi and come back to the hotel on her own.

By the time Nina got to Miami on November 8 to perform at the Gusman Center, she wanted to correct the public record. "The first thing I want to say is that music reviewers have been getting my age wrong. I am not sixty-seven. I am sixty-four going on five thousand." It got a laugh and reminded those familiar with Nina's history that she liked to refer to herself as a reincarnated Egyptian queen. But this was 2000, and she really was sixty-seven.

•

KATE WAYMON DIED April 4, 2001, six months shy of her one hundredth birthday. The loss devastated Nina. Clifton, Javier, and Juanita accompanied her back to Tryon for the funeral, arranging to stay in Charlotte, the nearest big city, and go by limousine back to her hometown. The hotel provided an additional escort so that Nina could mourn in private with her siblings and other family members, though Frances was both startled and hurt when Nina ignored her— apparently still angry over the 1996 incident in Los Angeles. When Frances started to say hello, Nina brushed by her with a withering "Who are you?"

More sobering news came when Nina returned home. Doctors discovered she had breast cancer, the diagnosis coming barely two months before she was to start another summer tour. Arrangements were made for surgery to be done in Aix-en-Provence to remove the tumor, and Nina refused to cancel the first date, which was in Paris on June 8. She treated the operation and the chemotherapy after-wards matter-of-factly, Javier said, as if the doctor visits were no more than going to the dentist. "She decided to continue her life."

Nina was making good progress until she picked up an infection shortly before the Paris concert. Despite talk again of canceling the show, Nina insisted on performing, but the evening did not go well, given how she was feeling.

Three weeks later Nina returned to perform at Carnegie Hall, invited back by George Wein as part of the JVC Festival. "We paid her very good money—$85,000 for the night," George remembered. "She went out onstage and they started cheering. She couldn't sing anymore. She was on the stage from eight to quarter past nine. Peo-ple paid $100 a ticket. She sang about six songs and waved her African fan. And the people—they never stopped cheering. The house is totally sold out, and nobody complained. The woman was worshipped. It was like they were cheering a goddess. She became an icon. She became a goddess of culture." Not unkindly, Gene San-toro mused in the *Daily News* that the evening was "a little like try-ing to glean the glory of Rome from its ruins. But the fact is," he wrote, "they don't make Nina Simones anymore."

Afterward, the singing duo Ashford & Simpson—Nick Ashford

and Valerie Simpson—hosted a party for Nina at their Upper West Side club. Chris White was there and had a chance to visit with Nina. He could see that she was struggling, and when he asked her how she was doing, all she said was, "I don't know, Chris. I just don't know." But she kept going. Javier and Clifton had arranged for a nurse to be on hand at each of the remaining dates to help change her dressings. Nina got a boost in Los Angeles when John and Carolle Waymon came down from Sacramento and stayed a few days with her at the Four Seasons hotel.

Perhaps because memories of the contested 2000 election were still fresh, Nina wove a harangue against President George W. Bush into the "Mississippi Goddam" she delivered in Seattle July 23. Then she sang Bob Marley's "Get Up, Stand Up" and instructed the crowd: "Now you heard me. So you go and do something about that man." She left the stage with one more instruction: "Continue to love me and buy my records."

Questions were raised every now and then, privately and sotto voce, about how wise it was for Nina to perform, not only for her health but her reputation, too. Juan knew she risked the kind of write-up that had appeared in the *Miami Times* the previous November, when Nina Korman talked about "the sad state of her voice—lacking in modulation and sometimes off key" and noted how she "wobbled precariously around the stage like a toddler" when she tried to shimmy during "See-Line Woman." Korman even took a swipe at Nina's gown: "a green spandex tube dress that made her hefty body look like a turtle." But the answer to the questions was easy. It wasn't only that Nina needed the money to support the house and staff in Carry. "My music is first in my life," she declared. "Nothing takes the place of my music. Nothing."

Juan understood. "It's hard to tell an artist to stop when they want to perform."

In her private moments, though, when fatigue diminished her defenses, Nina could admit that her music had limits. "See, Javier. Everybody loves me and wants me now," she had told him as he pushed her in a wheelchair after her June 23 concert in Washington, D.C. "When the lights are turned down, I go back to the hotel, and I am by myself." Javier found the statement no less poignant because

Nina was hardly the first entertainer to express the same thought. It reflected a lonesomeness that had lingered nearly half a century, ever since her first blush of fame.

BY LATE SPRING 2002 Nina wanted to perform again. Clifton and Javier took her to New York, where she made a brief appearance as part of a benefit for preserving rain forests. One of the sweetest moments occurred backstage when Nina held court with Elton John and the singer Sting. A few weeks later, on May 2, Nina performed in

Nina at Carnegie Hall, April 13, 2002
(K. Mazur/Getty Images)

Rome (the reception was mediocre), and then she performed June 29 in Sopot, Poland, a city northwest of Gdańsk. What stood out for Javier at these two concerts was not the few glistening moments of music but Nina's mood. She was calmer than he could remember and much more easygoing. What touched him was her acknowledgment to anyone she talked to of the care he and the others had given her. She introduced them, praised them, and called them her family. Nina knew that "Here Comes the Sun" was Juanita's favorite, and again in Sopot, she looked right at Juanita when she sang it. None of them, Nina included, knew that she would never appear on another concert stage.

Sometime in the summer, during a brief vacation with Juanita in Aix, Nina became ill. It was probably a stroke, and for a few weeks she could neither walk nor eat without assistance. "We nursed her back," Juanita recalled. "We got her out of bed, got her exercising on the lawn." She was nearly back to herself by the time John and Carolle arrived in Carry for Christmas, their third visit in sixteen months. They stayed through the end of January 2003, and Nina loved having them so much she wanted them to move to France. When the Waymons left, Nina's health was stable, and John and Carolle talked about when they could visit again. Juan was so encouraged that he had started to work on a tour in England. Nina told him she wanted to go to Asia, too. He had even sent a preliminary itinerary to Tony Jones, the bass player. But early in April Nina apparently suffered another stroke. Day by day, Javier said, "it was like a candle losing energy." She slipped away overnight April 20 with Juanita and Javier at her side. She had said more than once that she didn't want to live past seventy. "That's what's promised. That's all I want."

Nina's funeral was April 25. The small church in Carry was packed, most of the mourners people from town who had come to know her. Lisa flew over from New York, where she was appearing on Broadway in *Aïda*, and sang a gospel song. Miriam Makeba came from South Africa and offered praise for "a great artist, but she was someone who fought for liberty." Elton John sent a bouquet of yellow roses, and the government of South Africa sent a special message of condolence. Her remains were cremated after the ceremony.

Though Juanita and Javier wondered if Nina was serious, more than once she had announced a different plan for herself: "You put me in the fridge, and when you find a solution, you bring me back."

But Nina never really went away. Her spirit lives in her music, whose power to entertain, inspire, and provoke reveals the alloy of talent and turmoil that molded every performance. Hers was a troubled soul, tangled up in conflict that so easily diminished the joys that should come from success. "She held and carried the rage for her people, my people," Hannibal said. "But she was never able to transmute it." Perhaps Nina did not achieve all she wanted, and yet on May 18, 2003, barely a month after she died, the Curtis Institute of Music posthumously awarded her an honorary diploma for her "contribution to the art of music." Nina was aware of the school's plan and wanted to attend the ceremony in Philadelphia. Instead family members accepted her honor, the parchment representing nothing less than the dream come true for Eunice Waymon.

Notes

All of the interviews are my own unless a specific publication is cited as the source.

CHAPTER 1: CALLED FOR AND DELIVERED ~
JUNE 1898–FEBRUARY 1933

5   **Tryon, North Carolina:** Tryon information from various sources including *Polk County, North Carolina History*, Polk County Historical Association, Inc., pp. 75–77; Eunice Waymon birth certificate, Polk County records; Mike McCue interview.

6   **"a clever man":** John Irvin Waymon and Carrol Waymon interviews; Simone, *I Put a Spell on You*, pp. 1–3; Carrol Waymon comments from *La Légende*, a 1992 French-made documentary on Nina Simone.

6   **Kate's heritage:** Kate Waymon, written reminiscences, courtesy of John Irvin Waymon; *I Put a Spell on You*, pp. 1–4.

7   **a dry cleaning plant:** In *I Put a Spell on You*, Nina says her father moved to Tryon to open a barbershop. Her brother John, the oldest child, who was seven at the time—Nina had not yet been born—remembered that his father's first business was a dry cleaning shop on Trade Street. The ads in the *Tryon Daily Bulletin*, which ran almost daily in February and March 1929, suggest that John Davan moved to Tryon to open the dry cleaning business.

    For information about the black population in western North Carolina, see Davis, "The Black Heritage of Western North Carolina," probably published in 1984, courtesy of the University of North Carolina Asheville—D.H. Ramsey Library Special Collections. Also *Asheville Citizen*, December 11, 1932, Section B, p. 7, for a statistical breakdown of Polk County from the 1930 census. Ruth Hannon Hamilton interview; and *The Lanier Library, 1890–1965, Diamond Jubilee*.

8   **four gas stations:** John Irvin Waymon, Holland Brady Jr. interviews.

10   **nine-year-old Carrol:** Poem courtesy of Carrol Waymon.

10   **Reverend Scotland Harris:** Beryl Hannon Dade interviews.

11   **Ballenger's department store:** Holland Brady Jr. interview; *Tryon Daily Bulletin*, April 6, 1931, September 21, 1939, October 12, 1939, January 1, 1940, March 10, 1940.

13   **East Livingston Street:** John Irvin Waymon, Carrol Waymon, Blanche Lyles Solomon interviews.

14   **Simpson Quartet:** *Tryon Daily Bulletin*, August 18, 1930.

15   **the Depression:** In *I Put a Spell on You*, Nina writes that her father had lost everything during the Depression. Because she was not yet born, her narrative was necessarily based on others' accounts. John Irvin Waymon, who was eight when the Depression began, remembered it differently, and it is his firsthand account that I have used.

CHAPTER 2: WE KNEW SHE WAS A GENIUS ~
MARCH 1933–AUGUST 1941

16   **eight months old:** In the 1992 French-made documentary, Nina returned to Tryon and talked about her childhood. She stopped in front of one house on the east side of town and identified it as the house she was born in, but this is incorrect. The house she pointed to, which was demolished sometime after the documentary was made, was a temporary residence for the family, probably in 1940. Kate Waymon reminiscences, courtesy of John Irvin Waymon. See also *I Put a Spell on You*, p. 7.

17   **she slept:** Carrol Waymon, Dorothy Waymon Simmons interviews; *I Put a Spell on You*, pp. 14–17.

17   **Lake Lanier:** John Irvin Waymon interviews; Lake Lanier information, special edition of the *Tryon Daily Bulletin*—"Polk County Photo history—1885–2005," Vol. 1, p. 18.

18   **an intestinal blockage:** John Irvin Waymon, Carrol Waymon, Dorothy Waymon Simmons interviews; *I Put a Spell on You*, pp. 9–10.

21   **Episcopal Center:** In *I Put a Spell on You*, pp. 9–11, Nina presents a chronology of the family's moves in Tryon and to Lynn that is at odds with what her brothers John and Carrol remember. Some of their reminiscences are supported by contemporaneous documents. I have chosen to use their recollections in describing aspects of the family's life between 1933 and 1940.

21   **Lynn:** *I Put a Spell on You*, p. 11; Dorothy Waymon Simmons interview.

22   **heating stones:** Ruth Hannon Hamilton interview.

23   **moved back to Tryon:** John Irvin Waymon, Carrol Waymon, Dorothy Waymon Simmons interviews. Carrol and Dorothy are not clear about the sequence of moves after the family came back from Lynn. There may have been three temporary stops—one on what is now Beech Street, another in a house across the railroad tracks near the depot, and a third back on the east side, a house the family refers to as the Hunter house, where Lola Hunter lived. The family eventually settled in a house on what is now Jackson Street and stayed there until they left Tryon in 1950.

J.D.'s Social Security card application dated October 28, 1939, lists his place of employment as P.E. Christopher in Landrum, S.C., which was a dry cleaning business. Landrum is about fifteen miles south of Tryon.

23 **"ten a.m. coffee break"**: Holland Brady interview; *I Put a Spell on You*, p. 30.

24 **"one great commotion"**: *I Put a Spell on You*, pp. 18–19; John Irvin Waymon interviews.

25 **Tryon Colored School**: John Irvin Waymon interviews. The account of the school burning is taken from the contemporaneous reporting in the *Tryon Daily Bulletin*, June 9, 1940, June 14, 1940, June 20, 1940, June 21, 1940, August 24, 1940, August 26, 1940, August 27, 1942, December 4, 1942. Also *Asheville Times*, June 21, 1940, p. 12.

28 **a serious girl**: Eunice Waymon photo described from Stroud, *Nina Simone: Black Is the Color* . . .

28 **"number one"**: Fred Counts interviews; honor roll, *Tryon Daily Bulletin*, February 9, 1941.

CHAPTER 3: MISS MAZZY ~ SEPTEMBER 1941–AUGUST 1947

29 **Gillette Woods**: Gillette Woods promotional pamphlet, courtesy of Kipp McIntyre; David Johnson interview.

29 **Mrs. Miller**: In a *Philadelphia Bulletin* article of March 6, 1960, Nina told the story about Katherine Miller hearing her for the first time at a concert at the Tryon theater. In *I Put a Spell on You* (p. 21) Nina wrote that Mrs. Miller first heard her when she was "playing for a choir." Given that the March 1960 interview with the *Bulletin* was thirty years closer to the time of the event than the autobiography, that version seems the most likely.

31 **Muriel Mazzanovich**: *I Put a Spell on You*, p. 22; Garland Goodwin interviews, photos, and a drawing of the Mazzanovich house courtesy of G. Goodwin; Fred Counts interviews; *Thermal Belt News Journal*, February 11, 1985, p. 3A, "Mrs. Mazzy—Teacher, Friend Is Dead at 102"; *Tryon Daily Bulletin*, May 12, 1959, Lawrence Mazzanovich obituary.

36 **Eunice Waymon Fund**: Tom Moore interviews. In *I Put a Spell on You*, Nina writes that Miss Mazzy created the Eunice Waymon Fund: "She wrote to the local paper explaining the situation and asking for donations. . . . Every church took up a collection for the Fund, the paper started an appeal and the council collected on my behalf . . . " (p. 24). This account does not appear to be accurate, based on a review of the five relevant years of the *Tryon Daily Bulletin* and interviews with residents, white and black, who were Eunice's contemporaries.

The Waymon children's birth certificates help confirm the changes in J.D.'s work. By the time Sam was born in 1944, J.D. listed himself as a "handyman," as Tom Moore had remembered.

37 **played for her friends**: James Payne, Patricia Carson Caple interviews.

37 **a recital:** *I Put a Spell on You*, pp. 26–27.

38 **NAACP:** NAACP information, *Tryon Daily Bulletin*, July 27, 1944, November 22, 1944; Polk County chapter information from the NAACP state-by-state chapter files, 1940–1955, Library of Congress Manuscript Reading Room.

CHAPTER 4: WE HAVE LAUNCHED, WHERE SHALL WE ANCHOR? ~
SEPTEMBER 1947–MAY 1950

40 **their son Edney:** *I Put a Spell on You*, pp. 31–32; Edney Whiteside interviews.

41 **Allen School:** Information on Allen School from the school's file in the North Carolina Room of the Pack Memorial Library, Asheville, N.C.

42 **settled into a routine:** *Los Angeles Times*, March 5, 1967, p. C25, in which Nina talks to Leonard Feather about Hazel Scott; Scott obituary, *New York Times*, October 3, 1981; Patricia Carson Caple, Cordelia Pedew Chambers, Willie Mae Gaston Ferguson, Christine Ivey Jowers, Ruth Walther interviews; information on Eunice's activities at Allen from the school's yearbooks, courtesy of Ruth Walther; *Asheville Citizen*, February 8, 1949, p. 14. Nina did not mention Clemens Sandresky as a teacher in her autobiography, citing only "Joyce" Carroll, though her actual name was Grace. However, Nina referred to Sandresky in a 1960 interview with *Rogue* (March 1960), and in October 1990 sent a publicity photo to him inscribed "To Mr. Sandresky—I love you—merci for toute les leciones [*sic*]." Photo from www.ninasimoneproject.org.

45 **hosted a recital:** Garland Goodwin interview; Goodwin newspaper column reprinted in Goodwin, *A Boy in the Amen Corner*, pp. 26–29.

46 **long-distance romance:** Nina's account of her relationship with Edney Whiteside in *I Put a Spell on You* (pp. 31–36) contains several inaccuracies, according to Edney. While the thrust of the story is true about their teenage romance, he said he had gone to Cleveland for nearly two years and not just a few weeks. He noted that they were going in different directions and wanted different things. He did marry Annie Mae Burns, not immediately after Eunice/Nina went to Juilliard but in 1952, right before he went into the service. They remained married until he died unexpectedly on January 23, 2006. Nina's graduation with honors, *Asheville Times*, May 22, 1950, p. 4. See also *Rogue*, March 1960.

CHAPTER 5: PRELUDE TO A FUGUE ~ JUNE 1950–MAY 1954

48 **New York City:** Dorothy W. Simmons interviews; Social Security card application of Kate Waymon.

50 **Carl Friedberg:** Information about studying with Carl Friedberg from *I Put a Spell on You*, pp. 40–41; *New York Times*, September 13, 1955, p. 31, obituary; October 2, 1955, p. X9, Myra Hess letter about Friedberg; letter to a music magazine, January 1, 1956, from a student on Friedberg's death, Juilliard clip file on Friedberg.

52 **a B+:** According to documents from the Juilliard archives, Eunice studied at Juilliard only for six weeks, during the July 3–August 11, 1950, summer session. Accounts over the years have put her time of study at one year, one and a half years, even two years. But these do not seem to be accurate. It is probable that Eunice stayed in New York a full six months, studying privately with Carl Friedberg after summer school through the end of 1950.

52 **Curtis Institute:** Information about the audition procedures, including the timing, from the Curtis Institute library, based on the school's archives. In *I Put a Spell on You*, Nina writes of auditioning "at the end of the year," but this would appear to be an error. According to Curtis records, applications for the 1951–52 year, which would have been Nina's year, were due February 1, 1951, and auditions were in April.

53 **south Philadelphia:** Information on the Waymon family's early days in Philadelphia from *I Put a Spell on You*, pp. 40–41; Carrol Waymon, Doris Mack interviews.

54 **Natalie Hinderas:** Natalie Hinderas studied at Juilliard in the summer of 1946 and 1947 with Olga Samaroff and in the summer of 1950 with Edward Steurermann, according to the Juilliard archives.

55 **a photographer's darkroom:** Eunice Waymon's application for a Social Security card was dated April 24, 1951. She listed 2447 Grays Ferry Avenue as her address and her employer as Maurice E. Abuhove at 110 South Sixteenth Street, which was just a few blocks from where her uncle, Walter Waymon, lived.

55 **Town and Country Club:** *Philadelphia Tribune*, July 31, 1951, p. 5, August 11, 1951, p. 18.

55 **4221 Wyalusing:** *Philadelphia Bulletin* stories on the Mantua section of Philadelphia, which is adjacent to Wyalusing, December 7, 1951; February 2, 1956, from the Temple University Urban Archives; Philadelphia census information from 1950 courtesy of the Temple University Government Documents division. By 1953, when the Waymons moved to Wyalusing, blacks outnumbered whites by nearly three to one. *Philadelphia Tribune*, March 3, 1953, p. 14, for seventh-grade assembly Chopin performance.

58 **Mayer Sulzberger:** *Philadelphia Tribune*, March 31, 1953, p. 14.

58 **5705 West Master:** *I Put a Spell on You*, pp. 44–47; Carrol Waymon, Doris Mack interviews; Philadelphia phone book to confirm Eunice

Waymon's address at 5705 West Master; Taylor, *Notes and Tones*, p. 149, for Nina's observations about singers she had heard.

58 **New Century Auditorium:** Ticket to Philadelphia recital, Stroud, *Nina Simone: Black Is the Color*, p. 14; *Philadelphia Tribune*, September 25, 1954, p. 1; Doris Mack interview.

59 **Faith Jackson:** Carrol Waymon interviews; *I Put a Spell on You*, p. 48.

CHAPTER 6: THE ARRIVAL OF NINA SIMONE ~
JUNE 1954–JUNE 1956

60 **Atlantic City:** Davis, *Atlantic City Diary: A Century of Memories, 1880–1980*, pp. 109–11. Among those expected for the summer of 1954, Atlantic City's centennial, were Dean Martin and Jerry Lewis, Julius LaRosa, the Mills Brothers, and the Gene Krupa Trio. Paul Whiteman, who liked to be called the "King of Jazz," was originating his ABC-TV show in town.

61 **Midtown Bar:** *Atlantic City Press*, entertainment pages June–July 1954.

62 **"Nina":** *Philadelphia Bulletin*, March 6, 1960; *Rogue*, March 1960; *I Put a Spell on You*, p. 49. For the first few years when she was asked about her name, Nina stuck closely to the explanation she had given the *Bulletin*. She referred to the boyfriend as an inspiration for Nina in a 1969 interview and then first cited Simone Signoret as the inspiration for her last name in her 1991 autobiography. She had told the *New York Post* in a March 15, 1969, story that "I have no idea" where Simone came from. "It just fitted."

64 **"the two halves together":** *I Put a Spell on You*, pp. 50–53; Garland, *The Sound of Soul*, pp. 184–87; Taylor, *Notes and Tones*, pp. 149–53; Kenneth Hill interview.

64 **Word spread quickly:** *Atlantic City Press* entertainment pages, principally Wednesdays and Fridays for June, July, and August 1954. Precisely when Nina started to play at the Midtown is unclear. In *I Put a Spell on You* she says it was the summer of 1954. Carrol Waymon remembered that when she started, she only played weekends, which means she was not the Midtown's principal act. The ads in the *Atlantic City Press* seem to confirm this. The first ads mentioning Nina Simone are not until June 1955, and the first one appears on Wednesday, June 1, 1955, which suggests that she was performing several days a week. Stan Facey, who had gotten top billing in May, was listed in smaller type as the second act.

66 **"Why don't you pursue this":** Vladimir Sokoloff from *La Légende*, the French-made 1992 documentary.

68 **"Bohemian":** Kenneth Hill interview.

70 **Don Ross:** *I Put A Spell on You*, p. 55.

CHAPTER 7: LITTLE GIRL BLUE ~ JULY 1956–DECEMBER 1958

71 **Ed:** *I Put a Spell on You*, p. 47.

73 **Jerry Field:** *I Put a Spell on You*, p. 57. Though Nina refers to Jerry Fields in her autobiography, she most likely meant Jerry Field, who had an office in 1956, when they met, at 1619 Broadway in New York. He listed himself in the Manhattan phone book as "artists rep."

74 **Rittenhouse Hotel:** *Philadelphia Bulletin*, May 27, 1957, July 13, 1969, for history of the Rittenhouse Hotel; August 16, 1956, for police raid on the Queen Mary Room.

74 **intricate accompaniment:** These descriptions are taken from *Starring Nina Simone*, a bootleg album that was made up in part of a tape of one of Nina's Philadelphia club dates. *Philadelphia Tribune*, March 26, 1957, p. 5, for photo of Nina at a charity event.

75 **Al Schackman:** This account is based on newspaper articles that put Nina at the Rittenhouse in the spring of 1957 (*Philadelphia Bulletin*, May 27, 1957, March 6, 1960, which refers to the Rittenhouse job and the charity event) and ads in the *Bucks County Traveler*, September and October 1957 issues. The wording in the *Traveler*, ads suggests that the September job was Nina's first at the Playhouse; previous issues for the year list other musicians at the Inn in the main dining room and the Bistro. Nina was apparently incorrect in *I Put a Spell on You* (p. 58), when she said she went to the Playhouse Inn after Christmas in 1956. According to the *Traveler*, Stu Ross, a piano player, performed during the week, and Mickey Palmer's Trio played Friday and Saturday all through December. A story about Nina in the October 1960 *Sepia* (p. 30) also refers to the Playhouse Inn job as being in the summer of 1957.

Information also comes from Amram, *Vibrations: The Adventures and Musical Times of David Amram* (pp. 245–46). Amram writes about subbing at the piano for George Syran, who was part of a trio at a New Hope club that included Al Schackman through 1956. Al has said in interviews over the years that he played with his own trio while Nina was at the Playhouse Inn. See Schackman interview in *Fader*, May/June 2006, p. 92.

76 **Bethlehem Records:** Accounts of the Bethlehem session come from interviews with Bethlehem founder Gus Wildi, Albert "Tootie" Heath, Jimmy Bond, Vivian Bailey, and Irv Greenbaum; Greenbaum's self-published *In One Ear and In the Other*, pp. 68–72; and *I Put a Spell on You*, pp. 59–60. Nina writes in those pages that Syd Nathan owned Bethlehem and came to her home in Philadelphia with songs he wanted her to record at the New York session, and that she refused to do so and insisted on doing her own music. While Nina's description of Nathan as a bullying sort of man rings true with many who knew him, her account of the session is incorrect. Syd Nathan did not buy a piece of Bethlehem

Records until the middle of 1958, months after the session was held. Gus Wildi is firm on the fact that Nathan "had absolutely nothing to do with finding or recording Nina" and that he, Wildi, wanted Nina to record whatever songs she wanted. Wildi recalled meeting Nina only once at the Bethlehem offices at 1650 Broadway in New York when she signed the standard royalty contract the label gave its artists. Though Vivian Bailey said he made all the arrangements for the Bethlehem recording, he didn't remember meeting Gus Wildi, nor did Wildi remember meeting Bailey.

Jimmy Bond remembered the session as being difficult because Nina was cantankerous through much of it, threatening at one point to walk out. But Irv Greenbaum, the engineer, remembered an easy session. He did not recall any arguments, which he said he would have heard in the control room because the microphones were on. Bond also said he rather than Nina was responsible for most of "Central Park Blues," although it is credited to Nina. One of Bethlehem's publishing arms, Win-Gus, was listed as the publisher of the tune, giving it a right to a portion of any royalties.

78   **a cash crunch:** Gus Wildi interviews. Although Nina wrote in *I Put a Spell on You* (p. 68) that *Little Girl Blue* (BCP 6028, Neon NE 3541) was released in the middle of 1958, this is incorrect. Trade publications as well as several newspaper stories make clear that the album was not released until the first week in February 1959. Nina's subsquent discussion of events in response to the release is thus also chronologically in error.

79   **a brief civil ceremony:** *I Put a Spell on You*, pp. 62–63. A thorough check of Philadelphia marriage license records from 1957–59 unfortunately did not turn up any information about when Nina and Don were married. She could not remember the date, noting that "I have nothing from our time together to give me a clue. . . . "

CHAPTER 8: A FAST RISING STAR ~ 1959

80   **"talk poetry":** *I Put a Spell on You*, pp. 63–64.
81   *Little Girl Blue:* Gus Wildi interviews. Information about the release of *Little Girl Blue* comes from *Popular Record Aid*, the monthly digest of record releases, and the *Cash Box* issues cited in the text.
82   **five-act bill:** *Baltimore Afro-American*, March 7, 1959; *Washington Afro-American*, March 13, 1959, p. B9. Information about the Feld show that began March 28 from Gart, *First Pressings: The History of Rhythm and Blues*, Vol. 9, 1959, p. 30. For history on Feld see Guralnick, *Dream Boogie: The Triumph of Sam Cooke*, pp. 227–28. See *Philadelphia Tribune*, March 24, 1959, p. 12, for record ad.

83 **Syd Nathan:** Gus Wildi interviews.

83 **Colpix:** Judy Gail Krasnow interviews. Before doing the *Amazing Nina Simone* project, Hecky Krasnow had founded the children's records division at Columbia, during the heyday of "kid-disks," 1949 to 1956. One of his noteworthy accomplishments was persuading popular singers, movie stars, even baseball luminaries to record songs and albums for children, among them Gene Autry and Burl Ives. He also was behind the successful children's television show *Captain Kangaroo*, with Bob Keeshan.

84 **"scored brightly":** *Billboard*, July 22, 1959, p. 32; *Variety*, July 22, 1959, p. 51; Ben Riley interview.

85 **"Porgy" promotion:** *Cash Box, Pop Singles Charts, 1950–1993*, p. 316; *Cash Box*, August 1, 1959, p. 6, October 17, 1959, p. 6; Sid Mark, Gus Wildi interviews; *Chicago Defender*, August 1959, p. 18. Though stereophonic sound was just beginning to gain ground, *Cash Box* had recently started to show listings for "mono" and "stereo" sales. That *Little Girl Blue* didn't show up on the *Billboard* album chart said more about the vicissitudes of the music trades than it did about an artist's popularity.

In *I Put a Spell on You* Nina talks of the success of "Porgy" as happening in 1958 rather than in 1959, which all documentary evidence shows. The flip side was "Love Me or Leave Me" and not "He Needs Me," as she states on p. 62.

85 **"The piano is OK":** *I Put a Spell on You*, p. 65; July 5, 1959, letter from "Mrs. Lawrence Mazzanovich" to Garland Goodwin, courtesy of Garland Goodwin.

86 **Town Hall:** Description of the Town Hall event taken from *Nina Simone at Town Hall* (CP 409, COL-CD 6206).

87 **California:** *Los Angeles Times*, November 14, 1959, p. 9, for an ad promoting Nina's date at the Interlude, noteworthy for this mention in the city's mainstream newspaper.

88 **downtown Chicago:** *Chicago Defender*, December 15, 1959, p. A16; *Rogue*, March 3, 1960, for Frank Holzfeind comment; *Playboy's Penthouse*, Show #9, courtesy of Playboy Enterprises.

89 **a third single:** *Popular Record Aid*, November 1959 for the release of Bethlehem 1052, "Little Girl Blue"/"He Needs Me"; December 1959 for the release of Bethlehem 1055, "Don't Smoke in Bed"/"African Mailman."

90 **"wiry, moody girl":** *Ebony*, December 1959, pp. 168–72; Ben Riley interview.

CHAPTER 9: SIMONE-IZED ~ 1960

91 **two full-scale albums:** *The Amazing Nina* Simone (CP 407, COL-CD 6206); *Nina Simone at Town Hall.* See also *I Put a Spell on You*, p. 65;

Cash Box, February 27, 1960, p. 27. Chicago performance, *Chicago Defender,* February 10, 1960, p. 41. The Jazztet with Art Framer and Benny Golson and the Kirk Stuart Trio were the other acts.

92 **Today:** *Today* show information comes from the NBC Masterbooks, Box MT 996, for March 24, 1960, Library of Congress Motion Picture and Television Reading Room. Nina taped her performances on March 23.

94 **Milwaukee:** Interviews with Ron Carter, Ben Riley, Chris White; Storyville date, *Boston Globe,* April 7, 1960, p. 5; Henri's Show Lounge, *Milwaukee Journal,* April 21, 1960, Part 2, p. 13. See also *Atlanta Daily World,* May 29, 1960, p. 3, advance notice of Nina's shows at the Magnolia Ballroom June 3–5, 1960.

95 **"She had a good feel":** Ben Riley interview.

96 **Bertha Case:** Bertha Case information from publicity materials of GAC, which did some booking for Nina. *Today* show information comes from the NBC Masterbooks, Box MT 1013, for June 9, 1960, Library of Congress Motion Picture and Television Reading Room. Nina taped her performance on June 8; *Sepia,* October 1960, pp. 28–31, which includes photos from the *Today* show performance.

97 **Newport Jazz Festival:** Newport Jazz Festival information from *Nina Simone at Newport* (CP 412; COL-CD 4207); Library of Congress, Recorded Sound Reference Room; Goldblatt, *Newport Jazz Festival: The Illustrated History,* pp. 74, 267; Chris White interviews.

99 **Extended Play 45:** *La Musica,* April 1960, p. 17; translation courtesy of Catherine Re.

99 **Village Gate:** Art D'Lugoff interviews; *New York Times,* November 10, 1958, September 25, 1966, p. 339, March 23, 1980, p. D6; *I Put a Spell on You,* pp. 66–67, 73; *New York Citizen Call,* July 23, 1960, p. 21.

102 **Lake Meadows Restaurant:** *Chicago Defender,* September 24, 1956, p. 16, September 24, 1960, p. 16; *Chicago American,* October 7, 1960, p. 15; Chris White, Bobby Hamilton, David Sharpe, John Vinci, Brigitta Peterhans, Charles Walton, Bea Buck interviews.

104 **Hunter College:** *New York Amsterdam News,* October 29, 1960, p. 21; *New York Citizen Call,* October 29, 1960, p. 22; *New York Times,* October 22, 1960, p. 15; Chris White, Bobby Hamilton interviews.

105 **cabaret card regulations:** *New York Times,* November 14, 1960, p. 1; November 21, 1960, p. 1, January 17, 1961, p. 1, September 13, 1967, p. 27 ("Cabaret Card Use Ended by Council"); *Variety,* December 14, 1960, p. 50; December 7, 1960, letter from Nina Simone to Arthur J. D'Lugoff. See also Chevigny, *Gigs: Jazz and the Cabaret Laws in New York City,* pp. 57–67.

106 **"She is strange":** *Chicago Daily Defender,* week of December 18, 1960, p. 10 (editorial page).

CHAPTER 10: YOU CAN'T LET THEM HUMILIATE YOU ~
JANUARY 1961 — DECEMBER 13, 1961

107 **Apollo Theater:** Schiffman family Apollo Theater files, Smithsonian Museum of American History archives; *New York Citizen Call,* February 18, 1961, pp. 11, 15; *New York Post,* March 10, 1961, p. 52; *I Put a Spell on You,* pp. 74–75. In discussing the Apollo incident, Nina tells an imaginative story about "three Harlem ladies" walking to the stage and tossing coins at her feet. "Then they stuck their noses in the air, turned on their heels and walked out." None of the contemporaneous reports, including Nina's later interview with a reporter, mentioned the women.

109 **Chapel Hill:** *Daily Tar Heel,* February 7, 16, 17, and 18, 1961; *News and Observer,* February 16, 1961, p. 8; Chris White, Bobby Hamilton, Art D'Lugoff, Frank Craighill interviews; January 11, 2007, e-mail correspondence with Jonathan Yardley.

The concert at Memorial Hall was the highlight of the winter festival on campus called "Winter Germans," which was sponsored by a consortium of fraternities. It was a point of pride among young men like the current president, Frank Craighill, to present a good show for their classmates; he had also booked Louis Armstrong for a later event. The previous year's Winter Germans featured Duke Ellington and Count Basie and their orchestras, followed by Dizzy Gillespie for another concert.

110 **Roundtable:** March 25, 1961, newspaper clip from unnamed publication; *Negro Digest,* February 1962, p. 23; *New York Daily News,* June 9, 1961, p. 4; *Chicago Daily Defender,* April 11, 1961, p. 16; Bobby Hamilton, Chris White interviews. Andy Stroud interview, *Fader,* May/June 2006, p. 100; Stroud, *Black Is the Color,* p. 17; *I Put a Spell on You,* pp. 72–73.

111 **live recordings:** Chris White and Bobby Hamilton interviews; *Nina Simone at the Village Gate* (CP 421, Roulette Jazz/EMI CDP795058 2); *New York Times,* April 6, 1961, p. 30, for John Wilson review of a Gate performance. Wilson wrote that Nina treated her eclectic musical choices "with a fertile sense of the dramatic." But he found that her piano solos "are inclined to fall into a pattern of gradual, pounding crescendos that could qualify her as a female Dave Brubeck. These obvious instrumental routines are strangely out of character with her thoughtful, imaginative work as a vocalist."

Right before the Village Gate performance, Nina and the trio had made a trip to Toronto to be part of a new show, Impulse, that featured them and several other musicians, whose performances were to be tied together by the poet Brendan Behan. But the event was a bust, and contrary to plans never opened in New York after the Toronto run. *New York Times,* February 23, 1961; *New York Amsterdam News,* March 18, 1961, p. 17, March 25, 1961, p. 19, April 1, 1961, p. 15; *Chicago Defender,* March

23, 1961, p. 23; *Toronto Globe and Mail*, March 24, 1961, March 25, 1961, p. 10; *Toronto Star*, March 1, 1961, p. 21, March 23, 1961, p. 37; Chris White personal papers; Chris White, Art D'Lugoff interviews.

112 **Pye Records:** *Melody Maker*, February 4, 1961, p.2.

112 **Carnegie Hall:** *New York Times*, May 22, 1961, p. 37; May 5, 1961, p. 24.

113 **Andy Stroud:** *Philadelphia Tribune*, July 1, 1961, p. 1; *New York Post*, July 2, 1961, p. 18; *Pittsburgh Courier*, July 15, 1961, p. 12; *I Put a Spell on You*, pp. 75–76, although Nina remembered incorrectly when this episode occurred and where she was performing. Contemporaneous news articles show that her illness occurred the last few days of June 1961, when she was scheduled to perform at Pep's.

115 **Olatunji:** Chris White interviews.

115 **seventeen days:** *New York Amsterdam News*, July 22, 1961, p. 13; Stroud, *Black Is the Color*, pp. 22–23.

115 **American Jazz Festival:** *Detroit News*, August 7, 1961, p. 8B; *Detroit Free Press*, August 8, 1961, p. 21; *Variety*, January 25, 1961, p. 54, for "Afro-Simone."

115 *Camera Three*: *Camera Three*, August 13, 1961, courtesy of Creative Arts Television.

116 **Roberts Show Lounge:** *Chicago Defender*, August 18, 1961, p. 16; week of August 26–September 1, 1961, p. 12; Chris White, Brigitta Peterhans, John Vinci, David Sharpe interviews.

    Forbidden Fruit (CP 419, COL-CD6207), produced by Cal Lampley, featured three Oscar Brown songs, including the one picked for the title track, "Forbidden Fruit." The humorous up-tempo take on Adam and Eve was part nursery rhyme, part call and response. When Nina sang "Go on and eat" in every chorus, the trio shouted, "Forbidden fruit." At the end the roles were reversed. "Go ahead and taste it," they shouted. "You don't want to waste it," she sang. Nina stretched boundaries in her interpretation of "Gin House Blues," which Bessie Smith had recorded in a plaintive version copied by other singers. Nina turned the song into a finger-snapping gospel number, an unlikely combination of a tune that celebrated liquor and a musical treatment more at home in the church. Colpix released *Forbidden Fruit* in June, and though it didn't do much commercially, *Cash Box* gave it a nice plug on June 17, 1961, as a "Jazz Pick of the Week" (p. 24).

117 **Town Hill:** unnamed newspaper clip, October 28, 1961. Before the Brooklyn date, Nina had also played a job in Boston, *Boston Globe*, October 9, 1961, p. 10; Chris White plane ticket to Boston and back.

118 **$4,500:** *New York Amsterdam News*, November 11, 1961, p. 19; Schiffman family Apollo Theater files, Smithsonian Museum of American History archives.

118 **bumps in the road:** *I Put a Spell on You*, pp. 76–78; *Fader*, May–June 2006; Patti Bown, Judy Gail Krasnow interviews.

120 **Lagos:** *New York Times*, December 14, 1961, p. 54; *Chicago Defender*, January 6, 1962, p. 10, national edition.

CHAPTER 11: RESPECT ~ DECEMBER 14, 1961–DECEMBER 1962

121 **AMSAC:** *I Put a Spell on You*, p. 80; Langston Hughes papers, personal correspondence, James Weldon Johnson Collection in the Yale Collection of American Literature, Beinecke Rare Book and Manuscript Library.

Details for the AMSAC group's arrival from AMSAC papers at the Moorland Spingarn Research Center, Howard University. These include documents detailing the arrangements for the Lagos event and a summary of the program afterward written for the AMSAC Supplements newsletter, No. 22; *I Put a Spell on You*, p. 80; Hughes papers; Stroud, *Nina Simone: Black Is the Color*, for description of Lagos beach photo.

Nina's performance provoked additional commentary. Francesca Pereira wrote in the 1990 *Daily Times* that Nina "was right in being angry for she was determined to give the audience her best and it was necessary that she should have a calm audience and not one that had gone haywire." The music critic for the *Lagos Daily Express*, identified only as "Back-drop," also seemed to sympathize with Nina given his disdain for Hampton, whom he called "that great musical clown." See *Lagos Daily Times*, December 30, 1961, p. 8, and *Lagos Daily Express*, December 20, 1962, p. 3. During Nina's December 18 performance, Abdul Malik was on bass, Al Schackman played guitar, and Olatunji played drums. On the nineteenth, Clarence Stroman played the drums. See also *Ebony*, March 1962, pp. 87–94.

AMSAC itself ran into trouble in 1969 when information surfaced that the group had received money from foundations connected to the Central Intelligence Agency. The organization folded by 1970. *Ebony*, March 1962, pp. 87–94; AMSAC and the Central Intelligence Agency, *New York Times*, February 17, 1967, p. 1, February 20, 1967, p. 1; December 28, 1977, p. 1; Fierce, Milfred C., "Selected Black American Leaders and Organizations and South Africa," *Journal of Black Studies*, Vol. 17, No. 3, p. 316; Washington, Mary Helen, "Desegregating the 1950s: The Case of Frank London Brown," *The Japanese Journal of American Studies*, No. 10 (1999), pp. 28–30.

125 **Mount Vernon:** *I Put a Spell on You*, p. 81.

127 **"You folks":** *New York Daily News*, June 9, 1961, p. 4.

128 **"making any money":** Stu Phillips interview; Phillips, *"Stu Who?,"*

pp. 102–6. A few months before working on Nina's album, Malcolm Dodds and his singers had performed one of the proposed "official" state songs for the General Assembly, written by Manhattan Democrat Bessie Buchanan. Dodds would later write the arrangements for a Broadway show titled *Sophisticated Ladies*, based on Duke Ellington's music. *New York Times*, February 7, 1961, p. 24.

129 **Duke Ellington:** *Nina Simone Sings Ellington* (CP 425, EMI 7243 4 73220 2 0); *Cash Box*, October 20, 1962, p. 24; *Billboard*, October 20, 1962, pp. 32, 136. Nina's pregnancy, birth of Lisa, *I Put a Spell on You*, pp. 84–85; Stroud, *Black Is the Color*, p. 28; Art D'Lugoff interviews.

131 **Montego Joe:** Lisle Atkinson, Montego Joe, Warren Smith interviews.

132 **honeymoon:** *I Put a Spell on You*, p. 85. In *Down Beat*'s year-end poll for favorite female singer, Nina tied with Chris Connor for seventh place at 211 votes, well behind Ella Fitzgerald in first place, who had 2,720; December 20, 1962, p. 22.

CHAPTER 12: MISSISSIPPI GODDAM ~ 1963

133 **thirtieth birthday:** *Chicago Defender*, week of January 13–25, 1963, p. 14; week of February 2–8, 1963, p. 19; *Chicago Tribune*, February 17, 1963, p. F8; *Down Beat*, April 11, 1963, p. 34; Warren Smith, Onameega Doris Bluitt interviews; February 19, 1963, guest registry of Lake Meadows Art and Jazz society, courtesy of O. D. Bluitt; O. D. Bluitt; Langston Hughes papers.

See also *Atlanta Daily Journal*, February 8, 1963, p. 28, February 12, 1963, p. 12; *Atlanta Daily World*, January 27, 1963, p. 3 for Nina's date just before Chicago that included Gloria Lynne. Nina was apparently in a feisty mood, at one point reminding the audience, "I sing what I please."

135 **Nina's personal manager:** *I Put a Spell on You*, p. 82; Stroud interview, *Fader*, May/June 2006.

135 **a concert of her own:** April 12, 1963, Carnegie Hall concert information from Carnegie Hall archive materials, including the program and Felix Gerstman correspondence; *New York Times*, April 13, 1963, p. 11; *Nina Simone at Carnegie Hall* (CP 455, EMI 7243 4 73221 2 9); *New York Times*, October 20, 1963, p. 15, review. Hoping to capitalize on Nina's previous work, Colpix also released a nine-track LP, *Nina's Choice* (Colpix 443). Writing in the June 20, 1963, *Down Beat* (p. 30), Pete Welding didn't think much of the effort. Though several tracks were taken from live dates, he said they failed to capture "the excitement and spiraling intensity" that marked Nina's performances.

136 **Lorraine Hansberry:** *Notable Black American Women*, pp. 452–57; Carter, *Hansberry's Drama: Commitment and Complexity; see* Blakely, *Earl B. Dickerson: A Voice for Freedom and Equality*, Chapter 5 for a

discussion of *Hansberry v. Lee*; Federal Bureau of Investigation file on Lorraine Hansberry, secured via Freedom of Information Act inquiry #373742; *New York Times*, January 13, 1965, p. 25; Cheney, *Lorraine Hansberry* generally. See also *I Put a Spell on You*, pp. 86–87; Stroud, *Black Is the Color*, p. 29. Lorraine was Lisa's godmother and Max Cohen, Nina's longtime lawyer, was her godfather.

138 **"mammoth benefit"**: *New York Amsterdam News*, May 25, 1963, p. 14; the NAACP expected a big crowd for the fund-raising event, renting the grand ballroom of the Manhattan Center at Thirty-fourth Street and Eighth Avenue, a block from Macy's department store. *I Put a Spell on You*, pp. 88–89.

139 **Harry Belafonte, Lena Horne:** Black entertainers donating funds, *Jet*, May 30, 1963, p. 64 (Eartha Kitt); *Chicago Defender*, May 27, 1963, p. 5 (Mahalia Jackson benefit with Dinah Washington, among others); week of June 8–14, p. 24 (Nat King Cole pledges $50,000); July 11, 1963, p. A24; week of July 20–26, 1963, p. 11, (Johnny Mathis). See also *Los Angeles Sentinel*, June 11, 1963, p. B3. Los Angeles rally, *California Eagle*, May 30, 1963, p. 1; Detroit rally, *Detroit Free Press*, June 24, 1963, p. 1.

139 **SNCC:** The Student Non-Violent Coordinating Committee papers, 1959–72, B-1-12, Reel 45, Library of Congress, Manuscript Reading Room.

139 **Birmingham:** Birmingham event, *New York Times*, July 11, 1963, p. 11, AGVA announcement; July 16, 1963, p. 25, Birmingham denies use of city auditorium; *Chicago Defender* (Daily), July 23, 1963, p. 17, AGVA vows to put on show; August 14, 1963, p. 20, show a hit; *Show Business*, August 10, 1963, Vol. XXIII, No. 32, article by Leo Shull, via hungry blues.net; *New York Amsterdam News*, August 3, 1963, p. 20, August 10, 1963, p. 1; Bobby Hamilton, Lisle Atkinson interviews and transcript from Atkinson–Chris White conversation on Chris' Choice, his radio show from Bloomfield College.

142 **August 28:** Synopsis of the August 28, 1963, March on Washington taken primarily from Branch, *Parting the Waters*, Chapter 22; for a shorter well-crafted synopsis see Guralnick, *Dream Boogie*, pp. 509–12.

144 **Youth Sunday:** Sixteenth Street Baptist Church bombing, *New York Times*, September 16, 1963, p. 1; September 18, 1963, p. 1; for an extended discussion, see Branch, *Parting the Waters*, pp. 889–96; see also Bullard et al., from the Southern Poverty Law Center, *Free At Last: A History of the Civil Rights Movement and Those Who Died in the Struggle*.

144 **"I sat struck dumb"**: *I Put a Spell on You*, pp. 88–90.

146 **"Very sulky"**: Apollo, *New York Amsterdam News*, October 26, 1963, p. 17; Schiffman family documents, Smithsonian Museum of American History archives; Art D'Lugoff interviews.

146 **"folk & jazz wing ding"**: The Folk & Jazz Wing Ding, Carnegie Hall archives for programs; *New York Times*, November 2, 1963, p. 17.

146 **the first college dates:** Dartmouth University press release on CARavan, November 19, 1963; Bobby Hamilton interviews; *Philadelphia Bulletin*, November 24 and November 30, 1963; *Philadelphia Inquirer*, November 27, 1963, p. 14; *Philadelphia Tribune*, November 30, 1963, p. 11. *Hootenanny* information comes from the January–February 1964 *The Alkalizer*, published by Miles Laboratory, a sponsor of the event, courtesy of the Salem International University archives; *The Salem Herald*, December 19, 1963, p. 1; *Sunday Gazette-Mail*, Charleston, W.Va., January 12, 1964; *Clarksburg Exponent*, December 10, 1963, p. 1, December 11, 1963, p. 1.

CHAPTER 13: DON'T LET ME BE MISUNDERSTOOD ~ 1964

148 **Congress of Racial Equality:** *New York Times*, January 10, 1964, p. 28; Summit, N.J., *Dispatch*, January 16, 1964, p. 1; *I Put a Spell on You*, p. 94.

148 **appealing headshot:** *Variety*, January 8, 1964, p. 228.

149 **"Big Willy":** *I Put a Spell on You*, p. 106; Willem Langenberg information courtesy of Philips, via Andre Manning, Philips USA; *Cash Box*, February 22, 1964, p. 38.

149 **Phil Orlando:** Lisle Atkinson, Bobby Hamilton, Rudy Stevenson interviews.

150 **Nina had plenty of time:** *New York Times*, February 7, 1964, p. 38, Village Gate; Illinois Institute of Technology *Tech News*, February 28 and March 6, 1964; Lisle Atkinson interviews and Chris White radio show transcript.

150 **"See-Line Woman":** Although earlier versions of a song similar to "See-Line Woman" existed, George Bass claimed the copyright on the tune, registered February 24, 1964, EU812489; Bobby Hamilton, Rudy Stevenson interviews; Langston Hughes papers; Bernard Gotfryd interview, including discussion of his photographs of the Carnegie event.

153 **"Oh, Lord":** Horace Ott interview.

153 **Julia Prettyman:** Student Non-Violent Coordinating Committee papers, Library of Congress Special Collections, B1–12, Reel 45, Library of Congress Manuscript Reading Room.

154 **a "new" Nina:** *New York Amsterdam News*, June 27, 1964, p. 16; *Washington Post*, May 22, 1964, p. C10; Bernard Gotfryd interview.

155 **Cape Cod:** Cape Cod photos, Stroud, *Black Is the Color*; Langston Hughes papers; *New York Amsterdam News*, June 27, 1964, p. 16, August 8, 1964, p. 46.

155 **In mid-July:** *nina simone in concert* (Philips PHS 600-135); *Cash Box* review July 4, 1964, p. 24; *Folksy Nina*, (SCP 465); *Variety* review, July 8, 1964, p. 44. Nina's seven albums for Philips were later compiled into a four-CD package, *Four Women*, released by Verve Records (440 065 021 2).

155 **Allen had reconfigured:** Discussion of September 3 and September 10, 1964, Steve Allen performances from video, courtesy of Meadowlane Enterprises and Research Video. Nina had made another visit to a television variety show in the spring, appearing May 13 on *The Tonight Show* in New York. According to the NBC Masterbook, Box MT 1361, she performed an "African Rhythm," perhaps "Zungo," and "Porgy."

On September 20, Nina appeared at Carnegie Hall, opening for Harry James and his band. John Wilson wrote in the *New York Times* (September 21, 1964, p. 36) that she "sang, danced and played the piano with her trio with her customarily skillful sense of showmanship."

159 **a CORE benefit:** *New York Amsterdam News*, September 5, 1963, p. 26.

160 **Nina's second album:** *Broadway Blues and Ballads* (PHS 600-14B); Burdon, *Don't Let Me Be Misunderstood*, pp. 287–89; *Variety*, November 11, 1964, p. 56.

161 **"in poor taste":** *Chicago Defender*, October 17, 1964, p. 10.

161 **booklet of photographs:** Booklet from Schomburg Center, Nina Simone files; November 6, 1964, letter from Andy Stroud to Langston Hughes, Hughes papers.

161 **Premier Records:** *Nina Simone v. Philip Landwehr, Lewis Harris, et al.*, Case #18830/64, New York Supreme Court archives.

162 **Los Angeles fiasco:** *Los Angeles Times*, December 27, 1964, p. F1.

CHAPTER 14: MY SKIN IS BLACK ~ 1965

163 **an engaged performer:** Horace Ott, Lisle Atkinson interviews; Stroud, *Black Is the Color*, p. 49; *I Put a Spell on You* (PHS 600-172).

164 **another solo concert:** Nina entering Carnegie Hall and backstage, from Stroud, *Black Is the Color*; Dorothea Towles information, *New York Amsterdam News*, June 13, 1964, p. 23, June 27, 1964, p. 22; *New York Times*, July 30, 2006, p. 29, obituary; *New York Times*, January 16, 1965, p. 15, Wilson review; Langston Hughes papers; *I Put a Spell on You*, p. 103.

166 **"not quite as urgent":** *New York Times*, January 16, 1965, p. 15. Though federal indictments in the murders of the three civil rights workers were handed down in January 1965, no one was tried until 1967, when eighteen men were charged with conspiracy. Seven of the defendants were convicted, eight were acquitted, and a mistrial was declared for the remaining three. No one was tried on state charges for more than forty years. In 2005, one man was convicted of manslaughter for his part in the murders. *New York Times*, October 25, 1967, p. 1, June 22, 2005, p. 1.

166 **Lorraine had died:** Lorraine Hansberry's death, *New York Times*, January 16, 1965, p. 25, January 17, 1965, p. X3; *New York Amsterdam News*, January 16, 1965, p. 1, January 23, 1965, p. 6; *I Put a Spell on You*, pp. 87–88; Cheney, *Lorraine Hansberry*, pp. 33–34.

On January 22, 1965, the FBI, noting Lorraine's death, circulated a memorandum with copies of her obituary. "Subject is included on the Security Index of the NYO [New York Office] and because of her death on 1/12/65, the SI cards concerning her are being canceled . . . Subject's case file will be placed in a closed status."

168 **"Music chose me"**: *Nashville Tennessean*, February 14, 1965, Sunday Showcase.

168 **settled the suit**: *Nina Simone v. Philip Landwehr, Lewis Harris, et al.*, settlement confirmation; *New York Amsterdam News*, February 20, 1965, p. 13.

169 **Jesse H. Walker**: *New York Amsterdam News*, January 23, 1965, p. 9; February 13, 1965, p. 14; May 22, 1965, p. 23.

169 **Selma**: See Lawson, *Black Ballots: Voting Rights in the South, 1944–1969; Congressional Quarterly's Congress and the Nation*, Vol. I, p. 357; *New York Times*, March 5–25, 1965, for coverage of events in and around the Selma protest. Art D'Lugoff interviews; *I Put a Spell on You*, pp. 101–3. There is no independent confirmation in any contemporaneous reporting of the Montgomery event that the city airport was blockaded as Nina recounted in her memoir. Art D'Lugoff remembered that the private plane they took for the last leg of the trip left from Atlanta.

173 **"fierce integrity"**: *Billboard*, May 29, 1965, p. 10; *New York Times*, April 16, 1965, p. 32; *Cash Box* briefly noted *I Put a Spell on You* in its April 3 issue.

173 **Malcolm X**: *New York Amsterdam News*, April 17, 1965, p. 49; *New York Times*, March 24, 1965, p. 4X; Bobby Hamilton interviews; *I Put a Spell on You*, pp. 99, 194. Nina joined a benefit April 23, 1965, to raise money for Malcolm's family, a midnight event at the Apollo Theater. She had also joined another benefit April 11, 1965, at Philharmonic Hall for the Wiltwych School for disadvantaged children in the New York area; *New York Times*, April 12, 1965, p. 28.

175 **Annie's Room**: Annie Ross interview; *Pittsburgh Courier*, January 28, 1961, p. A22, Nina with Lambert Hendriks and Ross; *Melody Maker*, July 3, 1965, p. 12; Hampton, *Nina Simone: Break Down & Let It All Out*, pp. 24–25.

176 **"jolly good"**: Portion of July 15, 1965, letter from Nina to Sam Waymon, made available via www.ninasimone.biz/free-letter.html; *Evening Star and News*, July 9, 1965.

176 **"I read chapters"**: July 1965 letter from Nina Simone to Langston Hughes, Hughes papers.

177 **Antibes Juan-les-Pins**: *Jazz*, September 1965, pp. 47–48; *Jazz Hot*, September 1965, p. 7; translation courtesy of David Kaufman; Bobby Hamilton interviews; *Pastel Blues* (PHS 600-187).

179 **Andy sent regrets**: CORE papers, Atlanta collection, Reel 21, Section 62, Library of Congress Manuscript Reading Room.

CHAPTER 15: IMAGES ~ 1966

183 **"the rudder"**: Alfred Wertheimer interview.

184 **Ralph J. Gleason**: *San Francisco Chronicle*, November 5, 1965, p. 51.

184 **"the whole family"**: Stroud, *Black Is the Color*, p. 33.

184 **Haverford College**: *Haverford News*, February 25, 1966, p. 3; *Images* (PHS 600-202).

184 **at the East End:** *Philadelphia Tribune*, February 26, 1966, p. 18; March 8, 1966, p. 17. Writing about *Let It All Out* (PHS 600-202), the *Saturday Review*'s Martin Williams said he was at a loss to place Nina musically: "I confess I have no idea what Miss Simone's appeal is." He nonetheless admired "the variety of tempo and attitude on this LP."

The album felt as conventional as several of the meat-and-potatoes dates that filled up Nina's schedule right after the CORE concerts: that evening at Haverford College outside Philadelphia, four weeks at a new venue for Nina in New York City, Square East in the Village, and another evening concert at Hunter College. See *Saturday Review*, March 12, 1966, p. 130; Haverford date, *Philadelphia Bulletin*, February 7, 1966; Square East, Anne Fulchino press release; Hunter College, *New York Times*, April 15, 1966, p. 38.

185 **"Ohrbach's":** *Washington Post*, March 19, 1966, p. E3; *New York Amsterdam News*, April 2, 1966, p. 14; *Philadelphia Tribune*, July 19, 1966, second section front, for "freedom cap" reference.

186 **The new arrangements:** *Nina Simone with Strings* (CP 496), *Record Aid*, May 1966 for release date; June 24, 1965, recording date information courtesy of AFM Local 47 archives, Los Angeles, Calif.

187 **something special:** *Atlanta Journal*, May 27, 1966, p. 14 for the date before Newport; July 4, 1963, Newport Jazz Festival, Library of Congress, Recorded Sound Reference Room. In *Down Beat*, August 15, 1963 (p. 13), reviewer Ira Gitler, departing from audience reaction, was highly critical of her "overlong set in which her affected singing and out-of-the-academy piano playing succeeded in driving many to drink." "Porgy/Malindy" can be heard on *To Be Free: The Nina Simone Story* (RCA Legacy 88697 11009 2); Goldblatt, *Newport Jazz Festival*, pp. 132–33. For the 1966 festival, see *New York Times*, July 3, 1966, p. 11; *Down Beat*, August 11, 1966, p. 14; July 2, 1966, Newport Jazz Festival, Library of Congress, Recorded Sound Reference Room.

188 **Boston Globe's music critic:** *Boston Globe*, November 24, 1966, p. 86. Music critic William Buchanan said Nina had been "one of the top two or three performers" at the July Newport festival; *Boston Herald*, November 20, 1966, p. 14 of the Show Guide.

188 **another album:** *Wild Is the Wind* (PHM-200-207/PHS-600-207); the June 26, 1966, *Cash Box* (p. 44) gave it the magazine's usual positive spin:

"Interpreting either blues or ballads with depth and clarity, Nina has proven once again that she has her own special niche in the pop-blues-jazz field." Though the blurb cited a few tracks, it made no mention of "Four Women."

188 **Dolly Banks:** *Philadelphia Tribune*, October 8, 1966, second section front, October 15, 1966; *Pittsburgh Courier*, November 5, 1966, p. 5B; *Chicago Defender*, October 26, 1966, p. 16; *I Put a Spell on You*, p. 117.

189 **"Some people":** *Chicago Defender*, September 19, 1966, p. 10, September 29, 1966, p. 21; *New York Post*, September 2, 1966, p. 10; *Sepia*, March 1967, pp. 60–64; *New York Amsterdam News*, June 11, 1966, p. 20, anti-apartheid; September 17, 1966, p. 20, NAACP fashion benefit; *Philadelphia Tribune*, July 19, 1966, p.1; *Philadelphia Bulletin*, July 18, 1966; *Philadelphia Inquirer*, July 18, 1966; Stokely Carmichael comments from footage courtesy of Getty Images.

190 **almost midnight:** *Philadelphia Tribune*, November 15, 1966, p. 1, November 19, 1966, p. 4; *Philadelphia Bulletin*, November 14, 1966.

192 **Philharmonic Hall:** Ron Delsener, Bobby Hamilton, Lisle Atkinson interviews; *Chicago Defender*, May 21, 1966, p. 14, June 4, 1966, p. 14.

193 **"Backlash Blues":** Langston Hughes papers, concert program; *New York Amsterdam News*, December 3, 1966, p. 20; *New York Times*, November 23, 1966, p. 28, October 1, 1966, for "Khadejha."

194 **mainstream appeal:** *The Calling Card*, December 14, 1966 (Brooklyn College); Alan M. Nadel interview; *New York Amsterdam News*, December 3, 1966, p. 7. An honor Nina received at the end of the year seemed fitting given all the attention to her appearance in the previous months. Her friend Dorothea Towles had opened a charm school and was graduating her first professional models. At the mid-December ceremony the inaugural award for "excellence in dress" went to Nina.

CHAPTER 16: MY ONLY GROOVE IS MOODS ~ 1967

195 **RCA:** Move to RCA, *Cash Box*, December 31, 1966, p. 36B. Nina's champion at Philips, Willem "Big Willy" Langenberg, had resigned in April to accept an executive position with a Dutch ship-building consortium, so even if he had wanted the label to keep her, he no longer had any influence on such decisions. *Cash Box*, April 23, 1966, p. 45. Andy's management, *New York Amsterdam News*, January 7, 1967, p. 18, January 14, 1967, p. 16.

195 **Bill Cosby:** *Cash Box*, November 26, 1966, p. 25; *St. Louis Post Dispatch*, February 9, 1967, p. 8F; *St. Louis Globe Democrat*, February 11–12, 1967, p. 7F; *Baltimore Afro-American*, February 25, 1967, p. 20; *The Hilltop*, Howard University newspaper, February 22, 1967, p. 1; *New York Times*, February 20, 1967, p. 43. At least to John S. Wilson, Nina's offstage prob-

lems didn't hamper her performance. He found her "all fire and ice, playing and singing with a feline sense of power." *I Put a Spell on You*, pp. 110–11; Rudy Stevenson interviews.

197 **a cartoonlike drawing:** *The High Priestess of Soul* (PHM 200-219/PHS 600-219, Verve B0006004-02); *New York Amsterdam News*, December 3, 1966, p. 20; *Los Angeles Times*, January 20, 1967, p. C8. See *Cash Box*, January 28, 1967, p. 38 for a mini-review as "Pop Best Bets"; also *Los Angeles Times*, February 12, 1967, p. Q45.

197 **Nina Simone Sings the Blues:** (RCA Victor LPM/LSP 3789, RCA Legacy 82876 73334 2); Bernard Purdie interview, Danny Davis comments from the original liner notes. See *Cash Box*, April 24, 1967, p. 34 for a mini-review in "Jazz Picks"; also *Los Angeles Times*, May 14, 1967, p. C22, May 25, 1967, p. E10; *Down Beat*, October 5, 1967, p. 34.

"Day and Night," one of Rudy's compositions that RCA released as a single, found a home in Harlem. According to the *New York Amsterdam News* weekly charts in April, "Day and Night" made it into the paper's "Top Ten Records" for the month; *New York Amsterdam News*, April 18, 1967, p. 18, April 15, 1967, p. 19; *Washington Post*, May 14, 1967, p. L6; *Billboard*, August 5, 1967, p. 14; *Cash Box*, January 28, 1967, p. 38, April 24, 1967, p. 34, September 16, 1967, p. 48.

198 **singer-comedian:** Nina, Flip Wilson, and Miriam Makeba, *New York Amsterdam News*, February 24, 1967, p. 18; *Village Voice*, March 16, 1967, p. 18.

199 **Brixton:** Hampton, *Nina Simone: Break Down*, pp. 28–35; *Melody Maker*, April 22, 1967, p. 6; Stroud inteview, *Fader*, May/June 2006; Dick Gregory interview.

200 **"more out of myself":** *Washington Post*, May 14, 1967, p. L6.

200 **a tribute:** Langston Hughes's death, *New York Times*, May 23, 1967, p. 1; *New York Amsterdam News*, May 27, 1967, pp. 1, 29, June 3, 1967, p. 1; Nina Simone's July 1, 1967 Newport performance, Library of Congress Recorded Sound Reference Room.

201 **"entirely too apathetic":** *Sepia*, March 1967; *Down Beat*, January 11, 1968, p. 16, referring to October 1967 interview; *Billboard*, August 5, 1967, p. 14.

201 **Detroit:** *New York Times*, July 24, 1967, July 25, 1967, p. 1, riot coverage; *Chicago Defender*, August 5, 1967, p. 13; *Detroit Free Press*, August 15, 1967, p. 3B; *Detroit News*, August 14, 1967, p. 5C; *New York Amsterdam News*, July 29, 1967, p. 42, "Roundup of the 'Hot Summer' "; Bill Smith interview.

202 **express the blues:** *Silk & Soul* (RCA LPM/LSP 3837, RCA Legacy 82876733352). The album is notable for Nina's graceful, understated performances. One featured her alone at the piano on "Love O Love," which Andy had written. Its improvisations—a little Bach, a little blues,

a little gospel—evoked what Nina must have sounded like alone at the piano in 1954 at the Midtown in Atlantic City. Her quiet and contemplative reading of the Burt Bacharach–Hal David "Look of Love" gave the song a kind of charm missing from more sparkly renditions. Similarly, an elegant version of "Cherish," a hit for the Association, took the song from teenage crush to adult affection. *Silk & Soul* went on the *Billboard* Top 200 chart November 25, 1967, and stayed on the charts four weeks, though it rose only to number 158. *Washington Post*, May 14, 1967, p. L6; *New York Times*, December 31, 1967, p. D11, November 8, 2007, p. D11; see also www.corita.org.

203 **Las Vegas:** Rudy Stevenson, Sam Waymon interviews; *Las Vegas Sun*, October 1, 1967, p. 40.

204 **UCLA:** *Los Angeles Times*, November 14, 1967; listing for *Pat Boone in Hollywood*, *Washington Post*, November 30, 1967, p. D23.

204 **"You're not giving":** *New York Times*, December 31, 1967, p. D11.

CHAPTER 17: BLACK GOLD ~ 1968

206 **coronation:** Carnegie Hall concert, *New York Times*, January 8, 1968, p. 31; *Variety*, January 10, 1968, p. 51; *Billboard*, January 20, 1968, p. 16; *New York Amsterdam News*, January 6, 1968, p. 16, January 13, 1968, p. 17; *New York Post*, February 27, 1968, p. 29.

208 **Vancouver:** Henry Young interviews.

209 **"The great thing":** *Variety*, March 20, 1968, p. 66; Rudy Stevenson, Henry Young interviews.

210 **On April 4:** *Newsday*, April 4, 1968, p. 48; Henry Young interviews; *I Put a Spell on You*, pp. 113–14. RCA archives; Urban League of New York, *New York Amsterdam News*, May 11, 1968, p. 1; *'Nuff Said* (RCA LSP 4065, BMG RCA 82876596212); extended introduction and tribute to Dr. Martin Luther King Jr. from *Nina Simone: Saga of the Good Life and Hard Times* (RCA 07863-66997-2).

212 **"Breathe with me":** Nina talking to Buck Clarke, from *Nina*, a Peter Rodis documentary filmed in 1968–69 and eventually airing August 1972 on WOR in New York. This documentary is part of the 2008 CD/DVD package *To Be Free: The Nina Simone Story* (RCA Legacy 88697 11009 2). Lester Hyman, Henry Young, Fred Taylor interviews.

213 **In Amsterdam:** *Rotterdam Daily News* article, "NINA SIMONE, uitzonderlijk door feilloze 'timing' "—"NINA SIMONE, Exceptional through faultless timing"; *Amsterdam Daily News*, NINA SIMONE: INGETOGENHEID"—"NINA SIMONE: Modesty"; translations courtesy of Leonie van Raadshoove of the Embassy of the Netherlands, Washington, D.C., original articles courtesy of Henry Young.

214 **"Sigmund Freud, 24/7"**: Sam Waymon, Henry Young interviews; post-card from Nina to Henry Young, courtesy of Henry Young.

215 **"by sheer artistry"**: *High Fidelity*, September 1968, p. 104; *Melody Maker*, December 7, 1968, p. 7; Montreux materials, including a record-ing of the concert, courtesy of Henry Young. Years later Andy Stroud had apparently put out an album from the concert, *Nina Simone in Europe* (Trip Records, a Product of Springboard International Records, TLP-8020 2 SLX-00243).

In *I Put a Spell on You* Nina wrote that she had learned about Ken-nedy's assassination just as she arrived for her foreign dates and that by the time she got to Montreux, she was emotionally spent. She recounted in the memoir that she was so distraught that when she sat down to play the first number she started to sob, and Andy had to help her offstage. There is no mention of such an occurrence in the contemporaneous accounts of the concert or in the record of the live performance.

217 **"It's so wonderful"**: *New York Amsterdam News*, August 3, 1968, p. 16; *Christian Science Monitor*, July 13, 1968, p. 4; *Philadelphia Bulletin*, July 6, 1968, p. 4, *New York Times*, July 8, 1968, p. 45; *New York Daily News*, July 5, 1968, p. 38.

217 *Sound of Soul:* Nina's comments are from an interview that was pack-aged as part of the *Sound of Soul*, courtesy of WNET in New York.

219 **a new bass player:** Gene Perla interviews. Perla's personal calendar showed a busy schedule once he joined Nina the third week in October: October 26, Lake Forest, Ill., at the college; October 27, Detroit, Ford Auditorium; November 8, New York state, unknown venue; Novem-ber 9, Toledo, unknown venue; November 22, Pennsylvania, unknown venue; November 29, Miami, Dade County arena; November 30, Atlanta, unknown venue; December 1, Philadelphia, Spectrum "World Series of Jazz"; December 13, Long Island, unknown venue; December 27, Pittsburgh, Hilton Hotel, jazz workshop; December 28, Carnegie Hall in New York City. See also *Chicago Daily Defender*, October 24, 1968, p. 16; *The Stentor*, October 25, 1968, p. 1, student newspaper at Lake Forest College; Hampton, *Nina Simone: Break Down*, pp. 48–50; *Cash Box*, December 14, 1968, p. 62.

221 **"They seem to know"**: *Melody Maker*, December 7, 1968, p. 7, Decem-ber 21, 1968, p.13.

CHAPTER 18: TO BE YOUNG, GIFTED AND BLACK ~ 1969

222 **Nina's latest album:** *Nina Simone and Piano!* (RCA LSP-410, RCA 07863 68100 2); RCA archives for sessions September 16, 1968, October 1, 1968. Ralph J. Gleason was one of the few music writers who paid atten-

tion to it, noting with praise Nina's development as a pianist. In earlier years, he wrote, she "had a tendency to break loose and dominate a performance. Now, however, her playing is economical and exquisitely tasteful. Just right, in other words to frame what she is singing." *New York Post*, April 22, 1969; *Baltimore Afro-American*, January 11, 1969, p. 10.

223 **"We are the ones"**: *Time*, February 21, 1969, p. 63; *New York Times*, February 5, 1969, p. 37; *Village Voice*, February 13, 1969, p. 35. Along with a month of weekends at the Village Gate, Nina had also performed two well-received concerts with similar programs. The first was in New York at the Metropolitan Museum of Art, which used the event to kick off a new jazz series. No doubt by design, the museum was also featuring an exhibition called "Harlem on My Mind." The second was the Philadelphia Academy of Music.

224 **Nina and Andy arguing:** Gene Perla, Sam Waymon interviews.

224 **"nineteen people"**: *New York Post*, March 15, 1969, p. 29; "nineteen people," from footage probably shot late in 1968 for the Peter Rodis documentary; Andy Stroud interview, *Fader*, May/June 2006.

225 **ambitious three-week trip:** *Cash Box*, March 1, 1969, p. 6; *New York Amsterdam News*, February 8, 1969, p. 21. The packed UK-European schedule, courtesy of Gene Perla, was Dublin, March 12; Belfast, March 13; Amsterdam, March 14; Rotterdam, March 15; the Hague, March 16; Hillversum, March 18; Edinburgh, March 19; Cardiff, March 21; London, March 22; Manchester, March 23; Paris, March 25 with a television show on March 26; Geneva, March 31; Lucerne, April 1; Munich, April 2–3, including a live taping; and London, April 4.

Hampton, *Nina Simone: Break Down*, pp. 51–61; London *Sunday Times*, March 30, 1969; *Melody Maker*, March 29, 1969, p. 6; *Figaro*, March 27, 1969, p. 30; *Jazz Hot*, May 1969, p. 7, translation courtesy of David Kaufman; Gene Perla interviews; Taylor, *Notes and Tones*, p. 152.

226 **"a very rare evening"**: Gene Perla interviews; the Munich show was later released as a CD, *A Very Rare Evening* (Mambo Records, 804065144); Hampton, *Nina Simone: Break Down*, pp. 56–58.

227 **"Ten years ago"**: *Baltimore Afro-American*, January 11, 1969, p. 19; *Melody Maker*, April 19, 1969, p. 5.

227 **Berkeley:** By most accounts Nina was well received at the University of California–Berkeley jazz festival. See *The Daily Californian*, April 11, 1969; *New York Times*, May 11, 1969, p. D30; *Down Beat*, July 24, 1969, p. 28, which was a middling review; *New York Post*, June 20, 1969, p. 48, Ralph J. Gleason column; UCLA date, Leonard Feather review in the *Los Angeles Times*, May 1, 1969, p. 23. He had turned into a fan, calling Nina "a creature of our times. Her extraordinary faculty for communicating with an audience is based in part on the urgent topicality of her songs, and in equal measure on the power, sometimes tantamount to fury,

with which she drives home her point." See also *Boston Herald Traveler*, April 20, 1969, Show Guide, p. 19; *Boston Globe*, May 2, 1969, p. 23.

228 **"Get her together"**: *New York Amsterdam News*, May 24, 1969, p. 22. In June RCA released *To Love Somebody* (RCA LSP-4152, RCA 28765 9632) from those sessions earlier in the year. Beyond the title track there were three Bob Dylan tunes, Leonard Cohen's "Suzanne," and the two-part "Revolution." In its largely positive review, *Metronome*, the music trade, quipped that "the tigress learns to purr." "Revolution" notwithstanding, whatever hopes the label had for this album were overshadowed by a new Philips record, *The Best of Nina Simone*, which was released almost at the same time and spent a few weeks near the bottom of the Billboard Top 200 (at number 187). The new RCA album didn't register at all. However, "Revolution Part I," the single, did spend two weeks in April on the Billboard R&B chart. Chart information comes from Whitburn's collection of *Billboard* Top R&B and pop singles charts and the Top 200 album charts. The single "Ain't Got No Life," which had been so popular in England, had spent a month on the top pop chart in January but rose only to number ninety-four. Ralph J. Gleason gave *To Love Somebody* a glowing review in one of his columns, *New York Post*, June 20, 1969, p. 48; *Stereo Review*, September 1969, p. 94.

229 **"To be young"**: *Melody Maker*, December 21, 1968, p. 13; Hansberry information, *New York Amsterdam News*, January 18, 1969, p. 22, January 25, 1969, p. 21; *New York Times*, March 3, 1969, p. 18; *Baltimore Afro-American*, July 12, 1969, p. 5.

229 **Morehouse College**: *Black Journal*, aired October 1969, courtesy of WNET; *Baltimore Afro-American*, June 28, 1969, p. 10; *Baltimore Sun*, June 24, 1969, p. B6.

230 **David Frost**: July 15, 1969, *David Frost Show*, courtesy of Kingworld/CBS.

231 **Dallas**: Henry Young interviews, *Dallas Times Herald*, July 19, 1969, p. 4A; *Dallas Morning News*, July 18, 1969, p. C6; *Down Beat*, January 23, 1969, p. 34, for Nina's comments on white singers/blacks' music during a performance in Detroit; *Ebony*, August 1969, p. 159.

233 **blazing set**: *Jazz Hot*, September 1969, p. 23, translation courtesy of David Kaufman; footage via YouTube, though this post carries the incorrect date. The group of musicians Nina introduces did not begin to play with her until 1969. Beyond Antibes, Nina continued with regular festival work, performing August 15 in Philadelphia at the Spectrum, *Bulletin*, August 16, 1969, and then August 18 as part of the Schaeffer Music Festival in Central Park, *New York Amsterdam News*, August 16, 1969, p. 17.

235 **"how we feel as a race"**: *Ebony*, August 1969, pp. 156–59; Taylor, *Notes and Tones*, pp. 150–51; Hampton festival, *Washington Post*, June 30, 1969, p. B8.

235 **"more and more every day"**: Nina's remarks on "To Be Young, Gifted

and Black" taken from a live performance on *Black Gold* (RCA LSP-4248, BVCJ-37373 82876-60800-2); footage of an August 17, 1969, performance is available on *The Soul of Nina Simone* (RCA-Legacy, 82876 7193 2); *New York Amsterdam News*, August 23, 1969, p. 18; Philharmonic Hall concert, *New York Times*, October 27, 1969, p. 51; *Variety*, October 29, 1969, p. 60; *Billboard*, November 8, 1969, p. 22.

236 **"a work horse":** Hampton, *Nina Simone: Break Down*, pp. 67–68; *Melody Maker*, November 22, 1969, p. 6. In a sign of its continuing interest in Nina, RCA took out an ad in *Melody Maker* November 15 (p. 11) promoting the single of "To Be Young, Gifted and Black" "on her return to Britain."

Additional Stroud comments from *Nina*, the Peter Rodis documentary filmed in 1968–69. Prior to the Palladium concert, Nina had done two shows in Rotterdam, one in Amsterdam, and another in Stockholm, schedule courtesy of Gerrit DeBruin.

236 **number eight:** "To Be Young, Gifted and Black" (RCA 0269). The record also scored on the *Billboard* pop chart, though it peaked only at number seventy-six.

CHAPTER 19: I HAVE BECOME MORE MILITANT ~ 1970

238 **split up:** In *I Put a Spell on You*, Nina writes that she left Andy right after she played the Newport Jazz Festival on July 11 (pp. 118–19). But this appears to be in error, given stories in the black press in February about their separation. In addition, the May 14 *Jet* refers to Andy as Nina's "estranged husband." In the May/June 2006 *Fader* interview, Andy said that they separated from January 31, 1969, until 1970, when they returned from the European tour. But contemporaneous accounts refer to them together in 1969. He remembered that "she ran off the plane and I didn't see her for days or hear from her" (pp. 100–101).

See also *I Put a Spell on You*, pp. 119–20; *Fader*, May/June 2006, p. 98. Though Nina writes in her memoir that she left Mount Vernon immediately after leaving Andy, a profile in the November 1970 *Redbook* by poet Maya Angelou refers to Nina living with Lisa in suburban Westchester County in a "comfortable rambling house," which is an accurate description of the house on Nuber, and a 1971 interview in the *Philadelphia Inquirer* also refers to Nina living at the Mount Vernon house (March 28, 1971).

Lisa "Simone" Kelly myspace.com post, March 26, 2009, reflecting on living in North Carolina after her parents separated.

239 **a weekend performance:** Village Gate, *New York Amsterdam News*, January 17, 1970, p. 18, January 24, 1970, p. 18, January 17, 1970, p. 18, photo;

see Linda Yablonsky essay on Nina at the Gate, winter 1970, pp. 59–68, in Manning, ed., *Shows I'll Never Forget: 50 Writers Relive Their Most Memorable Concertgoing Experience*. On February 8 Nina performed at a benefit for the Union United Methodist Church in Brooklyn to raise money for a free breakfast program, *New York Amsterdam News*, January 31, 1970, p. 24.

240 **"I'm very proud":** *Philadelphia Bulletin*, March 29, 1970; *Washington Post*, March 22, 1970, p. K8.

In *I Put a Spell on You*, Nina writes that her first job after splitting up with Andy was in San Francisco, but that does not appear to be correct. They were separated by the end of January, and Nina performed at the Village Gate at the end of the month. It is possible she had a San Francisco job sometime in early March and made the date while she was visiting her brother Carrol in San Diego.

241 **Flip Wilson:** Stroud interview, *Fader*, May/June 2006, p. 101; *Jet*, May 14, 1970, pp. 60–61.

243 **Nina's modest schedule:** *Chicago Defender*, May 18, 1970, p. 10; *Variety*, June 6, 1970, p. 46; *New York Amsterdam News*, January 31, 1970, p. 24, February 7, 1970, p. 28; *I Put a Spell on You*, p. 118.

243 **Nassau:** Nassau *Tribune* coverage, June 30, 1970, p. 1, July 1, 1970, p. 1, July 2–3, 1970, p. 3; Nassau *Guardian*, July 2, 1970, p. 1, July 2–3, 1970, p. 2; *Life*, October 2, 1970, p. 11.

In *I Put a Spell on You* Nina talks about a March 1970 concert she played in Newark, New Jersey: "In front of a segregated audience—entirely black—and I was full of hate, tearing spitefully into political leaders of all races. Backstage after the show people said I was an inspiration to continue the struggle, but that was the end of it all for me—the beginning of my withdrawal from political performance." Nina probably remembered the venue incorrectly, and the outburst she spoke of was likely the Nassau event. Contemporaneous accounts show that Nina was in California for most of March until she returned for the Philadelphia concert on the twenty-ninth.

News of the fiasco in Nassau seems not to have traveled back to the United States. The *Chicago Defender* (July 9, 1970, p. 5) and the *New York Amsterdam News* (July 11, 1970, p. 20) each ran dispatches about the trip that spoke of red carpet treatment and a party on a fancy houseboat.

245 **"I have become more militant":** Taylor, *Notes and Tones*, pp. 150–56.

246 **Barbados:** *I Put a Spell on You*, p. 121.

246 **traced black music:** *& Beautiful II*, FBB 3198, Library of Congress collections, Motion Picture and Television reading room; *New York Amsterdam News*, September 12, 1970, p. 21, November 28, 1970, p. 29.

248 ***Essence:*** December 1970, pp. 28–33; Taylor, *Notes and Tones*, pp. 157–58.

CHAPTER 20: DEFINITE VIBRATIONS OF PRIDE ~ 1971

250 **Gerrit DeBruin:** Gerrit DeBruin, interviews, e-mail correspondence; *I Put a Spell on You,* p. 122; Hampton, *Nina Simone: Break Down,* pp. 74–76; *Blues & Soul,* January 1971, "Nina Simone—Superstar for 1971"; Sam Waymon interviews; Nina Simone, April 9, 1970, letter to Gerrit DeBruin, courtesy of Gerrit DeBruin.

252 **gentle scenes:** From *Great American Dream Machine; New York Times,* January 6, 1975, p. 75; *Los Angeles Times,* January 8, 1971, p. 21; Peter Rodis interview.

253 **back in the studio:** *Here Comes the Sun* (RCA LSP 4536, RCA BMG 82876 696252); Leopoldo Fleming, Nadi Qamar interviews.

255 **one of the AME churches:** Tad Hershorn interview, Dallas event; *Chicago Defender,* March 10, 1971, p. 4; *Chicago Tribune,* March 8, 1971, p. B16, for the Chicago performance.

256 **"susceptible to hurt":** *Philadelphia Inquirer,* March 28, 1971; April 5, 1971; schedule information courtesy Gene Perla.

Nina was in a better mood April 23 when she performed in Los Angeles with Miles Davis at what was billed as "Jazz à la Soul." Even a faulty sound system that made her ask "Can you hear me better now" and the fact that the seven-thousand-seat Shrine Auditorium was only two-thirds full didn't dampen her spirits. During her encore, "To Be Young, Gifted and Black," *Los Angeles Times* critic Leonard Feather said she virtually played the audience as if it were an instrument "hammered by her great, proud tones." *Los Angeles Times,* April 26, 1971, p. D18; *Melody Maker,* May 8, 1971, p. 32.

Prior to the Los Angeles date, Nina was the headliner April 4 for a Baltimore tribute to Dr. Martin Luther King Jr. held at the Lyric Theater, *Baltimore Sun,* April 4, 1971, Section D, p. 10.

257 **Mother's Day concert:** By several accounts, the Carnegie Hall show was unusual. The first part was padded with novelties rarely if ever seen in her previous performances. Lisa was brought out to dance, then a man came onstage, introduced by Nina as her swami, and he watched *her* dance. Nina even left a couple of times. Then she unveiled a plumped-up version of "Mr. Bojangles" that featured Sam doing a soft-shoe in tails, a top hat, and white gloves. *The New York Times's* Mike Jahn derided the event as a "shoddy uneven performance given to cliches of almost vaudeville proportions," *New York Times,* May 11, 1971, p. 46. Also *Billboard,* May 22, 1971, p. 22; Sam Waymon, Leopoldo Fleming interviews.

257 **Cairo, Illinois:** *Chicago Defender,* May 1, 1971, p. 2, June 22, 1971, p. 5, June 24, 1971, p. 15; Ewing and Roddy, *Let My People Go: Cairo, Illinois, 1967–1973,* p. 65; *East St. Louis Monitor,* June 17, 1971, June 24, 1971, July 1, 1971, starting on p. 6 of each issue, "Cairo news." *Daily Vidette,*

Illinois State University newspaper, May 21, 1971; Sam Waymon interviews; correspondence with Charles Koen; *Columbus Dispatch*, May 29, 1971, for Columbus, Ohio, performance.

259   **"She opened the door"**: Warren Benbow, Nadi Qamar interviews; *New York Times*, October 12, 1971, p. 49; *Variety*, October 20, 1971, p. 50; *Billboard*, October 23, 1971, p. 14.

Warren had hardly settled into the band when Nina and the group were flown to Paris for one performance. Leopoldo remembered it as a big gala for the International Red Cross. The venue was the ALCAZAR music hall, a competitor to the famed Folies Bergère. Nina and the band also did a television show, but only after Leopoldo insisted they be paid and Nina backed him. Warren Benbow, Leopoldo Fleming, Sam Waymon interviews; ALCAZAR, *Figaro*, September 30, 1971, p. 20. This date was sometime between September 19, 1971, when Nina performed at the Quaker City Jazz Festival in Philadelphia (*Philadelphia Bulletin*, September 20, 1971) and October 10, 1971, when she performed at Philharmonic Hall.

261   **"Operation Get Down"**: Pamphlet courtesy of Sam Waymon; Nina's July 25, 1971, letter to Gerrit DeBruin from Jamaica, courtesy of Gerrit DeBruin. Nina also was scheduled to play a jazz festival in Cleveland October 16 on a bill with Herbie Mann, Ramsey Lewis, and Eddie Harris, *Cleveland Call and Post*, October 16, 1971, p. 12A.

262   **Fort Dix**: Free the Army, *New York Times*, March 21, 1971, p. D1; November 23, 1971, p. 55; RCA archives, including the Donald Sutherland napkin note; "My Sweet Lord" from *Emergency Ward* (RCA LSP 4757, RCA/BMG 82876 596262 9); *I Put a Spell on You*, p. 125; *Trenton Times*, November 19, 1971, p. 3. See *Rolling Stone*, November 9, 1972, p. 64, and *Washington Post*, October 28, 1972, p. C1, for commentary.

CHAPTER 21: THIS AIN'T NO GERALDINE UP HERE ~ 1972

265   **Constitution Hall**: *Washington Star*, February 14, 1972, Section D, back page; *Washington Post*, February 14, 1972, p. B10; Peter Rodis documentary.

267   **Rainbow Sign**: *San Francisco Examiner*, April 3, 1972, p. 29; *San Francisco Chronicle*, April 3, 1972, p. 44; Peter Rodis documentary.

267   **"prancing and shaking"**: *Down Beat*, July 20, 1972, p. 50; *Chicago Tribune*, May 7, 1972, p. Q5; *Times-Picayune*, April 30, 1972, p. 39; Leopoldo Fleming, Ron Levy interviews.

In her write-up the *Chicago Tribune*'s Harriet Choice noted that Nina had dedicated "God Bless America" to another act on the bill, the Giants of Jazz, who included Dizzy Gillespie, Sonny Stitt, and Thelonious Monk. "These artists have played with mixed groups. Their choice of musicians is not a question of race. He's either a good musician or a bad one. I suspect they would have considered her behavior embarrassing."

At a Boston date two weeks before the New Orleans festival, Nina had exhibited more patience than usual when the sound system proved faulty and the auditorium was only half-full; *Christian Science Monitor*, March 23, 1972, p. 10.

268   **an homage to Nina:** Aretha Franklin, *Young, Gifted and Black* (Atlantic SD 7213), Whitburn, *Top Pop Albums*, p. 264; Hoffmann and Albert, *Cash Box Album Charts, 1955–1974*, p. 133.

268   **Malcolm X College:** *Chicago Defender*, June 7, 1972, p. 2, June 12, 1972, p. 16.

269   **a negative review:** *San Francisco Chronicle*, April 3, 1972, p. 44, June 12, 1972, p. 42; *Oakland Tribune*, June 12, 1972, p. 34. The *San Francisco Examiner*'s Phillip Elwood liked the Rainbow Sign show much better than Hunt. Calling her performance "magnificently theatrical," he said, "Miss Simone is a whole human being—singing, dancing, proclaiming her rage at the mistreatment of the black community." *San Francisco Examiner*, April 3, 1972, p. 29.

269   **a similarly receptive audience:** Hampton festival, *Virginian Pilot*, June 26, 1972, p. B3. The review, by Rick Patterson, said Nina's performance of "To Be Young, Gifted and Black" was the emotional high point of the evening: "Almost the entire audience stood to sing with her in an overwhelming tribute to black unity." In *Variety*, July 5, 1972, p. 44, the reviewer said, "It seems redundant to proselytize before crowds long since committed to her own ideals, but Miss Simone continues to do so and her performance suffers." See also *Cincinnati Enquirer*, July 24, 1972, p. 8; *Cincinnati Post and Times Star*, July 24, 1972, p. 22. *Post* reviewer John Eliot said that Nina "shouted rather than sang 'To Be Young, Gifted and Black' and other quasi-political songs at the crowd. Black pride is important, but can it not be communicated musically instead of by Nina's sledgehammer approach?"

Nina had been scheduled to perform July 7 at the Newport Jazz Festival, now moved to New York City, but she canceled because of laryngitis.

270   **Nina was still angry:** *New York Times*, July 27, 1972, p. 19, August 3, 1972, p. 25; *Variety*, July 26, 1972, p. 1.

273   **J.D. died:** *I Put a Spell on You*, pp. 122–28. Nina writes vividly about the break with her father, his death, and Lucille's, though some passages are at odds with verifiable facts—Lucille couldn't have told her that her father had passed away because she preceded him in death by two weeks. *The Washington Post*, October 28, 1972, p. C1, offers a long interview with Nina published the day of the Kennedy Center concert, in which she talks about having spent the previous week in North Carolina, October

30, 1972, p. B2. Concert review, *Washington Star and News*, October 30, 1972, p. B4; *Tryon Daily Bulletin*, October 10, 1972, Waddell obituary; October 25, 1972, John D. Waymon obituary.

274 **Geraldine:** *Chicago Tribune*, December 19, 1972, p. B3; Eugene Harvey hiring referred to in a May 12, 1973, profile in *Melody Maker*, p. 24.

CHAPTER 22: WHERE MY SOUL HAS GONE ~ 1973–1976

275 **expressed her gratitude:** *Nina Simone Sings Billie Holiday—Lady Sings the Blues* (SLP 1005, Stroud Records); *Cash Box*, December 30, 1972, p. 30; *New York Amsterdam News*, December 30, 1972, p. D3; Brecht program, *New York Times*, January 15, 1973, p. 23; *Opera News*, March 3, 1973, p. 25.

276 **performance at Lincoln Center:** *Variety*, August 8, 1973, p. 34. Using songs from this concert RCA created *It Is Finished* (RCA-APL 10241, RCA 82876 596272), along with three tracks from 1971 recording sessions, "The Pusher," "Funkier Than a Mosquito's Tweeter," and "Let It Be Me." It was released in the middle of 1974. See *Crawdaddy*, December 1974, pp. 80–81; *Stereo Review*, December 1974, p. 98; *Pittsburgh Courier*, September 28, 1974, p. 18.

Nina had done an earlier concert in Los Angeles April 11 at the Shrine auditorium on a bill with Miles Davis among others; *Los Angeles Times*, April 11, 1973, p. H17.

277 **Black Expo:** Prior to the Black Expo '73 in Philadelphia, Nina played a well-received concert at the Kennedy Center in Washington, *Washington Post*, August 6, 1973, p. B1. The Black Expo '73 had a number of problems, according to press accounts, and a week after the event, the main promoter was arrested on fraud charges. *Philadelphia Bulletin*, August 21, 1973, August 24, 1973; *Philadelphia Inquirer*, August 12, 1973, p. 7G, August 24, 1973, p. 2C; *Philadelphia Tribune*, August 18, 1973, p. 1, August 25, 1973, p. 1.

278 **Troubadour:** *Los Angeles Times*, October 6, 1973, p. A5.

278 **her Japanese fans:** *Japan Times*, October 28, 1973, p. 5; *The Age* (Melbourne, Australia), November 7, 1973, p. 22; *The Australian* (Canberra), November 27, 1973, p. 22, for a review of the November 25 Sydney concert; Nadi Qamar interview.

279 **"Empty afternoons":** The account of Nina's affair with Errol Barrow is taken from *I Put a Spell on You*, pp. 131–34. I could find no contemporaneous accounts to confirm what Nina described; however, in various interviews as an adult, Lisa talked about living in Barbados, and some interviews with Nina during this period talk about her living in Barbados. One long piece in the May 12, 1973, *Melody Maker*, p. 24, took place in

Nina's Manhattan apartment but refers to her having a tall man from Barbados with her, probably Paul. Nina also referred to her affair with Barrow, according to Sylvia Hampton in *Nina Simone: Break Down*, p. 80.

280 **"Human Kindness Day"**: Roscoe Dellums interview; poster courtesy of Roscoe Dellums, poem excerpt used by permission; *I Put a Spell on You*, pp. 136–37; *Washington Star*, May 12, 1974, pp. 1, B1, discusses in detail the vandalism that occurred on the National Mall as the day was ending; *Washington Post*, May 12, 1974, p. A10, May 13, 1974, p. C1; *Blues & Soul*, June 4–17, 1974, p. 136.

282 **unpaid taxes**: Mount Vernon house information, Westchester County tax assessor.

282 **Liberia**: *I Put a Spell on You*, pp. 138–50, for the time leading up to Liberia and her experiences there. Nina's account in her book is hard to verify. She says they arrived September 12, 1974, Lisa's twelfth birthday. News accounts in the *Liberian Age* note that President Tolbert was out of the country. Miriam Makeba had returned to Africa for the Zaire music festival September 21–24; *New York Amsterdam News*, September 19, 1974, p. 11, October 26, 1974, p. A1; *New York Times*, September 20, 1974, p. 27. Zaire was renamed Congo in May 1997 when a new government took over after forcing the previous leader from power.

283 **"I was twelve"**: *Telegraph Magazine*, October 2003, interview with Lisa "Simone" Kelly.

283 **Montreux Jazz Festival**: *Nina Simone Live at Montreux 1976* (Eagle Rock Entertainment DVD EE 39106-9). Shortly after the Montreux festival, a British company put out a compilation of Nina's RCA recordings, *Songs of the Poets*, featuring songs by George Harrison, Bob Dylan, Langston Hughes, and Nina and Weldon Irvine's "To Be Young, Gifted and Black." *New York Times*, August 20, 1976, p. 62.

285 **"I wasn't feeling that"**: Lisa "Simone" Kelly interview, *Fader*, May/June 2006, p. 96.

CHAPTER 23: I AM NOT OF THIS PLANET ~ 1977–1978

286 **"Everything was fine"**: Lisa "Simone" Kelly interview, *Fader*, May/June 2006, p. 96; Hampton, *Nina Simone: Break Down*, p. 166.

287 **MIDEM**: *Melody Maker*, February 8, 1977, p. 24; *Variety*, January 26, 1977, p. 2; Roland Grivelle interviews.

288 **Amherst College**: Interviews with Patricia Allen and Diane Piermattei at Amherst College; reference to Nina's degree, *New York Times*, June 28, 1977, p. 21.

289 **"She just freaked"**: *New York Times*, June 28, 1977, p. 21; *Jet*, July 14, 1977, p. 52; Darlene Chan and Gino Francesconi interviews; amount of

George Wein's potential claim against Nina from Appendix A, "Other Potential Liabilities," *United States of America v. Nina Simone*, 78CR770.

290 **"more mannered":** *Jazz Journal International*, November 1977, pp. 49–51.

290 **Drury Lane:** London *Sunday Times*, December 11, 1977. According to Gerrit DeBruin, Nina also performed at the North Sea Jazz Festival at the Hague.

290 **Christmas in Israel:** *New York Post*, January 3, 1978, p. 2; *Jerusalem Post*, January 4, 1978, p. 5.

291 **Creed Taylor:** *Baltimore* (CTI 7084, Sony 5127912); Creed Taylor comments from album jacket; Nina comments, *Blues and Soul*, August 1978; *Melody Maker*, September 29, 1979, p. 26; Dave Matthews, Jimmy Madison, John Beal, Chuck Israels interviews.

295 **he beat Nina:** *I Put a Spell on You*, pp. 156–58; Stroud interview, *Fader*, May/June 2006; news clips, March 31, 1978, April 1, 1978, London dateline, noting that Nina had collapsed and had been taken to a local hospital. Documents in *United States v. Simone* for Nina's May/June stay in London.

295 **a solo concert:** *Melody Maker*, July 29, 1978, p. 14; *Evening Telegraph* (London), July 14, 1978, p. 33; Nina's reconstruction of much of 1978 in *I Put a Spell on You* is unreliable. Contemporaneous documents put her trip to Israel in late December 1977, *before* the assault that took place in London. Similarly, documents filed in the criminal tax case against her show where she was staying in London and then in Switzerland during the summer and fall of 1978. The filings in the tax case show that Nina performed only twice in 1978, once at London's Festival Hall ($2,000) and at Avery Fisher Hall in New York ($10,000). She was supposed to have appeared on Swiss television but had to cancel because she lost her voice, forfeiting the $877 advance. Likewise, there is no contemporaneous account to confirm Nina's recollection (pp. 163–64) that the mayor of Tel Aviv met her at the airport along with a big crowd.

296 **financial problems:** *United States v. Simone*, 78CR770, United States District Court, Southern District of New York; Alan R. Naftalis, Elliot Sagor interviews. According to the IRS, Nina's income in 1971–73 dollars respectively was $35,288, $75,960, and $91,612.

By the time Nina pleaded guilty to failing to file her 1971 income taxes, her total liabilities as of December 1978, including those to the federal government, were estimated to be $87,500, or $293,125 in 2009 dollars. Her $10,602 in assets were roughly $35,517 in 2009 dollars.

Nina's dramatic account of her "booking" on pages 161–62 in *I Put a Spell on You* is at odds with what happened, according to Naftalis. Among the several things in error is the statement that Andy was involved on Nina's behalf. He was not present for any meeting or proceeding, Naftalis said. See also *New York Times*, November 10, 1978, p. C29; *Jet*, November 30, 1978, p. 57, January 18, 1978, p. 62; *Washington Post*, December 16, 1978, p. B3, December 23, 1978, p. B2.

300 **Avery Fisher Hall:** *New York Times*, December 12, 1978, p. C8; *New York Amsterdam News*, December 23, 1978, p. D12.

CHAPTER 24: LOVING ME IS NOT ENOUGH ~ 1979–1981

301 **"I must get my money":** *New York Times*, February 24, 1979, p. 19; *Village Voice*, March 12, 1979, pp. 63–64; Art D'Lugoff interviews.

304 **all her royalties:** A sample royalty statement from Nina's Philips recordings for 1982–83, courtesy of Sam Waymon.

304 **"Y'all are fickled":** Globe-Democrat-Knight News Service, August 4, 1979, from the *St. Louis Globe Democrat*, "Nina Simone is back with new form of performing," by Mary Martin Niepold; Stroud interview *Fader*, May/June 2006, p. 101; Shubert Theatre, *Philadelphia Tribune*, June 8, 1979, p. 8;

304 **antique necklace:** *Philadelphia Bulletin*, July 9, 1979, July 12, 1979.

305 **"When you fall":** *Melody Maker*, September 29, 1979, p. 26.

306 **Oakland Coliseum:** *Oakland* Tribune, December 17, 1979, p. C1; San *Francisco Examiner*, December 15, 1979, p. 8; *San Franciscio Chronicle*, December 17, 1979, p. 45; Hannibal Means interviews, e-mail correspondence.

308 **Locust Theater:** *Philadelphia Inquirer*, May 11, 1980, p. 10H; *Philadelphia Tribune*, May 9, 1980, p. 6.

308 **"I love Khomeini:"** *Washington Post*, June 7, 1980, p. B1, June 9, 1980, p. B11; Hollie I. West, Don Wilby, Wade Henderson interviews; Lisa "Simone" Kelly interview in Hampton, *Nina Simone: Break Down*, p. 167.

310 **"I'm a slave":** Lester Hyman interview; *Bubbling Brown Sugar*, *Washington Post*, July 3, 1980, p. C3.

311 **Montreal:** *Nina Simone: The Rising Sun Collection* (Just a Memory Records, RSCD 0004); Hannibal Means interviews, e-mail correspondence; *The Gazette* (Montreal), July 16, 1980, p. 80, ad for the jazz/blues festival.

312 **Grande Finale:** Hampton, *Nina Simone: Break Down*, p. 99; *Blues and Soul*, November 4–17, 1980, p. 33; *New York Times*, September 28, 1980, p. D43.

CHAPTER 25: FODDER ON HER WINGS ~ 1982–1988

314 **Jacques Brel:** *I Put a Spell on You*, p. 165; *Jazz Magazine*, September 1981, p. 10, translation courtesy of David Kaufman.

315 **Carrere label:** *Fodder on My Wings*, licensed to Sunnyside Communica-

tions, Inc. (SSC 114); *Rocky Mountain News*, December 2, 1983, p. 35W, discussion of "Fodder on My Wings."

315 **Barbican Hall:** *London Times*, May 10, 1982, p. 7.

316 **Pamplona:** *La Vanguardia*, Barcelona, July 25, 1982, "Nina Simone provoca un escándalo en Pamplona"; www.noticiasdenavarra.com, translations courtesy of Iliana Aguilar; Raymond Gonzales comments, *International Herald Tribune*, April 30, 2003, p. 18; Raymond Gonzales interviews.

317 **"I never got a dime":** Nina's meeting with the London lawyer courtesy of Hannibal Means.

318 **spiraled into such turmoil:** *Los Angeles Times*, October 29, 1982, p. J2; *Atlanta Daily World*, February 6, 1983, p. 6; Warren Benbow, Sam Waymon interviews.

319 **Swing Plaza:** *New York Times*, June 3, 1983, p. C4, June 6, 1983, p. 13; *Village Voice*, June 21, 1983, p. 69; Hannibal Means interviews, e-mail correspondence.

320 **European festival swing:** Performance contracts, courtesy of Sam Waymon; The Hague, *Haagsche Courant*, translation courtesy of Benno Groeneveld; Nice *Matin*, July 20, 1983, translation courtesy of David Kaufman.

320 **Pompeii:** Sam Waymon, Maria Carneglia, Roland Grivelle interviews; receipt from Maria Carneglia, wire to Hotel Intercontinental courtesy of Sam Waymon. In Pompeii, Nina was accompanied by bassist Sante de Briano.

321 **AREC:** Nina's agreement with Artists Rights Enforcement Corporation, signed September 15, 1983, from documents in the Estate of Nina Simone, Los Angeles County Superior Court, BP 079 597.

322 **Vancouver:** *The Sun*, November 26, 1983, p. D14; *The Province*, November 27, 1983, p. 64; *Rocky Mountain News*, December 2, 1983, p. 35W; *Denver Post*, December 6, 1983, p. 3B; Henry Young, Sam Waymon, Roland Grivelle interviews.

324 **Ronnie Scott's:** Nina's return to London was well covered with write-ups in several publications: *The Observer*, January 14, 1984, p. 40; *The Standard*, January 12, 1984; *Sunday Times*, January 15, 1984; *The Sun*, January 13, 1984, p. 14; *Jazz Journal International*, February 1984, p. 24; Paul Robinson interview, e-mail correspondence.

Nina wanted Leopoldo Fleming to join her, so he flew to London. But when he arrived, he learned that neither she nor the club management had arranged for a work permit, and he had to fly home the next day. Pete King told Leo that Nina had given the club so many potential sidemen that "they didn't know which one was real so they just canceled on everybody"; Leopoldo Fleming interviews.

324 **most of the year:** Though Nina stayed in London most of the summer,

she made a quick trip to New York to perform at the Blue Note. *Live at Ronnie Scott's*, DVD distributed by MVD Music Video. The date of the performance on the DVD appears to be incorrect. It was November 17, 1984, not 1985, which was confirmed by Paul Robinson, who was the drummer on the date. It was the last date of an engagement that had started on November 12, 1984.

325   **Anthony Sanucci:** *I Put a Spell on You*, pp. 169–70; *Jazz Times*, January 1985, p. 16.

325   **Beverly Theatre:** *Los Angeles Times*, January 27, 1985, p. N58, February 25, 1985, p. G4. The reviewer noted that Nina was "in uncharacteristically good humor." *Variety*, March 6, 1985, p. 370.

326   **all glitter:** *New York Times*, March 11, 1985, p. C17; *Washington Post*, March 12, 1985, p. C9; *Jet*, April 22, 1985, p. 54–55; *Nina's Back* (VPI 8453, also SNAP 040).

How productive Nina could be when she was happy was evident in the spring and summer schedule Anthony Sanucci had put together. It started with a month at Ronnie Scott's that ran from mid-April into May, which allowed Nina to stay in one place and do a nontaxing set each night for very good money. Then came a busy return to the United States: Avery Fisher Hall in New York as part of the Kool Jazz Festival, on to Hampton, Virginia, for the annual festival there, and to Chicago before coming back to New York for two concerts.

Despite the occasional hard stare and haughty pose, Nina was hardly sullen. Leaning close in to the microphone in Chicago, she encouraged her fans. "Please," she instructed, "I need that applause." Paul Robinson interview, e-mail correspondence, which detailed Nina's schedule: Ronnie Scott's from mid-April through May 11 (*London Times*, May 6, 1985, p. 7); New Morning in Paris, probably May 16–17; Savoy Theater in London, May 19; Avery Fisher Hall, New York, June 26 (*Variety*, July 3, 1985, p. 62). This concert had been billed as "Welcome back, Nina." Hampton, Va., festival, June 28, 1985 (*Virginian Pilot*, June 30, 1985, p. B4); Chicago's South Shore Country Club (*Chicago Sun Times*, July 1, 1985); Hunter College benefit, July 6, 1985 (*New York Amsterdam News*, July 6, 1985, pp. 27, 33).

326   **purchased a condominium:** *Los Angeles Times*, July 30, 1985, p. E1; Sam Waymon interviews; Nina's condominium was at 7250 Franklin Avenue, Los Angeles, 90046.

Nina was well received during her week at Vine Street. "Her pose of bitterness, which alienated her from supper clubs and white audiences in the late 60s and 70s, has changed to one of regal loneliness," *Variety* wrote (August 7, 1985, p. 77). A year later an album from live performances around this time was released, *Live & Kickin'* (VPCD 10012).

328 **"I found my roots"**: *Chicago Tribune*, November 10, 1985, p. K29, December 5, 1985, p. 4D. Nina's performance was November 14, 1985, at Park West. She was back for a week at Vine Street in Los Angeles on December 3, *Los Angeles Times*, November 29, 1985, p. G16.

329 **a terrible fight**: *I Put a Spell on You*, pp. 172–73; *Virginian Pilot*, June 30, 1985, p. B4, for kind words about Sanucci and Singleton; *London Standard*, February 6, 1985, p. 21; *Billboard*, February 22, 1986, p. 63; see also *Jazz*, January/February 1986, p. 10; Sam Waymon interviews.

330 **half-dressed**: Sam Waymon interviews; Hannibal Means interviews and e-mail correspondence; *Boston Globe*, March 17, 1986, p. 25 for March 16 performance at Symphony Hall.

330 **Playboy Jazz Festival**: *Los Angeles Times*, June 17, 1986, p. H8; Darlene Chan interviews. Nina was booked to play the New Orleans Jazz and Heritage Festival in the spring, but she did not make the booking, according to coverage of the festival in the *New Orleans Times Picayune*.

331 **"Is there any money in this?"**: *San Francisco Chronicle*, July 21, 1986, p. 54.

334 **Chanel No. 5**: *Nina Simone Live at Montreux* DVD; Hannibal Means interviews and e-mail correspondence. Nina apparently stayed in Los Angeles for a time after the dismal *Playboy* festival appearance. On January 29, 1987, she appeared at the Hollywood club Nucleus Nuance, and according to Leonard Feather was in a jovial mood. "Thank you for coming, you sweet things," she said. *Los Angeles Times*, January 31, 1987, p. 4. In mid-April she returned to the Vine Street Bar & Grill in part to unveil her part of the "Live at Vine Street" series, *Let It Be Me* (Verve 831-431-1). *Variety*, April 15, 1987, p. 210; *Jazz Journal International*, July 1988, p. 35, for an album review.

335 **early in 1988**: Sam Waymon, Gerrit DeBruin, Raymond Gonzalez, Roland Grivelle interviews; Nina in Barcelona, youtube.com clips; Nina in Hamburg, June 5, 1988, high-priestess.com; *Jazz Podium*, July 1988, p. 28, translation courtesy of James Huckenpahler; London, *Melody Maker*, June 11, 1988, p. 20, July 9, 1988, p. 27.

CHAPTER 26: NINA'S BACK . . . AGAIN ~ 1989–1992

336 **She was unkempt**: Chris White, Darryl and Douglas Jeffries interviews.

337 **Nijmegen**: Gerrit DeBruin interviews, e-mail correspondence; his interview in Hampton, *Nina Simone: Break Down*, pp. 170–72; Leopoldo Fleming interviews.

340 **Lycabettus Theater**: *Variety*, July 18, 1989, p. 93. A performance in Stuttgart later in 1989 was less charitably received than the show in Greece. A reviewer for *Jazz Podium* (September 1989, p. 29) said Nina

sang off-key and sounded brittle while the trio provided only weak accompaniment. "If only the benefit had been as immense as the honorarium." Translation courtesy of James Huckenpahler.

341 **still mad at Raymond:** Gerrit DeBruin, Chris White, Leopoldo Fleming, Paul Robinson, Raymond Gonzalez interviews; Hampton, *Nina Simone: Break Down*, pp. 142, 170–72.

341 **Steven Ames Brown:** *Billboard*, October 28, 1989, p. 105, December 19, 1990, p. 83. For details of the Bethlehem-Charly suit, see *Bethlehem Music Company, Inc., Nina Simone et al.* v. *Jean Lu Young et al.*, case CA001200, Los Angeles County Superior Court. For the Vine Street case see *Nina Simone v. Ron Berenstein et al.*, C755463, Los Angeles County Superior Court. Steven Ames Brown interview.

342 **1990 festival:** *Nina Simone Live at Montreux* DVD. Before Montreux, Nina was in Atlanta February 14, 1990, to be honored at the APEX Museum, *Atlanta Daily World*, February 22, 1990, p. 1.

342 **swing through Italy:** Roberto Meglioli, Odetta interviews. These were the concert dates: September 4, 1990, Rocca Normanna-Paterno, inside a stone castle near Catania, Sicily; September 6, 1990, Stadium Vestuti, Salerno; September 8, 1990, Exhibition Center, Calgiari, Sardinia; September 10, 1990, Arena Parco Nord Bologna. *Corriere Della Sera*, September 6, 1990, p. 27, translation courtesy of Catherine Re. Nina also performed at the One World Music Festival in Cologne in the fall of 1990, *Musica*, November–December 1990, pp. 386–87.

344 **less than stellar performances:** *Jazz*, December 1991, p. 9, reviewing a performance at the Olympia in Paris and noting that Nina seemed tired and almost robotlike, translation courtesy of David Kaufman. She had performed earlier in the year in London to a much more favorable notice, *Melody Maker*, January 24, 1991, p. 18.

344 **George Washington University:** Lester Hyman, George Wein interviews; *Washington Post*, June 23, 1992, p. C5; *New York Post*, June 27, p. 19; Carnegie Hall program, Carnegie Hall archives.

345 **back to Tryon:** *La Légende*, the 1992 French-made documentary. *San Francisco Chronicle*, July 21, 1986, p. 54, for Nina's comment about Lisa.

CHAPTER 27: A SINGLE WOMAN ~ 1993–1999

348 **She started to laugh:** Michael Alago interview.

350 ***A Single Woman:*** (Elektra, D-135417); *Pulse*, November 1993, pp. 53–54; *Philadelphia Tribune*, December 31, 1993, p. 7E.

351 **concerts in the Midwest:** Nina's spring concerts, *St. Paul Pioneer Press*, April 13, 1993, p. 8B; *Philadelphia Inquirer*, April 21, 1993, p. E1; *New York Newsday*, May 14, 1993, p. 59; *New York Amsterdam News*, May 8, 1993, p. 30; *Billboard*, June 5, 1993, p. 24.

The precise moment Nina left the United States is not clear, but by June 28 she was in France. An item appeared in the *Newark Star Ledger* on June 28 that she had suffered cuts from broken glass as she ran from a fire at her home "north of Marseille" that the paper said was apparently caused by an overheated fax machine.

351 **her testy responses:** *New York Times*, August 8, 1993, p. H24; Michael Alago interview.

352 **Jay Leno:** Michael Alago interview. The November 17, 1993, date was confirmed by NBC.

352 **40 percent:** *Nina Simone v. San Juan Music Group et al.*, 94-CV-01288-TEH, U.S. District Court for the Northern District of California (San Francisco); *Nina Simone v. Marshall Sehorn et al.*, 95-CV-03590-CAL, U.S. District Court for the Northern District of California (San Francisco).

Brown's arrangement with Nina is spelled out in a 2008 complaint against Andy Stroud over who has the rights to some of Nina's music, *Steven Ames Brown v. Andrew B. Stroud*, 08-CV-02348-VRW United States District Court for the Northern District of California. Point 4 in Brown's complaint states: "By virtue of a written contract made on or about July 30, 1990, between Dr. Simone and Plaintiff, plaintiff obtained a 40 percent ownership interest in all the Master Recordings that were the subject of Prior Actions." The prior actions refer to litigation cited above. See also *Billboard*, March 18, 1995, p. 90.

355 **"Quit it!":** Nina recounted the shooting encounter for a long profile in the London *Times* magazine June 26, 1999, p. 22; *Newark Star Ledger*, August 25, 1995; *Chicago Tribune*, August 25, 1995, p. 2; *Atlanta Daily World*, October 10, 1995, p. 4; Gerrit DeBruin, John and Carolle Waymon, Carrol Waymon interviews.

355 **hospitalized:** Clifton Henderson noted when he began to work for Nina, Estate of Nina Simone, BP 079 597, Los Angeles County Superior Court. Clifton comments on working for Nina from 2000 DirecTV program posted on www.nina-simone.com; Al Schackman interview, *Fader*, May/June 2006; Nina's November 20, 1996, letter to Gerrit DeBruin, courtesy of Gerrit DeBruin. Steven Ames Brown, Frances Fox, Carrol Waymon, Carolle Waymon interviews.

356 **returned to performing:** *Independent*, December 12, 1997, p. 6; *The Observer Review*, December 12, 1997, p. 14; *The Guardian Weekend*, December 6, 1997, pp. 28–32; 1997 schedule, ninasimone.com; Paul Robinson, Gerrit DeBruin interviews; Nina Simone letters to Gerrit DeBruin, January 10, 1996, November 20, 1996, courtesy of Gerrit DeBruin.

357 **"Desegregation is a joke":** *Interview*, January 1997, p. 79; *Details*, January 1997; *New York Times*, September 1, 1998, p. E1; *Newark Star Ledger*, September 1, 1998, p. 41; Eric Hanson interview.

359 **"you damned fool"**: *The National Post of Canada—Weekend*, May 15, 1999, p. 2, a reprint of an article that had run several months earlier in London's *The Big Issue*. Precious Williams, Javier Collados, Graham Ward interviews, e-mail correspondence; London *Times* magazine, June 26, 1999, p. 18; *Hard Talk*, March 1999, complete copy of the interview courtesy of the BBC.

CHAPTER 28: THE FINAL CURTAIN ~ 2000–2003

362 **"I continue to believe"**: Courtesy of Gerrit DeBruin.

362 **improved financial situation**: Income documents in the Estate of Nina Simone, Los Angeles County Superior Court BP 079 597.

364 **fired Raymond Gonzalez**: Al Schackman interview, *Fader*, May/June 2006; Juan Yriart, Javier Collados, Juanita Bougere, Hannibal Means, Gerrit DeBruin interviews, e-mail correspondence.

367 **put together a tour**: Juan Yriart interview, e-mail correspondence; interview in Brazil, from DirecTV program, nina-simone.com; *Details*, January 1997, interview with Brantly Bardin; 1999 BBC *Hard Talk*.

368 **A Nina Simone evening**: A complete list of Nina's 2000–2002 concert dates is found at ninasimone.com. For reviews see *Washington Post*, June 1, 2000, p. C5; *Boston Globe*, June 8, 2000, p. 3; *Chicago Tribune*, June 20, 2000, p. 2; *Los Angeles Times*, June 24, 2000, p. 2; *Miami Herald*, November 11, 2000, p. 3E; *Miami Times*, November 11, 2000, which is a very harsh review; *San Francisco Chronicle*, November 15, 2000, p. E1; Profile/interview, *Philadelphia Inquirer*, June 8, 2000, p. D1; Eric Hanson confirmed that these concerts were very lucrative. For example, Nina was paid $100,000 for the San Francisco date November 13, 2000, though not all of that was clear profit. She had to pay her musicians from that amount as well as some incidental expenses.

370 **Kate Waymon died**: Javier Collados, Juanita Bougere, Juan Yriart, Frances Fox interviews, which also cover Nina's bout with breast cancer.

370 **$85,000**: George Wein, Juan Yriart, Javier Collados interviews. See *New York Times*, July 8, 2001, p. E5, for Carnegie Hall performance, and June 24, 2001, p. 25, for commentary on Nina; *New York Daily News*, July 2, 2001, p. 34; *Chicago Tribune*, July 21, 2001, p. 31; *Seattle Post Intelligencer*, July 25, 2001, p. E4; *Seattle Times*, July 25, 2001, p. E8; Chris White interviews for Ashford & Simpson party.

370 **glory of Rome**: *La Republicca*, May 8, 2002, p. 43, a critical article whose tone is apparent from the headline: "The Myth of Nina Simone Only Shines in Our Memories; Live She Is the Shadow of Herself." *Il Messagero*, May 6, 2002, p. 18, was a more complimentary article: "Blues and Black, the colors of a unique singer." Translations courtesy of Luca

Favaro. Also *Dziennik Baltycki*, July 1, 2002, translation courtesy of Regina Frackowiak.

373 **She slipped away:** Juanita Bougere, Javier Collados, Juan Yriart, Carolle Waymon, Carrol Waymon, Sam Waymon interviews; funeral, *Atlanta Daily World*, May 1, 2003, p. 1; Curtis Institute, courtesy of Jennifer Rycerz, Curtis public relations manager.

Nina Simone, Briefly, on CD/DVD

Virtually all of Nina Simone's studio recordings, from her first with Bethlehem to her last with Elektra, are available on CD. The earliest recorded Nina is *Little Girl Blue* (Neon NE 3541). Her Colpix albums have also been reissued, and among the best is *Nina Simone at Town Hall* (COL CD 6208), which captures the performance that sparked her career.

Nina's seven albums during her Philips years have been compiled in a four-CD box set from Verve, *Four Women* (440 065 021 2). Nina's RCA years are compiled in a CD/DVD package *To Be Free: The Nina Simone Story* (RCA Legacy 88697 11009 2). In both of these packages Nina is at the height of her popularity and innovation. Nina recorded sporadically from the mid-seventies until 1993. Three of the albums illuminate a maturing if idosyncratic musician, *Baltimore* (Sony 5127912), released in 1978; *Fodder on Her Wings* (SSC 114), released in 1992; and *A Single Woman* (Elektra D-135417), the last.

A more freewheeling Nina is evident on two CDs from live performances, *A Very Rare Evening* (Mambo Records, 804065144) from April 1969 in Munich, and *Nina Simone: The Rising Sun Collection* (RSCD 0004), which captures Nina's performance at the July 1980 Montreal Jazz Festival.

Nina was at her most compelling live, and some of her performances are available on DVD. The earliest is a segment from her September 11, 1960, performance on *The Ed Sullivan Show*, titled *The Soul of Nina Simone* (RCA Legacy 82876 71973 2). Segments of Nina performing in Holland in 1965 and in London in 1968 are available on *Jazz Icons: Nina Simone Live in '65 & '68* (Naxos, 2.119014). Three of Nina's performances at the Montreux Jazz Festival are available on *Live at Montreux* (Eaglerock, EE 39106-9). An absorbing look at Nina, reflecting on her music and in performance, is contained in a half-hour documentary produced by Peter Rodis that is part of the *To Be Free* package from RCA Legacy.

Bibliography

Acker, Kerry. *Nina Simone*. Philadelphia: Chelsea House Publishers, 2004.

Amram, David. *Vibrations: The Adventures and Musical Times of David Amram*. New York: Thunder's Mouth Press, 2001.

Baldwin, James. *The Fire Next Time*. New York: Dial Press, 1963.

———. *Go Tell It on the Mountain*. New York: Dial Press, 1953; reprint 2005.

Bernard, Emily, ed. *The Letters of Langston Hughes and Carl Van Vechten, 1925–64*. New York: Alfred A. Knopf, 2001.

Blakely, Robert J. with Marcus Shepherd. *Earl B. Dickerson: A Voice for Freedom and Equality*. Evanston, Ill.: Northwestern University Press, 2006.

Branch, Taylor. *Parting the Waters: America in the King Years, 1954–63*. New York: Simon & Schuster, 1988.

———. *Pillar of Fire: America in the King Years, 1963–65*. New York: Simon & Schuster, 1998.

Burdon, Eric with J. Marshall Craig. *Don't Let Me Be Misunderstood*. New York: Thunder's Mouth Press, 2001.

Carter, Steven R. *Hansberry's Drama: Commitment and Complexity*. Urbana, Ill.: University of Illinois Press, 1991.

Cheney, Anne. *Lorraine Hansberry*. Boston: Twayne Publishers, 1984.

Chevigny, Paul. *Gigs: Jazz and the Cabaret Laws in New York City*. New York: Routledge, 1991.

Cleaver, Eldridge: *Soul on Ice*. New York: Dell Publishing, 1991.

Conner, Irma Pack. *Tryon: An Artist's & Writer's Sketch Book*. Chapel Hill: Tryon Publishing Co., 2001.

Davis, Ed. *Atlantic City Diary: A Century of Memories, 1880–1980*. Atlantic City, N.J.: Siracusa Real Estate & Insurance Co., c. 1985.

Davis, Lenwood. *The Black Heritage of Western North Carolina*. Asheville, N.C.: University of North Carolina-Asheville, c. 1984.

Downey, Pat, George Albert, and Frank Hoffmann. *Cash Box Pop Singles Charts, 1950–1993*. Englewood, Colo.: Libraries Unlimited, 1994.

Ewing, Preston and Jan Roddy. *Let My People Go: Cairo, Illinois, 1967–1973*. Carbondale, Ill.: Southern Illinois University, 1996.

Frost, Elizabeth Doubleday. *Tryon Memories*. Chapel Hill, N.C.: Tryon Publishing, Inc., 1995.

Garland, Phyl. *The Sound of Soul*. Chicago: Henry Regnery, 1969.

Gart, Galen. *First Pressings: The History of Rhythm and Blues, Vol. 9, 1959.* Winter Haven, Fla.: Big Nickel Publications, 2002.

Gillette Woods, Tryon, North Carolina. Publisher unknown, c. 1940.

Goldblatt, Burt. *Newport Jazz Festival: The Illustrated History.* New York: Dial, 1977.

Goodwin, Garland. *A Boy in the Amen Corner.* Spartanburg, S.C.: The Reprint Company, 1999.

Gotfryd, Bernard. *The Intimate Eye.* New York: Riverside Book Co., Inc., 2006.

Greenbaum, Irv. *In One Ear, and In the Other—Memories of 48 Years in Recording.* New York: Abraham I. Greenbaum, Inc., 2000.

Griffin, Farah Jasmine. *If You Can't Be Free, Be a Mystery: In Search of Billie Holiday.* New York: Ballantine Books, 2001.

Guralnick, Peter. *Careless Love: The Unmaking of Elvis Presley.* Boston: Back Bay Books, 2000.

———. *Dream Boogie: The Triumph of Sam Cooke.* Boston: Back Bay Books, 2006.

Hampton, Sylvia with David Nathan. *Nina Simone: Break Down & Let It All Out.* London: Sanctuary, 2004.

Hansberry, Lorraine. *A Raisin in the Sun.* New York: Vintage Books, 1987.

———. *To Be Young, Gifted and Black: An Informal Autobiography of Lorraine Hansberry,* adapted by Robert Nemiroff. New York: Signet, 1970.

Hoffmann, Frank, and George Albert. *The Cash Box Album Charts, 1955–1974.* Metuchen, N.J.: Scarecrow Press, 1988.

———. *The Cash Box Album Charts, 1975–1987.* Metuchen, N.J.: Scarecrow Press, 1987.

———. *The Cash Box Black Contemporary Album Charts, 1975–1987.* Metuchen, N.J.: Scarecrow Press, 1989.

Hughes, Langston, *The Big Sea.* New York: Thunder's Mouth Press, 1986.

Ind, Peter. *Jazz Visions: Reflections on Lennie Tristano and His Legacy.* London: Equinox, 2005.

Joseph, Peniel E. *Waiting 'Til the Midnight Hour: A Narrative History of Black Power in America.* New York: Henry Holt, 2006.

Killens, John Oliver. *'Sippi.* New York: Thunder's Mouth Press, 1967.

The Lanier Library: 1890–1965 Diamond Jubilee. Greenville, S.C.: Keys Printing Co., 1965.

Lawson, Steven F. *Black Ballots: Voting Rights in the South, 1944–1969.* Lanham, Md.: Lexington Books, 1999.

Manning, Sean, ed. *Shows I'll Never Forget: 50 Writers Relive Their Most Memorable Concertgoing Experience.* New York: Da Capo Press, 2007.

Mitchell, Joseph. *Up in the Old Hotel.* New York: Vintage, 1991.

Muller, Bill, and James Smethurst, eds. *Left of the Color Line: Race, Radicalism, and Twentieth-Century Literature of the United States.* Chapel Hill, N.C.: University of North Carolina Press, 2003.

O'Brien, Lucy. *She Bop: The Definitive History of Women in Rock, Pop and Soul.* New York: Penguin Books, 1996.

Phillips, Stu. *"Stu Who?" Forty Years of Navigating the Minefields of the Music Business.* Studio City, Calif.: Cisum Press, 2003.

Popular Record Aid. Philadelphia: RecordAid, Inc., 1959–1971.

Porter, Eric. *What Is This Thing Called Jazz: African American Musicians as Artists, Critics, and Activists.* Berkeley, Calif.: University of California Press, 2002.

Redfern, Michael. *The Unclosed Eye.* London: Sanctuary Publishing Limited, 1999.

Roberts, Gene, and Hank Klibanoff. *The Race Beat: The Press, the Civil Rights Struggle, and the Awakening of a Nation.* New York: Alfred A. Knopf, 2006.

Salvatore, Nick. *Singing in a Strange Land: C.L. Franklin, the Black Church, and the Transformation of America.* New York: Little Brown, 2005.

Simone, Nina, with Stephen Cleary. *I Put a Spell on You.* New York: Da Capo, 2003.

Smith, Jessie Carney, ed. *Notable Black American Women.* Detroit: Gale Research, 1992.

Stroud, Andy. *Nina Simone: Black Is the Color . . .* Xlibris Corporation, 2005.

Taylor, Art. *Notes and Tones.* New York: Da Capo, 1993.

Tcholakian, Arthur. *The Majesty of the Black Woman.* New York: Van Nostrand Reinhold Co., 1971.

Van Deburg, William L. *New Day in Babylon: The Black Power Movement and American Culture, 1965–1975.* Berkeley, Calif.: University of California Press, 1992.

Wallace, Michele. *Dark Designs & Visual Culture.* Durham, N.C.: Duke University Press, 2004.

Ward, Brian. *Just My Soul Responding: Rhythm and Blues, Black Consciousness, and Race Relations.* Berkeley, Calif.: University of California Press, 1988.

Whitburn, Joel. *Joel Whitburn's Top Pop Albums, 1955–1992.* Menomenee Falls, Wis.: Record Research, 1996.

———. *Joel Whitburn's Top Pop Artists and Singles.* Menomenee Falls, Wis.: Record Research, 1979.

———. *Joel Whitburn's Top R&B Singles, 1942–1995.* Menomenee Falls, Wis.: Record Research, 1996.

Much of the information on Nina's career came from contemporaneous reporting in music magazines and newspapers. Among the most important were: *Billboard, Cash Box, Melody Maker, The Atlantic City Press, Atlanta Daily World, Chicago Defender, Los Angeles Times, New York Amsterdam News, The New York Times, Philadelphia Bulletin, The Philadelphia Tribune, Pittsburgh Courier,* and *The Washington Post.*

UNPUBLISHED MATERIAL

Allen School archives, North Carolina Room, Pack Memorial Library, Asheville, N.C.

American Society of African Culture (AMSAC) papers, Moorland Springarn Research Center, Howard University.

Carnegie Hall programs, including contract materials, Carnegie Hall archives.

Congress of Racial Equality (CORE) papers, Library of Congress Manuscript Reading Room.

Juilliard School of Music archives, which include information on the 1950 six-week summer session that Nina—still Eunice Waymon—attended.

Langston Hughes papers, personal correspondence, James Weldon Johnson Collection in the Yale Collection of American Literature, Beinecke Rare Book and Manuscript Library.

NAACP state-by-state chapter files, 1940–1955, Library of Congress Manuscript Reading Room.

NBC television masterbooks, Library of Congress Motion Picture and Television Reading Room.

RCA archives, Sony-BMG headquarters, New York, N.Y.

Schiffman family Apollo Theater files, Smithsonian Institution, Museum of American History.

PRIVATE PAPERS

Onameega Doris Bluitt
Gerrit DeBruin
Roscoe Dellums
Garland Goodwin
Kipp McIntyre
Carrol Waymon
John Irvin and Carolle Waymon
Sam Waymon
Chris White
Henry Young

LEGAL DOCUMENTS

American Magnetics Corporation v. Nina Simone, et al., C613157, Los Angeles County Superior Court

Bethlehem Music Company, Inc., Nina Simone, et al. v. Jean Luc Young et al., case CA001200, Los Angeles County Superior Court.

Estate of Nina Simone, BP 079 597, Los Angeles County Superior Court.

Federal Bureau of Investigation file on Lorraine Hansberry.

Nina Simone v. Marshall Sehorn et al., 95-CV-03590-CAL, United States District Court for the Northern District of California (San Francisco).

Nina Simone v. Philip Landwehr, Lewis Harris, et al., Case 18830/64, New York Supreme Court.

Nina Simone v. Ron Berenstein et al., C755463, Los Angeles County Superior Court.

Nina Simone v. San Juan Music Group et al., 94-CV-01288-TEH, United States District Court for the Northern District of California (San Francisco).

Steven Ames Brown v. Andrew B. Stroud, an individual, and Stroud Productions and Enterprises, Inc., 08-CV-02348-VRW, United States District Court for the Northern District of California.

United States of America v. Nina Simone, 78CR770, United States District Court, Southern District of New York.

Acknowledgments

A host of people deserve thanks for their help in this years-long project. First among them are Peter Guralnick and Charlie McGovern. Peter encouraged me to write about Nina Simone, and throughout he has offered boundless support and wisdom, not only about the task of writing but about life, too. The same is true for Charlie, who listened, advised, prodded, and cajoled with a comforting and calming spirit. Their help and friendship, like the credit-card commercial, is priceless. I am and will be forever grateful.

John Irvin Waymon, Nina's oldest brother, and his wife Carolle; Carrol Waymon, another older brother; and Dorothy Waymon Simmons, Nina's older sister, provided invaluable information about the family's early life in Tryon, North Carolina. Sam Waymon, Nina's younger brother, fellow musician, and onetime manager, provided illuminating stories about their time together making music. Thanks, too, to Frances Waymon Fox, Nina's younger sister, for her insights about particular moments in Nina's life.

I appreciate having Nina's voice through her autobiography, written with Stephen Cleary, *I Put a Spell on You*, and through the remembrances of Sylvia Hampton and David Nathan in *Nina Simone: Break Down & Let It All Out*.

For the Tryon years, I received wonderful help from Kipp McIntyre, Mark Pumphrey, Cynthia Nanney, the late Edney Whiteside, Artie Hamilton, Holland Brady, Fred and Ulysses Counts, Beryl Hannon Dade, Garland Goodwin, Ruth Hannon Hamilton, David Johnson, Tom Moore, Joan Nash, James Payne, Blanche Lyles Solomon, and Crys Ambrust, creator of the website ninasimoneproject.org. Thanks, too, to the women who were classmates of Nina's—then Eunice Waymon—at the Allen School in Asheville: Patricia Carson Caple, Christine Ivey Jowers, Cordelia Pedew Chambers, and Willie Mae Gaston Ferguson, and one of their teachers, Ruth Walther.

Chris White, one of Nina's first bass players, set me on the path to many of the other musicians who played or worked with Nina either onstage or in the studio. My thanks to them, too: Michael Alago, Lisle Atkinson, John Beal, Warren Benbow, Jimmy Bond, the late Patti Bown, Leopoldo Fleming, Bobby Hamilton, Albert "Tootie" Heath, Chuck Israels, Tony Jones, Jimmy Madison, Dave Matthews, Hannibal Means, Montego Joe, the late Odetta, Horace Ott, Gene Perla, Bernard Purdie, Nadi Qamar, Ben Riley, Paul Robinson, Warren Smith, Rudy Stevenson, and Henry Young. Special thanks to Henry's wife

Yvonne for the hospitality in Vancouver and for keeping track of all the photos, documents, and e-mails when Henry, always patient, answered my questions.

My thanks also to Vivian Bailey, Onameega Doris Bluitt, Roscoe Dellums, the late Art D'Lugoff, Bernard Gotfryd, Irv Greenbaum, Eric Hanson, Wade Henderson, Tad Hershorn, Kenny Hill, Lester Hyman, Darryl and Douglas Jeffries, Judy Gail Krasnow, Alan Mitchell Nadel, Alan Naftalis, Peter Rodis, Elliot Sagor, Norm Schneider, Bill Smith, Chuck Stewart, Fred Taylor, George Wein, Alfred Wertheimer, Hollie West, and Gus Wildi, who first put Nina on vinyl on his Bethlehem label. Additional thanks to the late Charles Walton, still an inspiration, Brigitta Peterhans, Tim Samuelson, David Sharpe, and John Vinci for the Chicago stories.

Gerrit DeBruin provided illuminating stories, as did Nina's other European friends, Raymond Gonzalez, and Roland Griville. Thanks, too, to Roberto Meglioli and Maria Carneglia, and to Juan Yriart, Javier Collados, and Juanita Bougere.

This project could not have been completed without the help of many librarians and archivists around the country. My thanks and appreciation to all of them. At the Library of Congress: Jerome Brooks, Bryan Cornell, Liz Faison, Karen Fishman, Rosemary Hane, Jan McKee, Karen Moses, Sam Perryman, Mark Sweeney, Travis Westly, and to Regina Frackowiak, who went the extra mile by contacting a library in Warsaw for coverage of Nina's last concert and then translating two articles—*dziekuje*. Additional thanks to: Jeni Dahmus at Juilliard; Jennifer Rycerz, Sally Grant Branca, and Elizabeth Walker at the Curtis Institute of Music; Zoe Rhine, Pack Memorial Library, Asheville, North Carolina; Gino Francesconi, Rob Hudson, and Kathleen Sabogil of the Carnegie Hall archives; Karen Nangle—Beinecke Rare Book and Manuscript Library, Yale University; Donna Humphrey of the Bucks County, Pennsylvania, Historical Society; Monica Smith, Cairo, Illinois, Public Library; Diana Peterson at Haverford College; Barbara Allier at Brooklyn College; Wei-jie Cui at the Burlington County, New Jersey, library; John Slate, city archivist for the Dallas Municipal Archives; Lylian Morcos, WNET; Jane Klain at the Paley Center for Media; Jonathan Grant at Morehouse College in Atlanta; Christy Venham, West Virginia University Libraries; Becky Nesbitt, Benedum Library, Salem International University; Eleanor Krell and Lisa Greenhouse, Enoch Pratt Free Library, Baltimore, Maryland; Toni Tucker, Illinois State University; Patricia Woodard, Hunter College library; Patricia Allen and Diane Permattei at Amherst College; Octavio Olvera and Angela Riggio, Charles E. Young Research Library, UCLA; JoAnne El Bashir, Moorland Spingarn Research Center, Howard University; Ann Marie Wieland, Venechor Boyd, and Elmer Turner at the Cleveland Public Library; the library staff at the Illinois Institute of Technology; the staff at the Columbus, Ohio, public library; and the staff at the Temple University Urban Archives, whose collection was instrumental in understanding the early days of Nina's career.

To my translators: David Kaufman, *merci*; Catherine Re and Luca Favaro, *grazie*; Iliana Aguilar, *gracias*; James Huckenpahler, *danke*; and Leonie van Raadshoove and Benno Groeneveld, *dank u.*

Terrific help tracking down articles and court documents came from Emily Kelly, Susan Engstrom, and Jennifer Sepic. Additional thanks to Tom Tierney at the Sony-BMG archives.

My thanks to Wil Haygood and Richard Seidel for reading the manuscript, and to Michael Lydon, who was both blunt and right.

Flip Brophy, my agent, has represented me for twenty years and five books, and I renew my thanks for making each of these challenging adventures possible. At Pantheon, thanks to Deb Garrison, my editor, who was willing to do this a second time. Once again she provided encouragement at every turn and the astute observations and suggestions so valuable in bringing focus to a project. The very capable Caroline Zancan managed all the moving parts with impressive skill. Thanks also to the production team: Carol Carson, for designing a cover, as she did for the Dinah Washington book, that caught the essence of the story I have sought to tell; Iris Weinstein, whose design has the elegance Nina would surely have liked; managing editor Altie Karper; production editor Kathleen Fridella; production manager Marci Lewis; permissions administrator Caryn Burtt; and Holly Webber, the copy editor, who provided many graceful suggestions in her detailed read.

A final nod from the heart to Sylvia Cohodas, Howard Cohodas, and the late Arnold Cohodas.

Index

Page numbers in *italics* refer to illustrations.

A NOTE ON THE TYPE

The text of this book was set in Electra, a typeface designed by W. A. Dwiggins (1880–1956). This face cannot be classified as either modern or old style. It is not based on any historical model, nor does it echo any particular period or style. It avoids the extreme contrasts between thick and thin elements that mark most modern faces, and it attempts to give a feeling of fluidity, power, and speed.

COMPOSED BY
North Market Street Graphics,
Lancaster, Pennsylvania

DESIGNED BY
Iris Weinstein